Proceedings of the 15th World Sanskrit Conference

General Editor
Radhavallabh Tripathi

Vol. II
Vyākaraṇa Section
Vyākaraṇa Across the Ages

Vyākaraṇa
Across the Ages

Edited by

George Cardona

Rashtriya Sanskrit Sansthan

D.K. PRINTWORLD
Publishers of Indian Traditions

Cataloging in Publication Data — DK
[Courtesy: D.K. Agencies (P) Ltd. <docinfo@dkagencies.com>]

Vyākaraṇa across the ages / edited by George Cardona.
p. cm. — (Proceedings of the 15th World Sanskrit Conference ; v. II)
English and Sanskrit.
Includes bibliographical references.
ISBN 9788124606582

1. Sanskrit language — Grammar — Congresses. 2. Pāṇini. Aṣṭādhyāyī — Congresses. I. Cardona, George, 1936- II. Rashtriya Sanskrit Sansthan. III. Series: Proceedings of the 15th World Sanskrit Conference ; v. II.

DDC 491.25 23

ISBN 13: 978-81-246-0658-2 ISBN 10: 81-246-0658-7
First published in 2013

Published by:
RASHTRIYA SANSKRIT SANSTHAN
56-57, Institutional Area, Janakpuri, New Delhi - 110 058
Phones: (011) 2852 4993, 2852 1994, 2852 4995
e-mail: rsks@nda.vsnl.net.in
Website: www.sanskrit.nic.in

and

D.K. PRINTWORLD (P) LTD.
Regd. Office: *'Vedasri'*, F-395, Sudarshan Park
(Metro Station: Ramesh Nagar), New Delhi - 110 015-11
Phones: (011) 2545 3975; 2546 6019; Fax: (011) 2546 5926
e-mail: indology@dkprintworld.com
Website: www.dkprintworld.com

Printed by: D.K. Printworld (P) Ltd, New Delhi

Foreword

The 15th World Sanskrit Conference (WSC) was organized by Rashtriya Sanskrit Sansthan, New Delhi, in association with International Association of Sanskrit Studies (IASS) during 5 January–10 January 2012. The Conference was conducted through twenty sections including Veda; Linguistics; Epics and Purāṇas; Tantra and Āgamas; Vyākaraṇa; Poetry, Drama and Aesthetics; Sanskrit and Asian Languages and Literatures; Sanskrit and Science; Buddhist Studies; Jain Studies; Philosophies; Religious Studies; Ritual Studies; Epigraphy; Sanskrit in Technological World; Modern Sanskrit Literature; Law and Society; and Manuscriptology along with the Paṇḍitapariṣad and Kavisamavāya. Apart from these sections, the event was marked with some special panels on the themes — Models and Theories in Sanskrit Grammar and Linguistics; Electronic Concordance of the Great Epics; Re-interpreting Pāṇini; Nāṭyaśāstra in Modern World; New Perspectives on Scientific Literature in Sanskrit; Boundaries of Yoga in Indian Philosophical Literature; Śaiva Philosophy; Innovations in Sanskrit Pedagogy; Sanskrit Inscriptions in South-East Asian Countries; Manuscripts and Their Intellectual Preservation; and Sanskrit in Global Perspectives.

Right from its inception, Vyākaraṇa has been one of the most versatile sections of this conference. I am happy to note that during the 15th WSC, the Vyākaraṇa section remained vibrant for the vigorous exchange of ideas between traditional and modern scholars, and the deliberations covered a wide range of topics including lexical and grammatical positions, Pāli Vyākaraṇa as well as the non-Pāṇinian systems of Sanskrit grammar.

IASS has authorized Rashtriya Sanskrit Sansthan to bring out all the volumes of the proceedings of the 15th WSC. We are grateful to Prof. George Cardona for making a very judicious selection and for having edited the papers presented in the Vyākaraṇa section of the conference.

Radhavallabh Tripathi

Preface

The articles in this collection are those accepted for publication from the papers presented in the Vyākaraṇa section of the XVth World Sanskrit Conference. These cover a wide range of topics, centered about Sanskrit grammar, with major emphasis on vyākaraṇa, in particular Pāṇini's work.

The collection opens with a paper providing a general background, in which Iwona Milewska surveys currents in European traditions of Sanskrit grammars. Beginning with early works by missionaries, she proceeds to categorize and describe Sanskrit grammars composed with various aims: philological, comparative, and pedagogical.

The next group of contributions directly concerns Pāṇinian grammar.

Peter M. Scharf deals with an important theoretical issue: should a formal grammar like Pāṇini's Aṣṭādhyāyī countenance situations such that the proper application of certain rules to provide for particular forms requires looking forward instead of depending strictly on what is provided by rules for what is available at given stages of derivation.

Scharf considers the use of locative forms such as *ārdhadhātuke* in Aṣṭādhyāyī (A) 2.4.35: आर्धधातुके and *sārvadhātuke* in A 3.1.68: कर्तरि शप् (सार्वधातुके 67) and subsequent sūtras. According to the usual Pāṇinīya interpretation, *sārva-dhātuke*, stated overtly in A 3.1.67 (सार्वधातुके यक्) and understood to recur in the following rule, designates a right context before which an operation applies (A 1.1.66: तस्मिन्निति निर्दिष्टे पूर्वस्य): when a sārvadhātuka affix introduced on condition that an agent is to be signified follows a verbal base, the suffix ***śap*** (*a* with the markers *ś* and *p*) is introduced after the base. For example, *pac-a-ti* (← *pac-ti* ← *pac-l*) '... is cooking'. Similarly, A 3.1.71: तनादिकृञ्भ्य उः serves to introduce *u* after verbs of the set beginning with *tan* 'stretch' as well as *kṛ* (***ḍukṛñ***) 'do, make': *kar-o-ti* (← *kṛ-u-ti* ← *kṛ-ti* ← *kṛ-l*). As shown, the sārvadhātuka ending ***tip*** replaces an *l*-affix, here ***laṭ***.

Now, at each stage of deriving a form such as *karoti* an accentual adjustment is made: an accent that is newly introduced sets aside one which was there previously. The affix *u* brings its own high pitch and sets aside high pitch of the base *kṛ*. This accounts for *ka̱rotì,* with low pitch on *kar* and high pitch on the suffix vowel *o*. By the same principle the form *kur-u-taḥ* (3rd du. pres. act.) would have high pitch on *-u-* following the base, but the required form has high pitch on the ending: *ku̱ru̱taḥ*. Accordingly, Pāṇinīyas accept that the principle in question has an exception: a suffix such as *u*, which comes between a verbal base and an ending, does not set aside the previously present accent. They also invoke a Pāṇinian sūtra as making known that Pāṇini too operated with the exception. Scharf differs from the tradition. He argues for interpreting *sārvadhātuke* in the pertinent rules as a locative of domain (*viṣayasaptamī*). Under this interpretation, an operation applies in the domain where a given affix will occur. Accordingly, Scharf argues that in deriving *kurutaḥ* the post-verbal affix *u* is introduced on condition that a sārvadhātuka will occur, before this is actually allowed to occur as a replacement for an *l*-affix. In this way, the general principle is maintained without exception.

Ajotikar and Kulkarni also deal with this principle, except that they extend the range of exceptions. They consider rules that may apply in deriving forms of compounds such as *prāñc-* 'directed to the fore', *parāñc-* 'directed into the distance, afar' and conclude that the accentuation of *parăcaḥ* (acc. pl. masc.) requires recognizing an exception to the satiśiṣṭasvara principle.

Sharon Ben-Dor takes up a comparably general issue, with respect to sūtras in which *dā*, *mā*, and *gā* are used to refer to verbal bases. A term such as *dā* could refer not only to a base *dā* (***ḍudāñ***) that contains *ā* in its primitive form listed in the dhātupāṭha but also to bases with *ā* gotten through substitution, such as *dā* (← *dai**p***) 'clean'. For, according to A 6.1.45: आदेच उपदेशेऽशिति as traditionally interpreted, *-ā* unconditionally replaces *-e, -o, -ai* or *-au* of a verbal base unless this is used with an affix bearing the marker *ś*. In his richly detailed philological study Ben-Dor presents evidence to support the thesis that one need not look ahead to target forms in order to determine which particular bases *gā*, *dā*, and *mā* refer to in particular sūtras. On the contrary, it suffices to determine carefully the conditions under which the operations provided therein apply.

Tiziana Pontillo also takes up a general topic and disagrees with traditional Pāṇinīyas. According to Pāṇinīyas, the procedure in question is one whereby a single remainder (*ekaśeṣa*) is provided where two or more homophonous (*sarūpa*) items can occur with one ending or set of endings (A 1.2.64: सरूपाणामेकशेष एकविभक्तौ). For example, instead of a potentially indeterminately long dvandva compound *aśvāśvāśvāśva°*, the single remainder *aśva-* is allowed to occur with the ending ***jas***, to derive *aśvāḥ* (nom. pl.) 'horses'. Similarly, by A 1.2.68: भ्रातृपुत्रौ स्वसृदुहितृभ्याम्, instead of a dvandva *bhrātāsvasṛ-* the single remainder *bhrātṛ-* is allowed with the ending *au*: *bhrātarau* (nom. du.) 'brother and sister'. According to Pāṇinīyas, *sarūpāṇām* of A 1.2.64 is a genitive form designating a group out of which one entity is set apart specifically (A 2.3.41: यतश्च निर्धारणम्). Pontillo argues that this should be interpreted instead as a genitive referring to items that are replaced (A 1.1.49: षष्ठी स्थानेयोगा) by a single item. This argument is couched within general considerations about ellipsis and discussion of passages from the Mahābhāṣya.

Toru Yagi studies the use of instrumental forms such as *chātreṇa* ('student') in छात्रेणोपाध्यायमद्राक्षीत् ('... saw [that] ... [was] a teacher [*upādhyāya*], because of his student [*chātra*]'), where the instrumental *chātreṇa* serves to refer to a student as a characteristic (*lakṣaṇa*) whereby someone is known to be characterized as having a particular status (*itthambhūta* 'become thus, who has attained such and such a state'). A person is recognized as one who is a teacher by virtue of his relation to a student. Ancient scholars argued whether such instrumentals could justify formulating a distinct rule (A 2.3.21: इत्थम्भूतलक्षणे) or should instead be considered to refer to an instrument (*karaṇa*) in the performance of an act or an accompanying entity with (*saha*) which something is said to occur, thus being accounted for by other rules.

Still within the compass of Pāṇini's grammar, Dipesh Katira, Chinmay Dharurkar and Malhar Kulkarni take up the use of forms with *vat* in the Aṣṭādhyāyī. The data discussed mainly involve usages with derivates in the taddhita affix *vati* as accounted for by two major sūtras, A 5.1.116-117: तेन तुल्यं क्रिया चेद्वतिः, तत्र तस्येव. Examples generally considered to illustrate these in the object language and the Aṣṭādhyāyī are: ब्राह्मणवद्वर्तते ('... is like a brāhmaṇa'), पाटलिपुत्रवत्साकेते परिखा ('the moat in Sāketa is like the one in Pāṭaliputra'), A 1.1.56: स्थानिवदादेशोऽनल्विधौ ('A replacement behaves like the entity it replaces except with respect to an operation that depends on a sound'), A 1.1.21: आद्यन्तवदेकस्मिन् ('[An operation] occurs for a single [sound] as it does for an initial or final element'). The authors consider how modern lexicographers describe derivates with *vat*, how modern translators have interpreted sūtras with such terms, link the use of words with *vat* to simile (*upamā*), metaphor (*rūpaka*) and imaginative equating (*utprekṣā*) in Indian poetics, and account for ambiguities and indeterminacies in modern translations of the Aṣṭādhyāyī.

Subodh Sharma and George Cardona deal with questions concerning items called *nipāta* ('particle') and *upasarga* ('preverb'). The class of particles includes terms such as *ca* ('and') and a subset of preverbs such as *anu* and *pra,* used with verbal bases. There are two extreme views concerning these. All the terms in question signify certain meanings; they are signifiers (*vācaka*). Alternatively, all these terms serve merely as cosignifiers (*dyotaka* 'illuminator') which serve to bring out meanings that, for semantic and formal reasons, are attributed to items with which they are used. In addition, there is the position that nipātas other than upasargas are signifiers, while upasargas are cosignifiers. For example, in *idañ cādaś ca* ('this [*idam*] and that [*adas*]'), *ca* is said to signify a meaning. On the other hand, in *pra jayati* ('... is extremely victorious'), the preverb *pra* is said merely to bring out a qualification of being victorious, excellence, which is part of the meaning attributed to the base *ji* itself (*jayati* '... is victorious'). Difficulties arise in connection with pairs such as *āste* ('... is seated') : *upāste* ('... reveres'), *bhavati* ('... is'): *anu bhavati* ('... experiences'), *tiṣṭhati* ('... comes to a stand, remains') : *pra tiṣṭhate* ('... departs'). Here there is a stronger case for considering that the preverbs *upa*, *anu*, and *pra* separately signify particular meanings. Such questions occupied Indian thinkers over many years and the discussions involved grammarians, etymologists, logicians of the Nyāya school, and ritualists (*mīmāṁsaka*). Subodh Sharma considers a wide range of thinkers, succinctly pointing out major arguments. George Cardona's purview is more limited. He concentrates on the reasons for and consequences of adopting one of two views. First, a complex like *anu bhavati* involves a single lexical unit *anu-bhū* 'experience' distinct from *bhū* 'be, become'. Alternatively, this complex involves two syntactic words (*pada*), only one of which is included in the class of verbal bases (*dhātu*).

Hideyo Ogawa's study takes us into the general area of relations between speech forms (*śabda*) and their meanings (*artha*), with specific reference to Bhartṛhari's view. One of the verses of the Vākyapadīya outlining the topics of this treatise (1.25ab: कार्यकारणभावेन योग्यभावेन च स्थिता: ।) notes two of these. First, speech units and their meanings have the status of being cause and effect (*kāryakāraṇabhāva*): from a hearer's vantage, a perceived linguistic unit causes the understanding of a meaning this conveys, and from a speaker's vantage a meaning he wishes to express causes him to use a particular linguistic unit. Secondly, a term has the property of being fit, hence capable (*yogyatā*) of conveying a particular meaning. In addition, there is the relation of one being the other (सोऽयमिति सम्बन्ध:), conceived of as the result of a superimposition (*adhyāsa*) of one on the other, not in the same manner that in common usage one imputes imaginatively a property on someone — as when one says that a Vāhīka is an ox (गौर्वाहीक:) — but an identification that has been in place since language use began. Although Bhartṛhari does not mention this identity relation (*abheda*) in the passage noted, he does in his Mahābhāṣyadīpikā and auto-commentary on the Vākyapadīya. Helārāja notes that Bhartṛhari does not give separate status to this as opposed to the cause-effect and fitness relations, because it is ultimately the basis of these two, so that it is not merely a third possible relation. In his meticulously documented paper, Ogawa presents the textual evidence concerning this issue and refutes the claim that Bhartṛhari did not recognize the identity relation.

Yuki Tomonari takes up several points concerning which Prābhākaramīmāṁsakas and Naiyāyikas differ from and attack Pāṇinian grammarians. The arguments considered concern twelve sūtras of the Aṣṭādhyāyī. Seven of these are rules which assign to direct participants in actions (*kāraka*) category names — *apādāna*, *sampradāna*, *karaṇa*, *adhikaraṇa*, *karman*, *kartṛ*, *hetu* — and thereby assign participants to particular semantic-syntactic categories. Three rules serve to introduce the category names *dhātu* 'verbal base, root' (A 1.3.1: भूवादयो धातव:) and *prātipadika* 'nominal base' (A 1.2.45-46: अर्थवदधातुरप्रत्यय: प्रातिपदिकम्, कृत्तद्धितसमासाश्च). One is a major heading whereby taddhita affixes are optionally introduced and, where specified, are introduced after the first of semantically and syntactically related syntactic items (A 4.1.82: समर्थानां प्रथमाद्वा). Another rule (A 2.1.1: समर्थ: पदविधि:), traditionally considered a metarule with scope over the entire Aṣṭādhyāyī, provides that an operation concerning padas applies only to such terms as are syntactically and semantically related. Tomonari treats parallel arguments from Prabhākara's Bṛhatī on Śabara's Bhāṣya on Jaimini's Mīmāṁsāsutra and Jayanta Bhaṭṭa's Nyāyamañjarī. He considers the relations between the passages in question to each other and to what Pāṇinīyas said earlier, finally concluding that the arguments presented in the Bṛhatī and Nyāyamañjarī amount to cavilling (*vitaṇḍā*).

Vedmitra Arya's contribution brings in a non-Pāṇinian grammar, the Sārasvatavyākaraṇa of Anubhūtisvarūpa. Arya discusses the different formulations for describing nominal case forms (*subanta*) in the Sārasvatavyākaraṇa, contrasts these descriptions with those of Pāṇini, and argues that the Sārasvata procedures are simpler.

Finally, Paramanand Jha brings us into the area of modern Sanskrit literature, discussing the usage in the prose work Śivarājavijaya of Ambika Dutt Vyas. Jha surveys the use of forms in different categories and speaks of this work with admiration. He also notes some usages that do not conform to chaste Sanskrit in accordance with Pāṇinian grammar and suggests that a new revised edition is in order.

The thirteen articles in this collection thus cover a broad range of topics within the general area designated *vyākaraṇa*.

I am happy now to acknowledge the help of colleagues. As joint conveners, with me, of the vyākaraṇa section of the 15th World Sanskrit Conference, Professors Saroja Bhate and Dipti Tripathi read all the abstracts submitted and contributed to our final joint decisions for the program. In the course of my editing the papers which finally were invited, they also responded when I called on them to react to my comments on some papers. The authors of papers published here merit mention not only for their contributions but also for their cooperation. They responded to my comments and queries in ways that eased my task as editor. Finally, I am grateful to Professor Radhavallabh Tripathi and his aides for their prompt and helpful responses to my questions, help in organizing sessions during the 15th World Sanskrit Conference, and subsequent help in the publication stages. Their management of the entire conference has made it a pleasure to participate.

George Cardona

Contents

Main currents in the European tradition of Sanskrit grammars

Iwona Milewska

The subject of this article is an attempt to differentiate and briefly describe the main currents which have appeared in the European tradition of Sanskrit grammars. As this topic has never been discussed before in a concise form, let us look at it from both diachronic and synchronic perspectives.

The history of the European tradition of Sanskrit grammars is a comparatively long one as nearly four hundred years have passed since the first known book on Sanskrit grammar was composed. This was the grammar of father Heinrich Roth from 1660, which has survived until the modern day in manuscript form. Altogether we are dealing with nearly four hundred years of modern tradition of India–Europe contacts during which more than one hundred grammars were composed by Europeans and most of them were published, thanks to which they can be described and analyzed here. The only grammars not published at the time of their preparation are the first grammars which survived in manuscript form and which, it is worth stressing, only recently have come to light. Such is the case with the manuscript of *Grammatica grandonica* by Ernst Johann Hanxleden (1681-1723), discovered in 2010 in Convento di San Silvestro, a Carmelite monastery located in Montecompatri in the Province of Roma. The manuscript was found by a Belgian scholar Dr. Toon van Hal. Most probably there are also at least some more grammars, not accessible to the modern researcher, which have been composed but never published or presented to the general public in such a way that any traces of them could now be found. Probably some of these grammars were shared by their authors only with their "direct public", that is, with pupils who were taught by them as teachers — authors of materials who tried to invent their own solutions of the presentation of

Sanskrit grammar and add them to the existing written and published sources. However, the circulation of such grammars or materials was, even if meaningful for particular adepts, a limited one. They are unknown to others, and in most cases there is no information on them in any libraries. As a result, one can find them only in the memories of people who met their authors and who are still alive.[1] These facts show the possibility of still some more discoveries to be made in future by scholars who will focus on searching for them or of such a discovery being made by sheer chance. This can happen also to somebody not directly connected with the study of Sanskrit grammar, who may come across a grammar preserved in the form of a manuscript or, less probably, in printed form. From what we know so far, it seems that over one hundred grammars is quite an impressive number and certainly one which allows certain generalizations and classifications. It allows the attempt to deal with the topic of main currents which appeared during the years of the European modern tradition.

By "European tradition" we will understand here, first of all, grammars of Sanskrit composed in most cases by scholars coming from Europe. However, we will add also those composed in the nineteenth and twentieth centuries by researchers from America, Canada and Australia, as it seems that for historical reasons and dependencies these authors and the grammars written by them can be included in what we call here the European tradition. One of the readily visible features of these grammars is that European methods of exposition are used in them. Only in some of them, in

1. The author knows of at least one such case where the materials in written form of a Sanskrit grammar covering most major topics together with exercises was prepared but never published. It is a grammar entitled *First year Sanskrit course,* prepared, after many years of effort, by J. E. B. Grey, lecturer at the London School of Oriental and African Studies. The manuscript, more than two hundred pages long, is ready for publication but not published to date. The grammar, as mentioned above, is the result of many years of work by an eminent Sanskrit teacher who based its content on his own experiences of teaching Sanskrit. It contains several new solutions in presentation (e.g. of the alphabet) and certainly it is a loss that it still awaits publication.

rather rare cases, are there attempts to join European and Indian ways of presenting Sanskrit. These can be put into a separate group which, perhaps, will be one of the promising options for future attempts. This feature of what may be called the European method of presentation of Sanskrit grammar is, aside from the European origin of their authors, who took the grammars developed in Europe as their guides, also the fact which makes them very different from the traditional Indian ones. We must not forget, however, that many European grammars were, in their content, obviously based, at least partly, on Indian sources.

The main reason for the decision to describe here only works included in the European tradition of Sanskrit grammars is the need to limit the area covered by this investigation and the thesis of their particular features. An additional argument is that at least some of them are the result of the limitations faced by European scholars: their scope of access to the Indian sources, their generally European education, their lack of training in memorization techniques as a method of dealing with Sanskrit grammars, the influence of the European tradition of grammars developed and used for languages other than Sanskrit, to mention only a few.

One more limitation set here is the exclusion of grammars composed in Japan, China and other countries whose traditions are not connected with the European tradition. Such grammars obviously exist but they have to be excluded from this study, even if at least some of them probably use European methods of presenting grammatical content. This subject may open the field for an interesting future investigation.[2]

We have to add also that the main focus of this presentation will be to describe grammars in English and German, since they are most significant as examples of the main currents which have appeared during the modern years of the European tradition of

2. The author is conscious of these traditions but due to the lack of command of respective languages and lack of opportunity to visit libraries which may have these grammars even a bird's-eye view of them is not possible.

Sanskrit grammars. Grammars in other European languages, in the majority of cases, were copies or slightly changed versions based on Sanskrit grammars written in English or German.[3]

As already mentioned above, about a hundred grammars have been composed in what we call the European modern tradition. The reasons for preparing so many of them might have several explanations. Firstly, their authors were not satisfied with the existing sources of the European information on Sanskrit grammar. Secondly, they were, most probably, deeply convinced that their presentation had the value of being new and different in major features from others composed earlier or contemporaneously. Thirdly, and more commonly, their authors did not have the information or access to other grammars already composed and published. For obvious reasons such was the situation with the grammars which were composed in the first period, that is those which did not have any tradition preceding them. They were genuine, even if sometimes similar both in their content and presentation methods to others.

When we try to look at the European tradition diachronically we can differentiate several stages of its development as far as the content and methods of the exposition of Sanskrit grammar used in them are concerned. These stages covering the oncoming centuries are connected with the history of modern European-Indian contacts. These contacts, as we know, have a long lasting modern tradition starting from the period of first travelers who reached India at the end of the fifteenth century. We will not focus on this history of contacts here, since this is not our main subject and it has already been described in detail in many other books and

3. Of course there have been, especially in the twentieth century, at least some genuine attempts to deal with Sanskrit grammar in a new way in languages other than English or German (e.g., French or Italian), but it is impossible to discuss them here in detail. For more extensive information on some other grammars one can consult, for example, Milewska 2008.

articles.[4]

These stages in diachronic perspective can be described as follows:

- grammars composed in the seventeenth and eighteenth centuries by European Catholic missionaries (Heinrich Roth, Johann E. Hanxleden, Paulinus a Sancto Bartholomaeo)
- grammars coming from the beginning of the nineteenth century whose authors were connected with the activities of the East India Company (Charles Wilkins, Henry Thomas Colebrooke, William Carey, Horace Hayman Wilson)
- grammars from the same period written mostly by German scholars such as Franz Bopp, which were based on sources available in Europe in the nineteenth century but whose authors had never been in India themselves
- grammars from the second half of the nineteenth century based on direct Indian sources and personal visits to India resulting in studies undertaken there (Georg Buehler, Franz Kielhorn) and endeavours of particular scholars who worked in Europe and used both Indian and European sources of information (Adolf Friedrich Stenzler, William Dwight Whitney)
- grammars of the turn of nineteenth and twentieth centuries in which the search for simplicity and conciseness is visible (Arthur Anthony Macdonell)
- a grammar of the opposite kind, extensive, descriptive and historical, begun by Jakob Wackernagel at the end of nineteenth century, subsequently continued — though not yet completed — by the next generations of scholars, which was directed mostly to linguists
- twentieth century grammars that are examples of many different choices of methods used for presentation of Sanskrit grammar (Jan Gonda, Michael Coulson, Robert Goldman and

4. It will suffice to mention one: Halbfass 1981, which is one of the most popular sources of such information, translated into English (Halbfass 1988) and other languages, e.g., Polish (Nowakowska and Piotrowski 2008)

Sally Sutherland)

- twentieth century grammars whose authors are well acquaintened with European grammars used for teaching or learning European languages, both ancient (W. Maurer, D. Killingley) and modern (Ashok N. Aklujkar, Madhav M. Deshpande)

The diachronic method may be one way of presenting the currents which appeared in their respective periods. In our article, after this short resume showing the currents in their historical development, we will focus on the synhronic perspective, where the currents may be seen as having certain common features reappearing during the passage of time, having their own separate tradition of development. These currents will be shown in this way and then briefly described with a collection of examples illustrating these tendencies as evolving during consecutive years. We will use this method of description here as it seems more clear for a short presentation.

The current which seems to be the most popular in the European tradition of Sanskrit grammars is that of a descriptive nature. Sanskrit grammar is presented here in the form of chapters of a general nature divided into smaller units devoted to particular grammatical topics. Large chapters on particular grammatical categories (such as the categories of nouns or verbs) are organized as consecutive explanations of particular grammatical phenomena: declension tables, roles of cases, conjugation paradigms, tenses, moods etc. These constitute books which can be read in at least two possible ways: chapter by chapter or only select paragraphs, as necessary. Such grammars are called descriptive. Within chapters or smaller units they are synthetic in their description. Examples of certain forms are given but, in most cases, not in large numbers. Exceptional forms are added to the typical ones. We may observe that sometimes the right balance between typical and atypical forms is not achieved. The result of not giving the right view of the typical forms is the price for such a description. This "tradition" continues to the present day and hardly anywhere can one find any theoretical reflection on this problem.

The descriptive mode of presentation of grammar is popular not only for Sanskrit but also for other European languages. Grammars of this type can obviously be used not only by those who are starting their adventure with Sanskrit and want to become specialists in this language but also by linguists, specialists in philosophy or religious studies and so on. The European public is certainly well accustomed to such grammars and such ways of presentation.

In this presentation we will not give details of the earliest three manuscripts mentioned above, as they did not have much influence on the European tradition of Sanskrit grammars and our goal is to describe briefly only the most typical works. An exception will be made only for the grammar of Heinrich Roth (1620-1668), since it was, to our knowledge, the first one written by a European. His grammar, written most probably between the years 1660 and 1662, was an example of this kind. It is evident that Roth based his grammar on Indian grammars popular at the period of his stay in India. Roth most probably learned Sanskrit from the local pandits and the region he stayed in for most of his time spent in India was that close to Agra. The title of his grammar, written in Latin, was *Grammatica linguae Sanscretane Brachmanum Indiae Orientalis*. It was brought to Europe by Roth in 1664. Unfortunately, due to the policy of church superiors, for a long time his grammar did not become known to the greater public, being hidden in the depths of the library in Rome and kept there in manuscript form. In 1988, after its fortunate discovery this work was published and only since then have we the chance to analyze its structure.[5] This descriptive grammar consists of five large chapters covering the topics of orthography (De Ortographia), the declension of nouns, adjectives

5. The discovery was made by Arnulf Camps and Jean-Claude Muller after many-years of searching. Its facsimile was published together with an extensive introduction (1988).

and pronouns (De Declinacionibus Nominum), the conjugation of verbs (De Conjugacionis Verborum), nominal forms of verbs (De Verbalibus seu kridaṁtaḥ) and syntax of Sanskrit (De syntaxi huius Linguae). The last chapter contains a section devoted to the subject of adverbs. Roth added to his grammar also some information on major kinds of metres (Appendix ad universam grammaticam). The description of Sanskrit given by Roth seems to be versatile and comparatively complete. The presentation, based on direct Indian sources, follows the Indian tradition as far as particular grammatical forms are differentiated and as far as the choice of examples is concerned. It adopts the traditional Indian examples used for illustration of certain grammatical topics. However, the grammatical terms given by Roth are, in most cases, in Latin, and the theoretical parts are also written in Latin. This grammar, even if unknown to the later European tradition, is meaningful, since its structure is repeated in many descriptive grammars which followed. The way of gathering and presenting information on Sanskrit may be labelled a mixture of Indian and European ways of dealing with grammar (European structure, Indian examples).

It is a striking fact that one of the most famous authors of a Sanskrit grammar of this kind, very important for the later European tradition, Adolf F. Stenzler (1809-1877), in his work published over two hundred years later (1868), used a similar method in his description of grammar topics even if Roth's grammar was most probably not known to him. Stenzler covered the major topics of Sanskrit grammar in nine descriptive chapters devoted to separate large categories. The first three chapters dealt with the writing system (Schriftlehre), phonology (Lautlehre), and declension of nouns (Flexionslehre). He divided the last topic into vowel and consonant declensions, and within this division he differentiated nouns of one, two or three stems. In the next chapter he described the rules of comparison (Komparation), then the pronouns (Declination der Pronomina) and numerals (Zahlwörter).

Following this came the chapter on conjugation (Konjugation) where he described the systems of conjugation. Word formation, nouns and adjectives together with feminine forms (Wortbildung), were given in the next chapter. Stenzler devoted his last chapter to the explanation and classification of compounds of both verbal and noun character (Kompositionslehre). Within these large chapters Stenzler divided the information into smaller sub-chapters, adding also detailed cross references which might help navigating through the grammatical content. The construction of his grammar was very clear. The grammatical topics, as we have seen, were presented in a logical sequence and the choice of them was very well thought out. As mentioned above, the structure of the grammar resembles the one given nearly two hundred years earlier by Roth. As I have also noted, such a model of description most probably came out of the fact that both grammars were dependent on the Indian and also the European tradition of presentation. They were not dependent on each other, for the reasons described above. It is worth stressing, nevertheless, how good father Roth was in his pioneering effort to deal with Sanskrit grammar. The difference between these two grammars is that Stenzler added a short part with grammatical exercises, chrestomathies of fragments of Sanskrit texts and a glossary.

Stenzler's descriptive grammar has become a source of inspiration for many grammars written in other European languages.[6] It was also translated into other European languages more than one hundred years later, that is at the end of twentieth century, which shows its value also in modern times.[7] In Germany it has had, to my knowledge, eighteen editions, being probably the main Sanskrit grammar for many generations of both German and other Sanskritists. The last edition was published in 1995.[8]

6. See, e. g.,Gawroński 1932.

7. See Söhnen 1992, Krnic 1995.

8. 2nd ed. Breslau 1872; 3rd ed. 1875; 4th ed. Breslau 1880; 5th ed. 1885; 6th

The descriptive attitude is the feature of many other Sanskrit grammars published in Europe. Let me mention only some being published in the nineteenth and twentieth centuries. The first ones were composed by English scholars connected with the activities of the East India company. Such were the grammars of Charles Wilkins (1749-1836) (1808) and Henry Th. Colebrooke (1765-1837) (1805). Similar were the works by H. H. Wilson (1786-1860) (1841), M. Monier-Williams (1819-1899) (1846), and F. Max Mueller (1823-1900) (1866). All of these grammars appeared in the nineteenth century.

In the twentieth century the tradition of the descriptive approach continued to have exponents in the works of scholars from different countries of Europe; for example: V. A. Kocergina (1956), Louis Renou (1896-1966) (1968). The latest descriptive Sanskrit grammar, in German (Guhe 2008), stems from the beginning of twenty-first century. The popularity of this descriptive method of presenting the rules of Sanskrit grammar to the European public shows that this method is acceptable to large circles of readers with European philological training due not only to clarity but also well thought out structure and range.

The descriptive current which appeared in the European tradition of Sanskrit grammars, in addition to having its exponents in extensive grammars, was also used by some authors who decided to prepare them in a much more condensed way.

Shortening and simplifying Sanskrit grammar was the goal of Arthur Anthony Macdonell (1854-1930) in his work of 1901, in which he tried to simplify wherever possible and to present the content of his grammar in a user-friendly way. His main target was students of Sanskrit and he wanted to give them the tools necessary

ed. revised by R. Pischel, Breslau 1892; 7th ed. 1902; 8th ed. 1908; 9th ed. revised by K. F. Geldner 1915; 10th ed. 1923; 11th ed. 1939; 12th ed. 1943; 13th ed. 1952; 14th ed. revised by S. Biswas 1960; 15th ed. 1965; 16th ed. 1970; 17th ed. 1980; 18th ed. revised by A. Wetzler, Berlin-New York 1995.

for reading original Sanskrit texts. This was a pocket-sized book. It has had many editions since the day of its first publication, the last at the end of the twentieth century, reprinted in India. The main features of grammars similar to Macdonell's can be summarized as follows: a concise exposition of grammatical topics, clarity of presentation, a user-friendly form. Similar, and even more concise, is the grammar by Jan Gonda (1905-1991) (1941), in which the author covers the main topics of Sanskrit grammar in a pocket-sized book of only ninety-six pages. It is meaningful that his grammar gained huge popularity and was translated not only into major European languages like English (Ford 1966), French (R. Rocher 1966) and Spanish, but also into Japanese.[9] Another example of a descriptive but at the same time very concise Sanskrit grammar is the one by Klaus Karttunen (1984).

The next current which appeared comparatively early in the history of the European Sanskrit grammars was that which can be labelled comparative. Sanskrit has become one of the major languages used for comparisons with other languages of the Indo – Europan family of languages. The first scholar whose works are to be described here is certainly Franz Bopp (1791–1867). As we know, in his first book (1816), he already established the standards for comparative philology. His main goal was to trace the common origin of grammatical forms of inflection in Sanskrit, Greek, Latin, Persian and Germanic languages. Some years later (1828), Bopp also published a comparative dictionary which was meant to accompany his grammar. His last, extremely comprehensive work, in six parts (1833-1852), was a comparative grammar. The value of all Bopp's works for the history of the European approaches to Sanskrit is indisputable. He gave a new perspective to studies on

9. Spanish translation: *Gramática elemental de la lengua sánscrita*, México: El Colegio de México, 1982. Japanese translation: *Sanskuritto-go shoto bunpo* Tokyo, 1974. I have not been able to obtain additional information on these works.

Sanskrit grammar, established the standards for such study and also showed the importance of the knowledge of Sanskrit for the needs of comparative linguistics studies.

Descriptive but simultaneously comparative, even if not as wide-ranging as Bopp's, was the grammar of Monier Monier-Williams (1846). In addition to describing the forms, he compared them to the appropriate ones from ancient European languages in order to point to their common origin. Similar grammars were written in other European languages; to mention just some: in French: A. J. Carnoy (1925), in Italian: Vittore Pisani (1943), in Spanish F. R. Adrados (1953).

In all these works the Indo-European perspective used for comparative reasons takes precedence over other aspects of exposition of the content. The examples which are given in them come obviously from the above-mentioned languages and they are often shown in schemes or tables arranged in horizontal order, which is different from the traditional vertical exposition used in most other grammars. They are a perfect source of information for linguists who are interested in Sanskrit as compared to other languages of the Indo-European family.

Another type of comparative grammar is one that can be called historico–comparative. The first versatile book using this method of presentation was the one already mentioned above, by M. Monier–Williams (1846). But the one to become very popular was composed by the American Indologist William Dwight Whitney (1827-1894) and published in 1879. In his grammar, Whitney included not only a full descriptive presentation of Sanskrit grammar but also the earlier Vedic and Brahmanic forms in order to give information on them and to put stress on their origin.

Probably the most exhaustive grammar of this kind was begun by Jakob Wackernagel (1853-1938), then continued and revised by Albert Debrunner and Louis Renou — who composed on new general introduction to the work — as well as Richard Hauschild, who compiled an index to the published volumes. This work aims at covering all grammatical topics, including syntax, and in its presentation mode it is directed mostly to linguists.

Simultaneously with the currents mentioned above, though not so wide spread, there appeared a new current important for the history of European ways of describing Sanskrit grammar and the methods used for its presentation. This can be labelled a current of step-by-step presentation or a current of handbooks of grammars. It seems that one of the major reasons for preparing grammars of Sanskrit arranged in this way was pedagogic. The authors realized that if the goal of their works was to help potential readers learn the grammar mostly for practical reasons, among which the most important was reading original texts, they should invent another structure. As a result of such a defined target, in the opinion of these authors what can be called a good grammar should be arranged in a way that enables reaching this goal. Descriptive or comparative grammars were a very good source of information mainly as reference grammars, but they were most useful for seeing the language from a bird's-eye view or to check grammatical topics or particular forms which were already known to the reader from previous studies.

Probably the first one who tried to propose such a method was William Carey (1761-1834), a baptist missionary who went to India to convert its inhabitants to Christianity. He spent most of his stay in India in Calcutta and was appointed a teacher of both Bengali and Sanskrit. It is believed, though not known certainly, that with the help of local pandits he learned to speak Sanskrit and some other Indian languages. His task was to teach Europeans staying in India at this time and he tried to give them basic information in an easy-to-comprehend way. His grammar, published in 1806, did not become popular in India and it was hardly known in Europe, although we can note that in some French works on Sanskrit grammar dating from the mid-nineteenth century Carey's grammar is mentioned as a source of information.[10]

The single most widely known and popular for using such a didactic method was devised by Georg Buehler (1837-1898). Buehler also spent many years in India, and he was able to speak Sanskrit fluently. In his work Buehler (1883) divided the material into separate lessons in which he introduced particular grammatical topics in a concise form. Some grammatical problems — or what we can call items — were treated in one separate lesson while others continued through several of them. Small glossaries were added to each of the lessons. These lessons contained also collections of exercises meant to help in the active acquisition of the language. It is worth adding that these exercises were mostly artificially devised for training in particular grammatical topics. The method used in this book was what in modern applied linguistics is called grammar–translation. This was something new in the European tradition of Sanskrit grammars, although at this time it was already used for teaching and learning other European languages, including classical European ones like Greek or Latin. As mentioned above, Buehler's work was a handbook rather than what we call a descriptive grammar. It was soon translated to English by Edward Delavan Perry and published in the United States in 1885 to great acclaim.[11] Such grammars are meant to teach Sanskrit grammar step-by-step with the help of a teacher.

One step further were the grammars devised in the manner of teach-yourself books. The role of a teacher was limited and grammatical topics were explained in such a way as to enable a pupil to study them without any help. It is not widely known that the precursor of such an idea was James Robert Ballantyne (1813-1864), a professor of Moral Philosophy at the Sanskrit College in Benares. In 1843 he published a small booklet (only twenty-two pages long) in which Sanskrit grammar was explained

10. See, for example, M. Desgranges 1845-47.

11. To my knowledge Perry's work has had four editions (1885, 1886, 1901, 1936) and is still used in quite a few places where Sanskrit is taught.

in the form of questions and answers, with questions being asked by a potential student. It covered the topics of alphabet, sandhi, nouns, verbs and compounds in a very simplified way. Even if it was certainly too short and in many parts not accurate enough for learning Sanskrit, its main novelty and advantage were the new style in which it was written. In 1850 another of Ballantyne's books was published. This time the author explained the grammatical topics in twenty-three consecutive lessons. He included several extracts from the Hitopadeśa, and adjoined grammar exercises in the form of questions and answers. A small Sanskrit-English dictionary was appended at the end of the book. This work became popular, with at least four later editions (1862, 1865, 1885 and 1941). However, it was not very widely known in Europe even during Ballantyne's lifetime, and it took many years for Europeans to come back to the idea of teach-yourself grammars as applied to Sankrit.

Not until 1976 did any subsequent work of this kind appear. The next such book was by Michael Coulson (1936-1975). Published in the teach yourself series of grammars, Coulson's book appeared after the author's death, seen through the press by Richard Gombrich, then revised by Gombrich and James Benson. It is still very popular. This book is based on extracts of texts drawn from Sanskrit dramas. Its content is divided into fifteen chapters through which, step by step, the reader is prepared for independent work. It is very clearly designed, contains several appendices with grammatical paradigms, classical metres, exercises with key and small Sanskrit-English and English-Sanskrit glossaries. It also contains sandhi grids which due to their clearness of presentation are used by many modern-day Sanskritists. An important feature of this grammar is that it can prepare one for the reading of specialized kind of texts, in this case, dramas. In my opinion this current should be continued, and probably introduced to the process of learning after general introductory grammar courses. It may stand as a perfect tool for enabling work with particular kind of texts: literary, philosophical, religious or even more specialized, especially as far as Sanskrit literature or philosophy is concerned, covering different styles and structures used for particular works.

It is worth mentioning that at the end of the twentieth century the method of using courses in classical European languages as guides for the Sanskrit grammar books reappeared. Additionally, the methods widely used for teaching modern European languages, including exercises used, influenced works on classical European and Indian languages. Typical examples of such books are those of Walter Maurer (1995) and Dermot Killingley (1996-1997). Both of these, influenced by strategies used for teaching classical European languages, are oriented towards a much more active knowledge of a language. They are full of exercises, not only involving translation but also teaching particular grammatical structures.

This feature of a much more active command of Sanskrit is realized in the wider spectrum of proposals and is typical for most of the grammars coming from the end of the twentieth century. This is the dominant attitude also in the grammars in which European and Indian methods of teaching languages are mixed. Such is the work of Robert Goldman and Sally Sutherland, first published in 1980 and, as far as I know, published in a revised version in 1987 and yet again in 1992, 1999, 2002, 2004 and 2011. The authors of this primer take advantage of their fluency in spoken Sanskrit. Being influenced by Indian methods they suggest the memorization of parts of Sanskrit texts. This memorization should gradually cover larger and larger fragments. Their handbook is meant as a preparation for the reading of the epic Rāmāyaṇa by oneself, without any external help. Starting from artificially devised texts, step by step the student is faced with more and more complicated structures of the language. At the end of this process of learning an ability to read the original text of the epic should be achieved. Goldman and Sutherland's proposal is to use Indian grammatical vocabulary for the description of separate grammatical forms instead of Latin terminology. Their very good argument is that this is much more appropriate and, in many cases, helpful. This proposal is certainly worth considering in future grammars of Sanskrit to be developed by Europeans. Goldman and Sutherland's procedures are followed, most probably independently, by an Indian author working in the United States, Madhav Deshpande (1997). He also uses artificial Sanskrit sentences for the purpose of facilitating the approach to original texts. An innovation is that he adds to his handbook simplified versions of famous Sanskrit stories like those of Śakuntalā, Rāma, Nala and Damayantī and some others.

Another very interesting modern attempt to deal with Sanskrit grammar not only in the form of an introductory course but also as a primer which can be used with a particular, specialized kind of text is Scharf's primer (2003). This work is very well planned and has a versatile introductory part. General topics of grammar are discussed and suggestions of modes of usage for both students and instructors are included. Scharf presents the story of Rāma taken from the Mahābhārata with grammatical analyses of Mbh. 3.257-276, small glossaries added to each part, fragments of texts both in Devanāgarī and Roman transliteration, and English translations. Appendixes include a glossary of proper names with short characterizations of characters, genealogy tables, a word index and a short bibliography. From what I can see it seems this extremely extensive book (over nine hundred pages-long) is what I have foreseen as the next step to be worked on in the future history of grammars of Sanskrit.

To my knowledge, in the European tradition of Sanskrit grammars the only one composed in English in which the most recent European linguistic terms are used in the description of Sanskrit is the small book written by Siew-Yew Killingley (1940-2004) and Dermot Killingley (1995). Modern European linguistic terms like *phoneme* and *lexeme* are applied here to

Sanskrit grammar, enabling linguists trained in the West to look at Sanskrit from this perspective. The book includes a very precise and detailed description of Sanskrit syntax, which is a rarity in nearly all previous grammars. The question whether it will stand as the beginning of the new current in the exposition of Sanskrit grammar is an open one.

In 1990 Ashok Aklujkar, whose training was both traditional Indian and European (as was M. M. Deshpande's), composed and published a primer which includes the majority of methods of presenting Sanskrit. It covers most of the currents which have appeared during the years of the European tradition of Sanskrit grammars. In his book, in four volumes accompanied by six cassettes, Aklujkar includes both a descriptive grammar and a handbook of Sanskrit in which the language is presented step by step. The work abounds in exercises, paradigms of forms presented in manifold ways with different types of tables adjoining the main exposition of Sanskrit grammar rules. Small glossaries are also appended to the course. This is the first grammar in which the methods of teaching and learning are described and analyzed theoretically in the introduction and where the goals to be achieved by using the book are clearly described. Probably Aklujkar's is the first concise text of theoretical reflection over the strategies which can be or are being used in the exposition of Sanskrit grammar to European readers.

As might have been expected, modern day internet communication has already brought us some grammars of Sanskrit available for users of computers. One of these courses consists of Sanskrit grammar explained in separate lessons, with additional audio parts added. In this course the goal to be achieved is described as gaining the ability to read the original text of the Bhagavadgītā without any external help.[12] Most probably, the internet, which is becoming a more and more popular method of

12. This course is available at www.learnsanskrit.org.

obtaining information on every subject, will also become the major source on Sanskrit and its grammar. It is interesting to think of what influence it will have on future currents of description of Sanskrit. However, we should hope that the old tradition of books in paper form composed during the years of the European tradition of Sanskrit grammar is not to cease totally.

For reasons of space I have not touched here on an important field closely associated with the subject of grammars, that is the history of dictionaries, chrestomathies or collections of exercises planned, collected or invented by Europeans. All of these sources of information have been of major importance to the European public, but they require a separate treatment.

To summarize the European tradition of Sanskrit grammars described above, we can state that at least the following currents may be differentiated: descriptive grammars; comparative works, arranged synchronically and diachronically; didactic works, with several subtypes, namely handbooks or step-by-step grammars, teach yourself books, those in which only European methods of arrangement and presentation are used, and grammars which connect European and Indian ways of description and methods. The next currents, which appeared only in the twentieth century, are those in which techniques of modern methods of applied linguistics are used and the ones in which modern European linguistic categories and terms are applied to Sanskrit. Finally, we have the tendency of grammars in which the authors try to look at Sanskrit in a more active way. They prepare the reader not only for ancient texts but also for the creation of original Sanskrit sentences. This trend is most probably influenced by "Spoken Sanskrit" courses, which have been organized since the 1960s. Last but not least we have grammars in which most of the previously invented methods of description are used. Their authors take advantage of what, in their opinion, was the best and most productive in the previous traditions of both Indian and European origin. It is worth adding that the focus on audio methods as used simultaneously with the traditional ones is nowadays visible.

As mentioned above, the internet will without doubt bring opportunities for new ways of treating Sanskrit grammar. There will certainly be a time when any invention will have a chance of becoming immediately available globally. Will there perhaps be a time of virtual grammars and virtual teachers? A time of opportunity for virtual visits to distant countries? Or perhaps visits to ancient times? Will this bring something really genuine as far as the European tradition of Sanskrit grammars is concerned? Time will tell.

Bibliography

Adrados, Francisco Rodríguez

1953 *Védico y sánscrito clásico: gramática, textos anotados y vocabulario etimológico.* Manual de lingüística indoeuropea, cuaderno 2. Madrid: Consejo Superior de investigaciones científicas, Instituto Antonio de Nebrija. [Second edition 1992]

Aklujkar, Ashok

1990 *Sanskrit. An Easy Introduction to an Enchanting Language.* Three volumes in four parts. Vancouver, British Columbia: Department of Asian Studies, University of British Columbia. [volume one 1, Tools: Grammatical, part A, Tools: Grammatical, part B, volume two, Tools: Lexical, volume three, Tests and Transition] [Editions 2002, 2003, 2005]

Ballantyne, James Robert

1843 *A catechism of Sanskrit grammar.* London-Edinburgh. [Third edition 1851]

1850 *First lessons in Sanskrit grammar; with an introduction to the Hitopadeśa.* Mirzapore. [Second edition 1862, third edition 1865, fourth edition 1885, reprint 1941]

Baranowski, Bolesław

1977 *Podręcznik sanskrytu.* Warszawa: Akademia Teologii Katolickiej. [Translation of Buehler]

Benfey, Theodor

1852-54 *Handbuch der Sanskritsprache. Zum Gebrauch für Vorlesungen und zum Selbststudium.* Leipzig: F. A. Brockhaus.

Bopp, Franz

1816 *Ueber das Konjugationssystem der Sanskritsprache in Vergleichung mit jenem der griechischen, lateinischen, persischen und germanischen Sprache.*

Frankfurt am Main: Andreaische Buchhandlung.

1828 *Glossarium comparativum linguae sanscritae in quo omnes sanscritae radices et vocabula usitatissima explicantur et cum vocabulis graecis, latinis, germanicis, lituanicis, slavicis, celticis comparantur*. Berlin: Dümmler. [Second edition 1840-1844]

1832 *Kritische Grammatik der Sanskrita-Sprache in kürzerer Fassung*. Berlin. [Second revised edition 1845, third edition 1863, fourth edition 1868 Berlin: Nicolai]

1833-52 *Vergleichende Grammatik des sanskrit, send, griechischen, lateinischen, lituanischen, altslavischen, gothischen und deutschen*, Berlin: Dümmler.

Buehler, Georg

1883 *Leitfaden für den Elementarcursus des Sanskrit mit Übungsstücken und zwei Glossaren.* Wien: Carl Konegen. [Second revised edition Wien 1927]

Camps, Arnulf and Jean-Claude Muller

1988 *The Sanskrit Grammar and Manuscripts of Father Heinrich Roth S. J. (1620-1668). Facsimile Edition of Biblioteca Nazionale, Rome, Mss. Or. 171 and 172, with an introduction by Arnulf Camps and Jean-Claude Muller.* Leiden-NewYork-København-Köln: E. J. Brill.

Carey, William

1806 *A Grammar of the Sungskrit language, composed from the works of the most esteemed Grammarians, to which are added examples for the exercises of the student, and a complete list of the dhatoos, or roots.* Serampore: Mission Press.

Carnoy, Albert-Joseph

1925 *Grammaire élémentaire de la langue sanscrite*

comparée avec celle des langues indoeuropéenes. Louvain: Éditions Universitas. [Second édition revue et complétée 1937]

Colebrooke, Henry Thomas

1805 *A Grammar of the Sanscrit Language, vol. 1.* Calcutta: The Honorable Company's Press.

Coulson, Michael

1976 (Teach Yourself) *Sanskrit, an Introduction to the Classical Language.* London: Hodder and Stoughton. [Seen through press by Richard Gombrich, revised by Richard Gombrich and James Benson. Second edition 1992, re-issued 1995, 1996, 1997, 1998; third edition 2003, 2006; published in USA, 1992, 2003; available as an e-book: www.ebook3000.com/Teach-Yourself-Sanskrit-Complete-Course_75011.html]

Debrunner, Albert

1954 *Altindische Grammatik von Jakob Wackernagel, Band II, 2. Die Nominalsuffixe.* Göttingen: Vandenhoek & Ruprecht.

Desgranges, M.

1845-47 *Grammaire sanscrite-française.* Two volumes. Paris.

Deshpande, Madhav M.

1997 *Saṃskritasubodhinī. A Sanskrit Primer.* Michigan papers on South and Southeast Asia No. 47. Ann Arbor: Center for South and Southeast Asian Studies. [Reprinted 1999]

Ford, Gordon B., Jr.

1966 *A Concise elementary grammar of the Sanskrit language, with exercises, reading selections and a glossary*. Leiden: E. J. Brill. [Translation of Gonda]

Gawroński, Andrzej

1932 *Podręcznik sanskrytu. Gramatyka, wypisy,*

objaśnienia, słownik. Kraków: Polish Academy of Skills (PAU). [Second edition 1985, Lublin: Catholic University of Lublin; third revised edition 2004, Warszawa: Wydawnictwo Akademickie DIALOG]

Goldman, Robert P. and Sally J. Sutherland

1980 *Devavāṇīpraveśikā. An Introduction to the Sanskrit language.* Berkeley: Center for South and Southeast Asia Studies, University of California. [Revised editions 1987, 1992, 1999, 2002, 2004, 2011]

Gonda, Jan

1941 *Kurze Elementar-Grammatik der Sanskrit-Sprache mit Übungsbeispielen, Lesestücken und einem Glossar.* Leiden: E. J. Brill. [Second edition 1943, third edition 1948, fourth edition 1963]

Gray, John E. B.

nd *First year Sanskrit course.* [Undated manuscript]

Guhe, Eberhard

2008 *Einführung in das klassische Sanskrit. Ein Lehrbuch mit Übungen.* Wiesbaden: Harrassowitz.

Halbfass, Wilhelm

1981 *Indien und Europa, Perspectiven ihrer geistigen Begegnung.* Basel/Stuttgart: Schwabe & Co.

1988 *India and Europe. An Essay in Understanding.* Albany: State University of New York Press. [Enlarged version of *Indien und Europa ...*, translated by the author with the help of John Baker]

Hanxleden, Ernst Johann

nd *Grammatica grandonica.*

Hauschild, Richard

1964 *Register zur Altindischen Grammatik von J. Wackernagel und A. Debrunner (Bd. I-III).* Göttingen: Vandenhoek & Ruprecht.

Karttunen, Klaus

1984 *Lyhyt sanskritin kielioppi*. Helsinki: Suomen Itamainen Seura. [Revised edition 1987, third edition 1999]

Kielhorn, Franz

1870 *A Grammar of the Sanskrit Language*. [Fifth edition 1912, Bombay: Nirnaya Sagar Press; sixth edition 1970, Varanasi: The Chowkhamba Sanskrit Series Office]

Killingley, Dermot H. and Siew-Yue Killingley

1995 *Sanskrit*. Munich and Newcastle: Lincom Europa.

1996-97 *Beginning Sanskrit: A practical Course Based on Graded Reading and Exercises*. Two volumes. Munich and Newcastle: Lincom Europa. [Originally by D. H. Killingley, revised by D. H. Killingley and Siew-Yue Killingley.]

Killingley, Dermot H.

2009 *Beginning Sanskrit*. Volume 3. Grevat & Grevat.

Kocergina, Vera Aleksandrovna

1956 *Nacalnyj kurs sanskrita* (*ucebnik*). Moskwa: A.N. SSSR, In-t.jazykoznanja.

Krnic, Kresimir

1995 *Sanskrtska pocetnica*. Zagreb: Izdavac Nebo na zemlji d. o. o. [Translation of Stenzler]

Macdonell, Arthur Anthony

1901 *Sanskrit Grammar for Beginners*. London. [Third edition, entitled *A Sanskrit Grammar for Students*, Oxford, 1927; Indian reprints 1974, 1979, Delhi: Motilal Banarsidass]

Maurer, Walter Harding

1995 *The Sanskrit language: An Introductory Grammar and Reader*. Two volumes. Richmond: Curzon Press.

Milewska, Iwona

2008 How to teach Sanskrit? Didactic aspect of the European Sanskrit grammars — a historical survey, in *Cracow Indological Studies* X: 191-216.

Monier-Williams, Monier

1846 *An Elementary Grammar of the Sanskrit Language, Partly in the Roman Character, Arranged According to a New Theory in Reference Especially to the Classical Languages, with Short Extracts in Easy Prose*. London. [Fourth edition 1876]

1878 *A Practical Grammar of the Sanskrit Language : arranged with reference to the Classical Languages of Europe, for the use of English students*. London: The Clarendon Press. [Indian editions: 1962, Varanasi: Chowkhamba Sanskrit Series Office (Chowkhamba Sanskrit Studies 21), 1978, Oriental Books Reprint Corporation]

Mueller, F. Max

1866 *A Sanskrit Grammar for Beginners in Devanāgarī and Roman Letters Throughout*. London.

Nowakowska, Monika and Robert Piotrowski

2008 *Indie i Europa. Próba porozumienia na gruncie filozoficznym*. Warszawa: DIALOG. [Translation of Halbfass 1988]

Paulinus a Sancto Bartholomaeo

1790 *Sidharubam seu Grammatica Samscridamica. Cui accedit Dissertatio historico-critica in linguam Samscridamicam, vulgo Samscret dictam in qua huius linguae existentia, origo, praestantia, antiquitas, extensio, maternitas ostenditur, libri aliqui ex ea exarati critice recensentur, et simul aliquae antiquissimae gentilium orationes liturgicae paucis attinguntur, et explicantur*. Romae: S. C. de Propaganda Fide.

1804 *Vyàcarana seu locupletissima Samscrdamicae linguae institutio, in usum fidei praeconum in India orientali, et per virorum litteratorum in Europa adornata.* Romae: S. C. de Propaganda Fide.

Perry, Edward Delavan

1885 *Sanskrit Primer Based on the Leitfaden fuer den Elementar-cursus des Sanskrit of Professor Georg Buehler of Vienna.* Boston: Ginn. [Reprinted 1936, *A Sanskrit Primer,* New York and London: Columbia University Press, fourth edition Delhi 1936, reprinted Delhi: Motilal Banarsidass, 1978, 1982, 1986, 1988, 1992, 1994, 1997, 1999]

Pisani, Vittore

1943 *Grammatica sanscrita storica e comparativa.* Second, revised edition. Milano: Istituto editoriale "Cisalpino".

Renou, Louis

1957 *Jakob Wackernagel, Altindische Grammatik, introduction générale, nouvelle édition du text paru en 1896, au tome I.* Göttingen: Vandenhoek & Ruprecht.

1968 *Grammaire sanscrite.* Two volumes in one. Paris: Adrien-Maisonneuve.

Rocher, Ludo

1977 *Paulinus a Sancto Bartholomaeo, Dissertation on the Sanskrit Language: A reprint of the original Latin text of 1790, together with an introductory article, a complete English translation, and an index of sources.* Amsterdam Studies in the Theory and History of Linguistic Science 12. Amsterdam: Benjamins Publishing Company.

Rocher, Rosanne

1966 *Manuel de grammaire élémentaire de la langue sanskrite; suivi d'exercises, de morceaux choisis et d'un lexique*. Leiden: E. J. Brill. [Translation of Gonda]

Rodríguez Adrados, Francisco. See Adrados, Francisco Rodríguez.

Roth, H. See Camps, Arnulf and Jean Claude Muller.

Scharf, Peter

2003 *Rāmopākhyāna — the Story of Rāma in the Mahābhārata, An Independent-study Reader in Sanskrit*. London: RoutledgeCurzon. [sanskrit1.ccv.brown.edu/tomcat/sl/Kramapatha]

Söhnen, Renate

1992 *Primer of the Sanskrit language (translated into English with some revision ...)*. London: School of Oriental and African Studies, University of London. [Translation of Stenzler]

Stenzler, Adolf Friedrich

1868 *Elementarbuch der Sanskrit-Sprache. Grammatik, Texte, Wörterbuch. Breslau: Mälzer*. [Sixth edition, 1892, Breslau: Louis Koehler's Hofbuchhandlung]

Szczerbatskoj, F.

1923 Rukovodstvo k elementarnomu kursu sanskritskogo jazyka. Stokholm. [Translation of Buehler. Second edition, Lvov, 1960]

Wackernagel, Jakob

1896 *Altindische Grammatik, Band I: Lautlehre*. Göttingen: Vandenhoek & Ruprecht. [Nachträge zu Band I von A. Debrunner 1957]

1905 *Altindische Grammatik, Band II, 1: Einleitung zur Wortlehre. Nominalkomposition*. Göttingen: Vandenhoek & Ruprecht. [Nachtrage zur Band II,1 von A. Debrunner, 1957]

1930 *Altindische Grammatik*, III. *Band, Nominalflexion—Zahlwort—Pronomen*. Göttingen: Vandenhoek & Ruprecht.

Whitney, William Dwight
1879 *A Sanskrit Grammar, Including both the Classical Language, and the older Dialects of Veda and Brahmana*. Leipzig: Breitkopf & Härtel. [Second edition, 1875, eighth impression, 1955, London: Oxford University Press; subsequently reprinted, 1964, Cambridge, MA: Harvard University Press. Indian reprint, 1962, 1969, Delhi: Motilal Banarsidass.]

Wilkins, Charles
1808 *A Grammar of the Sanskrita Language*. London.

Wilson, Horace Hayman
1841 *An introduction to the Grammar of the Sanskrit Language for the use of early Students*. London. [Second edition 1847, London: J. Madden and Co.]

Teleology and the simplification of accentuation in Pāṇinian derivation

Peter M. Scharf

Considerable work has been undertaken over the past decade to create computational implementations of Pāṇinian derivational procedure. Shivamurthy Swamiji, P. Subrahmanyan, Amba Kulkarni, Anand Mishra, Girish Nath Jha, and I myself have all modeled segments of Pāṇinian grammar computationally. Others, such as Gérard Huet and Oliver Hellwig, are creating computational morphological generators and syntactic analyzers that do not attempt to model Pāṇinian procedure. The Sanskrit Computational Linguistics Consortium, which will hold its fifth symposium 3-8 January 2013 at IIT Bombay, provides a forum for sharing progress in this line of work. Attempts to model Pāṇinian procedure formulate determinative rules to produce finished speech forms from initial conditions consisting of semantic conditions and basic speech units such as roots and underived nominal stems. A computational implementation of Pāṇinian derivational procedure succeeds if the derivation of forms according to rules does not rely on knowledge of the finished form to be produced; that is, if the derivation is not circular. Robustness of the Pāṇinian linguistic description itself depends on the lack of circularity in the generative processes of the grammar.

Certain scholars have raised objections to the attempt to implement Pāṇinian procedure computationally on the grounds that Panini never intended his grammar to be a determinative generative grammatical device. Jan Houben, for instance, has recently argued that users of the grammar have certain speech forms in mind that they want to check for correctness and that these speech forms guide the derivational procedure which therefore does not proceed from semantic conditions and basic speech forms in a deterministic manner.

In Scharf 2011, I have demonstrated that Pāṇinian derivational procedure does indeed proceed from semantic conditions and basic speech forms. Yet I have also noted (Scharf 2011: 67-69) that there are three instances in which rules are formulated using the anticipatory device of the viṣayasaptamī. Patañjali escapes from the mutual dependence of the provision of an affix upon the presence of a preceding speech form and vice versa by stating that the affix in the locative is a locative of domain (*viṣayasaptamī*) rather than a right-context locative (*parasaptamī*).

Patañjali resorts to the locative of domain under A. 2.4.35 आर्धधातुके, A. 3.1.31 आयादय आर्धधातुके वा, and A. 4.1.90 यूनि लुक् (see Scharf 2011: 67–69). For example, A. 2.4.52 अस्तेर्भूः provides that the root *as* is replaced by the root *bhū* in the domain of an ārdhadhātuka-affix. A. 3.1.97 अचो यत् provides that the affix *yat* occurs after a vowel-final root, and A. 3.1.124 ऋहलोर्ण्यत् provides that the affix ***ṇyat*** occurs after roots that end in *ṛ* or in a consonant. The former affix conditions guṇa replacement of the final vowel of the root by A. 7.3.84 सार्वधातुकार्धधातुकयोः and high pitch on the first vowel of the derivate by A. 6.1.213 यतो ऽनावः, while the latter conditions vṛddhi replacement of the final vowel of the root by A. 7.2.115 अचो ञ्णिति and circumflex (*svarita*) on the affix vowel by A. 6.1.185 तित्स्वरितम्. In order to obtain the form *bhávyam* the affix *yat* must occur after the root *bhū*. However, the affix *yat* cannot occur until the root *as* is replaced by *bhū* since it only occurs after vowel-final roots; it does not occur after the root *as*, which ends in a consonant. If *ārdhadhātuke* were a parasaptamī, the replacement of the root *as* by the root *bhū* could only occur after the ārdhadhātuka-affix ***ṇyat*** had been provided. The result would be the erroneous form **bhāvyâm*, with vṛddhi replacement of the final *ū* of *bhū* and circumflex on the final vowel. The correct form *bhávyam* results if the replacement of the root *as* by the root *bhū* occurs in the domain of an ārdhadhātuka-affix, prior to its provision. The locative of domain permits the comprehension of the affix prior to its provision; it is a technique of looking ahead in the derivation and implies that the user of the grammar has some foreknowledge of the speech form to be derived. The locative of domain therefore implies that teleology plays a role in rule implementation in the grammar.

While the device of a locative of domain is admitted only under duress and is avoided as far as possible by commentators beginning with Patañjali, the fact that it is resorted to at all raises the question whether the rule set itself was not composed with the intent to utilize such a device more prevalently. Now, attempts to interpret Pāṇinian procedure independent of commentators, especially independent of Patañjali, inevitably inspire suspicion. If nearly two and a half millennia of astute grammarians do not consider an issue, it is unlikely to be relevant. Yet there are criteria to judge the correct interpretation of a system independent of commentary. These criteria are the simplicity and adequacy of the system to its intended domain. If an interpretation of the Pāṇinian linguistic description under one interpretation accounts for correct Sanskrit usage more efficiently, more simply than under a second interpretation, evidence is served in favor of the first interpretation. The case is strengthened if support for the interpretation is found in the discussion of commentators.

There is a major section of the grammar consisting of rules with locatives interpreted by commentators as right-context locatives (*parasaptamī*) which if interpreted as locatives of domain (*viṣayasaptamī*) would lead to a simplification of accentual rules. In the section of rules that introduces stem-forming affixes (*vikaraṇa*), namely A. 3.1.34–90, the locatives from *leṭi* in A. 3.1.35 to *liṅi* in A. 3.1.86 are accepted by commentators as right-context locatives. The verbal terminations are taken to be introduced prior to the stem-forming affixes. Table 1 shows the gloss of these rules in the Kāśikā, and Table 2 shows their gloss in the Siddhāntakaumudī, wherever the comment clarifies the case use. The commentaries do not mention or do not interpret the locative at all in the gloss of sūtras not listed; they never interpret any of these locatives as viṣayasaptamī. The Kāśikā utilizes the term *parataḥ* after a locative to show that it is a parasaptamī. Similarly, the Siddhāntakaumudī utilizes the term *pare*. For example, the Kāśikā paraphrases A. 3.1.68 कर्तरि शप्, "The affix ***śap*** occurs after a root when a sārvadhātuka affix denoting an agent (*kartṛ*) follows (*parataḥ*)." The Siddhāntakaumudī paraphrases the same rule (SK. 2167), "The affix ***śap*** should occur after a root when a sārvadhātuka affix meaning agent (*kartṛ*) follows (*pare*)." The use of the terms *parataḥ* and *para* implies that the verbal termination is already present following a root when the stem-forming affix is provided. In the derivations according to these commentators, therefore, the verbal terminations occur first and the stem-forming affixes subsequently.

Table 3 shows the derivation of *kurutaḥ*, the third person dual present indicative active of the root *kṛ*, according to Pāṇinian tradition. Steps 1-6 show the semantic conditions leading to the introduction of the *l*-affix ***laṭ*** after the root *kṛ*. Step 7 replaces the *l*-affix ***laṭ*** by the appropriate verbal termination; steps 7a-f determine the selection of the verbal termination *tas*. Steps 8-9 concern accent, which is the issue at hand. The affix has a high-pitched vowel in accordance with A. 3.1.3 (step 8).

Now, accents accompany items when they are introduced and are adjusted at each stage in a derivation in accordance with the principle, stated in 6.1.158 अनुदात्तं पदमेकवर्जम्, that a pada contains no high-pitched vowel save one (step 9). As Cardona (1997: 376) writes, "At each stage of derivation, an accentual adjustment is made such that, in general, the accentuation proper to the unit introduced at this stage cancels a previously existing accentuation." The principle is articulated by Kātyāyana under A. 6.1.158, in vt. 9: सतिशिष्टस्वरबलीयस्त्वं च (step 9a). Patañjali comments: सतिशिष्टस्वरो बलीयान्भवतीति वक्तव्यम् (MBh. III.99.23) (step 9b). Hence the accent of the verbal termination overrides the accent of the root.

An exception is made, however, to the accentuation principle that the accent of what is taught overrides the accent that was formerly present. The exception states that the accentuation of a stem-forming affix (*vikaraṇa*) does not override the accentuation of a sārvadhātuka verbal termination. Step 11 of the derivation introduces the stem-forming affix *u* which is high-pitched, just as was the verbal termination *tas*, in accordance with A. 3.1.3 (step 12). Yet instead of the accent of the newly introduced affix *u* overriding the accent of the verbal termination already present in accordance with the satiśiṣṭa principle, the accent of the stem-forming affix must yield to the accent of the verbal termination, even though stem-forming affix is introduced later. Kātyāyana notes this exception to the satiśiṣṭa principle in vt. 11, स्यादिस्वराप्रसङ्गश्च तासेः परस्यानुदात्तवचनात्, under A. 6.1.158 (step 13a). Patañjali comes to the point, "The accent of the stem-forming affix, even though it is taught while the other accent is already present, does not block the accent of the verbal termination." (step 13b).[1] The rest of the derivation culminates in step 24 with the form *kurutáḥ*, with the accent on the verbal termination rather than on the stem-forming affix.[2] In general the accent of a verbal termination prevails over the accent of a stem-forming affix.

In order to achieve the proper accentuation of verbal forms such as *kurutáḥ* — which are quite prevalent in ordinary Sanskrit as well as in Vedic — an exception to the principle that the accent of the item introduced later prevails must be stated. The statement of such an exception can be avoided, however, if the stem-forming

1. सति शिष्टो ऽपि विकरणस्वरो लसार्वधातुकस्वरं न बाधते । (MBh. III.100.8-11).

2. In Devanagarī,I use a vertical stroke above the headbar to indicate high pitch (*udātta*) and leave other pitches unmarked.

affix is introduced prior to the replacement of the *l*-affix by the verbal termination. Doing so requires understanding the locatives in the rules that introduce stem-forming affixes as locatives of domain rather than right-context locatives: the verbal terminations are not yet there but are anticipated. Table 4 shows the modifications necessary to the derivation. Step 7, instead of replacing the *l*-affix by an appropriate verbal termination, introduces the stem-forming affix *u*. The accent of the stem-forming affix overrides the accent of the root in accordance with the general accentuation principle that the accent of the item introduced later prevails (steps 9-9b). Then in step 10 the *l*-affix is replaced by the appropriate verbal termination *tas*. The accent of the verbal termination then prevails over the accent of the stem-forming affix by the same general accentuation principle (step 13-13b). No exception to the general accentuation principle is needed.

Now, the view that there is an exception to the general principle that the accent of what is taught overrides the accent that was formerly present in the case of vikaraṇas has a long history. The question comes up in the discussion of accentuation under A. 6.1.158. In vārttika 8 (सिद्धं तु प्रकृतिस्वरबलीयस्त्वात्प्रत्ययस्वरभाव:), Kātyāyana states that the accent of an affix overrides the accent of the base, and in vārttika 9 (सतिशिष्टस्वरबलीयस्त्वं च), that the accent of what is taught overrides the accent that was formerly present (the satiśiṣṭa principle). In vārttika 10 (तच्चानेकप्रत्ययसमासार्थम्), he states that the latter is necessary in the case of multiple affixes and in the case of complex compounds. The derivation of verbal forms such as *kurutáḥ* is a case where multiple affixes occur. Now, Patañjali raises an objection to the solution presented in vārttika 9. If the satiśiṣṭa principle applies, then the accent of the vikaraṇa would block the accent of the verbal termination in *sunutáḥ* and *cinutáḥ*.[3] This objection assumes that the vikaraṇa is taught after the replacement of an *l*-affix by a verbal termination because विप्रतिषेधे परं कार्यम् applies throughout the grammar so that replacements to *l*-affixes taught in 3.4.78 occur before the vikaraṇas taught in 3.1.33-90.

Kātyāyana's vārttika 11 on A. 6.1.158 (स्यादिस्वराप्रसङ्गश्च तासेः परस्यानुदात्तवचनात्) answers the objection. According to this vārttika, the mention of ***tāsi*** in A. 6.1.186 तास्यनुदात्तेन्ङिददुपदेशाल्लसार्वधातुकमनुदात्तमन्ह्विङोः is an indication (*jñāpaka*) of an exception for vikaraṇas. A. 6.1.186 teaches that a verbal termination after ***tāsi*** (which is a vikaraṇa), among other speech forms, is anudātta. Teaching that a verbal termination after ***tāsi*** is anudātta indicates that the accent of a vikaraṇa does not block the accent of a sārvadhātuka affix taught in place of an *l*-affix, even though the vikaraṇa is taught later than such a sārvadhātuka affix. The fact that one has to state that after ***tāsi*** such sārvadhātuka affixes are anudātta indicates that they wouldn't be anudātta just by the satiśiṣṭa principle. It implies an exception to the satiśiṣṭa principle for vikaraṇas, if one accepts that replacements to *l*-affixes taught in A. 3.4.78 occur prior to the vikaraṇas taught in A. 3.1.33-90.

However, this statement assumes that विप्रतिषेधे परं कार्यम् applies throughout the grammar so that replacements to *l*-affixes taught in 3.4.78 occur prior to the vikaraṇas taught in 3.1.33-90. Yet if this is not the case, if vikaraṇas occur first and verbal terminations subsequently, then the satiśiṣṭa principle itself lets the accent of the terminations take precedence, and there is no need for 6.1.186 to indicate it. Still A. 6.1.186 has to be stated to bring about the low pitch of the sārvadhātuka affixes in the specific cases mentioned because they would otherwise keep their high-pitched

3. यदि सतिशिष्टस्वरबलीयस्त्वमुच्यते स्यादिस्वरः सार्वधातुकस्वरं बाधेत । सुनुतः चिनुतः । (Mbh. III.100.6-7).

accent by the satiśiṣṭa principle. This is exactly what Kaiyaṭa states in his commentary on the MBh. on vt. 11. He writes,

> [A. 6.1.186] is said to be an indication by resorting to the derivation according to which the stem-forming affix *tā́si* occurs after replacements for *l*-affixes have already been made because the latter are provided by later rules. However, [A. 6.1.186] is not an indication if the sārvadhātuka (replacements) arise after the stem-forming affix *tā́si* has been added at the stage of the *l*-affixes because the provision of low pitch [by A. 6.1.186] serves the purpose of blocking accentuation of the sārvadhātuka replacements for *l*-affixes which would obtain because of the satiśiṣṭa principle."[4]

The satiśiṣṭa principle by itself, without special exception for vikaraṇas, applies to allow the accent of the verbal termination to remain; high-pitch accent is specifically overridden by 6.1.186.

In vārttika 12 (शास्त्रपरविप्रतिषेधानियमाद्वा शब्दपरविप्रतिषेधात्सिद्धम्), Kātyāyana considers an alternative explanation for the fact that the vikaraṇa does not get the accent in forms such as *sunutáḥ* and *cinutáḥ*. He states that because the principle that the later rule applies in cases of conflict cannot properly restrict the accent, it succeeds because of the principle that the later speech form gets the accent in cases of conflict. The details of the proposal, the objection raised to it, and its solution are not immediately relevant here.[5] What is relevant is that Kātyāyana and

4. परत्वाल्लादेशेषु कृतेषु तासिरिति प्रक्रियाश्रयेण ज्ञापकमुच्यते । लावस्थायां तु तासौ कृते सार्वधातुकोत्पत्तौ न ज्ञापकं भवति लसार्वधातुकस्वरस्य सतिशिष्टतया प्रसङ्गात् तद्बाधनार्थत्वाद् अनुदात्तविधानस्य ॥ (Pr. 4.492).

5. The proposal in vārttika 12 under A. 6.1.158 is objected to because in the case of the provision of dhātu-forming affixes such as *kāmya*, *āya*, and *īya*, the accent of the affix would take precedence over the accent of the root. Since the root is the whole sequence of base + affix while the affix is just the later part, the accent provided by 3.1.3 आद्युदात्तश्च would take precedence over the accent provided by 6.1.162 धातोः (अन्तः उदात्तः १५९). The latter provides that the final vowel of the root is high-pitched, the former that the first vowel of the affix is high-pitched. If the accent of the affix took precedence, one would then erroneously get **putrakā́myati*, **gopā́yati*, **ṛtī́yate* instead of the correct *putrakāmyáti*,

Patañjali consider an alternative to the principle that the later rule applies in cases of conflict throughout the grammar.

The principle that the later rule applies in cases of conflict is stated in A. 1.4.2 विप्रतिषेधे परं कार्यम् under the heading A. 1.4.1 आ कडारादेका सञ्ज्ञा. As Scharf (2012) discussed in detail, Patañjali applies the principle that the rule which is stated later prevails in cases of conflict throughout the grammar. Yet he concludes under A. 1.4.2 that it is the desired rule that applies rather than the later rule (MBh. 1.306.4–10) thereby casting doubt upon the use of the principle for rule ordering generally. Modern scholars limit the principle that the later rule applies in cases of conflict to the section of technical terms headed by A. 1.4.2 and do not accept that it applies generally throughout the grammar.

Although the principle that the later speech form gets the accent in cases of conflict is dismissed, the fact that an alternative to the principle that the later rule applies in cases of conflict is considered in the context of the satiśiṣṭa principle is pertinent. It is precisely this consideration that the present paper pursues. Since the principle that the later rule takes precedence in cases of conflict does not apply throughout the grammar, there is no reason to effect the replacement of *l*-affixes by verbal terminations prior to the provision of the vikaraṇa. Let the locatives such as *sārvadhātuke* in A. 3.1.67 सार्वधातुके यक् be viṣayasaptamīs. Let the vikaraṇas arise before the verbal terminations replace *l*-affixes. Then, since the verbal terminations occur subsequent to the vikaraṇas, the

gopāyáti, *ṛtīyáte*. The objection is dismissed on the grounds that the principle that the later speech form gets the accent in cases of conflict applies only where both accents are possible at once, but it is not the case that both accents are possible at once here. As Kaiyaṭa explains, the accent of the affix is taught outright at first, when the accent of the affix has already been effected, once the speech form ending in the affix has been termed *dhātu* by A. 3.1.32 सन्नाद्यन्ता धातवः, only then does the accent of the root take effect. Kaiyaṭa therefore conlcudes that one only needs to resort to the satiśiṣṭa principle, i.e., that the accent of what is taught overrides the accent that was formerly present.

satiśiṣṭa principle by itself accounts for the proper accent. There is no need for an exception to the satiśiṣṭa principle and no need to interpret A. 6.1.186 as an indication (*jñāpaka*) of such an exception. The interpretation of A. 6.1.186 as such an indication is only valid under the assumption that vikaraṇas occur subsequently to the replacement of *l*-affixes by verbal terminations. In the absence of such an assumption, that is, if the replacement of *l*-affixes by verbal terminations is provided subsequent to vikaraṇas, the accent of the termination takes precedence over the accent of the vikaraṇas just by the satiśiṣṭa principle alone. Thus the terminations *ḍā*, *rau*, and *ras* of the so-called periphrastic future (***luṭ***) after the vikaraṇa *tāsi* would be high-pitched by the default accentuation rule A. 3.1.3 and the satiśiṣṭa principle. In this situation, to avoid the undesired high-pitch in certain speech forms, A. 6.1.186 serves simply to effect the low pitch of the terminations *ḍā*, *rau*, and *ras* as well as of other verbal terminations following the specific items mentioned in the rule. A. 6.1.186 is just as much an indication (*jñāpaka*) that verbal terminations replace *l*-affixes subsequent to the provision of vikaraṇas as it is of an exception to the satiśiṣṭa principle. Verbal terminations can replace *l*-affixes subsequent to the provision of vikaraṇas if the locatives in A. 3.1.33-90 are understood as locatives of domain (*viṣayasaptamī*) rather than right-context locatives (*parasaptamī*).

The derivation of accent can be achieved more simply by understanding the locatives in rules that introduce stem-forming affixes as locatives of domain rather than right-context locatives. Simplification is a virtue in scientific description just as lāghava is in the ancient Indian grammatical tradition. Moreover, the approach proposed is supported by the fact that commentators suggest an alternative to the principle that the later rule applies in cases of conflict.

The Mahābhāṣya discusses the type of saptamī in stem-forming affixation rules only once (MBh. II.60.19-20 [on A. 3.1.78]) where reference is made to A. 1.4.13 यस्मात्प्रत्ययविधिस्तदादि प्रत्यये ऽङ्गम् in a pūrvapakṣa. The locative is there interpreted as a parasaptamī, paraphrasing यस्माच्च प्रत्ययविधिस्तदादिप्रत्यये परतो ऽङ्गसंज्ञं भवति. The fact that the affix ***śnam*** does not occur after roots such as *bhid* but after their last vowel (in accordance with A. 1.1.47 मिदचो ऽन्त्यात्परः), and that the stem with respect to the affix ***śnam*** does not terminate with that last vowel (for example *bhi* of *bhid*) shows that in fact *pratyaye* in A. 1.4.13 cannot be a parasaptamī.

Understanding the locatives as viṣayasaptamī implies a less mechanistic procedure of rule selection. Specific conditions for the occurrence of stem-forming affixes in the form of specific verbal terminations must be envisioned prior to the replacement of *l*-affixes by those verbal terminations. This implies that a foreknowledge of the form to be derived guides the derivational procedure teleologically. To this extent, it may be correct to assert that Pāṇinian derivation begins with speech forms: it is undertaken with the target speech form in mind, at least to the extent that the user envisions an affix to be used as a viṣayasaptamī prior to the introduction of the affix. Such envisioning does not compromise the robustness of the Aṣṭādhyāyī as a linguistic description of Sanskrit, but it does complicate the ability to undertake a computational implementation that closely models the rules. Computational implementation must rely on some procedure of rule implementation that permits anticipation of conditions.

Scharf (2010) describes such a procedure to implement a forward-looking rule where a decision at an early stage in the derivation requires evaluation of conditions that do not obtain until a subsequent stage in the derivation. The situation concerns the addition of the affix-initial augment *i* (*iṭ*) in the derivation of perfect active participle forms such as *jagmivān*. A. 7.2.67 वस्वेकाजाद्घसाम् provides the addition of the initial augment *i* to the affix *vas* (***kvasu***) on the condition that the root be single-syllabled after stem-internal changes and root doubling (A. 6.1.1 etc.) have applied. The problem is that stem-internal changes and root doubling require the prior addition of the augment *i*. The root is doubled by A. 6.1.8 लिटि धातोरनभ्यासस्य after 6.4.98 गमहनजनखनघसां लोपः क्ङित्यनङि applies. The latter in turn deletes the penultimate vowel of the mentioned roots *gam*, etc. followed by a vowel-initial affix other than *ṅ* marked with *k* or *ṅ*. Note that the root vowel is deleted only if the affix is vowel-initial. The affix is vowel-initial only *after* the augment *i* is added by A. 7.2.67. The problem is therefore that A. 7.2.67 must evaluate whether the root is going to turn out to be single-syllabled in order to determine whether to add the augment or not but the root can turn out to be single-syllabled only once the augment has already been added. Scharf (2010) describes implementation of a decision delay mechanism that produces both options, with and without the augment *i*, and eliminates the incorrect option at a subsequent point in the derivation where the monosyllabicity is able to be evaluated. Hence, although the decision whether or not to implement A. 7.2.67 is forward-looking, i.e., requires knowledge of a subsequent state in advance, it is not indeterminate.

The situation is similar in the case of the viṣayasaptamī. Just as the forward-looking condition in the case of the derivation of perfect active participles was not indeterminate, the viṣayasaptamī is not indeterminate either. A decision delay procedure is capable of determining the correct result in the same way. In the case of the derivation of the form *bhávyam* in the example above, one can produce both options, proceeding on one option as if the subsequent affix is ārdhadhātuka and on the other as if it is not, until the affix is introduced and its status is known. Then discard the incorrect option. In this way no indeterminism is introduced. The simplification of accentuation rules by the expanded use of the viṣayasaptamī therefore would not introduce the fault of indeterminacy into the grammatical procedure.

Table 1
Significance of the locative in rules introducing stem-forming affixes according to the Kāśikā

३।१।३३ स्यतासी ऌलुटोः	लृलुटोः	ऌरूपमुत्सृष्टानुबन्धं सामान्यमेकमेव । तस्मिँल्लुटि च परतो धातोर्यथासङ्ख्यं स्यतासी प्रत्ययौ भवतः ।
३।१।३४ सिब्बहुलं लेटि	लेटि	धातोः सिप्प्रत्ययो भवति बहुलं लेटि परतः ।
३।१।३५ कास्प्रत्ययादाममन्त्रे लिटि	लिटि	कासृ शब्दकुत्सायाम् । ततः प्रत्ययान्तेभ्यश्च धातुभ्य आम्प्रत्ययो भवति लिटि परतो ऽमन्त्रविषये ।
३।१।३६ इजादेश्च गुरुमतो ऽनृच्छः		इजादिर्यो धातुर्गुरुमानृच्छतिवर्जितस्तस्माच्च लिटि परत आम्प्रत्ययो भवति ।
३।१।३७ दयायासश्च		दय दानगतिरक्षणेषु । अय गतौ । आस उपवेशने । एतेभ्यश्च लिटि परत आम्प्रत्ययो भवति ।
३।१।३८ उषविदजागृभ्यो ऽन्यतरस्याम्		उष दाहे । विद ज्ञाने । जागृ निद्राक्षये । एतेभ्यो लिटि परतो ऽन्यतरस्यामाम्प्रत्ययो भवति ।
३।१।३९ भीह्रीभृहुवां श्लुवच्च		ञिभी भये । ह्री लज्जायाम् । डुभृञ् धारणपोषणयोः । हु दानादानयोः । एतेभ्यो लिटि परत आम्प्रत्ययो भवत्यन्यतरस्यां श्लाविव चास्मिन्कार्यं भवति ।
३।१।४० कृञ्चानुप्रयुज्यते लिटि	लिटि	आम्प्रत्ययस्य पश्चात्कृञनुप्रयुज्यते लिटि परतः ।
३।१।४३ च्लि लुङि	लुङि	धातोश्च्लिः प्रत्ययो भवति लुङि परतः ।
३।१।४८ णिश्रिद्रुस्रुभ्यः कर्तरि चङ		सिजपवादश्चङ्विधीयते । ण्यन्तेभ्यो धातुभ्यः श्रि द्रु स्रु इति एतेभ्यश्च परस्य च्लेश्चङादेशो भवति कर्तृवाचिनि लुङि परतः ।
३।१।५२ अस्यतिवक्ति-ख्यातिभ्यो ऽङ		असु क्षेपणे । वच परिभाषणे ब्रूञादेशो वा । ख्या प्रकथने चक्षिङादेशो वा । एभ्यः परस्य च्लेरङादेशो भवति कर्तृवाचिनि लुङि परतः ।
३।१।५४ आत्मनेपदेष्व-न्यतरस्याम्	आत्मने-पदेषु	लिपिसिचिह्व आत्मनेपदेषु परतश्च्लेरङादेशो भवत्यन्यतरस्याम् ।

३।१।५५ पुषादिद्युताद्यॢदितः परस्मैपदेषु	परस्मै-पदेषु	पुषादिभ्यो द्युतादिभ्य ॢदिद्भ्यश्च धातुभ्यः परस्य च्लेः परस्मैपदेषु परतो ऽङादेशो भवति ।
३।१।६० चिण्ते पदः	ते	पद गतौ । अस्माद्धातोः परस्य च्लेश्चिणादेशो भवति तशब्दे परतः ।
३।१।६१ दीपजनबुधपूरितायि-प्यायिभ्यो ऽन्यतरस्याम्		चिण्त इति वर्तते । दीपी दीप्तौ । जनी प्रादुर्भावे । बुध अवगमने । पूरी आप्यायने । तायृ सन्तानपालनयोः । ओप्यायी वृद्धौ । एतेभ्यः परस्य च्लेस्तशब्दे परतो ऽन्यतरस्यां चिणादेशो भवति ।
३।१।६२ अचः कर्मकर्तरि		अजन्ताद्धातोः परस्य च्लेः कर्मकर्तरि तशब्दे परतश्चिणादेशो भवति ।
३।१।६६ चिण्भावकर्मणोः		धातोः परस्य च्लेश्चिणादेशो भवति भावे कर्मणि तशब्दे परतः ।
३।१।६७ सार्वधातुके यक्	सार्व-धातुके	भावकर्मवाचिनि सार्वधातुके परतो धातोर्यक्प्रत्ययो भवति ।
३।१।६८ कर्तरि शप्		कर्तृवाचिनि सार्वधातुके परतो धातोः शप्प्रत्ययो भवति ।
३।१।८३ हलः श्नः शानज्झौ	हौ	हल उत्तरस्य श्नाप्रत्ययस्य शानजादेशो भवति हौ परतः ।
३।१।८६ लिङ्याशिष्यङ	लिङि	आशिषि विषये यो लिङ्तस्मिन्परतश्छन्दसि विषये ऽङ्प्रत्ययो भवति ।

Table 2
Significance of the locative in rules introducing stem-forming affixes according to the Siddhāntakaumudī

2167	३।१।६८	कर्तरि शप्	कर्त्रर्थे सार्वधातुके परे धातोः शप् स्यात् ।
2186	३।१।३३	स्यतासी ऌलुटोः	धातोः स्यतासी एतौ स्तो ऌलुटोः परतः ।
2239	३।१।४०	कृञ्चानुप्रयुज्यते लिटि	आमन्ताल् लिट्पराः कृभ्वस्तयो ऽनुप्रयुज्यन्ते ।
2269	३।१।५७	इरितो वा	इरितो धातोश्च्लेरङ वा स्यात् परस्मैपदे परे ।
2312	३।१।४८	णिश्रिद्रुस्रुभ्यः कर्तरि चङ	ण्यन्तात् श्र्यादिभ्यश्च च्लेश्चङ स्यात्कर्त्रर्थे लुङि परे ।
2321	३।१।७०	वा भ्राशभ्लाशभ्रमु-क्रमुक्लमुत्रसित्रुटिलषः	एतेभ्यः श्यन्वा स्यात्कर्त्रर्थे सार्वधातुके परे।
2328	३।१।६१	दीपजनबुधपूरि-तायिप्यायिभ्यो ऽन्यतरस्याम्	एभ्यश्च्लेश्चिण्वा स्यादेकवचने तशब्दे परे ।
2338	३।१।७५	अक्षो ऽन्यतरस्याम्	अक्षो वा श्नुप्रत्ययः स्यात्कर्त्रर्थे सार्वधातुके परे ।
2375	३।१।४९	विभाषा धेट्श्व्योः	आभ्यां च्लेश्चङवा स्यात्कर्तृवाचिनि लुङि परे ।
2513	३।१।६०	चिण्ते पदः	पदश्च्लेश्चिण् स्यात् तशब्दे परे ।
2557	३।१।८३	हलः श्नः शानज्झौ	हलः परस्य श्नः शानचादेशः स्याद् धौ परे ।
2756	३।१।६७	सार्वधातुके यक्	धातोर्यक् प्रत्ययः स्याद्भावकर्मवाचिनि सार्वधातुके परे ।
2758	३।१।६६	चिण्भावकर्मणोः	च्लेश्चिण् स्याद्भावकर्मवाचिनि तशब्दे परे ।
2768	३।१।६२	अचः कर्मकर्तरि	अजन्तात् च्लेश्चिण् वा स्यात्कर्मकर्तरि तशब्दे परे ।
3434	३।१।८६	लिङ्याशिष्यङ	आशीर्लिङि परे धातोरङ स्याच्छन्दसि ।

Table 3
The derivation of कुरुतः (the third person dual present indicative active of कृ)
according to Pāṇinian tradition

1	स्वतन्त्रताविशिष्ट-द्वित्वविशिष्टाश्रय-वर्तमानकालीन-करणानुकूल-व्यापारः			They two do
2	द्वित्वविशिष्टकर्तृक-वर्तमानकालीन-करणानुकूल-व्यापारः	1.4.54	स्वतन्त्रः कर्ता	The independent participant in the action is termed 'agent' (*kartṛ*).
3	कृ	MDhV. 8.12	डुकृञ् करणे	do, make
4	कृ[धातु]	1.3.1	भूवादयो धातवः	The items in the list beginning with *bhū* are termed *dhātu*.
5	कृ॑	6.1.162	धातोः (अन्तः उदात्तः १५९)	The last vowel of a root is high-pitched.
6	कृ॑-लट्	3.2.123	वर्तमाने लट्	The *l*-affix ***laṭ*** occurs after a root if the action it denotes occurs in present time.
6a		3.4.69	लः कर्मणि च भावे चाकर्मकेभ्यः (कर्तरि ६७)	The *l*-affixes occur when a direct object (*karman*) is to be denoted and, after roots without a direct object, when the action (*bhāva*) is to be denoted, as well as when the agent (*kartṛ*) is to be denoted.
7	कृ॑-तस्	3.4.78	तिप्तस्झि...इड्वहि-महिङ् (लस्य ७७)	The affixes ***tip*** etc. occur in place of an *l*-affix.
7a		1.4.22	द्व्येकयोर्द्विवचनैक-वचने	A dual or singular termination occurs to denote dual or singular number respectively.
7b		1.3.78	शेषात्कर्तरि परस्मैपदम्	A parasmaipada verbal termination occurs when an agent is to be denoted after the remainder, i.e., after any root under any conditions for which an ātmanepada termination has not been provided.
7c		1.4.99	लः परस्मैपदम्	A replacement for an *l*-affix is generally termed *parasmaipada*.

7d		1.4.101	तिङस्त्रीणि त्रीणि प्रथममध्यमोत्तमाः	Triplets of the affixes *tiṅ* etc. are termed respectively *prathama, madhyama* and *uttama*.
7e		1.4.102	तान्येकवचनद्विवचनबहुवचनान्येकशः	Affixes within each triplet are termed *ekavacana*, *dvivacana*, and *bahuvacana* respectively.
7f		1.4.108	शेषे प्रथमः	An affix termed *prathama* occurs in the remainder, i.e., where there is no correferentiality with a first or second person pronoun, whether such a pronoun is actually used or not.
8	कृ-तस्	3.1.3	आद्युदात्तश्च (प्रत्ययः १)	The first vowel of an affix is high-pitched.
9	कृ-तस्	6.1.158	अनुदात्तं पदमेकवर्जम्	A pada contains no high-pitched vowel save one.
9a		6.1.158 vt. 9	सतिशिष्टस्वरबलीयस्त्वं च	
9b		Patañjali	सतिशिष्टस्वरो बलीयान् भवति (MBh. III.99. 22-23)	
10	कृ-तस्[सार्वधातुक]	3.4.113	तिङ्शित्सार्वधातुकम्	The verbal terminations (*tiṅ*) and affixes marked with *ś* are termed *sārvadhātuka*.
11	(कृ-उ)-तस्[सार्वधातुक]	3.1.79	तनादिकृञ्भ्य उः (सार्वधातुके ६७, कर्तरि ६८)	The stem-forming affix *u* occurs after a root in the list beginning with *tan* and after the root *kṛ* followed by a sārvadhātuka affix if an agent is to be denoted.
12	(कृ-उ)-तस्[सार्वधातुक]	3.1.3	आद्युदात्तश्च (प्रत्ययः १)	(see step 8)
13	(कृ-उ)-तस्[सार्वधातुक]	6.1.158	अनुदात्तं पदमेकवर्जम्	(see step 9)
13a		6.1.158 vt. 11	स्यादिस्वराप्रसङ्गश् च तासेः परस्यानुदात्तवचनात्	

13b		Patañjali	सति शिष्टो ऽपि विकरणस्वरो लसार्वधातुकस्वरं न बाधते (MBh. III. 100.8-11)	
14	(कृ-उ[आर्धधातुक])-तस्[सार्वधातुक]	3.4.114	आर्धधातुकं शेषः	The remainder of affixes taught explicitly after a verbal root (*dhātu*) are termed *ārdhadhātuka*.
15	(कृ[अङ्ग]-उ[आर्धधातुक])-तस्[सार्वधातुक]	1.4.13	यस्मात्प्रत्यय-विधिस्तदादि प्रत्यये ऽङ्गम्	The speech form beginning with that after which an affix is provided is termed 'stem' (*aṅga*) with respect to that affix.
16	(कृ-उ)-तस्[सार्वधातुक]	7.3.84	सार्वधातुकार्ध-धातुकयोः (गुणः ८२, अङ्गस्य ६।४।१)	A stem followed by a sārvadhātuka or ārdhadhātuka affix is subject to replacement by a guṇa vowel.
16a		1.1.2	अदेङ्गुणः	*a, e* and *o* are termed *guṇa*.
16b		1.1.3	इको गुणवृद्धी	Guṇa and vṛddhi vowels occur in place of a vowel *i, u, ṛ* or *ḷ*.
16c		1.1.50	स्थाने ऽन्तरतमः	The most similar among possible replacements occurs in place of its substituend.
17	(कर्-उ)-तस्[सार्वधातुक]	1.1.51	उरण्रपरः	A vowel *a, i* or *u* that occurs in place of *ṛ* is followed by *r*.
18	करु[अङ्ग]-तस्[सार्वधातुक]	1.4.13	यस्मात्प्रत्ययविधिस्तदादि प्रत्यये ऽङ्गम्	(see step 15)
19	करु[अङ्ग]-तस्[ङ]	1.2.4	सार्वधातुकमपित् (ङित् १)	A sārvadhātuka affix not marked with *p* is marked with *ṅ*.
20	कुरु-तस्[ङ]	6.4.110	अत उत्सार्वधातुके (अङ्गस्य १, क्ङिति ९८, उतः प्रत्ययात् १०६, करोतेः १०८)	The *a* of the stem *karu* of the root *kṛ* ending in the affix *u*, followed by a sārvadhātuka affix marked with *k* or *ṅ* is replaced by *u*.

21	कुरु-तस्[ङ]	1.1.5	क्ङिति च (न ४, इको गुणवृद्धी ३)	Guṇa and vṛddhi do not occur if the affix that would otherwise condition them is marked with *k* or *ṅ*.
21a		7.3.84	सार्वधातुकार्ध-धातुकयोः (गुणः ८२, अङ्गस्य ६।४।१) blocked	
22	कुरुतस्[पद]	1.4.14	सुप्तिङन्तं पदम्	A speech form ending in a nominal termination (*sup*) or verbal termination (*tiṅ*) is termed *pada*.
23	कुरुतर्[उ]	8.2.66	ससजुषो रुः	The final *s* of a pada is replaced by ***ru*** (*r* marked with *u*).
24	कुरुतः	8.3.15	खरवसानयोर्वि-सर्जनीयः	Before a voiceless consonant or pause, pada-final *r* is replaced by *ḥ*.

Table 4
Alternative derivation of कुरुतः (third person dual present indicative active of कृ)

7	कृ́-उ-लट्	3.1.79	तनादिकृञ्भ्य उः (सार्वधातुके ६७, कर्तरि ६८)	The stem-forming affix *u* occurs after a root in the list beginning with *tan* and after the root *kṛ* in the domain of a sārvadhātuka affix if an agent is to be denoted.
8	कृ́-उ́-लट्	3.1.3	आद्युदात्तश्च (प्रत्ययः १)	The first vowel of an affix is high-pitched.
9	कृ-उ́-लट्	6.1.158	अनुदात्तं पदमेकवर्जम्	A pada contains no high-pitched vowel save one.
9a		vt. 9	सतिशिष्टस्वर-बलीयस्त्वं च	
9b		Patañjali	सतिशिष्टस्वरो बलीयान् भवति (MBh. III.99. 22-23)	
10	कृ-उ́-तस्	3.4.78	तिप्तस्झि...इड्वहिमहिङ् (लस्य ७७)	The affixes ***tip*** etc. occur in place of an *l*-affix.
10a-f				= Table 3, steps 7a-f
11	कृ-उ́-तस्	3.1.3	आद्युदात्तश्च (प्रत्ययः १)	The first vowel of an affix is high-pitched.
12	कृ-उ́-तस्[सार्वधातुक]	3.4.113	तिङ्शित्सार्वधातुकम्	The verbal terminations (***tiṅ***) and affixes marked with *ś* are termed *sārvadhātuka*.
13	कृ-उ-तस्[सार्वधातुक]	6.1.158	अनुदात्तं पदमेकवर्जम्	A pada contains no high-pitched vowel save one.
13a		vt. 9	सतिशिष्टस्वर-बलीयस्त्वं च	
13b		Patañjali	सतिशिष्टस्वरो बलीयान् भवति (MBh. III.99. 22-23)	

References and abbreviations

Abhankar, K. V.

1962–72 *The Vyākaraṇa=Mahābhāṣya of Patañjali, edited by F. Kielhorn, third edition, revised and furnished with additional readings, references and select critical notes.* Three volumes. Poona: Bhandarkar Oriental Research Institute.

Cardona, George.

1997 *Pāṇini: His Work and its Traditions.* Vol. 1, *Background and Introduction.* Second edition. Delhi: Motilal Banarsidass.

Cardona, George, Ashok Aklujkar and Hideyo Ogawa

2012 *Studies in Sanskrit Grammars (Proceedings of the Vyākaraṇa Section of the 14th World Sanskrit Conference, 1-5 September 2009, Kyoto University, Kyoto).* New Delhi: D. K. Printworld.

Dwarikadas Shastri

1983 The *Mādhavīyā Dhātuvṛtti* [A treatise on Sanskrit roots based on the *Dhātupāṭha* of Pāṇini] by Sāyaṇācārya. Second edition. Kamachha, Varanasi: Tara Book Agency.

Houben, Jan E. M.

2009 Pāṇini's grammar and its computerization: a construction grammar approach, in Kulkarni and Huet 2009: 6-25.

2012 Studies in India's Vedic grammarians, 1: Nārāyaṇabhaṭṭa's *Prakriyāsarvasva* and Pāṇini's *Śe*, in Cardona, Aklujkar, and Ogawa 2012: 163–194.

Huet, Gérard, Amba Kulkarni, and Peter Scharf

2009 *Sanskrit Computational Linguistics: First and Second International Symposia, Rocquencourt, France, October 2007; Providence, RI, USA, May 2008; Revised Selected and Invited Papers.* Lecture

Notes in Artificial Intelligence 5402. Berlin-Heidelberg: Springer-Verlag.

Jha, Girish Nath
2010 *Sanskrit Computational Linguistics: 4th International Symposium, New Delhi, India, December 2010, Proceedings*. Lecture Notes in Artificial Intelligence 6465. Berlin; Heidelberg: Springer-Verlag.

Kāśikā *Kāśikāvṛtti*. See Sharma, Aryendra, Khanderao Deshpande and D. G. Padhye

Kulkarni, Amba and Gérard Huet
2009 *Sanskrit Computational Linguistics: Third International Symposium, Hyderabad, India, January 15-17, 2009, Proceedings*. Lecture Notes in Artificial Intelligence 5406. Berlin; Heidelberg: Springer-Verlag.

Mbh. *Mahābhāṣya*. See Abhyankar, K. V.

MDhV. *Mādhavīyā Dhātuvṛtti*. See Dwarikadas Shastri.

Pansikar, Vasudev Lakshman Shastri,
1985 *The Siddhāntakaumudī with Tattvabodhinī commentary of Jñānendrasarasvatī and Subodhinī commentary of Jayakṛṣṇa*. [*Tattvabodhinī-samākhya-vyākhyā-saṃvalitā śiddhāntakaumudī nāma Bhaṭṭojidīkṣita-praṇītā pāṇinīya-vyākaraṇa-sūtra-vṛttiḥ. Jñānendrasarasvatī-viracitottarakṛdantāntaṃ Tattvabodhinī-vyākhyā, svara-vaidikyoḥ Jayakṛṣṇakṛtā Subodhinī. Vāsudevaśarmaṇā ṭippaṇyādibhiḥ pariṣkṛtā saṃśodhitā ca.*] New Delhi: Meharchand Lachhmandass Publications.

Pr. *Pradīpa*. See Vedavrata.

Scharf, Peter M.
2008 Pāṇinian accounts of the Vedic subjunctive: leṭ *kṛṇvaite*. *Indo-Iranian Journal* 51.1: 1-21.

2010 Rule-blocking and forward-looking conditions in the computational modeling of Pāṇinian derivation, in Jha 2010: 48-56.

2011 On the semantic foundation of Pāṇinian derivational procedure: the derivation of *kumbhakāra*. *Journal of the American Oriental Society* 131.1: 39–72.

2012 Rule selection in the *Aṣṭādhyāyī* or is Pāṇini's grammar mechanistic?, in Cardona, Aklujkar, and Ogawa 2012: 319–50.

Sharma, Aryendra, Khanderao Deshpande and D. G. Padhye

1969-70 *Kāśika, A Commentary on Pāṇini's Grammar by Vāmana & Jayāditya.* Two volumes. Sanskrit Academy Series 17, 20. Hyderabad: Sanskrit Academy, Osmania University. Reprinted in one volume, 2008.

Shivamurthy Swamiji

2010 *Gaṇakaṣṭādhyāyī.* Version 6.5 revised. http://www.taralabalu.org/panini/

Siddhāntakaumudī See Pansikar 1985.

SK *Siddhāntakaumudī*. See Pansikar 1985.

Vedavrata

1963 *Śrībhagavatpatañjaliviracitaṃ vyākaraṇa-mahā bhāṣyam [śrīkaiyyaṭakṛtapradīpena nāgojībhaṭṭa kṛtena bhāṣyapradīpodyotena ca vibhūṣitam].* Part 4 (adhyāyas 5-6). Rohatak: Haryana Sahitya Sansthan.

On the accent of the word पराँच: as stated by A 6.2.52

Anuja Ajotikar and Malhar Kulkarni

1 The verbal root *añcŪ* (meaning 'to go' and 'to worship') occupies a unique place in the grammar of Pāṇini. In the whole Aṣṭādhyāyī there are fifteen rules stating special operations related to this root and its derivates. These rules are:

1. अन्यारादितरर्तेदिक्शब्दाञ्चूत्तरपदाजाहियुक्ते ।	A 2.3.29
2. ऋत्विग्दधृक्स्रग्दिगुष्णिगञ्चुयुजिक्रुञ्चां च ।	A 3.2.59
3. अञ्चेर्लुक्।	A 5.3.30
4. विभाषाञ्चेरदिक्स्त्रियाम् ।	A 5.4.8
5. अञ्चेश्छन्दस्यसर्वनामस्थानम् ।	A 6.1.170
6. न गोश्वन्साववर्णराडङ्क्रुङ्कृद्भ्यः ।	A 6.1.182
7. चौ ।	A 6.1.222
8. अनिगन्तोऽञ्चतौ वप्रत्यये ।	A 6.2.52
9. विष्वग्देवयोश्च टेरद्र्यञ्चतावप्रत्यये ।	A 6.3.92
10. चौ ।	A 6.3.138
11. नाञ्चेःपूजायाम् ।	A 6 .4.30
12. अचः ।	A 6.4.138
13. उगिदचां सर्वनामस्थानेऽधातोः ।	A 7.1.70
14. अञ्चेःपूजायाम् ।	A 7.2.53
15. अञ्चोऽनपादाने ।	A 8.2.48

The special feature of this root is that when it means 'to go', inflected forms (*subanta*) of compounds containing it other than nominative forms as well as accusative singular and dual forms lose the nasal, but if the root means 'to worship' all the subanta forms retain the nasal, according to the rule A 6.4.30, a special rule blocking the deletion of penultimate *n*. Therefore accusative plural and subsequent forms differ in these two meanings. Thus, if the meaning is, 'to go', the accusative plural form will be *prācaḥ*, but if the meaning is, 'to worship' it will be *prāñcaḥ*. The grammatical process to derive these forms is given in Table I.

Another feature of the verbal root *añcŪ* is productivity according to the rules in Pāṇini's grammar. Later prakriyā texts have generated varied forms of an upapada compound *gonc/goc*, derived from the same root with the vigraha गामञ्चति ('one who goes to a cow'). In the normal paradigm of seven cases in three numbers, in the neuter, there are in all one hundred twelve subanta forms of this compound noted in these texts. In the Siddhāntakaumudī, five hundred twenty-seven possible forms of the same word are derived by applying rules stating phonological operations like duplication etc. These features also show how this verbal root occupies a special place in the Sanskrit grammar.

Another important aspect worth studying in connection with this root is rules stating accentual (*svara*) operations to the root and its derivates. There are four such rules:

1. अञ्चेश्छन्दस्यसर्वनामस्थानम्। (A 6.1.170)

KV: अञ्चेः परासर्वनामस्थानविभक्तिरुदात्ता भवति छन्दसि विषये।

SK: अञ्चेः परा विभक्तिरुदात्ता। "In the Chhandas, the case endings other than the *sarvanāmasthāna,* get the acute accent when coming after the *añc.*"[1]

2. न गोश्वन्साववर्णराडङ्क्रुङ्कृद्भ्यः। (A 6.1.182)

KV: गो श्वन् साववर्णः सौ प्रथमैकवचने यदवर्णान्तं राड् अङ क्रुङ कृद् इत्येतेभ्यो यदुक्तं तन्न भवति।

SK: एभ्यः प्रागुक्तं न। "The foregoing rules from (A VI.I.168) downwards have no applicability after go, śvan, and words ending in them; nor after a stem which before the case ending of the nominative singular has "*a*" or "*ā*", nor after *rāj*, or stem ending in *añca* nor as well as after *kruñc* and *kṛt*" (Vasu 1995: 132).

3. चौ। (A 6.1.222)

1. Translation according to Vasu 1995: 128.

KV: चावित्यश्चतिर्लुप्तनकारो गृह्यते । तस्मिन्परतः पूर्वस्यान्त उदात्तो भवति ।

SK: लुप्ताकारेऽश्चतौ परे पूर्वस्यान्तोदात्तः स्यात् । "In compounds words ending in añca, the final vowel of the preceding word has the acute accent in the weak cases in which only "c" of *añca* remains" (Vasu 1995: 91).

4. अनिगन्तोऽश्चतौ वप्रत्यये । (A 6.2.52)

KV: अनिगन्तो गतिः प्रकृतिस्वरो भवत्यश्चतौ वप्रत्यये परतः ।

SK: अनिगन्तो गतिर्वप्रत्ययान्तेऽश्चतौ परे प्रकृत्या । "An immediately preceding gati not ending in "i" or "u" retains its original accent before añc when an affix having a "v" follows" (Vasu 1995: 155).

In the same context, we wish to discuss in this paper a particular example, पराचः, which is provided by the traditional texts on A 6.2.52.

2 We discuss the examples of A 6.2.52 in this section so that salient points in the derivation and accent will be clear enough to serve as a basis for further discussion. Among the examples of the rule given in the Kāśikāvṛtti are *prāṅ* and *parāṅ*, nominative singular masculine forms of *prāñc-* and *parāñc-*, when either of the meanings of *añcŪ* is intended. In these examples, *añcŪ* is followed by suffix *KvIN* (null), which contains *v,* and preceded by *pra* and *parā*, members of the gati class. Thus, all the conditions required for the application of A 6.2.52 are met, so that the gati *pra* and *parā* retain their original accent, which is initial. The same situation holds true in the dual and plural forms of the words, cited as examples by the Kāśikāvṛtti. Since *parāṅ* is relevant to our discussion, we present its derivational process in Table II.

At the eighth step shown in this table, there is a single replacement (*ekādeśa*) by a long vowel *ā* for *-ā* and the following *a-*, with which it is homogeneous (*savarṇadīrgha*). *Párā* is a gati and its initial vowel is high-pitched (*udātta*); *rā* in *parā* has a low-pitched vowel (*anudātta*); and the verb has an anudātta vowel. This contrasts with *prá-añc-* (→ *prāṅ*), where anudātta *a-* is preceded by udātta *-á* of the gati. According to the Svaraprakriyā and Kāśikāvṛtti,[2] the single substitute *-ā-* of this word gets either a high pitch or the circumflex accent (*svarita*[3]) by A 8.2.6 (स्वरितो वानुदात्ते पदादौ [एकादेश उदात्तेन 5]).[4] But in the case of *parāṅ,* the first vowel of the word *parā* is high-pitched and is *-ā* is not. The vowel of *-añc* that follows is also low-pitched. Therefore the single replacement for *-ā* and *a-* is not subject to the alternation provided for in 8.2.6. The Nyāsa and Padamañjarī mention this clearly but in the Kāśikā and the Svaraprakriyā only the example is quoted.[5]

The counter example related to the word *aniganta* in the sūtra, as quoted by the Kāśikāvṛtti, is *pratyaṅ*, where the gati *prati* ends in a vowel denoted by *iK* (*iganta*), so that it is not referred to by *aniganta*;[6] hence, despite all other conditions being fulfilled, A 6.2.52 does not apply here. The Kāśikā states that since A 6.2.52 has no scope of application here, A 6.2.139 (गतिकारकोपपदात्कृत्) applies, implying that A 6.2.139 is a default rule to which A 6.2.52 is an exception. There is ample support for this view in the discussion in the Mahābhāṣya, where it is also stated that the word *aniganta* is used to prohibit the application of this rule in the cases like *pratīcaḥ*, the accusative plural form of *pratyañc.* But in the case of the first five forms, where semivowel replacement (*yaṇādeśa*) takes place, there is possibility of application of the accent that obtains for a term that does not end in a vowel denoted by *iK* (*aniganta*). However, this application is prohibited by the

2. See Svaraprakriyā 349 (Abhyankar 2001:142), Kāśikā 6.2.52 (Tripathi 1990: 347).

3. On this term, see Abhyankar and Shukla 1986: 440.

4. This rule requires a pada-initial low-pitched vowel preceded by a high-pitched vowel.

5. See Tripathi 1990: 347, Abhyankar 2001: 142. What the Svaraprakriyā says is similar to what the Kāśikā says.

6. This aspect happens to be the main theme of discussion on this sūtra in the Mahābhāṣya. Also there is another problem raised in the discussion on this aspect in the Svaraprakriyā which we do not enter into here.

statement इगन्तस्य यणादेशे कृतेऽपि प्रतिषेधः.[7] Hence, the initial vowel of *pratyaṅ* gets low pitch (*anudātta).*

One more case is discussed where conflict of accentual rules arises, namely, *parācaḥ.* Here no way out is found other than the Mahābhāṣya statement prohibiting the application of the rule चौ (A 6.1.222). Hence the author mentions the Mahābhāṣya and gives initial acute accent to the word पराचः.

3 The accent of *parācaḥ* is attested in the Ṛgveda and its padapāṭha,[8] and Sāyaṇācārya also mentions that *parācaḥ* will have an initial udātta vowel by A 6.2.52. Other forms, like *prācaḥ*, *avācaḥ*[9] are also attested and it is found that the initial vowel has high pitch in these examples too. Here also the prior component is a gati which does not end in *i or u* and *añcŪ* has a suffix added to it which contains *v.*

It is found that other accentual rules have scope of application in this example: अश्वेश्छन्दस्यसर्वनामस्थानम् (A 6.1.170) and चौ (A 6.1.222). Here we discuss this aspect of interrelation of sūtras in the svara section of the Aṣṭādhyāyī on the basis of the discussion found in various traditional sources: the Kāśikāvṛtti and Siddhāntakaumudī with their commentaries as well as two independent works related to the svara section, namely Svaraprakriyā and Svaramañjarī. Of the last two treatises, only the Svaraprakriyā is found to provide certain clues for discussion so that we focus on this work.

4 Svara rules and their application

The division of the four rules in question (see §1) according to the element whose accentuation is provided for is as follows:

1. A 6.1.170: case endings other than those called *sarvanāma-sthāna* (accusative plural through locative plural) get acute accent

7. See Svaraprakriyā 349 (Abhyankar 2001: 142).

8. E.g., ṚV 6.44.17 (Sontakke:1941: 143). See §4 below.

9. This form is also discussed in the Mahābhāṣya on A 6.2.52 (Guruprasad 2006: 747).

in Vedic (*chandasi*); this is applicable for *añcŪ* meaning 'to go' and 'to worship';
2. A 6.1.182: no acute accent for case ending (applicable to *añcŪ* meaning 'to worship');
3. A 6.1.222: the final vowel of a constituent preceding a derivate of *añcŪ* gets acute accent (applicable to *añcŪ* meaning ' to go')
4. A 6.2.52: a gati retains its original accent (applicable to *añc* meaning 'to go' and 'to worship').

The conditions required for application of the sūtras are:
1. A 6.1.170: *añc* is followed by a case ending other than a sarvanāmasthāna;
2. A 6.1.182: *añc* occurs before case endings;
3. A 6.1.222: compound member has only the *c* of *añc*;
4. A 6.2.52: a gati which does not end in *i* or *u* precedes *añc* followed by a suffix containing *v*.

From the above division it is observed that A 6.1.170 and A 6.2.52 are applicable to the root *añcŪ* in both its meanings. But when A 6.1.170 is applicable to *añcŪ*[10] 'to worship', A 6.1.182 cancels the application of A 6.1.170. On the other hand, when this rule is applicable to *añcŪ* meaning 'to go', the condition stated in A 6.1.170 becomes applicable and the final vowel of the ending will get the acute accent. This same condition is stated for the application of the rule चौ (A 6.1.222) which is a later (*para*) rule relative to A 6.1.170. Hence it is difficult to rule out the application of A 6.1.222. Commentators resolve this conflict by stating that the term *asarvanāmasthāna* in A 6.1.170 cancels the application of the later rule A 6.1.222. The term *asarvanāma-sthāna*[11] is used in order to include *Śas* (acc. pl.) among the endings referred to in A 6.1.170. If this rule were applicable only to forms like *dadhyagbhyām*, with endings in the third and

10. *dadhīcaḥ*. See Laghuśabdenduśekhara on 6.1.170 (SK IV. 513).
11. असर्वनामस्थानग्रहणं शस्परिग्रहार्थम् (SK:512-13), शस्परिग्रहार्थासर्वनामस्थानग्रहण-सामर्थ्यात्तत्रापि प्रवृत्ते: (Laghuśabdenduśekhara 513 [on A 6.1.170]).

following triplets, then *asarvanāmasthāna* would not be required, since *tṛtīyādir vibhaktiḥ* could be understood from A 6.1.168 (सावेकाचस्तृतीयादिर्विभक्तिः). According to them the term *asarvanāmasthāna* suggests that this expression is meant to include also the accusative plural suffix and the same is a cause to be an exception of the later rule A 6.1.222. The accent of the word *dadhīcaḥ* (gen. sg.)[12] (इन्द्रो दधीचो अस्थभिः ... जघान ... [ṚV 1.84.13] "Indra slew ... with the bones of Dadhyañc") illustrates a high-pitched case ending by A 6.1.170. The derivation process of this word is presented in table III.

A comparable conflict is observed in an example quoted for the rule A 6.2.52: परांचः. The Siddhāntakaumudī quotes two examples under this rule: ये परांञ्चस्तान्[13] (ṚV 1.164.19) and जहि वृष्ण्यानि कृणुहि परांचः (ṚV 6.25.3).[14] The word *parāñcaḥ* is a tatpuruṣa compound. The initial component parā is a *gati* by definition and the second constituent consists of a verbal root and the suffix *KvIN*. The initial component of this word does not end in *i* or *u* and *añc* ends in a suffix *v* (→ Ø). The first vowel of a gati is udātta by the phiṭ rule निपाता आद्युदात्ताः (Ph. 4.12). Therefore in the word *parāñcaḥ* the first vowel retains its accent by the rule A 6.2.52. But in the example परांचः, other accentuation rules are to be considered: A 6.1.170 and A 6.1.222. The latter is applicable to this example, as the nasal and the vowel *a* of the verbal root *añc* are deleted. Hence the word would get the accent on *rā*. The word *parācaḥ* contains *parā*, a word with the class name *gati*; this is followed by the derivate of the root *añc* to which a suffix (*KvIN*) is added which

12. This example of a genitive singular is provided on A. 6.1.170 in the Kāśikā and the Siddhāntakaumudī. An example of the accusative plural is ṚV 10.87.4: प्रतीचो बाहून् (padapāṭha: प्रतीचः । बाहून् ।) (Sontakke 1946: 596).

13. "Those who have turned ascending" (translation by H. H.Wilson : Sribaishnava.org/scripts/veda/rv/rvtop/htm).

14. "Annihilate, Indra, the strength of those who, whether kinsmen or unrelated, present themselves before us, exerting themselves as adversaries; enfeeble their prowess, put them to fight" (translation by H. H. Wilson).

has *v*. Hence the conditions stated in the A 6.2.52 are fulfilled in this example. Therefore the accent stated in the rule, namely, that the original accent of the gati will be retained. Let us look at the derivational process of the word परांच:, given in Table IV.

This shows that the operation stated by A 6.2.52 is applicable at a prior state (at the third step) as opposed to the rule A 6.1.222. Hence, the accent stated by A 6.1.222 is a sati śiṣṭasvara.[15] Therefore it is very difficult to avoid this rule. It is true that A 6.2.52 is a later (*para*) rule relative to A 6.1.222. The latter, however, is an exception to all the accent rules, since it provides a sati śiṣṭsvara. Hence, the application of this rule cannot be prohibited at all.[16] So to avoid the undesired application, there is a statement of the Mahābhāṣya which proposes a solution, namely, that A 6.2.52 cancels A 6.1.222 on account of it being later.[17] This statement helps to cancel the accentuation by A 6.1.222. In this way the conflict between A 6.1.222 and A 6.2.52 is solved traditionally. This solution also implies that, by default, a rule's being later than another (*paratva)* as a principle used to resolve conflict between sūtras dealing with accent refers to paratva in the derivational process and not to the paratva of the sūtra in the order of the Aṣṭādhyāyī. However, in this special case, on the authority of the statement of the Mahābhāṣya, this default rule is to be set aside and the place of the sūtra in the Aṣṭādhyāyī order is to be referred to by the paratva principle.

However, the traditional discussion does not seem to take into account another rule which is applicable after A 6.2.52 and before A 6.1.222. That rule is A 6.1.170, which is applicable at the fifth step in the derivation. Hence A 6.1.170 again provides a sati śiṣṭasvara relative to A 6.2.52. A 6.1.170 is applicable when the

15. सतिशिष्टस्वरबलीयस्त्वमन्यत्र विकरणेभ्य: । (SK IV. 457).

16. अक्रियमाणे हि प्रतिषेधे सर्वापवादोऽयं चुस्वर: । (Mbh. 6.2.52 [2006: 747]).

17. चुस्वरादनिगन्तोऽञ्चतौ वप्रत्यय इत्येष स्वरो भवति विप्रतिषेधेन । (Mbh. 6.2.52 [2006: 746]).

verbal root *añc* is followed by an ending other than one of the sarvanāmasthāna class. In this way A 6.1.170 provides a sati śiṣṭasvara and there is no way to stop the application of this rule. If we observe the conditions stated in the rules, it is found that the conditions stated by A 6.1.170 are more specific than the conditions of A 6.2.52. Hence A 6.2.52 has less chance to apply than A 6.1.170. Therefore, in the above example, it becomes difficult to defend the original accent of the gati by A 6.2.52.

The grammarians have not discussed the above conflict when discussing the example for A 6.2.52. They have discussed the clash between A 6.1.222 and A 6.2.52. Nageśabhaṭṭa[18] has mentioned in his commentary on A 6.1.170 that A 6.2.52 is also an exception to A 6.1.170 like A 6.1.222. But there is no strong reason given by any commentator in this regard. A 6.2.52 is not only restricted in application as compared to A 6.1.170 and A 6.1.222 but also an exception to the retention of the original accent of a kṛt suffix, by गतिकारकोपपदात्कृत् (A 6.2.138), which is a rule later rule than A 6.2.52.

5 A possible solution to resolve the conflict between A 6.2.52 and A 6.1.170 may be to state that, on the authority of a statement of the Mahābhāṣya, when a prior (*pūrva*) sūtra cancels a later (*para*) sūtra, even when the operation stated by the former is sati śiṣṭa, it cancels all pertinent later rules. However, this solution is not fully satisfactory and therefore requires further investigation and thought.

What we can certainly say is that whenever a conflict between sūtras stating accent arises, at different levels of a derivational process, by default the paratva that is equivalent to sati śiṣṭa overrules the paratva relative to rule order in the Aṣṭādhyāyī. It is only in exceptional cases like the one discussed in this paper that the statement of authority in the Mahābhāṣya, which cancels this

18. अनिगन्तोऽश्चतौ इति पूर्वपदप्रकृतिस्वरस्य सतिशिष्टचुस्वरबाधकत्ववदेतस्यापि बाधकत्वेन तत्रै-तदप्रवृत्तेरित्याहुः। Laghuśabdenduśekhara 513 (on 6.1.170).

default rule, has to be invoked to account for a desirable form. The tradition records the default rule by the statement सतिशिष्टस्वर-बलीयस्त्वमन्यत्र विकरणेभ्य: (see note 15). In this statement, one exception to this default rule is mentioned, namely, stem forming affixes in verb forms (*vikaraṇa*).

What we can also say after the discussion in the present paper is that there are other exceptions to the default rule as well. One such exception presented in this paper is the derivation rule related to the nominal termination added to a compound.

Table I. Derivation of accusative plural form of प्र+*अञ्चु* in two meanings

प्राच: 'to some who go directed forward (acc. pl.)'	प्राञ्च: 'some who worship extensively'
प्र अञ्चु क्विन् (A 3.2.59)	प्र अञ्चु क्विन् (A 3.2.59)
प्र अच् क्विन् (A 6.4.24)	प्र अञ्च् क्विन् (A 6.4.24, 6.4.30)
प्र अच् Ø (A 6.1.67)	प्र अच् Ø (A 6.1.67)
प्र अच् शस् (A 4.1.1, 4.1.2)	प्र अञ्च् शस् (A 4.1.1, 4.1.2)
प्र अच् अस् (A 1.3.8, A 1.3.9)	प्र अञ्च् अस् (A 1.3.8, 1.3.9)
प्र च् अस् (A 6.4.138)	प्र ञ्च् अस् (A 6.4.138)
प्रा च् अस् (A 6.3.138)	प्रा ञ्च् अस् (A 6.3.138)
प्राच रु (A 8.2.66)	प्राञ्च रु (A 8.2.66)
प्राच: (A 8.3.15)	**प्राञ्च:** (A 8.3.15)

Table II. Derivation of पराङ्.

1.परा अञ्च् क्विन्	A 3.2.59
2.परा अञ्च् व्	A 1.3.8, 1.3.3, 1.3.9
3. परा अञ्च् Ø	A 6.1.67
4.परा अच् Ø	A 6.4.24
5. परा अच् सु	A 1.2.46, 4.1.1, 4.1.2
6.परा अच् स्	A 1.3.9
7. परा अच् *Ø*	A 6.1.68
8. पराच् *Ø*	A 6.1.101
पराङ्	A 8.2.62

Table III. Derivation with accentuation of the form दधीचः

दधीचः [*dadhy añcati*]	
1. दधि अञ्चु क्विन्	A 3.2.59 1.3.8, 1.3.3, 1.3.9
2. दधि अञ्च् व्	A 6.4.24
3. दधि अच् Ø	A 6.1.67
4. दधि अच् Ø	A 1.2.46
5. दधि अच् ङस्	A 4.1.1, 4.1.2
6. दधि अच् अस्	A 1.3.8, 1.3.4, 1.3.9
7. दधी च् अस्	A 6.4.138, 6.3.138
8. दधीच रु	A 8.2.66
दधीचः	A 8.3.15

Table IV. Derivation and accentuation of परा॑चः[a]

1. परा॒ अञ्च् क्विन्	3.2.59
2. परा॒ अञ्च् व्	1.3.8, 1.3.3., 1.3.9
3. परा॒ अञ्च् Ø	6.1.67, 6.2.52
4. परा॒ अच् Ø	6.4.24
5. *परा॒ अच् शस्*	1.2.46, 4.1.1, 4.1.2, 6.1.170
6. **परा॒ Øच् अस्**	6.4.138, 1.3.8, 1.3.9
7. परा॒ च् अस्	6.3.138, 6.1.222
8. परा॒चस्	8.2.33
परा॑चः	8.3.15 ,6.2.52

[a] Italic, bold and underline show the application of three different accentuation rules.

References and abbreviations

A *Aṣṭādhyāyī of Pāṇini*. See Böhtlingk.

Abhyankar, K. V.

1953 *Śrīmadbhagvatpatañjaliviracitvyākaraṇa-mahābhāṣya muḷa āṇi maraṭhī bhāṣāṁtara, bhāṣāṁtarakāra Mahāmahopādhyāya Vāsudeva śāstrī Abhyaṁkara, saṁpādaka Kāśīnātha Vāsudeva Abhyaṁkara*, Volume 5. Pune: Deccan Education Society

1974 *Svopajñavyākhyayā-sahitā, Svaraprakriyā (śrīśeṣakulodbhavanāgāhvayapaṇḍitasūnurāmacandrapaṇḍitaviracitā)*, Kāśīnātha Vāsudeva Abhyaṁkara *ityetaiḥ prastāvanāpāṭhabhedasūtra-sūcyādibhir alaṅkṛtya saṁśodhitam*. Ānandāśrama Sanskrit Series 138. Pune: Anandashram Samstha. Reprinted 2001

Abhyankar, K. V. and Shukla, J. M.

1977 *Dictionary of Grammar*, Gaekwad's Oriental Series 134. Baroda: Oriental Research Institute. Reprinted 1986

ṚV *Ṛgvedasaṁhitā*. See Sontakke N.

Böhtlingk, Otto

1998 *Pāṇini's Grammatik. herausgegeben, übersetzt, erläutert und mit verschienden Indices versehen.* Two volumes in one. Delhi: Motilal Banarasidass. [First Indian Edition]

Caturveda, Giridharasharma and Parameshvaranandasharma

1941 (1997) *Śrīmadbhaṭṭojidīkṣitaviracitā Vaiyākaraṇa-siddhānta-kaumudī (Kṛdantaprabhṛti samāmptiparyantā) Śrīmadvāsudevadīkṣita-praṇītayā Bālamanoramākhya- vyākhyayā*

Śrīmajjñānendrasarasvatīviracitayā Tattvabodhinyākhyavyākhyayā ca sanāthīkṛtā Śekhara-subodhinīsuśobhitasvaravaidikīprakaraṇā tathā Bhairavīcandrakalāsamalaṅkṛta-liṅgānuśāsanā. Delhi: Motilal Banarasidass. [Reprinted 1997]

Devasthali, G. V.

1967 *Phiṭsūtras of Śāntanava, edited with Introduction, Translation and Critical and Exegetical Notes.* Publications of the Centre of Advanced Studies in Sanskrit, Class C, No.1. Poona: University of Poona.

1985 *Svaramañjarī* of *Śrīnarasihasūrī.* Bhandarakar Oriental Research Institute Research Unit Series No. 6. Poona: Bhandarakar Oriental Research Institute.

Katre, S. S.

1987 *A Grammatical Study of the Verbal forms in Ṛgveda with special referance to Maṇḍala II.* [[Unpublished University of Pune thesis]

KV *Kaśikāvṛtti.* See Tripathi, Jaya Shankar Lal.

Laghuśabdenduśekhara See SK (volume IV).

Mbh *Vyākaraṇamahābhāṣyam.* See Shastri, Guruprasad

Nyāsa See 1990, Tripathi Jaya Shankar Lal

Ph *Phiṭsūtra.* See Devasthali G. V.

Pradhan, Shubhangi

1988 *Verbal forms in Ṛgveda Maṇḍala III.* Two volumes. [Unpublished University of Pune thesis]

Ramachandradu., P. Sri

1981 *Śrīharadattamiśraviracitā Padamañjarī (Vāmana Jayāditya Viracitāyā Kāśikāyā Vyākhyā) Dvitīyo bhāgaḥ* (5–8 *adhyāyāḥ*). Sanskrit Academy Series 26. Hyderrabad: Sanskrit Academy, Osmania University.

Shastri, Guruprasad

2006 *Patañjali's Vyākaraṇa Mahābhāṣya with Kaiyaṭa's Pradīpa and Nāgojibhaṭṭa's Uddyota with the Notes by Guruprasas Shastri (Adhyāya Six)*. New Delhi: Rashrtiya Sanskarit Sansthan [Reprint of 1938 edition]

Shete, Suvarna

1998 *Verbal forms in Ṛgveda Maṇḍala VII*. [Unpublished University of Pune thesis]

SK *Vaiyākaraṇasiddhāntakaumudī*. See Caturveda, Giridharasharma and Parameshvaranandasharma.

Sontakke, N.

1933 *Ṛgveda-Saṁhitā with the Commentary of Sāyaṇāchārya. Volume I: Maṇḍal 1*. Poona: Tilak Maharashtra University Vaidic Samshodhan Mandala.

1941 *Ṛgveda-Saṁhitā with the Commentary of Sāyaṇāchārya. Volume III: 6-8 Maṇḍalas*. Poona: Tilak Maharashtra University Vaidic Samshodhan Mandala.

1946 *Ṛgveda-Saṁhitā with the Commentary of Sāyaṇāchārya. Volume IV: Mandalas IX-X*. Poona: Tilak Maharashtra University Vaidic Samshodhan Mandala.

Tripathi, Dr. Jaya Shankar Lal.

1990 *Kāśikā of Vāmana and Jayāditya with Nyāsa or Kāśikā-Vivaraṇapañjikā of Jinendrabuddhi and Padamañjarī of Haradatta Miśra with the Bhāvabodhinī by Jaya Shankar Lal Tripathi*. Vol.

VII. Pracya Bharatiya Granthamala 18. Varanasi: Tara Book Agency.

Vasu, Śrisa Chandra.

1905 (1995) *The Siddhānta Kaumudī Of Bhattoji Dīkṣita, edited and translated into English.* Vol. III. Allahabad: The Panini Office.

1963 (1995) *The Siddhānta Kaumudī Of Bhattoji Dīkṣita, edited and translated into English.* Vol. II. Allahabad: The Panini Office. Vol. II. [Reprinted Delhi: Motilal Banarasidass, 1995]

1891 (2003) The *Aṣādhyāyī of Pāṇini, edited and translated into English.* Vol II. [Reprinted Delhi: Motilal Banarasidass, 2003]

Vishvabandhu

1959 *A Vedic Word-concordance ... in five Volumes sub-divided into fifteen Parts.* Volume IV, part III. Hoshiarpur: V. V. R. Institute.

1964 *Ṛgveda,with the Padapāṭha and the Available Portions of the Bhāṣya-s by Skandasvāmin and Udgīthīa, The Vyākhyā by Veṅkaṭamādhava Mudgala's Vṛtti based on Sāyaṇa's Bhāṣya. Part-IV: Maṇḍala 5-6.* Hoshiarpur, Vishveshvarananda Vaidikshodhasamsthana.

Whitney,W. D.

1889 *Sanskrit Grammar Including both the Classical Language and the older Dialects of Veda and Brahmana.* Second edition. Leipzig: Breitkopf & Härtel. [Eighth issue of the second edition. Cambridge, Massashusetts: Harvard University Press; reprinted 1964. Indian reprint, 1962, 1969, Delhi: Motilal Banarsidass]

The use of the terms *dā*, *mā* and *gā* in the Aṣṭādhyāyī

Sharon Ben-Dor

0 Introduction

In the Aṣṭādhyāyī, Pāṇini uses the terms *dā, mā* and *gā* to refer to some verbal stems. These terms are mentioned without any marker. They are simply the form (i.e., *dā*, *mā*, *gā*) of the stems that they should refer to. In Pāṇini's system, there are quite a few verbal stems that have such forms. These stems are of two kinds: those which are mentioned in these forms already in the Dhātupaṭha, and others, which obtain such forms by the application of a grammatical rule. Commentators raise a question concerning which of the two kinds the terms *dā, mā and gā* refer to: whether they refer only to those which originally have that particular form, or also to those which obtain such forms by the application of a grammatical rule. An examination concerning which items these terms should desirably refer to shows that one cannot use the categories mentioned above for establishing a general rule in this respect. In some cases the term *dā*, *mā* or *gā* refers to one kind of an item and in other cases only to some items from each group. Consequently, commentators argue that with respect to the terms *dā*, *mā* and *gā* there are not any specifications concerning which item they refer to. They express this view by invoking the statement गामादाग्रहणेष्वविशेष: from the Mahābhāṣya[1], which in turn appears as a paribhāṣā ('interpretative principle') in most paribhāṣā collections.[2]

1. Bh I.74.21-22 (on A 1.1.20 vt. 1): दोष एवैतस्या: परिभाषाया लक्षणप्रतिपदोक्तयो: प्रतिपदोक्तस्यैवेति गामादाग्रहणेष्वविशेष इति ।।

2. The paribhāṣā गामादाग्रहणेष्वविशेष: is considered an exception to the paribhāṣā लक्षणप्रतिपदोक्तयो: प्रतिपदोक्तस्यैव ग्रहणम्, which in this context is taken to establish that a term refers primarily to original items (*pratipadokta*) and not to items which are acquired by the application of a grammatical rule (*lakṣaṇa/ lakṣaṇokta/ lākṣaṇika*).

Generally, commentators on Pāṇini agree that in order to know to which items the terms *dā, mā* and *gā* refer, one should look ahead and consider the desired target. In most cases, they argue that this is the only way to obtain this knowledge. In some cases, they mention other paribhāṣās or devices which according to them provide the desired knowledge.

In this paper, I show that in spite of the commentators' view, Pāṇini does not use the terms *dā*, *mā* and *gā* arbitrarily, and there are reasons for stating them as such. As we shall see, in each sūtra where a term *dā*, *mā* or *gā* is mentioned in the Aṣṭādhyāyī, it refers only to that stems which has the form *dā*, *mā* or *gā* in the particular situation where the sūtra is applicable. Thus, if one considers the requirements of the sūtra where the item is mentioned, one can know to which items the term refers. In other words, the context or the situation where the sūtra is applicable provides the knowledge about the correct application of the sūtra. Hence, contrary to the paribhāṣā गामादाग्रहणेष्वविशेषः, one can find a common feature with respect to the use of the terms *dā, mā* and *gā* in the Aṣṭādhyāyī. This allows knowing which items the term in question refers to without the aid of looking ahead and considering the desired target. In addition, there is no need of any device or paribhāṣā for obtaining this knowledge. Lastly, I will argue that the puzzlement with respect to the terms *dā, mā* and *gā* is due to an insertion of a notion from another school and that Pāṇini does not follows this notion.

1 A 6.1.145 and 6.1.150

Before discussing in detail the sūtras where these terms occur it is helpful to clarify the role of the sūtras आदेच उपदेशेऽशिति (A 6.1.45) and मीनातिमिनोतिदीङां ल्यपि च (A 6.1.50), which are involved in most of the cases mentioned below.

1.1 आदेच उपदेशेऽशिति (A 6.1.45)

According to this rule, *e o ai au* of stems are replaced by a long vowel *ā* when the stems occur before affixes which are not marked with the anubandha *ś*. Thus, for example, the stems ***deṅ*** 'to protect',[3] and ***meṅ*** 'to barter, to exchange'[4] obtain the forms *dā* and *mā* respectively when they are not followed by affixes which are marked with the anubandha *ś*. With respect to A 6.1.45, it is essential to specify the significance of the negation *aśiti* mentioned in the sūtra. According to Pāṇinīyas, *aśiti* is an instance of what is called *prasajya pratiṣedha*, that is, it prohibits what would occur otherwise. In other words, in any case where there is not an affix marked with the anubandha *ś* the replacement to long vowel *ā* provided for by A 6.1.45 should occur. As the Kāśikā argues, this replacement occurs unconditionally (*anaimittika*), before the occurrence of an affix.[5] By accepting this view, one can explain, as the Kāśikā does, how to derive *sugla* 'very tired' and *sumla* 'very weak'. These derivates contain the forms *gla* and *mla* of the verbal stems *glai*[6] and *mlai*,[7] respectively, with the preverb (*upasarga*) *su*. Both end with the affix ***ka*** provided by आतश्चोपसर्गे A (A 3.1.136), which requires a stem ending with long *ā*. For this sūtra to be applicable to the case of *sugla* and *sumla* it is necessary to consider the stems *glai* and *mlai* as ending with long vowel *ā* before any affix has been added. Considering the stems *glai* and *mlai* as ending with long vowel *ā* is allowed because A 3.1.136 involves the addition of the ***ka***. This affix is not marked with the anubandha *ś* and in this situation the replacement provided by A 6.1.45 takes place.

The case of उदीचाम्माङो व्यतीहारे (A 3.4.19) clearly illustrates Pāṇini's procedure. In A 3.4.19, he uses the term ***māṅ***. This refers

3. DhP I.1011.

4. DhP I.1010.

5. Kāśikā 6.1.45 (VII.72): अशितीति प्रसज्यप्रतिषेधोऽयम् । तेनैतदात्त्वमनैमित्तिकं प्रागेव प्रत्ययोत्पत्तेर्भवतीति । सुग्लः सुम्ल इत्यातश्चोपसर्गे (३.१.१३६) इति कप्रत्ययः । सुग्लानः सुम्लान इत्यातो युच् (३.३.१२८) इत्येवमादि सिद्धं भवतीति ॥

6. DhP I.952.

7. DhP I.953.

to the verbal stem ***meṅ*** 'to barter, to exchange',[8] as it is stated in the Dhātupaṭha. In this case also, A 6.1.45 provides the replacement by *ā*. Why does Pāṇini use ***māṅ*** to refer to ***meṅ***? For he could simply use the term ***meṅ*** as the stem is given in the Dhātupaṭha. A 3.4.19 involves cases where affixes other than those marked with the anubandha *ś* occur.[9] In such cases, according A 6.1.45, the replacement to long vowel *ā* takes place.

1.2 मीनातिमिनोतिदीङां ल्यपि च (A 6.1.50)

According to this rule, a final diphthong (***ec***) of the stems ***mīñ*** 'to injure',[10] ***ḍumiñ*** 'to scatter',[11] and ***dīṅ*** is replaced by a long vowel *ā*. Consequently, these stems obtain the form *mā* or *dā*. A 6.1.50 is applicable when the *i* or *ī* vowels of the stems have been replaced by an *ec* vowel. This occurs only in cases where an affix that causes a *guṇa* or *vṛddhi* replacement follows. Thus, Pāṇinīyas explain that the replacement provided for by A 6.1.50 should takes place in all cases where the stems ***mīñ***, ***ḍumiñ*** and ***dīṅ*** are followed by an affix which causes a *guṇa* or *vṛddhi* replacement (*ejvaviṣaya*), that is, affixes which are not marked with an anubandha *k* or *ṅ*. The Kāśikā adds that this replacement should take place already before the occurrence of the affix, that is, in the stage referred to as *upadeśa*.[12] In other words, ***mīñ***, ***ḍumiñ*** and ***dīṅ*** should be considered as having the form *mā* and *dā* respectively with respect to rules which concern cases where a replacement to *guṇa* or *vṛddhi* is anticipated to occur.

8. DhP I.1010.

9. Pāṇinīyas consider this instance as an indication of the existence of the paribhāṣā नानुबन्धकृतमनेजन्तत्वम्. Therefore, they argue that the negation ***adāp*** in A 1.1.20 refers also to the stem ***daip***. See Bh II.171.19-172.2 and Kāśikā 3.4.19 (IV.168).

10. DhP IX.4.

11. DhP V.4.

12. Kāśikā 6.1.50 (VII.76): उपदेश एवात्वविधानादिवर्णान्तलक्षण: प्रत्ययो न भवति । आकारलक्षणश्च भवति । उपदायो वर्त्तत ईषदुपदानमिति घञ्युचौ भवत: ॥ SK III 324-325 (on A 6.1.50): एषामात्वं स्याल्ल्यपि चकारादशित्येज्निमित्ते ॥

I shall now continue with a detailed discussion on the use of the terms *mā*, *gā* and *dā*.

2 *Mā*

In the Dhātupaṭha, there are three verbal stems which have the form *mā*: *mā* 'to measure',[13] ***māṅ*** 'to measure',[14] and ***māṅ*** 'to measure'.[15] The stem ***meṅ*** 'to barter, to exchange'[16] acquires the form *mā* according to A 6.1.45 (see §1.1). In addition, the stems ***ḍumiñ*** 'to scatter'[17] and ***mīñ*** 'to injure'[18] acquire the same form according to A 6.1.50 (§1.2).

The term *mā* occurs in ह्वावामश्च (A 3.2.2), घुमास्थागापाजहातिसां हलि (A 6.4.66), सनि मीमाघुरभलभशकपतपदामच इस् (A 7.4.54) and नेर्गदनदपतपदघुमास्यतिहन्तियातिवातिद्रातिप्सातिवपतिवहतिशाम्यतिचि – नोतिदेग्धिषु च (A 8.4.17).

In A 6.4.66, *mā* refers to *mā*, the two stems ***māṅ***, and ***meṅ***. It does not refer to ***ḍumiñ*** and ***mīñ***. This sūtra does not concern affixes marked with the anubandha *ś*, and since the stem ***meṅ*** acquires the form *mā* in this context, the term *mā* in this sūtra can refer to this stem in addition to *mā* and ***māṅ***. Moreover, A 6.4.66 requires a stem that is followed by an affix marked with *k* or *ṅ*. As

13. DhP II.53.

14. DhP III.6.

15. DhP IV.34. It should be noted that *Sāyaṇa* doubts the existence of the stem ***māṅ*** of the *divādi* group. He bases his doubt on Kṣīrasvāmin's commentary on this stem and on the Nyāsa on Kāśikā 6.4.66, 7.4.40, and 7.4.54, which does not mention this stem. MDhV IV.34 (p. 412) on the stem ***māṅ***: अयं कैश्चिदेव पठ्यते । यदाह स्वामी माङः मान इति दुर्ग इति । तथा घुमास्थादिसूत्रे न्यासेऽपि मेति कस्येदं ग्रहणं किं मेङः प्रणिदान इति भौवादिकस्य उत माङः मान इत्यस्य जौहोत्यादिकस्याहोस्विन्मा मान इत्यस्यादादिकस्य । गामादाग्रहणेष्वविशेष इति त्रयाणामपि ग्रहणमिति । तथा द्यतिस्यतीत्यत्र सनिमीमेत्यत्राप्युक्तानामेव त्रयाणां ग्रहणमित्युच्यते ॥

16. DhP I.1010.

17. DhP V.4.

18. DhP IX.4.

the stems ***ḍumiñ*** and ***mīñ*** do not acquire the form *mā* in such a situation, the term *mā* in this sūtra does not refer to these stems. Thus, by considering the context where A 6.4.66 is applicable, one can know that here *mā* refers only to *mā*, the two stems ***māṅ*** and ***meṅ***.[19]

The same feature as in A 6.4.66 occurs also with respect to the term *mā* in A 7.4.54, where *mā* refers to *mā*, the two stems ***māṅ***, and ***meṅ***.[20] This sūtra requires a stem followed by the affix ***san***. This affix is not marked with *ś* and in such a situation the stem ***meṅ*** has the form *mā*. Therefore, *mā* in A 7.4.54 can refer also to this stem. Moreover, this term cannot refer to the stems ***ḍumiñ*** and ***mīñ***. According to इको झल् (A 1.2.9), the affix ***san*** occurring after a verbal stem ending with a vowel *i*, *u*, *ṛ* or *ḷ* (***ik***) is considered marked with the anubandha *k*. Consequently, after ***ḍumiñ*** and ***mīñ***, ***san*** is considered marked with *k*. Since A 6.1.50 does not apply in such cases, these stems do not obtain the form *mā* in the

19. The Nyāsa provides some explanations with respect to the use of the term *mā* in A 6.4.66. It says that some (*kecit*) argue that according to the paribhāṣā निरनुबन्धकग्रहणे न सानुबन्धकस्य, the term *mā* refers to the stem *mā*. Others (*anye*) argue that according to the paribhāṣā लुग्विकरणालुग्विकरणयोरलुग्विकरणस्य, this term refers to ***māṅ*** (DhP IV.34) and ***meṅ***. Still others (*apare*) say that according to the paribhāṣā गामादाग्रहणेष्वविशेषः, this term refers also to the stem ***māṅ*** (DhP III.6), ***māṅ*** (DhP IV.34) and ***meṅ***. According to the Nyāsa, this last view is the opinion of the Kāśikā. Nyāsa on Kāśikā 6.4.66 (VIII.235-236): अथ मेति कस्येदं ग्रहणं किं मेङ प्रणिदान इत्यस्य भौवादिकस्य उत माङ मान इत्यस्य जौहोत्यादिकस्याहोस्विन्मा मान इत्यस्यादादिकस्य । तत्र केचिदाहुर्निरनुबन्धकग्रहणे न सानुबन्धकस्येत्यादादिकस्य ग्रहणम् । अन्ये त्वाहुर्लुग्विकरणालुग्विकरणयोरलुग्विकरणस्यैव ग्रहणमित्यलुग्विकरणयोर्माङमेङोरिति । अपरे ब्रुवते गामादाग्रहणेष्वविशेष इति त्रयाणामपीत्येतदेव वृत्तिकारस्याभिमतमिति लक्ष्यते ॥ It seems that the Nyāsa accepts the Kāśikā's view, as in its commentary on A 7.4.40 and A 7.4.54, it mentions only the paribhāṣā गामादाग्रहणेष्वविशेषः. This may also be said with regard to Sāyaṇa, who mentions only this paribhāṣā when quoting the Nyāsa.

20. The Nyāsa explains that this is on the basis of the paribhāṣā गामादाग्रहणेष्वविशेषः. Nyāsa on Kāśikā 7.4.54 (IX.332): मेति गामादाग्रहणेष्वविशेष इति मेङ प्रणिदाने पूर्वोक्तानां त्रयाणां ग्रहणम् ॥

context where A 7.4.54 is applicable. Therefore, the term *mā* in A 7.4.54 cannot refer to them. Yet, it is desired that A 7.4.54 should apply also to these stems. Therefore, in order that this sūtra be applicable with respect to these stems, Pāṇini mentions also the term *mī*, which refers to ***ḍumiñ*** and ***mīñ***.[21]

In addition, with respect to *mī* used in A 7.4.54 another dilemma arises. This term should refer also to the stem ***ḍumiñ***. How can *mī* refer to ***ḍumiñ***? The vowel *i* of ***ḍumiñ*** is replaced by a long vowel *ī* when it is followed by the affix ***san*** according to अज्झनगमां सनि (A 6.4.16), so that in this context the stem has the form *mī*. As A 7.4.54 concerns the same situation, where stems are followed by ***san***, the term *mī* can refer also to this stem.

The same feature as in A 6.4.66 and 7.4.54, occurs in A 7.4.40 and A3.2.2. In A7.4.40, the term *mā* again refers to the stems *mā*, the two stems ***māṅ***, and ***meṅ***. However, it does not refer to the stems ***ḍumiñ*** and ***mīñ***.[22] A 7.4.40 concerns cases where an affix marked with the anubandha *k* follows. Such an affix prohibits *guṇa* or *vṛddhi* replacement and thus A 6.1.50 is not applicable to provide the long vowel *ā* replacement. Therefore, the term *mā* in A 7.4.40 cannot refer to these stems, since they do not obtain the form *mā* in the context where A 7.4.40 is applicable.

In A 3.2.2, *mā* refers to the two stems ***māṅ*** and to ***meṅ***. As this sūtra concerns only transitive verbs, commentators explain that *mā*

21. The Padamañjarī and Bhaṭṭoji Dīkṣita present this reasoning. PM on Kāśikā 7.4.54 (IX.332): मा माने माङ माने मेङ प्रणिदाने त्रयाणामपि ग्रहणम् । मीनातिमिनोत्योः सनः कित्त्वे सत्यनेज्विषयत्वात् मारूपासम्भवात्पृथग्ग्रहणम् ॥ SK III.451 (on A 1.2.9): एज्विषयत्वाभावान्मीनातिमिनोति (सू २५०८) इत्यात्वं न । अत एव सनिमीमा (सू २६२३) इति सूत्रे माधातोः पृथङ्मीग्रहणं कृतम् ॥ The Kāśikā, however, uses the paribhāṣā गामादाग्रहणेष्वविशेषः in order to explain how this term refers to all these stems. Kāśikā 7.4.54 (IX.332): मा इति गामादाग्रहणेष्वविशेषः ॥

22. The Nyāsa explains that this is on the basis of the paribhāṣā गामादाग्रहणेष्वविशेषः. Nyāsa on Kāśikā 7.4.70 (IX.322): मा माने माङ माने मेङ प्रणिदाने गामादाग्रहणेष्वविशेष इति त्रयाणामपि ग्रहणम् ॥

does not refer to the stem *mā* not marked with *ṅ*, because it is intransitive.[23] Moreover, A 3.2.2 is considered as an exception to आतोऽनुपसर्गे कः (A 3.2.3), which provides the affix ***ka*** after stems ending with a long vowel *ā*. This affix is marked with the anubandha *k*, which prohibits *guṇa* or *vṛddhi* replacement. In such a situation, A 6.1.50 is not applicable to provide the long vowel replacement. Therefore, A 3.2.3 is not applicable to the stems ***ḍumiñ*** and ***mīñ***, since they do not end with a long vowel *ā* in the context where A 3.2.3 is applicable.[24] Consequently, it is unnecessary to prevent the application of this sūtra to these stems in A 3.2.2. This is the reason why the term *mā* in A 3.2.2 does not refer to them.[25]

3 *Gā*

There are two verbal stems which have the form *gā* in the Dhātupaṭha: ***gāṅ*** 'to go'[26] and *gā* 'to praise'.[27] In addition, the stem *gai* 'to sing'[28] obtains this form when an affix which is not marked with the anubandha *ś* follows, according to A 6.1.45 (§1.1). Moreover, the stem ***iṇ*** 'to go'[29] is replaced by *gā* in the aorist (***luṅ***)

23. PM on Kāśikā 3.2.2 (III.407): माङः मान इति । ङितो मारूपस्योपलक्षणमेतत्तेन मेङः प्रणिदाने (धा०पा० ९६१) इत्यस्यापि ग्रहणम् । मा माने (धा०पा० १०६२) इत्यस्य तु संभावनार्थस्याकर्मकत्वादग्रहणम् ॥ PrM II.1657(to SK on A 3.2.2): माङमेङोरिह ग्रहणम् । न तु मा मान इत्यस्याकर्मकत्वाद् ॥
24. In addition, the addition of the affix ***aṇ*** to stems ending with a long vowel *ā* involves the addition of the augment ***yuk*** according to आतो युक्चिण्कृतोः (A 7.3.33).
25. The Nyāsa also explains that these stems get the affix ***aṇ*** according to कर्मण्यण्(A 3.2.1). Nyāsa on Kāśikā 3.2.2 (III.407): ननु यदि गामादाग्रहणेष्वविशेषस्तदा मीञ् हिंसायां डुमिञ् प्रक्षेपण इत्येतयोरपि ग्रहणं प्राप्नोति यस्मान्मीनातिमिनोतिदीङां ल्यपि चेति तयोरप्येज्विषय आत्त्वे कृते मेत्यतद्रुपं सम्पद्यते । भवत्येवाभ्यामणेवेति पूर्वसूत्रेण प्राप्तस्य ॥
26. DhP I.998.
27. DhP III.25.
28. DhP I.965.
29. DhP II.36.

according to इणो गा लुङि (A 2.4.45).[30] The stem (*adhi*) ***iṅ*** 'to study'[31] is replaced by ***gāṅ*** in the perfect (***liṭ***) according to गाङ् लिटि (A 2.4.49). This replacement occurs also optionally in the aorist and in the conditional (***lṛṅ***) according to विभाषा लुङ्लृङोः (A 2.4.50), and when this stem occurs with ***ṇic*** before ***san*** or ***caṅ***, according to णौ च संश्चङोः (A 2.4.51).

The term *gā* is used in घुमास्थागापाजहातिसां हलि (A 6.4.66), स्थागापापचां भावे (A3.3.95) and गापोष्टक् (A3.2.28).

In A 6.4.66, *gā* refers to all the five stems mentioned above.[32] However, with respect to ***iṇ*** and ***iṅ***, it refers only to these stems when they obtain the form *gā*. This does not have any significance concerning the application of A 6.4.66 but it affects the application of the following sūtra, एर्लिङि (A 6.4.67), where *gā* occurs by anuvṛtti. In A 6.4.67, this term refers only to the stems *gā* and *gai*,[33] since this sūtra is applicable in the context of ***liṅ***. As in this context ***iṇ*** and ***iṅ*** do not obtain the form *gā*, the term *gā* in A 6.4.67 does not refer to these stems.[34]

30. But before the causative affix ***ṇic***, when this stem does not denote 'understanding', it is replaced by ***gami*** according to णौ गमिरबोधने (A 2.4.46).

31. DhP II.37.

32. However, it does not concern the stem ***gāṅ*** because गाङ्कुटादिभ्योऽञ्णिन्ङित् (A 1.2.1) does not refer to this stem. See SK III.225, on the stem ***gāṅ*** (I.950).

33. This sūtra does not concern the stem ***gāṅ*** (I.998 ***gāṅ*** *gatau*), since this does not conjugate in *parasmaipada* (यासुट्परस्मैपदेषूदात्तो ङिच्च [A 3.4.103]).

34. The Nyāsa provides this explanation. Nyāsa on Kāśikā 6.4.66 (VIII.235-236): गेति । गाङ् गतौ के गै शब्दे एतौ भौवादिकौ गा स्तुतौ छन्दसीति जौहोत्यादिक इणो गा लुङीतीणो गादेश इण्वदिक इति वक्तव्यमितीको गादेशो गाङ् लिटि विभाषा लुङ्लृङोरिति चेङो गाङादेश एषां पूर्ववत्सर्वेषामविशेषेण ग्रहणम् । सत्यपि सर्वेषां ग्रहणे यस्य क्ङिदार्धधातुकपरं सम्भवति तस्यैवेत्वं भवति नेतरस्य निमित्ताभावात् ॥ Nyāsa on Kāśikā 6.4.67 (VIII.238): कै गायित्यस्योदाहरणं न तु गाङः तस्य परस्यमैपदासंभवात् । नापीणिगिङादेशानां (नापीणीङादेशानां/नापीणीङ्गादेशानां ?) तेषामपि लिङ्यसम्भवात् । इङादेशस्य तु पूर्वस्माच्च हेतोः ॥

In A 3.3.95, the term *gā* refers to the stems *gāṅ*[35] and *gai*. This sūtra provides for the addition of the affix ***ktin*,** which is not marked with the anubandha *ś*. In this situation, the stem *gai* obtains the form *gā* according to A 6.1.45 (§1.1). Therefore, the term *gā* in A 3.3.95 can refer also to the stem *gai*. Moreover, the affix ***ktin*** does not cause *iṇ* or *iṅ* to obtain the form *gā*. Therefore, *gā* in A 3.3.95 does not refer to the stems *iṇ* or *iṅ*. This also corresponds to the fact that Pāṇinīyas consider A 3.3.95 an exception to आतश्चोपसर्गे (A 3.3.106),[36] which generally concerns stems ending in a long vowel *ā*.[37]

The same issue that obtained for A 3.3.95 obtains also in the case of गापोष्टक् (A3.2.8). Here too, *gā* does not refer to the stems *iṇ* and *iṅ*, since they do not get the form *gā* before the affix ***ṭak***.[38] Moreover, in A 3.2.8 the term *gā* refers only to the stem *gai*. The affix *ṭak*, provided for by this sūtra, is not marked with the anubandha *ś* and in such a case this stem gets the form *gā*. Thus, the term *gā* in A 3.2.8 can refer to the stem *gai*. Yet, here the question arises why this term does not also refer to the stems *gā* and *gāṅ*.[39]

35. On this sūtra the Kāśikā presents only the examples *udgīti* and *saṃgīti* (← *ut/sam gī+**ktin*** [A 6.4.66]) ← *ut/sam gā+ti* (6.1.45) ← *ut/sam gai+**ktin***) 'singing' for the term *gā*. According to the Nyāsa, this term also refers to the stem *gāṅ*: अत्र च गामादाग्रहणेष्वविशेष इति गै शब्दे गाङ्गताविति द्वयोरपि ग्रहणम् ॥ Nyāsa on Kāśikā 3.3.95 (IV.68). However, none of the commentators present an example of this stem.

36. This holds for the stems *sthā*, *gā* and *pā*. With respect to the stem *pac* 'to cook'. A 3.3.95 is considered an exception to षिद्भिदादिभ्योऽङ् (A 3.3.104).

37. This sūtra provides for the addition of the affix ***aṅ*** after stems ending with a long vowel *ā*.

38. In addition, this sūtra is also considered an exception to आतोऽनुपसर्गे कः (A 3.2.3), which generally concerns stems ending in the long vowel *ā*.

39. Bhaṭṭoji Dīkṣita raises this question and answers that, in the case of these stems, such a form does not occur in ordinary usage. PrM II.1659 (on SK to A 3.2.8): गायतेरेव ग्रहणं न तु गाङ्गतौ गा स्तुतावित्यनयोरनभिधानात् ॥

Concerning the term *gā*, the case of गातिस्थाघुपाभूभ्यः सिचः परस्मैपदेषु (A 2.4.77) should be mentioned, where Pāṇini uses *gāti* (*gā*+***śtip***) instead of *gā*. This term refers here to *gā* that substitutes for ***iṇ*** (A 2.4.45). A 2.4.77 concerns ***sic***, which comes between verbal stems and endings that replace ***luṅ***, so that *gā* can refer to *gā* which replaces ***iṇ***. Moreover, if instead of *gāti* the term *gā* were used, this would refer to the stems ***gāṅ*** and *gā*, as well *gai*, which obtains the form *gā* in this context.[40] The use of *gā,* with ***śtip***, in A 2.4.77 prevents this term from referring to all the stems that have the form *gā*. This is based on the convention that when a stem is referred to with ***śtip***, it is also mentioned with the vikaraṇa affix according to the class to which the root belongs. The fact that the term *gāti* does not include a vikaraṇa affix shows that it refers to a stem belonging to the class in which the dropping (*luk*) of the vikaraṇa affix occurs, that is, to the stem ***iṇ***, which belongs to the *adādi* class.[41]

4 *Dā*/*Dhā*

The case of the terms *dā* and *dhā* differs from the case of the term *mā*. By दाधा घ्वदाप् (A 1.1.20), Pāṇini assigns the name *ghu* to *dā*

40. This is also in accordance with the paribhāṣā गामादाग्रहणेष्वविशेषः. In his Laghuśabdaratna, Nāgeśa argues that this paribhāṣā does not apply here since it is *anitya*, and, he adds, because it concerns only the term *gā* and not *gāti*. LŚR II.1302 (on SK to A 2.4.77): गामादाग्रहणेष्विति तु न प्रवर्त्तते । अनित्यत्वात्तस्याः । केवलगाग्रहणविषयत्वाच्च ॥

41. This is explained already in the Bhāṣya on A 2.4.77 vt. 1 (Bh I.495.12-16): इणो यो गाशब्दः पिबतेर्यः पाशब्द इति वक्तव्यम् । इह मा भूत् । अगासीन्नटः । अपासीद्धनमिति । तर्त्तर्हि वक्तव्यम् । न वक्तव्यम् । इणो ग्रहणे तावद्वार्त्तम् । निर्देशादेवेदं व्यक्तं लुग्विकरणस्य ग्रहणमिति । पाग्रहणे चापि वार्तम् । वक्तव्यमेव एतत्सर्वत्रैव पाग्रहणेऽलुग्विकरणस्य ग्रहणमिति ॥ The Nyāsa (on Kāśikā 2.4.77 [III.187]) presents the same reasoning: गापोर्ग्रहण इण्पिबत्योर्ग्रहणमिति । इणादेशस्य ग्रहणं तावद्गातीत्यत एव श्तिपा निर्देशाद्विज्ञायते । श्तिपा हि विकरणशून्य एवमर्थो निर्देशः क्रियते लुग्विकरणस्यैव ग्रहणं यथा स्यादिति । अन्यथा हि यदि गायतेर्ग्रहणमिष्टं स्यात्तदा गा इत्येवं ब्रूयात् । एवं तर्हि गामादाग्रहणेष्वविशेष इत्युभयोरपि ग्रहणं भविष्यति । किं श्तिपा निर्देशेन । तस्मादयमेव श्तिपा निर्देशो ज्ञापयतीणादेशस्यैवेदं ग्रहणं न गायतेरिति ॥

and *dhā* excluding *dā**p***. According to Pāṇinīyas, the terms *dā* and *dhā* refer to the verbal stems ***ḍudāñ*** 'to give',[42] *dā**ṇ*** 'to give',[43] *do* 'to split',[44] *de**ṅ*** 'to protect',[45] ***ḍudhāñ*** 'to place, to provide'[46] and *dhe**ṭ*** 'to suck'.[47] Here the question arises: how do *dā* and *dhā* refer to the verbal stems *do*, *de**ṅ***, and *dhe**ṭ***, since these are not mentioned with such forms in the Dhātupaṭha? The stems *do*, *de**ṅ*** and *dhe**ṭ*** obtain the form *dā* (← *do*/*de**ṅ***) or *dhā* (← *dhe**ṭ***) by आदेच उपदेशेऽशिति (A 6.1.45 [§1.1]) when they are not followed by affixes which are marked with the anubandha *ś*; e.g., *dā-tṛ-*, *dhā-tṛ-*.[48] In other cases, where an affix marked with *ś* follows (e.g., ***ś**a**p*** or ***ś**ya**n***), they do not obtain this form. For example: *praṇidayate* (← *prani+daya+te* ← *prani+de**ṅ**+**ś**a**p**+te* ← *prani+de**ṅ*** *+te* (***laṭ***),[49] *praṇidyati* (← *prani+dya+ti* ← *prani+do+**ś**ya**n**+ti* ← *prani+do+ti**p*** (***laṭ***)[50] and *praṇidhayati* ← *prani+dhaya+ti* ← *prani* *+dhe+**ś**a**p**+ti* ← *prani+dhe**ṭ**+ti**p*** (***laṭ***).[51] Moreover, the difficulty concerning *dā* and *dhā* in A 1.1.20 with respect to the verbal stems *do*, *de**ṅ*** and *dhe**ṭ*** occurs also with the term *dā**p*** (in the negation *adā**p***) mentioned in the sūtra. *Dā**p*** should refer to the verbal stems

42. DhP III.9.
43. DhP I.977.
44. DhP IV.40.
45. DhP I.1011.
46. DhP III.10. 47.
47. DhP I.951.
48. The affix *tṛc* is added according to ण्वुल्तृचौ (A 3.1.133).
49. In the derivation process for this form, the following sūtras apply (given in their order of application): वर्त्तमाने लट् (A 3.2.123)/तिप्तस्झिसिप्थस्थमिब्वस्म-स्तातांझथासाथांध्वमिड्वहिमहिङ् (A 3.4.78) / टित आत्मनेपदानां टेरे (A 3.4.79), कर्तरि शप् (A 3.1.68), एचोऽयवायाव: (A 6.1.78), नेर्गदनदपतपदघुमास्यतिहन्तियातिवाति-द्रातिप्सातिवपतिवहतिशाम्यतिचिनोतिदेग्धिषु च (A 8.4.17).
50. In the derivation process for this form, the following sūtras apply (given in their order of application): A 3.2.123/A3.4.78, दिवादिभ्य: श्यन् (A 3.1.69), ओत: श्यनि (A 7.3.71), A 8.4.17.
51. In the derivation process for this form, the following sūtras apply (given in their order of application): A 3.2.123/A3.4.78, A 3.1.68, A 6.1.78, A 8.4.17.

dāp and ***daip***. As in the case of *do*, ***deṅ*** and *dheṭ*, the diphthong of the stems ***daip*** is replaced by a long vowel *ā* according to A 6.1.45. Thus, here again there arises not only the question of how ***dāp*** can refer to ***daip*** but also another key question: how is the knowledge obtained that *dā* and *dhā* in A 1.1.20 refer to the verbal stems ***ḍudāñ***, *dāṇ*, *do*, ***deṅ***, ***ḍudhāñ*** and *dheṭ* and that ***dāp*** refers to ***dāp*** and ***daip***?

There are two indications which show that in addition to ***ḍudāñ***, *dāṇ*, ***ḍudhāñ*** and ***dāp***, the terms *dā*, *dhā* and ***dāp*** in A 1.1.20 refer also to *do*, ***deṅ***, *dheṭ* and ***daip***, which get the form *dā* or *dhā* when not followed by affixes marked with *ś*, by A 6.1.45. In the Dhātupaṭha, the stem ***daip*** is marked with *p*. According to Pāṇinīyas, this anubandha does not have any purpose other than to provide a common reference (i.e., by ***dāp***) for both ***dāp*** and ***daip***.[52] Thus we know that A 1.1.20 concerns also a stem which does not have the form *dā* or *dhā* in the Dhātupaṭha but acquires such a form by the application of a grammatical rule. Another indication which provides the same knowledge involves the expression *daḥ* '(in the place) of the *dā* (named) *ghu*' used in दो दद्घोः (A 7.4.46). This sūtra provides the replacement *dad* for a stem *dā* with the name *ghu* before an affix in *t*- that is marked with *k: datta*- (← *dad*-***kta***) 'given'. Here, *daḥ* is obviously intended to exclude only *dheṭ*. दधातेर्हिः (A 7.4.42) provides *hi* for ***ḍudhāñ*** in the same

52. According to the Nyāsa on Kāśikā 1.1.20 (I.207), this indicates that the paribhāṣā गामादाग्रहणेष्वविशेषः is used: ननु च लक्षणप्रतिपदोक्तयोः प्रतिपदोक्तस्यैव ग्रहणम् । न तु लाक्षणिकस्येत्यनया परिभाषया दो अवखण्डने देङ रक्षणे धेट् पान इत्येतेषां ग्रहणं न स्यात् । नैतदस्ति । तस्या हि परिभाषाया गामादाग्रहणेष्वविशेष इत्यपवादोऽस्ति । तेन सत्यपि लाक्षणिकत्वे दोदेङौ तावद्गृह्येते । धेटोऽपि लिङ्गाद्ग्रहणमनुमीयते । तत्पुनर्लिङ्गं दैपः पकारानुबन्धः । स ह्यदाबिति दाप्प्रतिषेधसामान्यग्रहणार्थः क्रियते । यदि चास्याः परिभाषाया इह व्यापारः स्याद्दैपः पकारानुबन्धकरणमनर्थकं स्यात् । लाक्षणिकत्वादेव ह्यस्य ग्रहणं न भविष्यतीति किं प्रतिषेधेऽस्य ग्रहणेन ॥ Kaiyaṭa too presents this explanation (Pradīpa I.261a): गामादाग्रहणेष्विति । अस्य चार्थस्य दैपः पित्त्वमदाबिति पित्प्रतिषेधे सामान्यग्रहणार्थं लिङ्गम् । अन्यथास्य लाक्षणिकत्वादत्र ग्रहणं न भविष्यतिति किं प्रतिषे-धार्थेन पित्वेन ॥

context as A 7.4.46 provides *dad* for *dhā*, so that *daḥ* in the latter is not intended for excluding ***ḍudhāñ***. Thus, the use of the expression *daḥ* in A 7.4.46 is meant only to prevent its application to the stem *dheṭ*. This instance, as well as the use of the anubandha *p* in *dai**p***, indicates that A 1.1.20 concerns not only stems with original *ā* but also stems which do not have the form *dā* or *dhā* in the Dhātupaṭha and acquire such forms by the application of a grammatical rule.[53]

The two indications mentioned above show that *dā*, *dhā* and *dā**p*** refer both to stems with original *ā* and to those which do not have such forms in the Dhātupaṭha. One may say that these terms refer also to the stems which acquire these forms by A 6.1.45 simply because this rule is traditionally accepted to be applicable unconditionally, that is, before the addition of any affix. This may be the reason why Pāṇini did not mention in A 1.1.20 the stems *do*, *de**ṅ***, *dhe**ṭ*** and *dai**p*** with the form they have in the Dhātupaṭha and refers to them by the general terms *dā* and *dhā*.[54] Yet, a question

53. Pradīpa I.261a: दो दद्घोरित्यत्र वा द इत्येव धेटो निवृत्त्यर्थं सद्धेटो घुसंज्ञां ज्ञापयति । न हि दधातिनिवृत्त्यर्थं द इत्येतत्तस्य दधातेर्हिरिति ह्यादेशविधानाद्दद्भावाप्रसङ्गात् ॥

54. Some Pāṇinīyas provide an elaborate explanation on this issue. In his Mahābhāṣyadīpikā, Bhartṛhari argues that the compound *dādhā* in A 1.1.20 is actually a compound of all the six verbal stems. In that case, the form *dā* is a single reminder (*ekaśeṣa*) of the stems ***ḍudāñ***, *dā**ṇ***, *do* and *de**ṅ*** and the form *dhā* is a single reminder of the stems ***ḍudhāñ*** and *dhe**ṭ***. The basis of this assumption is that at the first stage this compound had the form *dādādodedhādhe*. Afterward, the diphthongs of the stems *do*, *de* and *dheṭ* have been replaced by a long vowel *ā*, as this replacement occurs unconditionally. Dīpikā II.21.3-9 (on Bh I.73.22): अस्यायमभिप्रायः प्रणिददातियच्छतिदयतिधातिधयतीनामनुकरणशब्दैर-नुक्रियमाणक्रियापदर्थाकेनार्थवत्त्वादर्थवदिति प्रतिषेधशब्द (?) प्रातिपदिकसंज्ञैः ... प्रागेव विभक्त्युत्पत्तेरनैमित्तक आत्वे शिति च प्रतिषेधे विहितैकशेषैरुपदेशादिहायं प्रकृतिग्रहणं कर्तव्यतया चोदयति । कथं प्रकृतीनां घुसंज्ञा स्यात् । प्रकृतिषु च लब्धघुसंज्ञासु प्रकृत्यन्वयाद्विकाराणां स्थानिवद्भावशास्त्राद्वा विकराणामपि यथा स्यादिति ॥ Kaiyaṭa presents this solution. Pradīpa (I.259a): किं प्रयोजनमिति । दोदेङ्धेटामेजन्तानाम-नुकरणानि व्यवस्थाप्यात्वे कृते ददातिदधातियच्छत्यनुकरणानां चैकशेषे कृते द्वन्द्वनिर्देशात्सिद्धा दोदेङ्धेटामपि घुसंज्ञा कृतात्वानां चैषां स्थानिवद्भावेन सिद्धेति प्रश्नः ॥ This explanation is also given in the Nyāsa and the Padamañjarī on Kāśikā

arises with respect to the stem ***dīṅ***. This stem obtains the form *dā* by the application of मीनातिमिनोतिदीङां ल्यपि च (A 6.1.50 [§1.2]), which is also traditionally accepted to be applicable unconditionally. In fact, Kātyāyana and later commentators agree that the term *dā* in A 1.1.20 may refer to this stem too. In the sixth vārttika on A 1.1.20, Kātyāyana argues for an additional statement that would prohibit the name *ghu* in the case of forms such as *upādāsta*,[55] which is derived from ***dīṅ***. Here, if *ghu* also referred to this stem, स्थाघ्वोरिच्च (A 1.2.17) would be applicable to provide the replacement of the long vowel *ā* of *dā* in *upādāsta* by a short

1.1.20 (I.107). This solution is also mentioned by Bhaṭṭoji Dīkṣita in his ŚK I.141 (on A 1.1.20): इह दोदेङ्धेटामेजन्तानामनुकरणानि व्यवस्थाप्य तत्र प्रकृतिवदनु-करणमित्यतिदेशादादेच उपदेशेऽशिति (६.१.४५) इत्यात्वं क्रियतेऽनैमित्तिकमात्वं शिति तु प्रतिषेध इति सिद्धान्तात् ॥ It is clear that Kātyāyana did not hold this view. Otherwise he would not argue that A 1.1.20 may be wrongly applicable in the case of the forms *pranidārayati*, *pranidhārayati* and *upādāsta*. *pranidārayati* and *pranidhārayati* are derived from the verbal stems ***dṛṅ*** and ***dhṛṅ*** respectively and the replacement by a long vowel *ā* provided for in A 6.1.45 does not concern them. *upādāsta* is derived from the verbal stem ***dīṅ***. The fact that Kātyāyana recognizes that A 1.1.20 may be applicable in these cases shows that he did not hold this view. Nāgeśa refers to this fact. Uddyota (I.259a): दारयतिधारयत्योश्च नातिप्रसङ्गः । तयोरनुकरण आत्वासंभवेनेह दृधृ इत्यनयोरनुपात्तत्वाद् । दीङोऽपि नेह ग्रहणम् । एज्विषयाभवेन तदनुकरणे आत्वासंभवादिति बोध्यम् । दोदेङ्धेटामेजन्तानामिति । एषां चात्र प्रकृतिवदनुकरणं भवतीति न्यायादशिति प्रसज्यप्रतिषेधाश्रयणाच्चात्वमिति भावः। अत्र च पक्षे लक्षणप्रतिपदोक्तपरिभाषानिरनुबन्धकपरिभाषादीनां न प्रवृत्तिः । सर्वेषां स्वरूपेणैवानुकृतत्वात् ॥ The argument is also given by Bhaṭṭoji Dīkṣita (ŚK I.141 [on A 1.1.20]): अत एव दारयतिधारयत्योर्नातिप्रसङ्गः तयोरनुकरणे आत्वासंभवेनेह दृ धृ इत्यनयोरनुपात्तत्वात् ॥

55. A 1.1.20 vt. 6 (Bh I.75.15) दीङः प्रतिषेधः स्थाघ्वोरित्त्वे॥ *upādāsta* derives from the verbal stem ***dīṅ*** 'to waste', 'to decay': *upādāsta* (←*upa adā+s+ta* ← *upa ade+s+ta* ← *upa adī+s**ic**+ta* ← *upa adī+cli+ta* ← *upa aṭdī+ta* ← *upa **dīṅ** +ta* (←***luṅ***)). In the derivation process for this form, the following sūtras apply (given in their order of application): लुङ् (A 3.2.110)/A 3.4.77/A3.4.78, लुङ्लङ्लृङ्क्ष्वडुदात्तः (A 6.4.71), च्लि लुङि (A 3.1.43), च्लेः सिच् (A 3.1.44), सार्वधातुकार्धधातुकयोः (A 7.3.84), मीनातिमिनोतिदीङां ल्यपि च (A 6.1.50), अकः सवर्णे दीर्घः (A 6.1.101).

vowel *i*. The commentaries mention solutions to this difficulty which involve the use of a paribhāṣā or an additional statement.[56] Yet, these solutions are not needed. In addition to the replacement by an *i* vowel, A 1.2.17 assigns to the affix ***sic*** the property of being marked with the anubandha *k*.[57] Considering ***sic*** as being marked with *k* prevents the application of मीनातिमिनोतिदीङां ल्यपि च (A 6.1.50 [§1.2]) because this is not applicable where an affix marked with *k* occurs. In that case, ***dīṅ*** cannot obtain the form *dā* which is acquired after the application of the *guṇa* or *vṛddhi* replacement provided by सार्वधातुकार्धधातुकयोः (A 7.3.84). In fact, all the sūtras[58] that are related to the name *ghu* or mention the term *dā* involve affixes which are marked with *k* or *ṅ*. When such affixes are concerned, A 6.1.50 does not apply and consequently *dīṅ* does not obtain the form *dā*. Moreover, all these sūtras do not involve affixes which are which are marked with the anubandha *ś*. In such a situation आदेच उपदेशेऽशिति (A 6.1.45 [§1.1]) is applicable so that the stems *do*, ***deṅ*** and *dheṭ* obtain the form *dā* (← *do*/***deṅ***) or *dh!* (← *dheṭ*). Thus, also with respect to *ghu*, if one considers the context where the sūtras that include the term *ghu* are applicable, one can know to which items the term refers.

56. Generally, Pāṇinīyas provide two solutions to this case. First, by the paribhāṣā सन्निपातलक्षणो विधिरनिमित्तं तद्विघातस्य (Bh I.75.21-23 [on A 1.1.20 vt. 6]: स तर्हि प्रतिषेधो वक्तव्यः॥ न वक्तव्यः। घुसंज्ञा कस्मान्न भवति। सन्निपातलक्षणो विधिरनिमित्तं तद्विघातस्येत्येवं न भविष्यति॥). Alternatively, they accept the additional statement suggested by Kātyāyana (Bh I.98.12-13 [on A 1.1.39 vt. 8]: एतदपि नास्ति प्रयोजनम्। उक्तमेतत् दीङ्प्रतिषेधः स्थाघ्वोरित्त्व इति ॥

57. Cf. क्ङिति च (A 1.1.5).

58. They are: स्थाघ्वोरिच्च (A 1.2.17), गातिस्थाघुपाभूभ्यः सिचः परस्मैपदेषु (A 2.4.77), उपसर्गे घोः किः (A 3.3.92), घुमास्थागापाजहातिसां हलि (A 6.4.66), ई हल्यघोः (A 6.4.113), सनि मीमाघुरभलभशकपतपदामच इस् (A 7.4.54), घोर्लोपो लेटि वा (A 7.3.70), दो दद्घोः (A 7.4.46), नेर्गदनदपतपदघुमास्यतिहन्तियातिवातिद्रातिप्सातिवपति-वहतिशाम्यतिचिनोतिदेग्धिषु च (A 8.4.17).

5 नेर्गदनदपतपदघुमास्यतिहन्तियातिवातिद्रातिप्सातिवपतिवहतिशाम्यति-चिनोतिदेग्धिषु च (A 8.4.17)

The case of A 8.4.17 is hard to explain. This sūtra does not require an occurrence of any affix. It concerns cases where the stems are preceded by an upasarga *ni* that follows another upasarga containing a sound that conditions retroflexion, namely *r*. Here, *ghu* refers to ***ḍudāñ***, *dā**ṇ***, *do*, *de**ṅ***, ***ḍudhāñ*** and *dhe**ṭ***. For example, *praṇidātā* (← *praṇidātṛ+**su*** ← *praṇidātṛ* ← *prani+do/de**ṅ**+tṛ**c***) and *praṇidhātā* (← *praṇidhātṛ+**su*** ←) *pranidhātṛ* ← *prani+dhe**ṭ**+tṛ**c***).[59] A 8.4.17 applies also in cases where *do*, *de**ṅ***, and *dhe**ṭ*** do not obtain the form *dā* or *dhā*; e.g., *praṇidayate* (← *prani+daya+te* ← *prani+de**ṅ**+**ś**a**p**+te* ← *prani+de**ṭ**+te* [*la**ṭ***]),[60] *praṇidyati* (← *prani +dya+ti* ← *prani+do+**ś**ya**n**+ti* ← *prani+do+ti**p*** [*la**ṭ***])[61] and *praṇidhayati* (← *prani+dhaya+ti* ← *prani+dhe+**ś**a**p**+ti* ← *prani +dhe**ṭ**+ti**p*** [*la**ṭ***]).[62] In these cases, the stems are followed by an affix marked with *ś* (i.e., ***ś**a**p*** or ***ś**ya**n***). Therefore, they do not acquire the forms *dā* or *dhā*. Yet, it is desired that also in such cases these stems get the name *ghu* in order to apply the replacement by *ṇ* provided for by A 8.4.17. Thus, arguing that the terms *dā* and *dhā* refer to their own forms and not to specific verbal stems would lead to an undesired result, since in the case of *praṇidayate*, *praṇidyati* and *praṇidhayati* we do not have the forms *dā* or *dhā* at any stage of their derivation.

With respect to the term *mā* used in the A 8.4.17, one of three

59. The affix *tṛc* is added according to ण्वुल्तृचौ (A 3.1.133).

60. In the derivation process for this form, the following sūtras apply (given in their order of application): वर्त्तमाने लट् (A 3.2.123)/तिप्तस्झिसिप्थस्थ-मिब्वस्मस्तातांझथासाथांध्वमिड्वहिमहिङ् (A 3.4.78) / टित आत्मनेपदानां टेरे (A 3.4.79), कर्तरि शप् (A 3.1.68), एचोऽयवायावः (A 6.1.78), A 8.4.17.

61. In the derivation process for this form, the following sūtras apply (given in their order of application): A 3.2.123/A3.4.78, दिवादिभ्यः श्यन् (A 3.1.69), ओतः श्यनि (A 7.3.71), A 8.4.17.

62. In the derivation process for this form, the following sūtras apply (given in their order of application): A 3.2.123/A3.4.78, A 3.1.68, A 6.1.78, A 8.4.17.

alternatives should be expected.[63] First, *mā* in this sūtra should refer not only to the stems *mā*, ***māṅ*** (DhP III.6), ***māṅ*** (DhP IV.34), but also to the stems ***ḍumiñ***, ***mīñ*** and ***meṅ***. Secondly, in case this term refers to the form which is actually in use, it should refer only to cases where these stems have the form *mā*. Thirdly, this should refer only to the stems *mā*, and the two stems ***māṅ*** which have such a form originally. However, none of these alternatives applies in this case. The term *mā* in A 8.4.17 refers only to the two stems ***māṅ*** and ***meṅ***.[64]

63. See, for example, the Nyāsa on Kāśikā 8.4.17 (X.425-426).मेति माङ मान मेङ प्रणिदान इत्येतयोर्ग्रहणं न तु मीञ् हिंसायां डुमिञ् प्रक्षेपण इत्येतयोर्मीनातिमिनोतिदीङां ल्यपि चेति कृतात्त्वयोर्नापि मा मान इत्येतस्य । ननु च गामादाग्रहणेष्वविशेष इति सर्वेषामेव ग्रहणेन भवितव्यं तत्कथं माङमेङोरेव ग्रहणं लभ्यते । नैतदस्ति । इह द्वन्द्वे घ्यल्पाच्तरमिति वचनमनपेक्ष्य घ्वित्येतस्य पूर्वनिपातमकुर्वता नात्र वचनानुरोधेन प्रवर्त्ति-तव्यमपि त्विच्छयेति सूचितम् । तेन यत्रेच्छा भवति स एव गृह्यते ॥

64. The Bhāṣya on A 1.1.20 vt. 1 refers to the case of this term with respect to A 8.4.17. The first solution that the Bhāṣya (Bh I.74.15-16 [on A 1.1.20 vt. 1]) offers is to add the term *prakṛti* 'original' to A 8.4.17.: अवश्यं तत्र मार्थं प्रकृतिग्रहणं कर्तव्यं प्रणिमयते प्रण्यमयत इत्येवमर्थम् । तत्पुरस्तादपक्रक्ष्यते घुप्रकृतौ माप्रकृतौ चेति ॥ Patañjali argues that this term should be placed between the terms *ghu* and *mā* mentioned in A 8.4.17. This would provide the knowledge that these terms refer to items which have the forms *dā dhā* and *mā* originally and also to items which obtain such forms during the process of derivation. However, in that case, the term *mā* should refer also to the stems ***ḍumiñ*** (in cases such as *praniminoti*), ***mīñ*** (in cases such as *pranimīnāti*) and *mā* (in cases such as *pranimātā*), so that such a solution does not solve this difficulty. Therefore, Patañjali says that the term *mā* in A 8.4.17 should be stated with the anubandha *ṅ*. In that case, this term would not refer to the stem *mā*. Bh I.74.16-20 (on A 1.1.20 vt. 1): यदि प्रकृतिग्रहणं क्रियते प्रनिमिनोति प्रनिमीनात्यत्रापि प्राप्नोति । अथाक्रियमाणेऽपि प्रकृतिग्रहण इह कस्मान्न भवति प्रनिमाता प्रनिमातुं प्रनिमातव्यमिति । आकारान्तस्य ङितो ग्रहणं विज्ञास्यते । यथैव तर्ह्यक्रियमाणे प्रकृतिग्रहण आकारान्तस्य ङितो ग्रहणं विज्ञायत एवं क्रियमाणेऽपि प्रकृतिग्रहण आकारान्तस्य ङितः ग्रहणं विज्ञायते।। In the *vṛtti* 8.4.17, the Kāśikā refers to this issue and says that the term *mā* refers to ***māṅ*** and ***meṅ***. Kāśikā 8.4.17(X.426): माङ प्रणिमिमीते परिणिमिमीते । मेङ प्रणिमयते परिणिमयते । मा इति माङमेङोर्ग्रहणमिष्यते ॥ According to the Nyāsa and the Padamañjarī, the Kāśikā argues that this involves simply acceptance (*iṣṭi* 'desire, acceptance') of what is required. PM on Kāśikā 8.4.17 (X.425-426): गामादाग्रहणेष्वविशेष इति

6 Conclusion

As we have seen, Pāṇini uses the term *dā, mā* and *gā* with a consideration of the context where each sūtra is applicable. Thus these terms are not used arbitrarily. There are reasons for their particular use in the Aṣṭādhyāyī. These reasons also provide the knowledge of which items *dā*, *mā* or *gā* refer to. This position is contrary to the commentators' view that with respect to the use terms *dā, mā* and *gā* there are no specifications and in order to know to which items the terms refer one should look ahead and consider the desired targets.

The question remains why this puzzlement occurred in the first place. This is due to the fact that after the time of Kātyāyana, a view which originally did not belong to Pāṇini's system was introduced to his system. According to this view, the terms in the Aṣṭādhyāyī primarily refer to original items.[65] This is why the commentators struggled to explain why and how, for example, *dā* and *dhā* refer also to the stems *do*, *deṅ*, ***ḍudhāñ*** and *dheṭ*. In the Mahābhāṣya, there may be a clue that shows that this view does not belong to Pāṇini's system. This clue also points to its source. In the Bhāṣya on दाधा घ्वदाप् (A 1.1.20 [§4]), the section leading to the conclusion that with respect to the terms *dā*, *mā* and *gā* there are not any specifications concerning which item they refer to starts with the expression *bhāradvājīyāḥ paṭhanti* ('members of the school of the Bhāradvājas teach'). According to this school, *dā* and *dhā* cannot refer to forms which are acquired by the application of grammatical rules, as its followers presuppose that

वचनान्मीनातिमिनोतिदीङामिति कृते यन्मारूपं यच्च मा मान इति तेषामपि ग्रहणप्रसङ्ग इत्याशङ्क्याह माङ्मेङोर्ग्रहणमिष्यत इति । इष्टिरेवेयम् ॥

65. I discuss this issue at length in my dissertation (Ben-Dor. 2009; 101-232). I give some evidence which shows that Kātyāyana did not hold this view and that Pāṇini's procedures do not follow this view.

the terms refer primarily to original forms.[66] Moreover, in the Bhāṣya under A 1.1.56, the same school is quoted as arguing that a partially changed form is not same as the original items.[67] Thus, the school of the *bhāradvājīyas* values a 'pure' untouched original item, yet it does not conform to Pāṇini's method, which accepts that terms refer also to items which are acquired by the application of a rule in addition to original items.

66. Bh I.73.26-74.1-2 (on A 1.1.20 vt. 1): भारद्वाजीयाः पठन्ति घुसंज्ञायां प्रकृतिग्रहणं शिद्विकृतार्थम् । घुसंज्ञायां प्रकृतिग्रहणं क्रियते । किं प्रयोजनम् । शिदर्थं विकृतार्थं च । शित्युदाहृतम् । विकृतार्थं खल्वपि प्रणिदाता प्रणिधाता ॥

67. Bh I.136.15-18 (on A 1.1.56 vt. 11): भारद्वाजीयाः पठन्ति । एकदेशविकृतेषूपसंख्यानम् । किं च कारणं न स्यात् ॥ अनादेशत्वात् ॥ आदेशः स्थानिवदित्युच्यते न चेम आदेशाः । रूपान्यत्वाच्च ॥ अन्यत्खल्वपि रूपं पचतीत्यन्यत्पचत्विति ।

References and abbreviations

A *Aṣṭādhyāyī.*

Abhyankar, K. V.

1962-72 *The Vyākaraṇa=Mahābhāṣya of Patañjali, Edited by F. Kielhorn. Third Edition, Revised and Furnished with Additional Readings, References and Select Critical Notes.* Three volumes. Poona: Bhandarkar Oriental Research Institute.

Ben-Dor, Sharon

2009 *The paribhāṣās arthavadgrahaṇe nānarthakasya, lakṣaṇapratipadoktayoḥ pratipadoktasyaiva grahaṇam and ekadeśavikṛtam ananyavat, Studies on some Metarules in Pāṇinian system.* Publications of the Institute for Asian and African Studies 9. Helsinki: Helsinki University Print. (https:// www.doria.fi/bitstream/handle/10024/45136/ theparib.pdf?sequence=1)

Bh *Mahābhāṣya.* See Abhyankar, K. V.

Bhagavat, V. B. and Saroja Bhate

1986 *Mahābhāṣyadīpikā of Bhartṛhari, Fascicule III: Āhnika VI, Part I.* Poona: Bhandarkar Oriental Research Institute.

Bhaṭṭoji Dīkṣita

1997 *Mahāmahopādhyāyaśrīmadbhaṭṭojidīkṣitaviracitā Vaiyākaraṇa-Siddhānta-Kaumudī, Śrīmajjñānendrabhikṣuviracitayā Tattvabodhinīṭīkayā, Śrīvāsudevabhaṭṭadīkṣitaviracitayā bālopakāriṇyā Bālamanoramākhyayā vyākhyayā,* (*tatpuruṣādārabhya*) *mahāmahopādhyāyaśrīnāgeśabhaṭṭaviracitayā Laghuśabdenduśekharaṭīkayā ca samanvitā, Mahāmahopādhyāyaśrīmadbhaṭṭojidīkṣitaviracitā Vaiyākaraṇa-Siddhānta-Kaumudī, Śrīmajjñānendra-bhikṣuviracitayā prauḍhopakāriṇyā Tattvabodhiny-ākhyaṭīkayā, Śrīvāsudevadīkṣitaviracitayā chātropakāriṇyā

Bālamanoramākhyaṭīkayā, mahāmahopādhyāya Śrīnāgeśa (Nāgojī) bhaṭṭaviracitena vidvatpriyeṇa Laghuśabdendu-śekharākhyena tilakena, svaravaidikabhāge Śrījayakṛṣṇamauniviracitayā Subodhinyākhyayā ṭīkayā, liṅgānuśāsanabhāge Śrībhairavamiśrakṛtayā Candrakalākhyaṭīkayā, ante ca gaṇapāṭhasūcīpatrādina pariśiṣṭena ca virājitā. Two volumes Delhi: Bhāratīya Book Corporation. [No editor is named.]

Caturveda Giridharaśarmā and Parameśvarānandaśarma Bhāskara

1987-91 *Vaiyakāraṇa Siddhāntakaumudī of Bhaṭṭojidīkṣita with Bālamanoramā of Vāsudevadīkṣita* and *Tattvabodhinī of Jṇānedrasarsvatī.* Four volumes. Varanasi: Motilal Banarsidass.

DhP *Dhātupāṭha.* (Reference by gaṇa and serial number as in Sumitra M. Katre, *Aṣṭādhyāyī of Pāṇini.* Delhi: Motilal Banrsidass, 1989)

Dīpikā *Mahābhāṣyadīpikā.* See Bhagavat, V. B. and Saroja Bhate; Limaye, V. P., G. B. Palsule and V. B. Bhagavat; Palsule, G. B, and V. B. Bhagavat.

Dvivedī , Vindhyeśwarī Prasād and Gaṇapati Śāstrī Mokāte

1991 *Śabda Kaustubha of Bhaṭṭoji Dīkshita.* Three volumes. Chowkhamba Sanskrit Series 2. Varanasi: Chowkhamba Sanskrit Series Office.

Gokhale, Gaṇeśa Śāstrī

1978 *Bhaṭṭanāgeśaviracitaḥ paribhāṣenduśekharaḥ (vaidyanāthakṛtagadāṭīkopetaḥ).* Ānandāśrama Sanskrit Series 72. Poona: Ānandāśrama.

Kāśikā *Kāśikāvṛtti.* See Tripathi, Jaya Shankar Lal and Sudhakar Malaviya.

Limaye, V. P., G. B. Palsule and V. B. Bhagavat

1985 *Mahābhāṣyadīpikā of Bhartṛhari, Fascicule III: Āhnika V.* Poona: Bhandarkar Oriental Research Institute.

LŚR *Laghuśabdaratna.* See Shastri, Sitaram.

LŚŚ *Laghuśabdenduśekhara.* See Bhaṭṭoji Dīkṣita;

Shastri, Bal.

MDhV *Mādhavīyā Dhātuvṛtti*. See Shastri, Swami Dwarikadas.

Nene, Gopal Śāstrī

1994 *The Prauḍhamanoramā of Bhaṭṭoji Dikśita with its gloss called Laghuśabdaratna by M. M. Śrī Hari Dikśita with three commentaries, the Bhairavi, Bhāvaprakāśa & Saralā by M. M. Pandit Śrī Bhairava Miśra, Vaidyanātha Payagunde and Gopāl Śastri Nene.* Kashi Sanskrit Series 125. Varanasi: Chaukhambha Sanskrit Sansthan.

Palsule, G. B, and V. B. Bhagavat

1991 *Mahābhāṣyadīpikā of Bhartṛhari, Fascicule VIII: Āhnika VII*. Poona: Bhandarkar Oriental Research Institute.

PbhŚekh *Paribhāṣenduśekhara*. See Gokhale, Gaṇeśa Śāstrī.

PM *Padamañjarī*. See Tripathi, Jaya Shankar Lal and Sudhakar Malaviya.

Pradīpa See Raghunath Kashinath Shastri and Sivadatta D. Kudala.

PrM *Prauḍhamanoramā*. See Nene, Gopal Śāstrī.

Raghunath Kashinath Shastri and Sivadatta D. Kudala.

1994 *Mahamuni Patanjali's Vyākarana Mahābhāsya with Kaiyata's Pradipa, and Nagesha's Uddyota edited with foot notes, collected from the Chhaya, Padamanjari and Shabdakaustubha as well as supplied by the editor's own originality*. Volume 1, Navāhnika. Varanasi: Sudhi Prakashan, 1987.

Shastri, Bal

saṁ. 2048 *Laghu Shabdendu Shekhar of Nagesh Bhatt with six rare commentaries (Candrikā, Cidasthimālā, Vivṛtisaṃgraha, Jyotsnā, Viṣamapadavivṛtī, Varavarṇinī) & explanatory notes by Guru Prasad Shastri*. Two volumes. Varanasi: Vāṇī Vilās Prakāśan. [through the avyayībhāvaprakaraṇa]

Shastri, Swami Dwarikadas

2000 *The Mādhavīya Dhātuvṛtti [A Treatise on Ṣanskrit Roots based on the Dhātupāṭha of Pāṇini]*. Varanasi: Tara Book Agency, 2000.

Shastri, Sitaram

1992 *Prauḍhamanoramā of Mahāmahopādhyāya Śrī Bhaṭṭojī Dīkṣita together with Bṛhachchhabdaratna, and Unpublished Commentary of Mahāmahopādhyāya Śrī Hari Dīkṣita and Laghuśabdaratna of Mahāmahopādhyāya Śrī Nāgeśa Bhaṭṭa.* Second volume. Prāchya Vidyā Series 5. Varanasi: Banaras Hindu University.

ŚK *Śabdakaustubha.* See Dvivedī, Vindhyeśwarī Prasād and Gaṇapati Śāstrī Mokāte.

SK *Siddhāntakaumudī.* See Caturveda Giridharaśarmā and Parameśvarānandaśarma Bhāskara.

Tripathi, Jaya Shankar Lal and Sudhakar Malaviya

1988 *Kāśikā of Vāmana and Jayāditya with Nyāsa or Kāśikā-Vivaraṇapañjikā of Jinendrabuddhi and Padamañjarī of Haradatta Miśra with the Bhāvabodhinī by Jaya Shankar Lal Tripathi.* Ten volumes. Varanasi: Tara Book Agency.

Uddyota See Raghunath Kashinath Shastri and Sivadatta D. Kudala.

vt. vārttika of Kātyāyana. See Abhyankar, K. V.

“Where the sense is intended although the corresponding speech unit is not employed”: the ekaśeṣa case

Tiziana Pontillo

1 Ekaśeṣa as an exception to the one-to-one symmetry between artha and śabda.

Deshpande (1985: 37-9) reserves a special place for ekaśeṣa, which he classifies as a case of “prescribed word-deletion in Pāṇini”, putting it on an equal footing with the uttarapadalopa taught by A 5.3.82. He concludes (p. 38) that the “obligatory ‘one constituent retention’” is “different from natural ellipsis” for the following reasons: a) because it is “prescribed by rules of the system, and is not simply taken for granted”; b) “by being obligatory, it shows that only the abbreviated expression is grammatical”; c) “there is a clear sense of directionality in the process of retention of a constituent.”[1]

As is well known, the ekaśeṣa rule (A 1.2.64: *sarūpānām ekaśeṣa ekavibhaktau*) teaches that just one of a possible series of items having the same form occurs, as a single remainder, provided that a single ending is used. As a consequence the denotation of many objects (which for instance belong to the same class, such as many trees) corresponds to the unique plural word form *vṛkṣāḥ*. In other words the remainder *vṛkṣa-*, i.e. the unique word form which

1 With regard to ekaśeṣa, there is a partly ambiguous distinction introduced by Kiparsky (1982: 37 n. 38) on the subject of the “free deletion process” for which “Pāṇini’s grammar contains no rules that substitute anything for the personal pronouns” mentioned as *sthānin* in A 1.4.105: “This is distinct from the conjunction rule that drops repeated items in parallel expressions, which Pāṇini states explicitly (1.2.64 [...]).” I wonder whether, by focusing on the explicit feature of rule A 1.2.64, Kiparsky means that it deals with a lopa rule, or an ādeśa rule or an (explicit) something else. I agree with all three conclusions about ekaśeṣa expounded by Deshpande (1985: 38), provided that ekaśeṣa is not classified as a case of lopa but of ādeśa, as I shall propose below.

remains, conveys the sense of all objects denoted by the other word forms which do not remain.

Thus, some objects are denoted even though the matching word-forms are not overtly used, which seems to contradict some well known presupposed grammatical points that are enunciated — possibly in their earliest statement — partly in the very first vārttika in Kielhorn's Edition of the *Mahābhāṣya* (M I.6:16: *siddhe śabdārthasambandhe lokato 'rthaprayukte śabdaprayoge śāstreṇa dharmaniyamaḥ*)[2] and partly in the first two vārttika*s* on the ekaśeṣa-rules (M I.233:16 [vt. 1], 20 [vt. 2] ad A 1.2.64)[3]: *pratyartham śabdaniveśān naikenānekasyābhidhānam*; *tatrānekārthābhidhāne 'nekaśabdatvam*), as follows:

- there is a well established relation between words (*śabda*) and the knowledge of their objects (*artha*),[4] which relies on everyday linguistic usage;

2. Both Abhyankar-Shukla 1975 and Joshi-Roodbergen 1986 divide this vārttika into three parts, as they are repeated and commented on separately by Patañjali. With regard to the place occupied by this first vārttika and his supposed author, see Cardona 1999: 223-5.

3. A 1.2.64: *sarūpānām ekaśeṣa ekavibhaktau* "A single remainder of [many] items having the same form occurs, provided that a single ending is used."

4. Of course this analysis of *śabdārthasambandhe* as a tatpuruṣa-compound is taken apart from Patañjali's interpretation; cf., e.g., Scharf 1996: 22. In fact Patañjali's analysis as a samāhāra dvandva implies a more compelling interpretation as "words, meanings and [their] relations". As many scholars have noticed, the interpretation of this compound as a samāhāra dvandva seems to contradict the current use of vārttikas. Cf. Joshi-Roodbergen 1986: 90 n. 331; Biardeau 1964: 36; Houben 1995: 37, n. 59. Furthermore, Patañjali glosses *siddha* as *nitya* ('permanent'). Surprisingly enough, this passage is the only one, out of almost 150 occurrences of the term *nitya* in the *Mahābhāṣya*, where *nitya* is attributed to the object meant by a word, instead of to linguistic forms (*nitya* vs. *kārya*); cf. Candotti - Pontillo 2010: 42. Additionally, word forms (*śabda*) are considered as causes giving rise to the cognition of objects (*artha*) (in the mind of the participants in the communicative event); that is, the addresser actually needs to employ words, for instance to utter them, in order to arouse the relevant mental image in the buddhi of the addressee. Without this perceptible input no meaning could ever be brought about (M I.18:19-20 [ad Śivasūtra 1 vt. 12]: *śrotropalabdhir buddhinirgrāhyaḥ prayogeṇābhijvalita ākāśadeśaḥ śabdaḥ*).

- the use of words is prompted by the thing-meant; i.e. it depends in the end on the intention of making something known, of conveying some meaning (through a verbal expression);[5]

- words as a rule apply per object; i.e. one and only one word-form matches with one and only one object.[6]

By contrast the statement hinted at in my title is exactly what is questioned in the very long discussion that Patañjali devotes to this ekaśeṣa rule (A 1.2.64). Since the analysis of the context of this statement seems to be crucial, I shall now take a step backwards, in order to reconstruct at least a part of this complex discussion. This reconstruction will not, however, deal with the very important part proposing the view that a generic term denotes a class property, because this goes beyond the scope of the present study.[7]

The starting point is vt. 27 on A 1.2.64 which introduces the topic of the number of ekaśeṣa formations. The objection envisioned is that the dual and plural desinences cannot be realized because the object of an ekaśeṣa is just one.[8] However, vt. 28

5. Cf. Deshpande 1989: 113.

6. Just as a corollary, early grammarians seem to apply this one-to-one relationship not only to words but to all meaningful (*arthavat*) linguistic units, that is, according to A 1.2.45, verb roots (*dhātu*), nominal bases (*prātipadika*), and affixes (*pratyaya*). In fact Patañjali plainly expounds the grammatical process on which this presupposed one-to-one symmetry between the semantic and the phono-morphological level of language is based, by involving the two well known complementary systematic actions, namely anvaya (lit. 'association') and vyatireka (lit. 'distinction'), aimed respectively at catching the continuity and discontinuity between different compared units (M I.219:19-25 [ad A 1.2.45 vt. 9]). Thus morphemic linguistic units also might have been basically supposed by Patañjali to convey their meaning only if actually uttered within the word.

7. This is the object of Scharf 1996, in particular pp. 47-50.

8. M I.240:16 (vt. 27 ad A 1.2.64): *dvivacanabahuvacanāprasiddhiś caikārthatvāt* "And the dual and plural desinences cannot be realized because the object [of an ekaśeṣa formation] is just one." M I.240:17-18 (ad vt. 27 on A 1.2.64): [...] *eko' yam avaśiṣyate / tenānena tadarthena bhavitavyam / kimarthena / yadarthaḥ ekaḥ* [...] "'Just one' means that [just] this [word form] is left as a remnant. This [word form] which denotes this object should be realized. - What object? - That which is denoted by this single [word form] (i.e. the remainder)."

denies that a single remainder (*ekaśeṣa*) denotes a single object,[9] since if it did denote a single object, the rule itself would have no purpose.[10] As a consequence, in order to account for this double object matching a single word form, the discussion shifts to a dichotomy between two devised explanations for this anekarthatā, raised by vt. 29, which assumes that a single word might correspond to more than one object simply by nature (M I.240: 23): *aśiṣya ekaśeṣa ekenoktatvāt* "The single remainder should not be taught because [the other objects] are already denoted by one and only one word form." Nevertheless, in this case no input could determine the usage of a second or a third word form denoting some object which is, on the contrary, already denoted, in accordance with the general principle which prohibits the use of more words to express the same meaning which has been expressed by one word (*uktārthānām aprayogaḥ*).[11] As a consequence, there would be no word form to which this rule could apply; that is, no word form would be generated apart from "that which does remain."

The two opposing explanations of anekarthatā which Patañjali enunciates as an introduction to vt. 29 (M I.240:21-22 [ad vt. 28 on A 1.2.64]) are the following: *iha hi śabdasya svābhāvikī vānekārthatā syāt vācanikī vā* "Indeed in this case this feature of

9. Cf. Patañjali's introduction (M I.241:19 [ad vt. 27 on A 1.2.64]): *naikārthyam / nāyam ekārthaḥ / kiṁ tarhi / dvyartho bahvarthaś ca* "This feature of denoting a single object does not occur. This [single word form] (i.e. the remainder) does not denote one object What is it then? It denotes two or many objects."

10. M I.241:19-20 (vt. 28 ad A 1.2.64): *naikārthyam iti ced ārambhānarthakyam* "If we say that this feature of denoting a single object does not occur there, the effort [made in enunciating this rule teaching that one word-form remains] would have no purpose."

11. M I.240:24-25 (ad vt. 29 on A 1.2.64): *ekenoktatvāt tasyārthasya dvitīyasya prayogeṇa na bhavitavyam uktārthānām aprayoga iti* "Since [the other objects] are already denoted by one and only one word form, the usage of a second word form denoting this (same) object would not occur, according to this (principle): 'Usage of [word forms denoting] objects which have already been denoted does not occur'."

denoting more than one object might be either svābhāvika or vācanika".

This terminological pair *svābhāvika* vs. *vācanika*, both in Kātyāyana and in Patañjali's work, does not result as being secondary. On the basis of a complete survey of the occurrences, published in Candotti-Pontillo 2010, this pair does indeed result as somehow matching with the more known pair *nitya* 'permanent' / *kārya* 'created by means of rules'. Nonetheless, while *nitya* and *kārya* refer to words (*śabda*), *svābhāvika* / *vācanika* refer to their denotation (*abhidhāna*). Accordingly, the denotation of an inflected word can be defined as svābhāvika, if it is autonomous, that is, independent of its morphs, even though these morphs can be regularly abstracted by means of the process of anvaya and vyatireka. Otherwise, if denotation is conditioned by the morphology, that is, if denotation clings to the morphological structure of the corresponding word form — often, but not always, according to some express grammatical rules — it is defined as vācanika. This opposition employed for explaining a special case of denotation seems to anticipate the perspective of the more recent one between *arthādhyāhāra*, 'suppletion of meaning' / *śabdādhyāhāra* 'suppletion of words'.[12]

With regard to ekaśeṣa, this vācanika hypothesis consists in a morphological condition which does not need to be established by an additional explicit mention of this special denotation of ekaśeṣa, because the sole provision for a single remainder, alone, is sufficient to assure the right denotation.

M I.240:25-241:1 (ad vt. 29 on A 1.2.64): *atha vācanikī tad vaktavyam eko 'yam avaśiṣyate sa ca dvyartho bhavati bahvarthaś ceti / na vaktavyam / siddham ekaśeṣa iti eva /*

12. With regard to some other different pieces of evidence for the assumed anticipation by Patañjali, cf. Deshpande 1985:54 and 1989: 114-5, 119-20, even though the Nyāya-, Mīmāṁsā- and Kāvyālaṁkāra-traditions which involve them, are of course generally interested in these methods in the context of hermeneutics rather than with respect to the grammatical derivation.

katham punar eko 'yam avaśiṣyate ity anena dvyarthatā bahvarthatā vā śakyā labdhum / tac caikaśeṣakṛtam / na hy antareṇa tadvācinaḥ śabdasya prayogaṁ tasyārthasya gatir bhavati / paśyāmaś ca punar antareṇāpi tadvācinaḥ śabdasya prayogaṁ tasyārthasya gatir bhavatīti agnicit somasud iti yathā "Otherwise [if this feature of being endowed with more than one object is not autonomous], it is founded on word forms', but it has to be expressly mentioned [in this way]: 'only this one remains and it denotes two objects or many objects. - It does not have to be stated. It is realized, just stating that one remains. - But how could the denotation of two objects or of many objects be obtained by means of this statement: 'This one word form remains.'? - This is also brought about by means of the statement according to which 'just one word form remains'. In fact there is no comprehension of an object without employing the word-form denoting this. And yet we see that there is comprehension of an object even without employing the word-form denoting this, as we use [words such as] *agnicit* 'one who has arranged the fire altar' or *somasut* 'one who has pressed soma (for the relevant sacrifice)'".

2 Ekaśeṣa compared with lopa

Thus paradoxically, this passage seems, on the one hand, to emphasize the correspondence between śabda and artha, by recalling their well-established relation, and the need of a physical input to cause verbal cognition, and on the other, to present ekaśeṣa as one among the rare exceptions to this rule itself, comparable with the lopa cases, which are presented as standard exceptions. The examples pointed out here are precisely *agnicit* 'one who has arranged the fire altar' and *somasut* 'one who has pressed soma (for the relevant sacrifice)', i.e., two examples of lopa of the affix *KvIP*, which could be defined as two extreme cases of zero-replacement.[13] In fact, as is well-known, all the affixes referred to by terms containing the syllable *vi* are always devoid of a perceptible form of their own, in accordance with A 6.1.67 which teaches a zero-replacement of *vi*[14]. Nevertheless this specific zero-substitute mentioned by Patañjali is perceptible at least with regard to its 'effect' on the pre-affixal base (*aṅga*), because it deals with a case of zero denoted by *lopa* and not with one that concerns a zero referred to by a term containing *lu* (*lumat)*.[15] In fact, thanks to the convention governing replacements (recalled by *sthānivad ādeśaḥ analvidhau* [A 1.1.56]),[16] the zero-affix will have the properties of its substituend. Thus, since the substituend is marked with *p* (*KvIP*), its substitute receives the final augment *tuK* (*-t*), as if it were a unit marked with *p* (*pit*), according to A 6.1.71.[17]

In my opinion, it is exactly this specific choice that allows Patañjali to emphasize, some lines below, that a difference between

13. *agni- + ci- + Ø* (*KvIP*) + *-t* > *agnicit* 'one who has arranged the fire altar' is derived according to rule A 3.2.91: *agnau ceḥ (upapada = sup = karman* 86*; bhūte* 84*, kvip* 87) "When *agni* occurs as an upapada which is a direct object, the affix *KvIP* occurs after the verbal base *ci-*." *soma- + su- + Ø (KvIP) + -t > somasut* 'one who has pressed soma (for the relevant sacrifice)' is derived according to rule A 3.2.90: *some suñaḥ* "When *soma* occurs as an *upapada* which is a direct object, the affix *KvIP* occurs after the verbal base *su-*." It deals with two *kṛt* nominal bases which convey the sense of agent, both being taught in the section included between A 3.1.93: *kṛd atiṅ* and A 3.4.67: *kartari kṛt.*

14. *vI* is a one-sound affix. Cf. A 6.1.67: *ver apṛktasya,* A 1.2.41 *apṛkta ekāl pratyayaḥ.*

15. A 1.1.63 (*na lumatāṅgasya*) blocks the effect of affixes replaced by zero on their bases: "An affix which is subject to lopa when it is termed with a name which contains *lu* (i.e., *LuK, Ślu* and *luP*) does not condition operations in the place of (a part of) the pre-affixal base."

16. This inclusion of lopa in the domain of substitution would not have been so obvious at Kātyāyana and Patañjali's time, but it is a fact that some lopa*s* are mentioned by Patañjali among the exceptions to A 1.1.56 itself. See Candotti-Pontillo: 122ff. For some other Mahābhāṣya pieces of evidence, see Candotti-Pontillo 2012: 119ff., Pontillo 2008 and Freschi-Pontillo 2012: 136f. Contemporary research on the Aṣṭādhyāyī also speaks of 'zero replacements' for describing the various lopa phenomena. See, e.g., Cardona 1997: 46 (§ 79).

17. A 6.1.71: *hrasvasya piti kṛti tuk* "The final augment *tuK* is added to a short vowel before a *kṛt* affix marked with *p*."

ekaśeṣa and lopa does exist, at least with regard to operational rules, when the sūtra's rejector underlines how, on the contrary, both ekaśeṣa and lopa in the end depend on everyday language usage as far as the denotation of terms is concerned, so that teaching them could be useless. In fact, the augment *t* applied to the mentioned couple of nouns subject to lopa might appear to be ultimately considered as a perceptible input to cause the verbal cognition of a *kartṛ* instead of a *dhātu.*

> M I.241:8-11 (ad vt. 29 on A 1.2.64): *yadi tarhi loko 'vaśyaṁ śabdeṣu pramāṇaṁ kimartham ekaśeṣa ārabhyate / atha kimartham lopa ārabhyate / pratyayalakṣaṇam ācāryaḥ prārthayamāno lopam ārabhate / ekaśeṣārambhe punar asya na kiṁcit prayojanam asti* "Then, if the common usage is certainly the standard, as regards words, with what aim is the rule according to which 'just one word form remains' undertaken? - Then, with what aim is zero-replacement undertaken? The teacher undertakes zero-replacement, aiming at applying the rules determined by the affix (which is replaced by zero), but there is no scope for him to undertake the remainder-rule."

By contrast, the special denotation of both *somasut* and of *vṛkṣāḥ*, which contradicts the general *pratyartham* statement, is respectively defined as an effect which is produced by lopa (*lopakṛtam*) and by ekaśeṣa (*ekaśeṣakṛtam*). In other words, from the denotational point of view, they are perfectly comparable, since as the provision for zero-replacement assures the meaning-extension of the unit which is replaced by zero to zero itself, the provision for a remainder also assures the possibility of denoting the objects whose matching word-forms do not remain.

In the example mentioned above, the meaning of the whole analytic string (*vigrahavākya*) *vṛkṣaś ca vṛkṣaś ca vṛkṣaś ca* is denoted by the single plural form *vṛkṣāḥ* 'trees', but even more evidently in some other classical examples,[18] such as the plural form *akṣāḥ* of the polysemic noun *akṣa-* — which denotes an axle, a die and a rosary seed — corresponding to the prakriyā formula *akṣaś cākṣaś cākṣaś ca*, instead of many axles or many rosary seeds and so on: *akṣaś cākṣaś cākṣaś ca* > *akṣāḥ*.

Analogously, the dual *brāhmaṇau* may denote not only two male *brāhmaṇa*s but also a male *brāhmaṇa* and a female *brāhmaṇa*, according to the rule *pumān striyā* (A 1.2.67). That is, a masculine term optionally occurs as a single remainder of two items with the same base meaning that only differ in that one denotes a male and the other a female: *brāhmaṇaś ca brāhmaṇī ca* > *brāhmaṇau*.

Moreover, even the meanings of two lexically distinct items, which, however, denote a male and female of the same type, can be optionally denoted just by the prior constituent of a compound inflected as a dual noun (or optionally by a dvandva compound); e.g., *pitarau* 'mother and father, parents': *pitā ca mātā ca* > *pitarau* "mother and father" / *mātāpitarau* (A 1.2.70 *pitā mātrā* [*anyatarasyām* 69]).

In fact, there is no contradiction at all between the *śabda-artha* correspondence and the ekaśeṣa procedure. Only if it is maintained that there is full correspondence between śabda and artha does the ekaśeṣa provision consistently entail that the meaning denoted by the whole series of terms (i.e. by the relevant prakriyā formula), has to be automatically extended to the remainder, so that more than one object is denoted by a single word form. Nonetheless, this would be the way a substitution works, since it ensures the meaning extension of the substituend (*sthānin*) to the replacement (*ādeśa*), but this is contradicted by Patañjali and later commentators, as we shall see below.

As in the case of *lopa, ekaśeṣa* denotation works in the absence of a part of its perceptible input, because — as we have just seen

18. Cf. KV 1.2.64 with M I.233: 2-4 (ad A 1.2.64).

— some parts of the meaning (*artha*) are comprehended (*arthasya gatiḥ*), even without employing the word-form denoting them (*antareṇa api tadvācinaḥ śabdasya prayogam*). This similarity of the ekaśeṣa device with the lopa device probably induced Deshpande (1985) to also classify the former one as a case of lopa, but I really wonder what principle underlies this sort of meaning extension.

In any case, the need for an additional rule to ensure the anekarthatā explained according to the vācanika explanation was rejected by Patañjali himself. Therefore it must depend on some existing rule. Moreover, a mere grammatical device taken apart from actual linguistic usage could not ensure a good shared and understandable denotation, just as a rule stating that a cow has to be called a horse and vice-versa would be in manifest contradiction with the ordinary usage. For this reason one mainly has to turn one's attention to common usage.

> M I.241:5-8 (ad vt. 29 on A 1.2.64): *ucyeta tarhi na tu gamyeta / yo hi gām aśva iti brūyād aśvaṁ vā gaur iti na jātucit sampratyayaḥ syāt // tenānekārthābhidhāne yatnaṁ kurvatāvaśyaṁ lokaḥ pṛṣṭhato 'nugantavyaḥ / keṣv artheṣu laukikāḥ kāñ śabdān prayuñjate iti / loke caikasmin vṛkṣa iti prayuñjate dvayor vṛkṣāv iti bahuṣu vṛkṣā iti* "It could be stated (that the word form which remains, denotes two or many objects), but it would be not understood. If one calls a cow a horse or a horse a cow, there would possibly be no comprehension (of the intended sense). For this reason, whosoever makes the effort to denote more than one object has to follow common usage, by turning his attention to this (and by wondering): 'Which words do common people use to denote which objects?' In the common usage, *vṛkṣaḥ* is employed in the case of a single object, *vṛkṣau*, in the case of two objects, *vṛkṣāḥ* in the case of many objects."

Thus, the grammatical effort of describing this specific relationship between word form and its object merely aims at providing the correct nominal ending, which is consequent to this passing over the general one-to-one principle, while denotation is independent from grammatical rules. As a consequence, Kātyāyana will conclude in vt. 33 (*abhidhānaṁ punaḥ svābhāvikam*) that "denotation is on the other hand autonomous",[19] after suggesting in vt. 32 the interesting comparison with dvandva compounds such as *plakṣanyagrodhau.*

3 Ekaśeṣa compared with dvanda compounds

This comparison, which is intentionally and explicitly propounded by Kātyāyana — whose vt. 32 and vt. 33 furthermore match almost word by word respectively with vt. 14 and vt. 15 on A 2.2.29 — is really enlightening.

> M I.241:26-27 (vt. 32 ad A 1.2.64 [= M I.433:17-18 (vt. 14 ad A 2.2.29)]): *ekenoktatvād aparasya prayogo 'nupanna iti ced anuktatvāt plakṣeṇa nyagrodhasya nyagrodhaprayogaḥ* "If it is said that because [the object] has already been denoted by one word form, usage of the other [word form] cannot arise, (the reply is that) there is usage of the word form *nyagrodha* because the object of *nyagrodha* has not already been denoted by the word form *plakṣa.*"
>
> M I.242:4 (vt. 33 ad A 1.2.64): *abhidhānaṁ punaḥ svābhāvikam* "denotatation is on the other hand autonomous" (cf. M I.433:25 [vt. 15 ad A 2.2.29]: *abhidhānaṁ ca punaḥ svābhāvikam*).

Actually, these two vārttikas on A 2.2.29 (*cārthe dvandvaḥ*) conclude a long discussion about a problem tackled in vt. 1. In fact, since rule A 2.2.29 teaches the formation of compounds called

19. M I.242:4 (vt. 33 ad A 1.2.64). This assertion of course suggests the rejection of the *sūtra*, as conclusively advanced by Kātyāyana but not by Patañjali. Vts. 34-35 reinforce Kātyāyana's position on the matter. In particular, vt. 35 states that if a word denotes a class property (*ākṛtyabhidhanāt*), even the possibility of using more than one speech form completely vanishes. For a clear and detailed synthesis of the long and complex discussion by Kātyāyana and Patañjali on A 1.2.64, see Scharf 1996: 40-58.

dvandva under the meaning-condition of *ca*, even when the compound is not formed, a possible undesired involvement of this name *dvandva* occurs, because the meaning of *ca* is understood (although the word *ca* is not used).[20] A possible solution is advanced early in vt. 2,[21] which proposes a different phrasing of the sūtra itself: *yugapad-adhikaraṇa-vacane* instead of *cārthe.* A dvandva would be accordingly formed, only provided that each single constituent refers to both the denoted items simultaneously.[22] Hence these kinds of compounds are considered from a very peculiar point of view. In fact, in a compound like *plakṣa-nyagrodha-* (nom.-acc. du. *plakṣanyagrodhau*) the prior constituent *plakṣa-* is also supposed to denote the object denoted by the other, i.e. the *nyagrodha*, and vice versa.[23]. However, a fresh shortcoming arises: in this case the word form denoting *nyagrodha*

20. M I.431:1 (vt. 1 *ad* A 2.2.29): *cārthe dvandvavacane 'samāse'pi cārthasaṁpratyayād aniṣṭaprasaṅgaḥ.*

21. M I.431:6 (vt. 2 *ad* A 2.2.29): *siddhaṁ tu yugapadadhikaraṇavacane dvandvavacanāt* "But this is solved if a dvandva rule is taught under this (following condition): when the objects meant are simultaneously referred to (by each single constituent)."

22. This view is generally opposed to the view of denotation of meanings in sequence (*paurvāparya*).

23. In order to keep the general statement about the per-object (*pratyartham*) denotation as valid, vts. 30 and 31 state that even one word denoting many objects is still precisely per object: vt. 30: *pratyartham śabdaniveśād ekenānekasyābhidhānād apratyartham iti cet tad api pratyartham eva* "If it is said that it is so (i.e., that one word cannot denote many objects) from the fact that words apply per object, (the reply is that) the application of words is actually stated per object"; vt. 31: *yāvatām abhidhānam tāvatāṁ prayogo nyāyya iti ced ekenāpy anekasyābhidhānam* "If it is said that it is a common practice that as many word forms are used as there are objects to be denoted, (the reply is that) it is also a common practice that more than one object is denoted just by one word form". This argumentation of course relies on the *avyayībhāva* nature of the compound *pratyartham* itself, which can be supposed as derived from *prati* followed by a second *pada* which is inflected in the singular, dual or plural number, so that *pratyartham* could convey the sense of application of a word form to one object or to two objects or to many objects. As a consequence, the statement in question might include some specific but ordinary linguistic usage such as ekaśeṣa denotation itself or other apparent exceptions like this.

itself could not be used anymore, according to the recurring grammarians' statement that a word form can be used only if its meaning has not yet been conveyed (*uktārthānām aprayogaḥ*). Vt. 15 ad A 2.2.29, which has just been quoted as corresponding to vt. 33 on A 1.2.64, is the final and conclusive view about the proposal of the so-called *yugapad-adhikaraṇa-vacanatā* view of a dvandva, which will finally be declared by Patañjali to be painful and hard to justify.[24] In fact, the simultaneous reference to the sense of *plakṣa* and *nyagrodha*, both by the word form *plakṣa* and by the word form *nyagrodha*, could only be accepted provided that the former member of the compound does not stand for the latter one without it and vice versa, even though each single word form aims at denoting the meaning of the whole pair. Otherwise, the analytical string including both word forms could not be justified. In fact we would know the meaning of *plakṣa* but we could not know why *nyagrodha* is used, since the former pada already denotes the latter object too. In fact, differently from the classic examples of ekaśeṣa, since it deals with two words whose form and meaning are completely different, it is impossible to guess which is the latter member, merely on the basis of the former, unless ordinary linguistic usage currently registers this combination.

Thus, Patañjali mentions two intriguing options in the use of śabdas: they can potentially stand for an object (*artha*) which is prāthamakalpika, that is, for an object which is primarily conceived as it is, or merely for some activity or quality of this object, which is shared by another object. As a consequence, we can use the word form *plakṣa* in order to denote a tree of the genus ficus infectoria or even to compare, e.g., a ficus indica (*nyagrodha*) with a ficus infectoria (*plakṣa*) because of some shared features of these two trees.[25] Therefore, by always using the dual *plakṣau* we

24 M I.434:3 (ad vt. 15 on A 2.2.29): *iyaṁ yugapadadhikaraṇavacanatā duḥkhā ca durupapādā ca.*

25. M I.433:25-26 (ad vt. 15 on A 2.2.29): *atha veha kaucit prāthamakalpikau plakṣanyagrodhau kaucit kriyayā vā guṇena vā plakṣa ivāyaṁ plakṣe nyagrodha*

would be able to denote two plakṣas, as a current dual-inflected noun, and one *plakṣa* and one *nyagrodha*, as if it were an *ekaśeṣa*. Nevertheless, if we want to avoid the doubt derived from these two options, we have to prefer the dvandva *plakṣa-nyagrodhau*, that is, to also perceptibly use the word *nyagrodha* and this preference is merely determined by the indisputable fact that daily usage does not support the latter possibility.[26] It is a noteworthy coincidence that the only two occurrences of this already highlighted term *svābhāvika* by Katyāyana are included here precisely in the commentary on the ekaśeṣa rule (vt. 33 ad A 1.2.64), and in the context of dvandva compounds (vt. 15 ad A 2.2.29), which is compared with it here. Actually, these two formation-rules overlap to a great extent: their vigraha and the conveyed meaning are largely coincident with each other. The respective final word forms are different, governed by different morphological procedures merely in accordance with everyday usage. As a consequence, in both cases, at least from Kātyāyana's and Patañjali's point of view, there is surely no bi-univocal correspondence between artha and śabda; that is, their respective abhidhāna mostly coincides, even though their morphological features diverge from each other.

With regard to Pāṇini's view, in conclusion, I shall try to assume that ekaśeṣa and dvandva rules (or better, compound rules in general) are simply two operatively distinct substitution rules.

ivāyaṁ nyagrodha iti "In fact there are some words which stand for an object which is primarily conceived as it is, such as *plakṣanyagrodhau*, some other words which stand for some activity or quality of this object, which is like that which pertains to another object. If ficus infectoria (*plakṣa*) is mentioned, it could be in the sense of 'like a ficus infectoria'. If ficus indica (*nyagrodha*) is mentioned, it could be in the sense of 'like a ficus indica'."

26. M I.433:26-434.2 (ad vt. 15 on A 2.2.29): *tatra plakṣāv ity ukte saṁdehaḥ syāt kim imau plakṣāv evāhosvit plakṣanyagrodhāv iti / tatrāsaṁdehārthaṁ nyagrodhaśabdaḥ prayujyate* "Therefore if *plakṣau* is said, there could be the doubt, whether it deals with two plakṣas or with a plakṣa and a nyagrodha. In order to avoid this doubt, the word *nyagrodha* is also used.

4 Rule A 2.1.1 is a governing rule for the derivational procedure (*prakriyā*) of some derivates, referred to as *vṛtti*. If we continue to follow the pattern of discussion raised by commentaries on the nature of the denotation of compounds and other vṛttis,[27] we find another important Mahābhāṣya context involving this category of the svabhāva feature of abhidhāna: the commentary on A 2.1.1: *samarthaḥ padavidhiḥ*, commonly interpreted as "A provision concerning inflected words [is said] of words having semantic and syntactic connection (*samartha*)"[28] and traditionally considered a heading (*adhikāra sūtra*) or metarule (*paribhāṣā*) which teaches the so-called *samartha* principle for all compounds or even for all the types of vṛtti.[29]

Of course the discussion of this long commentary goes beyond the scope of the present communication. It is interesting, however, that with a different formulation, which nonetheless involves the term *svabhāva*, the principle of the one-to-one application of word forms is again questioned by Kātyāyana in precisely this context. In particular, Kātyāyana does indeed propose an interpretation of the category of samartha, looking for a synonym of *samartha* that is more suitable for compounds. Thus, vt. 1 tells us that *samartha* refers to the merging in a single integrated meaning (*ekārthībhāva*) of words having separate objects (*pṛthagarthānām*):[30] *pṛthagarthā-*

27. These are compounds (*samāsa*), derivates with kṛt and taddhita affixes, derivative verbal bases, single remainder (*ekaśeṣa*) and a nominal and a following vocative being treated as a single accentual unit (*paraṅgavadbhāva*). As is well-known, not all commentators include the last two in the category.

28. Cf. the interpretation by Cardona (1997: 66 [§ 109]): "an operation pertaining to padas applies to padas that are syntactically and semantically related"; by Katre (1987: 105): "An operation on padas (takes effect) only when they are semantically and syntactically connected"; by Sharma (1995: vol. 3:1): "An operation concerning fully inflected words is to be syntactically related".

29. Patañjali considers the rule itself as an adhikāra, i.e. working only for compounds, yet he is also open to a wider application of the sāmarthya principle for all the vṛttis, treating it as a paribhāṣā.

30. As is well known, this term constitutes a pair together with *vyapekṣā* 'the mutual expectation / connection' mainly focused as the distinctive samartha feature for sentences (*vākya* / *vibhaktividhāna*).

nām ekārthībhāvaḥ samarthavacanam (M I.361:26 [vt. 1 ad A 2.1.1]) "The expression *samartha* is the merging in a single integrated meaning of words having separate objects."[31]

According to Patañjali's examples, this proposed ekārthibhāva could describe the phenomenon according to which, in a sentence such as *rājñaḥ puruṣaḥ*, the separated objects of the words stay as such, while the compound *rājapuruṣaḥ* denotes one single object, namely a royal servant.[32] Thus the distinction between the analytical and the synthetical form is so sharp that it entails the autonomous (*svabhāva*) formation of both.

> M I.364:1 (vt. 2 ad A 2.1.1): *vāvacanānarthakyaṁ ca svabhāvasiddhatvāt* "And the expression of optionality could be vain because of the established autonomous feature [of *padas*]."

This could therefore lead, as suggested by vt. 2, to the rejection of the optionality, which, on the contrary, Pāṇini teaches elsewhere; for example a string of *padas* is taught as optional with respect to a compound by A 2.1.11 (*vibhāṣā*), to a desiderative verb by A 3.1.7 (*dhātoḥ karmaṇaḥ samānakartṛkād icchāyāṁ vā*), to a taddhita by A 4.1.82 (*samarthānāṁ prathamād vā*). In fact, no option can subsist between a vākya and a vṛtti if their denotation is not equivalent.

Furthermore here too, once again in the context of the problem addressed with respect to the dissymmetry between the semantic and the phono-morphological level of language, the topic of the number of the padas obtained by composition is introduced by vt. 3, because it could not correspond to the number of objects

31. Patañjali also mentions (M I.364:23-4 [ad vt. 2 ad A 2.1.1]) another interpretation of the samartha condition: bheda versus saṁsarga, that is, respectively as an expression of the meaning by means of distinct words or while they are related to each other: *apara āha / bhedasaṁsargau vā sāmarthyam iti*.

32. M I.361:28 (ad vt. 1 on A 2.1.1): *vākye pṛthag arthāni / rājñaḥ puruṣa iti / samāse punar ekārthāni / rājapuruṣa iti* "In a sentence, objects are separated: e.g. the man/servant of the king; on the other hand, in a compound, objects constitute a single object: e.g. the royal servant."

involved in the corresponding analytical string (*vigrahavākya*).[33] At this point, it seems to be clear that the abhidhāna which raises problems and induces Kātyāyana and Patañjali to depict it as an autonomous feature of words — i.e., independent from their morphological constituent analysis (*svābhāvika*) — really pertains to the dissymmetry between the combination of inflected padas which constitute the vigrahavākya and the newly formed pada. Nevertheless, both of these might have failed to appreciate what their problem really was with the vṛtti, so that they meet some difficulties in interpreting A 2.1.1, and vt. 18 even proposes a new wording as *samarthānām padavidhiḥ*,[34] on which the current translation, questioned above, is based.

By contrast, if *samarthaḥ padavidhiḥ* simply teaches that "A provision which depends on (/involves/mentions) inflected words denotes the same object [of the output of rule]",[35] the target becomes the equivalence of the denotation which is taught by the formation-rule and the output of the formation itself, i.e. between

33 M I.365:7 (vt. 3 ad A 2.1.1): *saṁghātasyaikārthyān nāvayavasaṁkhyātaḥ subutpattiḥ* "if there is just one single word object for the collection, there is no question of production of the case endings following the number of the constituent parts." As far as the specific terminology is concerned and its possible Sarvastivādin source see Candotti-Pontillo 2010: 43; n. 8-10, 49, n. 33. With regard to the term *svabhāva* in the history of Buddhism, see Cox 2004 and Tillemans 2007; for *saṁghāta,* see Bronkhorst 1987.

34. M I.369:10 (vt. 18 ad A 2.1.1): *siddhaṁ tu samarthānām iti vacanāt.*

35. *samartha* is overtly explained as *tulyārtha* in the Kāśikāvṛtti on A 1.3.42: *propābhyāṁ samarthābhyām.* With regard to the etymology, since the word form which is expected is actually *samārtha* and not *samartha* in the sense of 'whose meaning is equivalent', Joshi-Roodbergen 1994: 70-71 also recall two possibilities, the first of which is suggested by the Padamañjarī, which recalls vt. 4 (*śakandhvādiṣu ca*) ad A 6.1.94 (*eṅi pararūpam* "A single substitute i.e. the latter of two contiguous phonemes [replaces both the former phoneme-class *a* as a final phoneme of a pre-verb and the latter one, i.e.] a vowel *e* or *o*") in order to extend the list *śakandhvādi* to the nominal base *samartha.* The relevant note for the second supposed explanation by Joshi-Roodbergen (1994: 71) is: "Alternatively, the form can be derived as *sam* + *artha* in which *sam* means *sama.*" I wonder if they hint at A 6.3.84-7 which teach the substitution of *samāna* 'equal, common, similar' with *sa-* in various contexts or at some other rule which they omit to quote.

the *vigraha* enunciated or suggested by *vṛtti*-rules and the newly formed (and then inflected) *pada*. Thus, moving from the everyday linguistic setting to the metalinguistic one, the targeted equivalence of A 2.1.1 might include all the cases where this dissymmetry between the denotative and the phono-morphological level of language is apparent,[36] provided that the relevant rules teach that specific denotation.[37] In other words this equivalence is independent from the need of supplying some words more than the segmented constituents and it is furthermore indifferent to the nature attributed to the relationship among the constituents of the uncompounded string, if this relationship is classified as either ekārthibhāva or vyāpekṣā. Thus the questioned abhidhāna would not be svabhāva but consistently predicted by means of the vigrahavākya.

This interpretation of A 2.1.1 is not unprecedented, since Joshi-Roodbergen (1996: 1) translated the rule, "An operation involving finished words conveys the same meaning", signalling that this fresh translation "deviates substantially from the two translations offered" in their work published eighteen years before (Joshi-Roodbergen 1968: 1). In fact, these two translations, matching the two different traditional classifications of this rule as an adhikāra and a paribhāṣā, agree with the current translation expounded above. As Joshi-Roodbergen (1996: 1) remark, the fresh translation is based on the five other Pāṇini occurrences of the term *samartha*, four of which — that is, in A 1.3.42; 2.3.57; 3.3.152 and 8.1.65 — self-evidently mean "which conveys the same meaning", and the last of which (A 4.1.82) deals once again with a vṛtti, exactly as in the case of A 2.1.1. They conclude (1996: 1-2):

36. It might even imply the metaphorical level of meaning - see e.g. the meaning of *plakṣaḥ* as 'like a *plakṣa*' supposed by Patañjali (see above).
37. Cf. Bronkhorst 1987b: 297: "His (= Pāṇini's) grammar ... does not primarily attempt to describe the surface forms of the Sanskrit language, it rather shows how these surface forms manifest the real elements underlying them, the grammatical elements which directly express the meanings to be expressed." Cf. Bronkhorst 1981.

"Here both the non-integrated wordgroup and the newly derived, integrated word are regarded as meaning-equivalents. By the non-integrated wordgroup what is meant in this connection is the formally corresponding wordgroup as represented by the technical constituent analysis, the *alaukikavigrahavākya*, not the meaning-paraphrase, the *laukikavigrahavākya*".

An additional piece of evidence for a part of this interpretation could be supplied by the analysis of the five other occurrences of the noun *vidhi* used in the Aṣṭādhyāyī as a second member of a compound: *alvidhi-* (A 1.1.56: *sthānivad ādeśo 'nalvidhau*); *pūrvavidhi-* (A 1.1.57: *acaḥ parasmin pūrvavidhau*[38]), *padānta-dvirvacana-vareyalopa-svara-savarṇānusvāra-dīrgha-jaś-car-vidhi-* (A 1.1.58: *na padānta-dvirvacana-vareyalopa-svara-savarṇānusvāra-dīrgha-jaś-car-vidhiṣu*), *pratyayavidhi-* (A 1.4.13: *yasmāt pratyayavidhis tadādi pratyaye 'ṅgam*), *sup-svara-saṁjñā-tug-vidhi-* (A 8.2.2: *nalopaḥ sup-svara-saṁjñā-tug-vidhiṣu kṛti*). The focus of these expressions is regularly some unit mentioned in the rules themselves, no matter if this unit constitutes the object or the condition of the rule itself. By means of the compounds x-*vidhi*, Pāṇini seems to merely point to a starting "level", which represents the real consistency of the rule taken as a sentence. Thus, this lexically internal evidence reinforces the supposition that *padavidhi* in A 2.1.1 refers to a provision that depends on *pada*s, almost by mentioning them; a detail which is only indirectly highlighted by Joshi and Roodbergen (1996), who — as we have seen above — propose to replace, as a second term of the *abhidhāna* equivalence in question, the *laukikavigrahavākya* with

38. Pāṇini seems to point to defining the crucial term *aṅga* which governs the section A 6.4.1-7.4.97. Note that a number of Kātyāyaṇa's doṣas relative to the discussion of A 1.1.56 can be solved merely by literally taking into account the term *aṅga*, mentioned in the wording of the rules in question. Note also the quasi-coincidence with the section (A 6.1-8.1) which Buiskool (1939: 19) considered the object of the supposed *sarvatra siddham* principle.

the *alaukikavigrahavākya*, i.e. with the string of *pada*s taught as *vigraha.*[39]

Further, in my opinion, there is more to this than simply changing the reference string on which the *vṛtti*s are based — if we consider A 2.1.1 to be a paribhāṣā rule. First of all, the equivalence taught by A 2.1.1 has to be restricted to the types of vṛtti which are actually taught by means of a rule which mentions a string of pada*s*.

For instance, as is well known, sūtras devoted to the formation of compounds as a rule indicate two padas, in accordance with the pattern taught by the heading A 2.1.4 (*saha supā* [*sup* 2]): an upasarjana expressed by a nominative and a non-upasarjana by an instrumental form. For example, in A 2.1.34: *annena vyañjanam* "A pada denoting a flavor (*vyañjanam* [= upasarjana]) combines with a pada denoting food (*annena* [= non-upasarjana])", this pair of inflected nominal forms is represented by two common nouns, *vyañjana* and *anna*. With regard to the specific classical example *dadhyodanaḥ*, the constituent padas *dadhi* and *odanaḥ* would have to be considered in a way hyponyms of *vyañjanam* and *annam*. Nonetheless, yogurt (*dadhi*) is not lexically a vyañjana by nature. By contrast, the meaning handed down by Patañjali himself (on the basis of vt. 4) — *dadhnopasikta odanaḥ* 'rice sprinkled with yogurt' — actually corresponds to the general combination expressed as *annena vyañjanam*, since, for instance, yogurt is

39. Furthermore, this seems to contradict Kiparsky's (1982; 2002) distinction of different linguistic levels in the system of Pāṇini's grammar. By contrast, it is consistent with Cardona's (2009: 14) explanation of Pāṇini's derivational grammar not as a 'compartmentalized system' but rather as 'a continuum starting from meanings that a speaker is to convey through to utterances'. Indeed these rules are organized following the units they mention, not in terms of levels to which or from which they map. Often — and there is an increasing awareness in Kiparsky's position itself — not all the parts of a rule pertain to the same level. See e.g. A 7.2.35 *ārdhadhātukasyeḍ valādeḥ* that uses a unit which belongs at the same time to level 3 ("abstract morphological representation"), ārdhadhātuka affix], and 4 ("phonological output form"), an affix beginning with a semivowel except *y*.

understood as a flavoring for any kind of food, if the noun *dadhi* is used to express an instrument (*dadhnā*) connected to the passive participle *upasiktaḥ* 'sprinkled with'. In this sense the vidhi A 2.1.34, which depends on the two padas mentioned (*annena vyañjanam*), shares the same meaning of the compounds which it goes on to form, such as *dadhyodanaḥ* which denotes a kind of food, namely *odanaḥ*, whose condiment is precisely the *dadhi.* Additionally, albeit from a different point of view, it is a fact that *dadhyodanaḥ* is an option with respect to the string *dadhnopasikta odanaḥ*, but this optionality, whose maintenance Kātyāyana (vt. 2 ad A 2.1.1) is so worried about, is indeed taught elsewhere by means of Pāṇini's specific technical terms (*vā, vibhāṣā, anyatarasyām*).[40] Of course, both these options are based on everyday language and as a consequence, a speaker might feel the compound as a shorter or even elliptical substitute for the matching analytical sentence, which is not always literally enunciated in the formation rule. Nonetheless, this optionality does not depend on rule A 2.1.1.

An easier case is that of a tatpuruṣa, such as *vṛkabhayam* 'fear of wolves' or *rājapuruṣaḥ* 'king's man, royal servant', whose relevant formation rules are A 2.1.37: *pañcamī bhayena* and A 2.2.8: *ṣaṣṭhī* respectively. In accordance with the general formula taught by A 2.1.4: [*sup*] *saha supā*, padas with fifth and sixth vibhaktis are regularly mentioned in the rule as upasarjana padas in the nominative case and the second pada, in the instrumental case, is the generic *supā* and *bhayena* respectively. Thus the crucial feature of being a padavidhi, as a rule depending on padas, is

40. With regard to the option between a string (*vākya*) and a compound (*samāsa*) taught by the anuvṛtti of *vā* included in A 2.1.18 and the denial of the traditional yogavibhāga of *vibhāṣā* included in A 2.1.11, see Kiparsky 1979: 39 and Radicchi 1985, 1988: II.56-58. On the contrary Cardona 1997: 219 (§ 316) maintains that *vibhāṣā* "could remain a heading to be understood in subsequent sūtras, just as *ātmanepadam* of A 1.3.12 is understood to recur in a long series of sūtras that follow", therefore independently from the yogavibhāga. With regard to a short comparison with other modern descriptive models of compounds, based on this option, see also Pontillo 2005: 228-35.

ensured for all these compounding rules by the formula supplied by the adhikāra 2.1.4, that is, *padam saha padena.*

Analogously with respect to taddhitas, the set of padas such as A 4.1.92: *tasyāpatyam* suggests exactly the equivalent of a taddhita as far as the meaning is concerned. For instance, *upagor apatyam* is the meaning of *aupagavaḥ.* Both the syntagma and the derivate can denote one of Upagu's descendants. Once again the fact that it deals with two concurring expressions from the syntactical point of view, is of course not determined by A 2.1.1, but the equivalence between these two expressions is granted by the string of padas mentioned in the relevant taddhita rule. Furthermore, it is tempting to consider *aupagavaḥ* as a sort of replacement (*ādeśa*) with respect to the samartha string of pada*s* *upagor apatyam*, especially after focusing on the non-prescribed substitutions, which compulsorily have to be taken for a given datum, being explicitly mentioned as conditions for some other rules. Furthermore, the initial genitive *samarthānām* in the general taddhita rule A 4.1.82: *samarthānām pathamād vā* seems to suggest this substitution frame, as if it taught "In the place of the padas which convey the same meaning (on which the relevant taddhita rule depends, by mentioning them) (according to A 2.1.1) (in order to form a taddhita-final base) [a taddhita affix] is optionally introduced after their first pada".

As regards single remainders (*ekaśeṣa*) and the strict relationship between the vigraha taught by each ekaśeṣa rule as an input and their corresponding output, the hypothesis here advanced consists in interpreting them as a case of substitution. For instance, according to A 1.2.70 which depends on the padas *pitā mātrā*, the denotation of this group of padas is equivalent to *pitarau.* Once again the initial genitive *sārūpānām* of A 1.2.64: *sarūpānām ekaśeṣa ekavibhaktau* seems to suggest — in just the same way as *samarthānām* of A 4.1.82 — a substitution frame for the ekaśeṣa procedure too, something that is explicitly denied by tradition.

M I.233:7-12 ad A 1.2.64: *atha śeṣagrahaṇaṁ kimartham / sarūpāṇām eka ekavibhaktāv itīyaty ucyamāna ādeśo 'yaṁ vijñāyeta*[41] */ tatra ko doṣaḥ / aśvaścāśvāśvau / āntaryato dvyudāttavataḥ sthānino dvyudāttavān ādeśaḥ prasajyeta / lopyalopitā ca na prakalpate / tatra ko doṣaḥ / gargāḥ vatsāḥ / bidāḥ urvāḥ / añ yo bahuṣu yañ yo bahuṣv ity ucyamāno lug na prāpnoti / mā bhūd evam / añantam yad bahuṣu yañantaṁ yad bahuṣv ity evaṁ bhaviṣyati / naivaṁ śakyam / iha hi doṣaḥ syāt / kāśyapapratikṛtayaḥ kāśyapā iti* "- Then, for what purpose is the mention of *śeṣa* made? If it is said that 'Just one of a possible series of items having the same form occurs, as a single remainder, provided that a single ending is used', the rule would be recognized as a substitution. In this case, what is the fault? *Aśvaḥ* 'horse' and *aśvaḥ* 'horse' are *aśvau* two horses". Since the substituend has two high pitched sounds, a substitute with two high pitched sounds might automatically be involved, because of its close relationship.[42] And that which has to be zeroed would not succeed in being zeroed. In this case, what is the fault? [In order to form e.g. these padas] *gargāḥ* and *vatsāḥ* or *bidāḥ* and *urvāḥ*.[43] The LUK-zero-replacement which is stated

41. The genitive form *sarūpāṇām* is interpreted as a sthānin in accordance with A 1.1.49: *ṣaṣṭhī sthāneyogā.*
42. Cf. A 1.1.50: *sthāne 'ntaratamaḥ.*
43. According to A 4.1.104 *anṛṣyānantarye bidādibhyo 'ñ,* both after *bida* and after *urva* the affix *aÑ* applies to denote a gotra descendant, or an immediate descendant provided that it does not deal with a ṛṣi, so that *baidaḥ* and *aurvaḥ* are respectively the name of a gotra descendant of Bida and of Urva; analogously, according to A 4.1.105: *gargādibhyo yañ*, after both *garga* and *vatsa* the affix *yaÑ* applies to denote a gotra descendant, so that *gārgyaḥ* and *vatsyaḥ* are respectively the name of a gotra descendant of Garga and of *Vatsa*. A 2.4.64: *yañaños ca* also teaches a LUK-zero replacement of the affixes *yaÑ* and *aÑ* concerning a gotra name (*gotre* 63) used to denote a plurality (*bahuṣu* 62) which only has to do with such an affix meaning (*tenaiva* 62) except in the feminine (*astriyām* 62), so that the plural names quoted by Patañjali, namely *gargāḥ, vatsāḥ, bidāḥ* and *urvāḥ* are plural names designating the group of all

> when *aÑ* is in the plural sense and when *yaÑ* is in the plural sense could not be obtained.[44] - Let it not be so! On the contrary it will be thus: 'That which ends in *yaÑ* in the plural sense and that which ends in *aÑ* in the plural sense'.[45] - It cannot be so. In this case there would really be

gotra descendants of Garga, Vatsaḥ, Bidaḥ and Urvaḥ, respectively, almost as if *gargaḥ* etc. were used aiming at denoting the official representative descendant of Garga and all descendants who are represented by him. The argument of the sūtra-proposer is explained in a more complex way in P on A 1.2.64 (I.2.98): *lopasambandhȯ na prāpnotītyarthaḥ / gargā iti / prakṛtir arthābhedād ekaiva / yañpratyayās tu bahavaḥ / yañākṛteś ca ekatvād vyavadhānābhāvād anekasyāpi pratyayasya paratvaṁ na virudhyate / tatra garga ya ya ya iti sthite yadā gargaśabdaṁ muktvā pratyayānām evaiko yaśabda ādeśaḥ kriyate tadā tasya bahvarthatvāl luk sidhyati / yadā tu virūpāṇām api samānārthānām ekaśeṣavad eka ādeśaḥ saprakṛtikaḥ kriyate tatra garga ya ity asyānyayoś ca 'yaśabdayor gargayaśabda ādeśaḥ* "The meaning is that the relationship with the zero-replacement could not be obtained. With regard to *gargāḥ*, the base is just one because of the non-difference of meaning, but the affixes *yañ* are many. And since there is only one generic form *yaÑ* and absence of anything which intervenes (between the nominal base and this form), the fact that more than one affix follows is not excluded. In this case in the place of *garga* followed by three *ya,* after leaving the word-form *garga*, when just one word-form *ya* applies as a substitute of the affixes, then LUK is realized because of the plural meaning of this affix. On the contrary, when only *garga ya,* as a single substitute along with the base, takes place as a substitute of many word forms, with the same meaning but different form, such as an ekaśeṣa, the word form *garga ya* is a substitute in the place of *garga ya* and of the other two *ya.*" With regard to the interpretation of *tenaiva* in A 2.4.62 ff., see Cardona 1997: 308 (§ 465), who does not make use of the process taught in A 1.1.72. Somehow, the sūtra's proponent and rejecter also rely on the ambiguity of *tenaiva* connected to the condition of the plural denotation *bahuṣu*, which is meant as a modifier to the affix or to the nominal base, for their following discussion about the risk of interpreting A 1.2.64 as an *ādeśa* rule.

44. If *gārgyāḥ* designates a plurality, namely the gotra descendants of Garga by means of an ekaśeṣa procedure according to A 1.2.64 and this ekaśeṣa formation is considered as a substitute, so that the plurality is conveyed by the whole form *gārgya-* before the plural ending. The affix *yaÑ* of the form *gārgyāḥ*, does not convey the sense of plurality, which here is assumed to be required as a condition for the LUK-replacement taught by A 2.4.64. This is the reason mentioned by the sūtra's proponent, in order to exclude that ekaśeṣa is a substitution-rule.

45. Thus, the sūtra's rejecter denies that the plurality condition taught by A 2.4.64 has to be referred only to the affix *yaÑ* instead of to the whole form

a fault: *kāśyapāḥ* would denote many images of Kāśyapa."[46]

The last counter-objection propounded by the sūtra-proponent which should manage to persuade the sūtra-rejector not to consider the *ekaśeṣa* as a substitution rule is in fact rejected by Patañjali himself. Actually, the affix *aÑ* of *kāśyapāḥ* meaning 'images of the gotra descendant of Kaśyapa' denotes no plurality. In fact, Kāśyapa is only one and his images are many. Furthermore, M

gārgya, by relying on A 1.1.72: *yena vidhis tadantasya* "The unit by means of which a provision is made denotes a unit which ends in that unit." Cf. P on A 1.2.64 (I.2.98-99): *tatra yaśabdāntasya bahuṣu vṛttiḥ na tu pratyayamātrasyeti bhāvaḥ / yañantaṁ yad bahuṣv iti / ādeśapakṣe 'pi vacanasāmarthyāt sārūpyād yañbuddyutpādād yañantam etad ity āśrīyate* "In this case the vṛtti of that which ends in the word form *ya* is in the sense of plurality, but this is not a condition of the mere affix. With regard to 'that which ends in *yaÑ* is in the sense of plurality': once again from the substitution point of view, by dint of its mention, because of the same form, and since the cognition of *yaÑ* is produced, it resorts to that which ends in *yaÑ* (as an ādeśa)."

46. According to A 5.3.96: *ive pratikṛtau* (*kan* 95), the affix *kaN* would occur after a nominal base when an image similar to what the nominal base denotes, is to be denoted, but A 5.3.99: *jīvikārthe cāpaṇye* (*lup* 98) teaches a LUP zero replacement of this affix when it is intended for earning a living, though not through its sale. Therefore *kāśyapaḥ* can denote an image similar to Kāśyapa, whose name is formed according to A 4.1.104 (see n. 43), i.e., by means of the affix *aÑ* taught to denote a gotra descendant. If A 1.1.72 is taken into account and the ekaśeṣa procedure is applied, the plural form *kāśyapāḥ* might be subject to a LUK zero replacement in accordance with A 2.4.64, since an affix *aÑ* occurs and that which ends in this affix denotes a plurality. Cf. P on A 1.2.64 (I.2.99): *kāśyapā iti / kāśyapa ivāyaṁ tatpratikṛtir itīve pratikṛtāv iti vihitasya kano jīvikārthe cā'paṇye iti lup / tataḥ kāśyapaś ca kāśyapaś ca kāśyapaś ceti pratikṛtipracayavivakṣāyām ekaḥ kāśyapaśabdaḥ prayujyate / sa bahvarthe 'ñantaśceti lukprasaṅgaḥ / laukikasya gotrasya tatra grahaṇam iti parihāra uttaratra vakṣyate itīha noktaḥ* "With regard to *kāśyapāḥ*, according to A 5.3.99 *jīvikārthe cāpanye* 'If the object denoted is an image when it is intended for earning a living, though not through its sale', zero replacement occurs in the place of the affix *kaN* taught after a nominal base to denote an image similar to that which is denoted by the nominal base *kāśyapa*. Therefore, when it is desired to denote a multiplicity of these images, i.e., *kāśyapaś ca kāśyapaś ca kāśyapaś ca*, only one word form *kāśyapa-* is employed. And this is a [word form]) ending in *aÑ* in the plural sense: there is a potential involvement of LUK zero replacement. The exclusion (of this fault) will be stated elsewhere, since there is a mention of the current sense of gotra; thus it is not enunciated here."

I.238:24-28 (ad vt. 20 on A 1.2.64) underlines how A 2.4.64 includes the denotation of a gotra among its conditions and this is not relevant for the example of *kāśyapāḥ*:

> *mā bhūd evam / añantaṁ yad bahuṣu yañantaṁ yad bahuṣv ity evaṁ bhaviṣyati / nanu coktaṁ naivaṁ śakyam iha hi doṣaḥ syāt kāśyapapratikṛtayaḥ kāśyapā iti / naiṣa doṣaḥ / laukikasya tatra gotrasya grahaṇaṁ na caital laukikaṁ gotraṁ / athavā punar astv ekā prakṛtir bahavaś ca yañaḥ / nanu coktam asārūpyād ekaśeṣo na prāpnotīti* "Let it not be so! On the contrary it will be so: 'That which ends in *yaÑ* in the plural sense and that which ends in *aÑ* in the plural sense.' Nonetheless it is said: 'It cannot be so. Here there would be a fault, when it is said *kāśyapāḥ* as 'many images of *Kāśyapaḥ*'. Here there is a mention of the current denotation of *gotra*. On the contrary this (*kāśyapāḥ*) is not a current name of a *gotra*. Or better, once again let there be a only nominal base and many *yaÑ*!".[47]

Thus only the first shortcoming is not refuted anywhere by Patañjali and consistently the *Kāśikāvṛtti* only quotes this one. Nevertheless the accentuation of *sthānin* should be included among the provisions dependent on phonemes; that is, the fact of having two high-pitched sounds is a *vidhi* of *sthānin* which cannot be extended to the *ādeśa aśvau* in accordance with the *sthānivadbhāva*-rule. Therefore, there is no fault if the ekaśeṣa-rule which determines the formation of *aśvau* for *aśvaścāśvaś ca* is considered as an ādeśa-rule.

Analogously, with regard to the example presented by Cardona (1997:11), i.e., the dual nominative / accusative form *gārgyau* which designates Gārgya (the elder descendant of Garga) and Gārgyāyaṇa (the younger descendant of Garga) together, according

47. Cf. M I.492:12-15 (ad vt. 8 on A 2.4.62): *mā bhūd evam añ yo bahuṣu yañ yo bahuṣv iti / añantaṁ yad bahuṣu yañantaṁ yad bahuṣv ity evaṁ bhaviṣyati / nanu coktaṁ naivaṁ śakyam iha hi doṣaḥ syāt kāśyapapratikṛtayaḥ kāśyapā iti / naiṣa doṣaḥ / laukikasya tatra gotrasya grahaṇaṁ na caital laukikaṁ gotram.*

to A 1.2.65: *vṛddho yūnā tallakṣaṇaś ced eva viśeṣaḥ* ("When a derivate denoting the elder descendant combines with one denoting the younger descendant of a *gotra*, only the former remains, provided that the only denotation difference between the two units is this [i.e. the different age]"). The nominal base of the first name is derived by applying the taddhita suffix *yaÑ* in accordance with the sūtra A 4.1.105 cited above. Its first vowel is high-pitched according to A 6.1.197: *ñnityādir nityam.* The nominal base *gārgyāṇa-* is derived by applying the taddhita suffix *phaK* in accordance with A 4.1.101: *yañiñoś ca*, ("[The *taddhita*-affix *phaK*] occurs after a nominal base ending in *yaÑ* and *iÑ* to denote a gotra descendant"). Its final vowel is high-pitched according to A 6.1.165: *kitaḥ* (*antodattaḥ* 159 *taddhitasya* 164) ("The final vowel of a nominal base ending in a taddhita affix with marker *K* is high-pitched").

If *gārgyau* is treated as a substitute of the two names mentioned, there is the possibility of applying the accentuation of the substituend (*sthānin*) to the replacement (*ādeśa*) according to A 1.1.56.[48] Actually, if the niyama *analvidhau* of A 1.1.56 is literally taken into account, A 6.1.165 is an alvidhi, as is each rule which

48. See Cardona 1997: 11: "In accordance with the usual convention governing replacements, the substitute would have the properties of substituends. Consequently, although the base in question should have a high-pitched initial vowel only, one would allow a substitute *gārgya* with high pitch not only on its first vowel but also on its suffix, or on both." Cf. Sharma 1990: II.134: "The *śeṣa* is used to indicate that *ekaśeṣa* is not *ādeśa* 'replacement' in place of the similar forms. This means that the genitive of *sarūpāṇām* has to be interpreted not as a *sthānaṣaṣṭhī*, or genitive denoting 'in place of' (I.1.49 *ṣaṣṭhī sthāneyogā*). It should rather be interpreted as the genitive of specification (*nirdhāraṇa*), thereby giving the meaning 'one from among many which are similar in form'." These kinds of comments agree with KV 1.2.64: *śeṣagrahaṇam kim? ādeśo mā bhūt*; and with PM 1.2.64 (I.378-379): *ādeśo mā bhūt / asati śeṣagrahaṇe ṣaṣṭhī sthāneyogā iti vacanāt sthānaṣaṣṭhī syāt, tataś cādeśaḥ syād / astu; śabdato'rthataś cāntaratamo bhaviṣyati / sarūpāṇām iti sthānaṣaṣṭhī syāt / naivaṁ śakyam / svare hi doṣaḥ syāt / dvayor aśvaśabdayoḥ samudāyaḥ sthānī / tatra ca dvāv udāttāv iti dvyudātta ādeśaḥ syāt / etena dvyanudāttatvaṁ vyākhyātam.*

provides for the accentuation of a vowel.[49] As a consequence, this transference of the accentuation of the sthānin to the ādeśa is precisely blocked by A 1.1.56 and there is no fault in classifying ekaśeṣa rules as substitution rules.

By contrast, in my opinion, the mention *śeṣa* is rather necessary to provide for a phono-morphological feature — the accentuation of the ekaśeṣa formation — which is not taught elsewhere, since these ādeśas governed by the ekaśeṣa rules are not directly taught. In fact we know, e.g., the accent of the nominal base *aśva-* or *gārgya-* only as śeṣas (of *aśvo' śvaś ca* and of *gārgyo gārgyāyaṇaś ca* respectively),[50] because of the basic provision of *aśvaḥ* which is included in the speaker's lexical competence with a high-pitched first vowel or because of the provision of *gārgyaḥ*, which is taught with its high-pitched first vowel according to A 6.1.197. Accordingly, that this discussion on the ādeśa-classification of A 1.2.64 actually starts with questioning the use of the term *śeṣa* might be supposed to be a trace of this specific role of ekaśeṣa rules as apavāda cases of substitution. Ekaśeṣa would now be an example of ādeśa which is not grammatically taught, since it is actually merely supposed by the śeṣa-procedure taught by the general rule A 1.2.64, just as the zero replacements which are supposed but not directly taught both in A 1.4.105 (*yuṣmady upapade samānādhikaraṇe sthāniny api madhyamaḥ*) and 2.3.14 (*kriyārthopapadasya ca karmaṇi sthāninaḥ*)[51] as well as in A 8.1.45 (*lope vibhāṣā*), 8.1.62 (*cāhalopa ehety avadhāraṇam*) and 8.1.63

49. Cf. Candotti-Pontillo 2004, Appendix (Analysis of doṣa-vārttikas 18-30 ad A 1.1. 56), e.g., vt. 23.

50. I consider here the prātipādikas corresponding respectively to the padas *aśvaḥ* and *gārgyaḥ* (actually obtained by means of the ekaśeṣa procedure), because nominal endings (which are required in the relevant sentence) only apply to prātipādikas, which are the result of a LUK zero replacement in accordance with A 2.4.71: *supo dhātuprātipadikayoḥ* "LUK zero replacement in place of a nominal ending of a *pada* constituting a verbal stem or a nominal base."

51. These two cases are classified as "ellipsis" by Kiparsky 1982: 24-25; 37-51, and Deshpande 1981, 1985, 1989.

(*cādilope vibhāṣā).*[52] In fact, there is no regular use of a genitive case teaching the sthānin in the ekaśeṣa rules, apart from the expression sarūpāṇām included in their general rule. For instance, *vṛddho yūnā* or *pitā mātrā* could also be the regular prakriyā of a dvandva or a correct copulative syntagma. Furthermore, in the second case, the matching dvandva formation is optional. A 1.2.65 and A 1.2.70 might respectively teach a śeṣa procedure for two assumed replacements that are not explicitly taught.

As zero replacement ensures the meaning-extension of the unit which is replaced by zero to zero itself — for instance the sense of agent for the zeroed affix *KviP* — analogously, the absent but potentially present pada *mātrā*, which, furthermore, is present elsewhere combined with *pitṛ*, ensures the additional denotation of this second object (whose matching word-form does not remain) to *pitarau.*

What is the principle underlying this meaning extension which both grammatical devices ensure? I propose that it could be spotted in the so-called laukika part of substitution, precisely in its more spontaneous side,[53] which Patañjali himself emphasizes in his extremely long commentary (M I.133:22-24) on the main rule of substitution, A 1.1.56: *sthānivad ādeśo 'nalvidhau*:

> *guruvad asmin guruputre vartitavyam iti gurau yat kāryaṁ tad guruputre 'tidiśyate/ evam ihāpi sthānikāryam ādeśe 'tidiśyate* "We have to behave in the presence of the preceptor's son as if we were in the presence of the preceptor, i.e., that which has to be done (*kārya*) in the presence of the preceptor is extended in the presence of the preceptor's son. Analogously, that which has to be done

52. Cf. Candotti-Pontillo 2012: 99f., 122ff.

53. Cf. Cardona 2007: 704: "This appeal to the Laukika status of the most basic principles governing how Pāṇini's Sūtras are to apply, principles which Pāṇini obvious[ly] observes but does not need to formulate explicitly, brings up a general issue regarding grammar, other Vedāṅgas, and their status in Indian thought". For a supposed spontaneous side of *lopa* see Candotti-Pontillo 2012: 122ff.

(the rule/-s which has/have to be applied) when there is the sthānin, is extended when there is its ādeśa."

Consistently afterwards, Patañjali objects to the necessity of teaching sthānivadbhāva for ādeśas because this kind of extension of rules is actually a common practice, and there is no need for its specific enunciation, as in common life when one obtains the privileges which are due to the person one has been associated with. For instance, a pupil gets the seat of honor etc. when he reaches the clan for which he is going to perform a sacrifice. In fact, Patañjali concludes that rule A 1.1.56 merely aims at a restriction (*niyama*), that is, the prohibition of extension 'in case of a rule concerning (or conditioned by) sounds (*analvidhau*)':

M I.133:24-134:2 (ad A 1.1.56): *lokata etat siddham / tad yathā / loke yo yasya prasaṅge bhavati labhate 'sau tatkaryāṇi / tad yathā / upādhyāyasya śiṣyo yājyakulani gatvāgrāsanādīni labhate* "This is also established from the point of view of common life. As in common life when one obtains the privileges which are due to the person one has been associated with. For instance, a pupil gets the seat of honour etc. when he reaches the clan for which he is going to perform a sacrifice."

References and Abbreviations

A *Aṣṭādhyāyī* : see Sharma 1987-2003.

Abhyankar, Kashinath Vasudev and Jayadev Mohanlal Shukla

1975 *Patañjali's Vyākaraṇa-Mahābhāṣya. Āhnikas 1-3. With English Translation and Notes*. Poona: Bhandarkar Oriental Research Institute.

Biardeau, Madeleine

1964 *Théorie de la connaissance et philosophie de la parole dans le brahmanisme classique*. Paris: Mouton.

Bronkhorst, Johannes

1981 *Nirukta* and *Aṣṭādhyāyī*: their shared presuppositions. *Indo-Iranian Journal* 23: 1-14.

1987a *Three Problems pertaining to the Mahābhāṣya*. Post-Graduate and Research Department Series, No. 30. "Pandit Shripad Shastri Deodhar Memorial Lectures" [Third Series]. Poona: Bhandarkar Oriental Research Institute.

1987b Review of Deshpande 1985. *Indo-Iranian Journal* 30: 296-301.

Buiskool, Herman Eildert

1939 *The Tripādī — being an abridged English recast of Pūrvatrāsiddham (An Analytical-synthetic Inquiry into the System of Pāṇini's Aṣṭādhyāyī)*. Leiden: Brill. [*Pūrvatrāsiddham: Analytisch Onderzoek aangaande het systeem der Tripādī van Pāṇinii's Aṣṭādhyāyī*. Amsterdam 1934].

Candotti, Maria Piera and Tiziana Pontillo

2004 Substitution as a descriptive model in Pāṇini's grammar: towards an opposition between fonological and morphological level?, in *Atti del Secondo Incontro Genovese di Studi Vedici e Pāṇiniani* (Genova, 23 luglio 2003-15 ottobre

2003), a cura di R. Ronzitti e G. Borghi, Recco, Le Mani, pp. 1-45.

2010 The autonomous Process of Denotation: Kātyāyana and Patañjali on the Limits of analysis, in P. Caracchi, A.S. Comba, A. Consolaro and A. Pelissero (eds.) *Tīrthayātrā. Essays in Honour of Stefano Piano,* Alessandria: Edizioni dell'Orso, pp. 41-61.

2012 The earlier Pāṇinian tradition on the imperceptible sign, in Candotti and Pontillo (eds.), pp. 99-153.

Cardona, George

1997 *Pāṇini. His Work and Its Traditions. Volume 1*: Background and Introduction. Second edition. Delhi: Motilal Banarsidass.

1999 *Recent Research in Pāṇinian Studies*. Delhi: Motilal Banarsidass. (Second edition 2004).

2007 On the Position of Vyākaraṇa and Pāṇini, in Preisendanz 2007: 693-710.

2009 On the structure of Pāṇini's system, in Huet, Kulkarni and Scharf 2009: 1-32.

Cox, Collett

2004 From Category to Ontology: the changing Role of Dharma in Sarvāstivāda Abhidharma. *Journal of Indian Philosophy* 32: 543-97.

Deshpande, Madhav M.

1981 Sanskrit gerund constructions: some disputations. *Indo-Iranian Journal* 23: 167-185.

1985 *Ellipsis and Syntactic Overlapping: Current Issues in Pāṇinian Syntactic Theory*. Poona: Bhandarkar Oriental Research Institute.

1989 Ellipsis in modern Linguistics and Pāṇini. *Annals of Bhandarkar Oriental Institute* 70: 103-124.

Freschi, Elisa and Tiziana Pontillo

2012 When one thing applies more than once: tantra and

prasaṅga in *Śrautasūtra, Mīmāṃsā* and *Grammar*, in: Pontillo and Candotti 2012, pp. 33-98.

Houben, Jan E. M.

1995 *The Saṃbandha-samuddeśa (Chapter on Relation) and Bhartṛhari's Philosophy of Language*. Gröningen: Egbert Forsten.

Huet, Gérard, Amba Kulkarni and Peter Scharf (eds.)

2009 *Sanskrit Computational Linguistics, First and Second International Symposia, Roquefort, France, October 29-31, 2007, Providence, RI, USA, May 15-17, 2008, Revised and Selected Invited Papers*. Lecture Notes in Artificial Intelligence, Subseries Lecture Notes in Computer Science. Berlin/ Heidelberg/New York

Joshi, Shivra Dattatray and Jouthe Anthon Fokko Roodbergen

1968 *Patañjali's Vyākaraṇa-Mahābhāṣya. Samarhāhnika*. Publications of the Centre of Advanced Study in Sanskrit Class C no. 3. Poona: University of Poona.

1986 *Patañjali's Vyākaraṇa-Mahābhāṣya. Paspaśāhnika*. = Publications of the Centre of Advanced Study in Sanskrit Class C no. 7. Poona: University of Poona.

1994 *The Aṣṭādhyāyī of Pāṇini*, Vol. III. New Delhi: Sahitya Akademi.

1996 *The Aṣṭādhyāyī of Pāṇini*, Vol. V. New Delhi: Sahitya Akademi.

Katre, Sumitra Mangesh (ed. and transl.)

1987 *Aṣṭādhyāyī of Pāṇini*. Austin: The University of Texas Press. (Reprinted 1989, Delhi: Motilal Banarsidass)

Kielhorn, Franz

1880-85 *The Vyākaraṇa-Mahābhāṣya of Patañjali* Third edition, 1962-75, revised and furnished with additional readings, references, and select critical notes by K. V. Abhyankar. [I: 1962, II: 1965, III: 1972]

Kiparsky, Paul

1979 *Pāṇini as a Variationist*. Poona: Centre of Advanced Study in Sanskrit, University of Poona, in collaboration with the MIT Press, Cambridge (Mass.) University Press. (Edited by S. D. Joshi).

1982 *Some theoretical problems in Pāṇini's grammar*. Post-graduate and Research Department Series no.16 "Professor K.V. Abhyankar Memorial Lectures", 2nd Series. Poona: Bhandarkar Oriental Research Institute.

2009 On the Architecture of Pāṇini's grammar, in Huet, Kulkarni and Scharf 2009: 33-94.

KV *Kāśikāvṛttii* : see Shastri and Shukla 1983-85.

M *Mahābhāṣya* : see Kielhorn 1880-1885.

P *Pradīpa* : see Shastri 1938.

PM *Padamañjarī* : see Shastri and Shukla 1983-85.

Pontillo, Tiziana

2005 *I cosiddetti "composti sintetici" nella grammatica di Panini*. ACME. Annali della Facoltà di Lettere e Filosofia dell'Università degli Studi di Milano" LVIII, 2: 225-44.

2008 The edible part of the rice in the Mahābhāṣya imagery: what are the husks of rules? What is a-tantram, in Jaroslav Vacek (ed.), Pandanus 2008, Prague: Triton, pp. 79-96.

Pontillo, Tiziana and Maria Piera Candotti (eds.)

2012 *Signless Signification in Ancient India and Beyond*, edited by Tiziana Pontillo and Maria Piera Candotti. Cultural, Historical and Textual Studies of Religions. London: Anthem.

Preisendanz, Karin, ed.

2007 *Expanding and Merging Horizons. Contributions to*

South Asian and Cross-Cultural Studies in Commemoration of Wilhelm Halbfass Österreichische Akademie der Wissenschaften. Philosophisch-Historische Klasse Denkschriften, 351. Band, Beiträge zur Kultur- und Geistesgeschichte Asiens Nr. 53. Wien: Austrian Academy of Sciences Press.

Radicchi, Anna

1985-88 *La teoria pāṇiniana dei Samāsa secondo l'interpretazione delle scuole grammaticali indiane dal quinto all'ottavo secolo d.C.* Two volumes. Firenze: Elite.

Scharf, Peter M.

1996 *The Denotation of Generic Terms in Ancient Indian Philosophy: Grammar, Nyāya, and Mīmāṃsā.* Transactions of the American Philosophical Society 86, Pt. 3. Philadelphia: American Philosophical Society.

Sharma, Rama Nath

1990-2003 *The Aṣṭādhyāyī of Pāṇini, English Translation ... with Sanskrit Text, Transliteration, Word-boundary, Anuvṛtti, Vṛtti, Explanatory Notes, Derivational History of Examples and Indices.* Five volumes. Delhi: Munshiram Manoharlal (= volumes II-VI).

Shastri, Bal

1938 *Patañjali's Vyākaraṇa Mahābhāṣya with Kaiyaṭa's Pradīpa & Nāgojibhaṭṭa's Uddyota and Bhaṭṭoji Dīkṣita's Śabdakaustubha. With the Commentary Abhinava Rājalakṣmī by Acharya Guruprasad Shasti, edited by Dr. Bal Shastri.* Six volumes. Delhi: Pratibha Prakashan (reprint 2001).

Shastri, Swami Dwarikadas and Kalika Prasad Shukla

1983-85 *Nyāsa or Pañcikā Commentary of Ācārya Jinendrabuddhipāda and Padamañjarī of*

Haradatta Miśra on the Kāśikāvṛtti [*Commentary on the Aṣṭādhyāyī of Pāṇini*] *of Vāmana-Jayāditya* critically edited. Six volumes. Varanasi: Prachya Bharati Prakashan.

Tillemans, Tom
2007 Trying to be Fair to Mādhyamika Buddhism, in Preisendanz 2007, pp. 507-23.

vt. vārttika(s) of Kātyāyana cited in M.

On the so-called predicative instrumental

Toru Yagi

parihāsavijalpitaṁ sakhe paramārthena na gṛhyatāṁ vacaḥ.
O friend, let not (my) words, uttered in jest, be taken in earnest (as of true import). (Śak II 18^{cd})

0 Introduction

Examples of the so-called predicative instrumental are enumerated by, among others, Speijer[1] and Renou.[2] The former refers to P. 2.3.21: *itthaṁbhūtalakṣaṇe (tṛtīyā* 18*)* as the rule relevant to the present instrumental. On the other hand, the latter seems to attribute it to P. 2.3.18: *kartṛkaraṇayos tṛtīyā.*[3] The former, however, emends the manuscript reading *dūtena* to *dūtyena*, referring to §237 only.[4] With regard to the text reading *coreṇa*, Kangle notes that *coreṇa* obviously is used for *cauryeṇa.*[5] On the other hand, Ghanaśyāma comments on the above-mentioned *paramārthena* (see note 3), as follows: *paramārthena paramārthatveneti bhāvapradhāno nirdeśaḥ, ata eva malinaṁ pramārṣṭīti rājaśekharaḥ. tathā ca sarvam alīkam iti bhāvaḥ.*[6] (Rājaśekhara [says]: "*paramārthena*, that is, *paramārthatvena*, is a

1. For example, Speijer 1998: 51 (§67 Rem.2): *dravībhūtaṁ manye patati jalarūpeṇa gaganam* (methinks, the firament dissolves and falls down as rain), 184 (§237 Rem): *prayāti sma dūtyayā, ... prayātu dautyena* «in the quality of messenger».
2. For example, Renou 1968: 293 (§219 C): *paramārthena gṛhyate* «est compris comme vérité», *tad agninaiva deveṣu brahmābhavat* «le *b*. est apparu chez les dieux en tant qu'A.», *snuṣātvena svīkṛ-* «choisir pour bru».
3. Renou 1968: 293.
4. Aś 325, 11-12: *anyatamaḥ puruṣo dūtyenāhūyoktah..* Cf. BHSG §7.38. With regard to the word-form *dūtyena*, cf. Kāśikā on P. 5.1.126 and SK 1791.
5. Kangle 1992: II 275, note 7 on 4.8.7: *coreṇābhiśasto vairadveśābhyām apadiṣṭakaḥ śuddhaḥ syāt.*
6. Raval-Bhatt 1997: 75.

wording having as the essential the property of being [verities].[7] For this very reason, the poet wipes off a fault in grammar."[8] And, in this way, the intention [of the second half of the verse] is: All [I say] is false.)

In this paper, basing myself on Nāgeśa, I would like to examine by what rule and on what conditions the instrumental functions as predicative.

1 P. 2.3.21

1.1 Bhaṭṭoji's and Nāgeśa's comments

On P. 2.3.21: *itthaṁbhūtalakṣaṇe* (*tṛtīyā* 18) Bhaṭṭoji comments as follows: *kañcit prakāraṁ prāptasya lakṣaṇe tṛtīyā syāt. jaṭābhis tāpasaḥ. jaṭājñāpyatāpasatvaviśiṣṭa ity arthaḥ.*[9] (The third case ending should occur [after a nominal stem denoting] the attribute of someone or something that has already attained the property of being someone or something. [For example,] "an ascetic with [the attribute in the form of] matted hair", the meaning of which is "[he who is] qualified by the property of being an ascetic to be perceived by matted hair").

Nāgeśa's comment is:

itthambhūta. idamas thamupratyayānta itthamśabdaḥ prakṛtyarthaṁ vihāya prakāramātre lākṣaṇikaḥ. prāptyarthakabhūdhātoḥ karttari ktaḥ. karmavibhaktyantena itthamśabdena bhūtaśabdasya samāsaḥ. lakṣaṇaśabdaḥ karaṇasādhanaḥ. tasya karmaṣaṣṭhyantenetthambhūtaśabdena samāsaḥ. tad āha kañcid ityādi. evaṁ ca sahaiva putrair ityādau vidyamānatāvācisahaśabdayoge itthambhūtalakṣaṇe iti tṛtīyeti keśāñcid uktiś cintyeti bhāvaḥ. lakṣaṇe iti. tatra vartamānād iti śeṣaḥ. jaṭābhir iti. jñāpyatvarūpaḥ sambandhas tṛtīyārthaḥ. tad āha jaṭājñāpyeti. yat tu jaṭābhis tāpaso jñāta ityarthāj jñānakriyāyāṁ jaṭādīnāṁ karaṇatvād eva tṛtīyāsiddher idaṁ

7. P. 5.1.119: *tasya bhāvas tvatalau* and Cardona 1997: 243 (§348), '*tva* or *tal* follows a pada with a sixth-triplet ending (*tasya*) to form a derivate that denotes the property of being (*bhāvaḥ*) what the base of the pada denotes.' Cf. Ogawa 2005: 107-114.

8. I could not identify the quotation.

9. SK 566.

vyartham iti. tan na. karaṇatvāvivakṣāyāṁ ṣaṣṭhībādhanārtham āvaśyakatvāt. etena hetutṛtīyayedaṁ siddham ity apāstam. lakṣyalakṣaṇabhāvasyaiva vivakṣitatvāc ceti dik.[10]

On [SK 566] *itthaṁbhūta* ...: The word *ittham-*, which ends in the secondary suffix *-tham* <*tham*u> [laid down by P. 5.3.24] after *idam-*, expresses secondarily "mode in general", having given up the meaning ["this mode"] of the nominal stem [*ittham-*]; *-ta* <k*ta*>, [laid down by P. 3.2.102] after the root *bhū-*[11] meaning "attainment", refers to an agent [by P. 3.4.72]; [the word in question is] a compound [by P. 2.1.24] of the word *bhūta-* [ending in *-s* <*s*u>] with the word *ittham-* ending in the second case ending which refers [by P. 2.3.2] to a direct object. The word *lakṣaṇa-* includes a primary suffix referring [by P. 3.3.117] to a means; [therefore, the word *itthambhūtalakṣaṇa-* is] a compound [by P. 2.2.8] of it with the word *itthambhūta-* ending in the sixth case ending which refers [by P. 2.3.66] to a direct object; so he says: *kañcid* ...; and thus his intention is that the following assertion of some grammarians is contestable: [They assert:] The third case ending by P. 2.3.21: *itthambhūtalakṣaṇe* functions as such when it is construed [by P. 2.3.19: *sahayukte 'pradhāne*"] with the word *saha* expressing existence,[12] as in examples such as "[a father to whom some sons really exist, i.e. a father] with some sons." On *lakṣaṇe*: After [a nominal stem denoting ...;] *occurring* [in the meaning ...] remains [to be supplied]. On *jaṭābhis*: The meaning of the third case ending is the relationship [of matted hair with an ascetic] in the form of property of being an object to be perceived [by means of matted hair]; so he says: *jaṭājñāpyeti*. However, [others assert]: Because [the phrase "an ascetic with matted hair"] means "an ascetic perceived by matted hair", matted hair, among others, is the very means with regard to the action of perceiving [the ascetic]; accordingly [the application of] the third case ending [to the nominal stem *jaṭā-*,etc.] is realized [by P. 2.3.18: *kartṛkaraṇayos tṛtīyā*]; therefore, the present rule [P. 2.3.21] is of no use. This [assertion of them] is not correct. [First of all, the formulation of the present rule] is inevitable in order to set aside [P. 2.3.50: *ṣaṣṭhī śeṣe*, which lays down the value "relationship in general"

10. Bś II.879.

11. DhP. 10.235: *bhū prāptāv ātmanepadī.*

12. Cf. Aneka, Pariśiṣṭakāṇḍa 60^{cd}-61^{ab}: *saha sambandha-sādṛśya-yaugapadya-samṛddhiṣu, sākalye vidyamāne ca.*

of] the sixth case ending [and which is expected to take effect] when a speaker [of the present phrase] does not desire to express that matted hair is a means [of perceiving the ascetic]; by this [very reason the following assertion of the rest of grammarians] has also been set aside: The [phrase "an ascetic with matted hair" means "an ascetic perceived because of matted hair",[13] so the] present problem has been resolved by [P. 2.3.23: *hetau* which lays down] the third case ending referring to a cause. And, [secondly,] only the relationship between someone or something to be characterized and his or its attribute [to characterize him or it] has been desired to express [by the speaker]. Such is a right direction [in the present argument].

P. 2.3.19, 18, 50 and 23 have been rejected by Nāgeśa, so that we can proceed to verify on what conditons the instrumental by P. 2.3.21 can function as predicative.

1.2 Conditions for a predicative instrumental by P. 2.3.21

1.2.1 First condition

The other examples which Pāṇinians quote are: *api bhavān kamaṇḍalunā chātram adrākṣīt* "Did you see a pupil with [the attribute in the form of] a water-pot?", *chātreṇopādhyāyam* "a teacher with a pupil", *śikhayā parivrājakam* "a religious mendicant with a tuft" and *śvetacchatreṇa rājānam* "a king with a white parasol".[14] It is quite natural that these instrumentals do not function as predicative because *kamaṇḍalunā*, for example, does not refer to one and the same substratum that *chātram* does to. Therefore one condition under which an instrumental functions as predicative is: one word denoting a lakṣaṇa and the other word denoting a lakṣya refer to one and the same substratum. Instrumentals interpreted on this condition as predicative by modern scholars are: *tad agninaiva deveṣu brahmābhavat* «le *b.* est

13. Cf. Bś II.879: *ādinā guṇakriyayoḥ saṅgrahaḥ* (on SK 568: *dravyādisādhāraṇaṁ ... ca hetutvam*).

14. Kāśikāvṛtti, Haradatta, Annambhaṭṭa, Puruṣottamadeva. All these lakṣaṇas are material objects and differ from lakṣyas. They substantially correspond to "3. A material object recognized as appropriate to, and thus symbolic of, any office or actor; *spec.* in *Painting, Sculpture*: A conventional symbol added, as an accessory, to denote the character or show the identity of the personage represented" (The Oxford English Dictionary, *s.v.* attribute).

apparu chez les dieux en tant qu'A.»[15] and *coreṇābhiśasto vairadveṣābhyām apadiṣṭakaḥ śuddhaḥ syāt* "Ein als Dieb Angeklagter (*coreṇābhiśasta*), der zu seiner Verteidigung zeigt, daß Feindschaft oder Haß (der Beschuldigung) zugrunde liege, soll gereinigt sein."[16] and so on. By the way, with regard to the relationship between a lakṣya and a lakṣaṇa in the example *api bhavān kamaṇḍalunā chātram adrākṣīt*, Nāgeśa explains: *itthaṁbhūtaś* [i.e.] *chātratvaṁ prāptaś* [i.e.] *chātras tasya* [*chātrasya*] *lakṣaṇaṁ* [i.e.] *kamaṇḍaluḥ* ("A water-pot is the attribute of a pupil who has already got into such-and-such a mode, i.e., who has already attained the property of being a pupil.")[17] And an attribute (*lakṣaṇa*) is a means to characterize a person or a thing in question (*lakṣya*).

Agni or a thief is an attribute [by means] of [which to characterize] Brahman or the accused that has already attained the property of being Brahman or the accused. Keeping this in mind, a speaker, who desires to express only the relationship between a lakṣya and a lakṣaṇa [where the latter is the essential in comparison with the former], applies the third case ending to a nominal stem such as *agni-* or *cora-*, which denotes a lakṣaṇa.[18] Therefore "The Brahman with the attribute of Agni appeared among gods" amounts to "The Brahman appeared among gods in the quality of Agni" and "The accused with the attribute of thief" amounts to "the accused as thief". In connection with this type of example, the opinions of Speijer (*dūtena* > *dūtyena*) and Kangle (*coreṇa* > *cauryeṇa*) are not compatible with those of Renou, Meyer and Rājaśekhara, though an instrumental of a derivate

15. Renou1968: 293.
16. Meyer 1977: 342.
17. Nāgeśa on the Mahābhāṣya ad P. 2.3.21 (Shivdatta Sharma 1988: 503b).
18. *Lakṣaṇe iti* = *lakṣaṇe vartamānād* [*ṅy-āp-prātipadikāt*]. This type of attribute substantially corresponds to "1.A quality or character ascribed to any person or thing, one which is in common estimation or usage assigned to him; hence, *sometimes*, an epithet or appellation in which the quality is ascribed" (The Oxford English Dictionary, *s.v.* attribute).

formed with a suffix denoting the property of being such-and-such or the activity/office of such-and-such (*bhāva-, bhāvakarma-pratyaya*[19]) is preferred in many cases.

The wording *prakṛtyā* occurs as such in P. 6.2.1, 2.137, 3.75, 83 and 4.163 and it occurs by reiteration in, among others, P. 6.1.125 *plutapragṛhyā aci nityam* (*prakṛtyā* 115). This rule provides, I believe, that protracted vowels[20] and items called *pragṛhya*[21] remain with the attribute of their original form necessarily before a vowel. This amounts to "A protracted vowel and pragṛhya necessarily remain original forms [or in the quality of original form] before a vowel." The present interpretation is, I believe, tenable, because Patañjali remarks on the third vārttika to P. 6.1.125 as follows: *yad ayaṁ plutaḥ prakṛtyā iti* [*plutasya*] *prakṛtibhāvaṁ śāsti tad* ... ("Because [of the fact that] this [great Master Pāṇini himself] teaches the property of being an original form [or the office of original form] [of a protracted vowel by the rule] 'A protracted vowel remains an original form …'"). If such is the case, his remark suggests the following. First, the three munis (*munitraya*) are of the same opinion. Secondly the wording *prakṛtyā* is an expression whose essential meaning is the property of being such-and-such or the activity/office of such-and-such (*bhāvakarmapradhānanirdeśa*), with which Rājaśekhara's opinion perfectly corresponds. Like *prakṛtyā*, the instrumentals *dūtena, coreṇa* and *paramārthena* lack an overt affix denoting the meanings noted (*bhāvakarmapratyaya*), although a bhāvakarma-pradhānanirdeśa denotes an attribute. This causes, I believe, Speijer and Kangle to regard these instrumentals as grammatically faulty.[22]

19. P. 5.1.119-136. Cf. Bś II.1437 (on SK 1788 [= P. 5.1.124]): *karmeha kriyā* [activity], *kāryaṁ* [office] *ca*.
20. P. 1.2.27.
21. P. 1.1.11-19.
22. The word *malinam* used by Rājaśekhara can be interpreted as "dirt, i.e. a fault" either in grammar or in meter. In the former case, he is of the same opinion as Speijer and Kangle. In the latter, he is consistent. I should translate,

If one condition under which an instrumental functions as predicative is that one word denoting a lakṣaṇa and the other word denoting a lakṣya refer to one and the same substratum, should both these words not be put in the same case, for example, *tad agnir eva deveṣu brahmābhavat*?

By the token, in the sentence *api bhavān kamaṇḍalupāṇiṁ chātram adrākṣīt* ("Did you see a pupil with a water-pot in his hand?"), the prior constituent *kamaṇḍalu-* denotes a lakṣaṇa of a pupil. Therefore, should the third case ending not be applied to *kamaṇḍalu-*? Patañjali removes the doubt, remarking: *tathāhy ayaṁ prādhānyena lakṣaṇaṁ pratinirdiśati: itthaṁbhūtasya lakṣaṇam itthaṁbhūtalakṣanaṁ, tasminn itthaṁbhūtalakṣaṇa iti.*

> For this [great Master Pāṇini himself] refers to a lakṣaṇa [with the attribute in the form of property of being the essential, i.e.] as the essential, in this way: the compound *itthaṁbhūtalakṣaṇa-* is analyzed into *itthaṁbhūta-as lakṣaṇa-s* (the attribute [by means] of [which to characterize] someone that has already attained the property of being someone); that [compound in this sense is referred to in the present rule thus:] *itthaṁbhūtalakṣane.*

Normally there is no attribute (*lakṣaṇa*) without a substratum in the form of lakṣya to which it belongs. In this sense, a lakṣaṇa is subordinate while a lakṣya is essential. In spite of this fact, according to Patañjali, a speaker, who desires to express a lakṣaṇa as the essential, i.e., to emphasize a lakṣaṇa in the relationship between a lakṣya and a lakṣaṇa, applies the third case ending to a nominal stem denoting a lakṣaṇa. In addition, one word denoting a lakṣaṇa as the essential must be also the essential. These two are revealed by Pāṇini's wording and the latter does not hold for the word *kamaṇḍalu-* that is a subordinate member.

for example, "From this very fact, the poet wipes off an expected fault in meter in advance." The present meter is called *Vaitālīya* (6 moras, – ⏑ –, ⏑, –/8 moras, – ⏑ –, ⏑, –//). Cf. Piṅgala 4.33: *vaitālīyaṁ dviḥsvarā ayukpāde, yugvasavo 'nte r-l-g-aḥ* .

To return to the main subject, Patañjali's opinion is, I believe, applicable to *agni-*. Agni is an attribute of Brahman and so, in fact, Agni is subordinate while its substratum Brahman is essential. In spite of this fact, a speaker, desiring to express Agni as the essential, uses the instrumental *agninā*.

1.2.2 Second condition

The other condition under which an instrumental functions as predicative is that one word denoting an attribute ends in a bhāvakarmapratyaya as in *dūtyena, cauryeṇa, paramārthatvena* or the like. In this case, we can understand at first sight that the instrumental is a bhāvakarmapradhānanirdeśa and thus functions as predicative. By the way, in connection with *kamaṇḍalupāṇi-*, Nāgeśa refers to some grammarians' opinion: *kecit tu kamaṇḍalupāṇiśabdād atra tṛtīyāpattiḥ. kamaṇḍalupāṇitvasyaiva lakṣaṇatvāt, sakṛd asau kamaṇḍalupāṇiś chātro dṛṣṭas tasya tad eva lakṣaṇaṁ bhavatīty anur lakṣaṇa iti sūtre* (P. 1.4.84) *bhāṣyāt. tad evety asya kamaṇḍalupāṇitvam evety arthaḥ. anyathā sa eveti vadet ... ity āhuḥ.*[23]

> But some grammarians assert: "The third case ending occurs, in the present phrase, after the word *kamaṇḍalupāṇi-* because the very property of being [a pupil] who has a water-pot in the hand is an attribute [of the pupil]. For it is stated in the Mahābhāṣya on P. 1.4.84: *anur lakṣaṇe* that, once the pupil, having a water-pot in the hand, was seen, that is nothing else but his attribute." The meaning of this phrase "that is nothing else but" is "the very property of being [a pupil] who has a water-pot in the hand". Otherwise, Patañjali would say: that very [water-pot]...

According to them, if a speaker desires to express only the relationship between a lakṣya and a lakṣaṇa and thus to emphasize the latter, not only *kamaṇḍalupāṇitvena* but also *kamaṇḍalupāṇinā* is allowable. A word such as this, expressing a quality, as in *buddhyā/prajñayā muktaḥ* or *pāṇḍityena muktaḥ*, refers to a property only, not to a substratum which the property belongs to. On the other hand, *śukla-* in an expression like *śuklaḥ paṭaḥ* ("The

23. Nāgeśa on the Mahābhāṣya ad P. 2.3.21 (Shivdatta Sharma 1988: 503b).

cloth is white, a white cloth") refers not only to a property but also to a substratum which the property belongs to. So does a bahuvrīhi compound. In this connection, a bahuvrīhi corresponds, I believe, to "a type of nominal which he [Pāṇini] called *guṇavacana*, as in **A**. 4.1.44 (**271**) and elsewhere. These are nominals that denote properties and things qualified by such properties."[24]

2 Conclusion

I have discussed constructions involving two nominals that meet either of the following conditions:

1. one denotes a lakṣaṇa (such as *agni-* [instr. sg. *agninā*]) and the other denoting a lakṣya (such as *brahman-*) and both refer to one and the same substratum.

2. one nominal, denoting a lakṣaṇa (such as *caurya-* [instr. sg. *cauryeṇa*]), ends in a *bhāvakarmapratyaya*.

An instrumental form, by P. 2.3.21, in a construction meeting one of these conditions can function predicatively.

24. Cardona 1997:185 *(*§275).

References and abbreviations

Abhyankar, K. V.

1962-72 *The Vyākaraṇa=Mahābhāṣya of Patañjali Edited by F. Kielhorn, Revised and furnished with additional readings, reference, and select critical notes, third edition.* Three volumes. Poona: Bhandarkar Oriental Research Institute.

Aneka *Anekārthasaṁgraha.* See Hośiṅga, Jagannātha Śāstrī, Pt. Ghanānanda Pāṇḍeya, and Pt. Janārdana Jyotirvit.

Aś *Avadānaçataka.* See Speyer, Jacob Samuel.

BHSG *Buddhist Hybrid Sanskrit Grammar*; see Edgerton, Franklin.

Bś *Bṛhacchabdenduśekhara.* See Shastri, Sitaram.

Cardona, George

1997 *Pāṇini, his Work and its Tradtions, vol. I: Background and Introduction.* Second edition, revised and enlarged. Delhi: Motilal Banarsidas.

Caturveda, Giridhara Śarmā and Parameśvara Śarmā Bhāskara

1977 *Śrībhaṭṭojidīkṣitaviracitā Vaiyākaraṇa-siddhāntakaumudī Śrīmadvāsudevadīkṣitapraṇītayā Bālamanoramākhyavyākhyayā Śrīmajjñānendra-sarasvatīviracitayā Tattvabodhinyākhyavyākhyayā ca sanāthitā.* Four volumes. Delhi: Motilal Banarsidass, 1958-61. Reprinted 1997.

DhP *Dhātupāṭha.* See Shastri, Dwarikadas.

Edgerton, Franklin

1972 *Buddhist Hybrid Sanskrit Grammar and Dictionary, volume I: Grammar.* New Haven: Yale University Press, 1953. Reprinted 1970, 1972, Delhi: Motilal Banarsidass.

Hośinga, Jagannātha Śāstrī, Pt. Ghanānanda Pāṇḍeya, and Pt. Janārdana Jyotirvit

1969 *Anekārthasaṁgraha of Śrī Hemacandrācārya.* Kashi Sanskrit Series 68. Varanasi: The Chowkhamba Sanskrit Series Office, 1929. Reprinted 1969.

Joshi, Bhargava Shastri

1988 *Patañjali's Vyākaraṇa Mahābhāṣya with Kaiyaṭa's Pradīpa and Nāgeśa's Uddyota.* Vol.V. Bombay: Nirnaya-Sagar Press. 1945. Reprinted 1988, Delhi: Chauwkhamba Sanskrit Pratishthan.

Kāle, Moreshvar Ramchandra

1969 *The Abhijñānaśākuntalam of Kālidāsa*, with the commentary of Rāghavabhaṭṭa, various readings, introduction, literal translation, exhaustive notes, and appendices. Tenth edition. Delhi: Motilal Banarsidass.

Kangle, R.P.

1992 *The Kauṭilīya Arthaśāstra.* Three volumes. University of Bombay Studies, Sanskrit, Prakrit and Pali, Nos. 1-3. Bombay: University of Bombay, 1960-1965. Second edition 1969. Reprinted 1986, 1988, 1992, Delhi: Motilal Banarsidass.

Kāśikā *Kāśikā*. See Miśra, Śrī Nārāyaṇa.

Mahābhāṣya See Abhyankar, K. V., Joshi, Bhargava Shastri, Sharma, Shivdatta.

Meyer, Johann Jakob

1977 *Das altindische Buch vom Welt- und Staatsleben: das Arthaçāstra des Kauṭilya, aus dem Sanskrit übersetzt und mit Einleitung und Anmerkungen versehen.* Leipzig: Harrassowitz, 1926. Reprinted 1977 , Graz: Akademische Druck-u. Verlagsanstalt.

Miśra, Śrī Nārāyaṇa.

1996 *Pāṇinīyavyākaraṇasūtravṛtti Kāśikā of Pt. Vāmana and Jayāditya* ... Kashi Sanskrit Series 37. Varanasi: Chaukhambha Sanskrit Sansthan.

Ogawa, Hideyo

2005 What is *bhāva*? A Grammatical Analysis of the Term *bhāva*. *The Annals of the Research Project Center for the Comparative Study of Logic* (Hiroshima University), III: 107-114.

P. Pāṇini.

Piṅgala See Vijayapāla.

Renou, Louis

1968 *Grammaire Sanscrite*. Two volumes in one. Paris: Adrien Maisonneuve, 1961. Reprinted 1968 by the same publisher.

Raval, Poonam Pankaj and V. M. Bhatt

1997 *Abhijñānaśākuntalam (South-Indian Recension) with the critical edition of the commentary of Ghanaśyāma Paṇḍita* (*viz. Sañjīvan-Ṭippaṇa*). Ahmedabad: Saraswati Pustak Bhandar.

Śak *Abhijñānaśākuntalam*. See Kāle, M. R.

Sharma, M.M.Pandit Shivdatta

1988 *Vyākaraṇamahābhāṣya of Patañjali with the Commentary Bhāṣyapradīpa of Kaiyaṭa Upādhyāya & the Super Commentary Bhāṣyapradīpoddyota of Nāgeśa Bhaṭṭa.* Vol. II. Bombay: Nirnaya-Sagar Press, 1912. Reprinted 1988, Delhi: Chauwkhamba Sanskrit Pratishthan.

Shastri, Sitaram

1960 *Bṛhat-śabdenduśekhara by Nāgeśa Bhaṭṭa*. Three volumes (continuous pagination). Sarasvati Bhavana Granthamala 87. Varanasi: Varanaseya Sanskrit Vishvavidyalaya.

Shastri, Dwarikadas

1964 *The Mādhavīyā Dhātuvṛtti* [*A Treatise on Sanskrit Roots based on the Dhātupāṭha of Pāṇini*]. Prāchya Bhāratī Series 1. Varanasi: Prāchya Bhāratī Prakāshana.

SK *Siddhāntakaumudī*. See Caturveda, Giridhara Śarmā and Parameśvara Śarmā Bhāskara.

Speijer, Jacob Samuel
1998 *Sanskrit Syntax*. Leyden: E. J. Brill, 1886. Reprinted 1968: Kyoto: The Rinsen-Shoten Bookstore, 1973, 1980, 1988, 1993, 1998, Delhi: Motilal Banarsidass.

Speyer, Jacob Samuel
1992 *The Avadānaçataka a Century of Edifying Tales Belonging to the Hīnayāna*. Two volumes. Bibliotheca Buddhica III. St. Pétersbourg : Commissionnaires de l'Académie impériale des sciences, 1906-1909. Reprinted 1958: 's Gravenhage: Mouton, 1970: Osnabrück: Biblio Verlag, 1992, Delhi: Motilal Banarsidass.

Vijayapāla
1988 *Piṅgalachandaḥsūtram Yādavaprakāśapraṇītena-Piṅgalachandovicitibhāṣyeṇa Samupetam* (*anekaiḥ pariśiṣṭaiḥ samalaṁkṛtam*). Bahalgarh, Sonipat (Harayana): Ram Lal Kapoor Trust.

Vat: a textual study

Dipesh Katira, Chinmay Dharurkar and Malhar Kulkarni

0 Introduction[1]

This paper studies the occurrences of the suffix *vat*, whose meanings are stated in the Aṣṭādhyāyī of Pāṇini (P. 5.1.115-117: तेन तुल्यं क्रिया चेद्वतिः । तत्र तस्येव । तदर्हम् ।). We survey the occurrences and study the function(s) of *vat* in rules of the Aṣṭādhyāyī. Based on the senses provided for in P. 5.1.115-117, we classify the occurrences of *vat* in Pāṇini's sūtras. Various interpretations of *vat* have been set forth within and without the tradition (e.g., Bronkhorst 1980). Certain issues also come up within the tradition that would compel modern thinkers to reconsider their arguments pertaining to the interpretation of *vat*. This raises the issue of the translation of *vat*, ambiguities that surround it, and the interpretations of *vat* reflected in the translations.

Based on the three Pāṇinian sūtras (P. 5.1.115-117) that exhaust the possible usages of *vat*, we can see that *vat* which occurs elsewhere across the sūtras is based on P. 5.1.115 and 116. This is because the main function of *vat* in the Aṣṭādhyāyī is extension (*atideśa*). In several cases, one can paraphrase the interpretation of the sūtra and of *vat* that occurs therein based on either of the sūtras P. 5.1.115 and 116. The translation of *vat* would depend on which sūtra-based meaning of *vat* a translator accepts. All the variations that we see in the translations of *vat* are an outcome of this. P. 5.1.115 concerns attributive predicates that are verbal (*kriyā* 'action'), so that the rule disallows *vatI* where *tulya* has scope over a term denoting a quality (*guna*) or thing (*dravya*). P. 5.1.116 is meant for attributive predicates other than actions. But we can still

1. An earlier draft of the paper was divided between main body and the appendices. The appendices included several translations considered and an xls-sheet dealing with the typology of *vat* at various levels. We had to omit them due to space constraints.

derive the sense of action (*kriyā*: 115) in P. 5.1.116, by nominalization of a verbal term expressing an action. Once this is established, we can see why translators differ in their translations.

This paper has 10 principal sections. Sections 1 to 8 cover the various aspects of the discourse on *vat*. Section 9 has the main argument, which traces the roots of differences in translations and interpretations of *vat*, due to ambiguity (section 10). The main function of *vat* being extension, the paper problematizes the idea of a unitary translation of *vat* as either 'same as' or 'as if'. We argue that even in cases where *vat* is absent its function is found to be carried out, so that its occurrence cannot serve as absolute evidence for its unitary meaning.

1 *Vat* in Pāṇini

There are three *vat* suffixes mentioned in the Aṣṭādhyāyī, as follows.

i. In words like *vidyāvat*, the suffix is *matUP*, according to P. 5.2.94 (तदस्यास्त्यस्मिन्निति मतुप्). Its *m* is replaced by *v* (*vat*) in accordance with P. 8.2.9 (मादुपधायाश्च मतोर्वोऽयवादिभ्यः). Words ending in *matUP* are adjectives. P. 8.2.43 (संयोगादेरातो धातोर्यण्वतः) is an example of a sūtra where a word ending in *matUP* has been used.

ii. In words like *yāvat*, the suffix is *vatUP*, used, according to P. 5.2.39-40 (यत्तदेतेभ्यः परिमाणे वतुप् । किमिदंभ्यां वो घः।) in the sense of 'measure'. It can be added to *yad, tad, etad, kim* and *idam*. Words ending in *vatUP* are adjectives. P. 2.4.15 (अधिकरणैतावत्त्वे च) is an example of a sūtra where a word ending in *vatUP* has been used.

iii. In examples like ब्राह्मणवदधीते, मथुरावत् स्रुघ्ने and राजवत्पालनम्, the suffix is *vatI*, according to P. 5.1.115-117 (तेन तुल्यं क्रिया चेद्वतिः, तत्र तस्येव, तदर्हम्). Abhyankar and Shukla's (1977: 339a) entry on *vatI* is as follows:

(1) tad. affix वत् in the sense of similar activity or thing; e.g. राजवद्वर्तते, मथुरावत् स्रुघ्ने प्राकारः ; cf. तेन तुल्यं क्रिया चेद्वतिः। तत्र तस्येव P. V.1.115,116; (2) tad. affix वत् in the sense of deserving; e.g. राजवत् पालनम् ; cf. तदर्हम् P. V.1.117; (3) tad. affix वत् applied to prefixes in Vedic Literature without any sense of its own; e.g. यदुद्वतो निवतो याति बप्सत् ; cf. उपसर्गाच्छन्दसि धात्वर्थे P. V.1.118.

We conceptualize two propositions: 1) 'x is y' or 'x is equal to y' and 2) 'x is y-vat'. We wish to study the second proposition in contrast with the first one, to investigate various shades of meanings that such a proposition using terms with *vat* can deliver and various ways in which it can be understood and translated. Only the third sense (the first two meanings explained in Abhyankar and Shukla) is relevant to such a discussion of 'x is y-vat' in contrast with the proposition 'x is y'. The first two senses, though associated with *vat*, would fall under the type 'x is y', since the word ending in *vat* would then be an adjective.

2 Deliberation on 'x is y'

When a śāstra says 'x is equal to y', there are two possibilities:

i. x has no connection with y in reality. That is why we never hear one say, 'x is x'. For example: (a) That part of a word beginning with its final vowel is called *ṭi*. (b) let *ā, ai* and *au* be called *vṛddhi*.[2]

ii. The śāstra informs us about the identity of x and y in some way, at a deeper level of reality, under the following circumstances: (a) the identity may not appear to hold; for example, तत् त्वम् असि, प्रज्ञानं ब्रह्म (b) we may come to know this from that śāstra itself; for example, कर्तुरीप्सिततमं कर्म (P. 1.4.49).

2. Cf. अचोऽन्त्यादि टि (P. 1.1.64) and वृद्धिरादैच् (P. 1.1.1).

Statements like ‘x is y’ are used by Pāṇini to lay down technical terms in following contexts:

iii. When x is equal only to y and y is equal only to x; for example: यू स्त्र्याख्यौ नदी (P. 1.4.3), क्तक्तवतू निष्ठा (P. 1.1.26), शेषो घ्यसखि (P. 1.4.7).

iv. When we say that x is y, the following may obtain: (a) There is also a chance that w is also y, so that x is one subset in y; for example, उपदेशेऽजनुनासिक इत् (P. 1.3.2); by हलन्त्यम् (P. 1.3.3) a final consonant is also labeled *it*; अर्थवदधातुरप्रत्ययः प्रातिपदिकम् (P. 1.2.45), कृत्तद्धितसमासाश्च । (P. 1.2.46); by the second rule items ending with kṛt and taddhita affixes (*kṛdanta*, *taddhitānta*) as well as compounds also are given the name *prātipadika*. (b) x can also be z, apart from being y. Here one of y or z may be a subset of the other; for example, (P. 1.1.26) *tavyat*, *tavya* and *anīyar* are not only members of the class called *kṛtya* but also of the group called *kṛt*: all kṛtya*s* are kṛt.

When a śāstra says ‘x is y-*vat*’ all the above mentioned relations are to be ruled out.

3 *Vat* in dictionaries

i. Apte (2004: 1383): “वत् *ind.* An affix added to nouns or adjectives to denote ‘likeness’ or ‘resemblance’ and may be translated by ‘like’, ‘as’.”

ii. Monier Williams (2005: 915): “वत् An affix (technically termed वति; see Pāṇ. v,1,115 &c.) added to words to imply likeness or resemblance, and generally translatable by ‘as’, ‘like’ (e.g. *brāhmaṇa-vat,* like a Brāhman; *pitṛi-vat* = *pitêva, pitaram iva, pitur iva* and *pitarîva*).”

Macdonell (1993: 212): “**vat** forms adverbs meaning *like* from substantives and adjectives; e.g. **manu-vát** *like Manu* ; **pūrva-vát, pratna-vát** *as of old.*”

4 Relevant Pāṇinian sūtras

Three sūtras of Pāṇini are relevant in this regard.

i. तेन तुल्यं क्रिया चेद्वतिः (P. 5.1.115). Jijnāsu (2008): तेनेति तृतीयासमर्थात् प्रातिपदिकात् तुल्यमित्यस्मिन्नर्थे वतिः प्रत्ययो भवति यत्तत्तुल्यं क्रिया चेत्सा भवति । ... स्थानिना तुल्यं वर्तते क्रिया = स्थानिवत् ॥ Vasu (2003b: 892): ब्राह्मणेन तुल्यं ब्राह्मणवदधीते । क्रियाचेदिति किम् । गुणतुल्ये मा भूत् । पुत्रेण तुल्यः स्थूलः।

ii. तत्र तस्येव (P. 5.1.116). Jijnāsu (2008): तत्रेति सप्तमीसमर्थात् तस्येति षष्ठीसमर्थाच्च प्रातिपदिकादिवार्थे वतिः प्रत्ययो भवति । Vasu (2003b: 892): मथुरायामिव मथुरावत् स्रुघ्ने प्राकारः। चैत्रस्येव चैत्रवन्मैत्रस्य गावः । A point to be noted here is that the word *kriyā* does not come into this sūtra by anuvṛtti. Hence, the object that is compared when one says *tatra iva* and *tasya iva* may or may not be an action (*kriyā*).

iii. तदर्हम् (P.5.1.117). Jijnāsu (2008): तदिति द्वितीयासमर्थात् प्रातिपदिकात् अर्हणविशिष्टक्रियायां सत्यां वतिः प्रत्ययो भवति । उदा.- राजानमर्हति राजवत्पालनम् । ब्राह्मणवद् विद्याप्रचारः । Vasu (2003b: 893): विधिमर्हति विधिवत्पूज्यते। क्रियाग्रहणं मण्डूकप्लुत्यानुवर्तते । तेनेह न राजानमर्हति छत्रम् । Two points are to be noted here. First, *vatI* by this sūtra is to be added to a nominal which denotes an object something is worthy of, not one to which something is similar. Second, what is worthy of that object is an action. For example: विधिम् अर्हति पूजा = विधिवत् पूजा (विधियोग्या पूजा इति) । राजानम् अर्हति स्थितिः = राजवत्स्थितिः (राजोचिता स्थितिः), but राजानम् अर्हति छत्रम् ≠ राजवत् छत्रम् ।

5 Sūtras considered

There are in all thirty-seven sūtras where words ending in *vat* (*vatI*) occur. Apart from these sūtras, terms with *vat* occur in more than one hundred-fifty others through anuvṛtti. Only the former have been considered in this study.

6 *Vat* and extension

6.1 Atideśa using *vat*

From the examination of the type of sūtras that contain words ending in *vat,* one can easily observe that most of them are extension rules (*atideśasūtra*). Thus, no matter what purpose this suffix serves in the rest of Sanskrit literature, it seems to work as a tool used by Pāṇini for making extension rules. Abhyankar and Shukla (1977: 10b) say the following about atideśa and the role of *vat* therein:

> अतिदेश extended application; transfer or conveyance of application of character or qualities or attributes of one thing to another. Atideśa in Sanskrit grammar is a very common feature prescribed by Pānini generally by affixing the tad. affix मत् (sic) or वत् to the word whose attributes are conveyed to another, e.g. लोटो लङ्वत् P. III 4.85.

The Mahābhāṣya under P. 1.1.56 (Joshi and Roodbergen 1990: ३) also elucidates the purpose of *vat* in atideśasūtras, as follows: वत्करणं किमर्थम्? स्थान्यादेशोऽनल्विधावितीयत्युच्यमाने संज्ञाधिकारो ऽयम् तत्र स्थानी आदेशस्य संज्ञा स्यात् । तत्र को दोषः? आङो यमहनः आत्मनेपदं भवतीति वधेरेव स्यात्, हन्तेर्न स्यात् । वत्करणे पुनः क्रियमाणे न दोषो भवति । स्थानिकार्यमादेशेऽतिदिश्यते । गुरुवद्गुरुपुत्रे इति यथा ।[3]

> "What is the purpose in adding *vat* (in *sthānivat*)? If (the rule) is stated as *sthāny ādeśo 'nalvidhau* 'the ādeśa is

3. Charudeva Shastri (1968: 497) in his commentary on the Mahābhāṣya mentions 7 types of atideśa, namely- nimitta, vyapadeśa, tādātmya, śabda, rūpa, kārya and artha.

sthānin except in a rule (prescribing an operation) conditioned by a speech-sound', (we have to keep in mind that) this is the section dealing with *saṁjñā* 'technical designations'. This being so, *sthānin* would be the designation of the *ādeśa* 'substitute'. This being the case, what is the difficulty? (The difficulty is that) the ātmanepada endings (prescribed) by P. 1.3.28 would be (applied) after (the verbal base) *vadh-* 'to kill' only, not after *han-*. But when we add *vat* (in *sthānivat*), this difficulty is not there. (The effect of adding *vat* is that) an operation applicable to *sthānin* is extended to the substitute, like (we have in) *guruvat guruputre* "towards the son of the teacher (one should behave) like towards the teacher" (Joshi and Roodbergen 1990: 7, 9).

6.2 Atideśa without using *vat*

At several places, atideśa is intended even without using *vat*. For example:

i. बहुगणवतुडति संख्या (P.1.1.23). Here, *saṁkhyā* is a class name (*saṁjñā*) that is assigned to the words *bahu, gaṇa,* words ending in *vatU* and *ḌatI* as well as number words. The term *saṁkhyā* here is anvartha, hence the sūtra is interpreted as बहुगणवतुडति संख्यावत्.

ii. गाङ्कुटादिभ्योऽञ्णिन्ङित् (P. 1.2.1). The meaning of *ṅit* is to be understood as that of *ṅidvat*. Even in असंयोगाल्लिट् कित् (P. 1.2.5) *kit* has the meaning of *kidvat*. This is known from a jñāpaka, as follows. If we do not consider *kit* equivalent to *kidvat*, a second option is to consider P. 1.2.1 a saṁjñāsūtra. P. 1.2.1 is one of a series of sūtras that includes न क्त्वा सेट् (P. 1.2.18). Now, the saṁjñā *kit* was never assigned to *Ktvā*. This tells us that *kit* is to be interpreted as *kidvat*.

7 Translating *vat*

7.1 Translating *vat* ordained by तेन तुल्यं क्रियाचेद्वतिः (P. 5.1.115)

The sentence

(1) He walks **like** an old man

conveys that someone's act of walking is comparable to the walking of an old man. This is an exact equivalent of सः वृद्धवत् चलति । or सः वृद्धः इव चलति । (according to तेन तुल्यं क्रिया चेद्वतिः)

Another way of saying the same thing is

(2) He walks **as if he were** an old man.

However, we cannot say

(3) *He walks **as** an old man.

Nevertheless, one can say

(4) He works **as** a director of a company

but

(5) *He works l**ike** a director of a company

is not acceptable in the same sense.

From the above exercise we can conclude that 'like' is used for indicating similarity in action whereas 'as' indicates similarity in agency. That is why sentence (1) seems to be an exact equivalent of a sentence using a term with *vat*. However, (2) also conveys the same sense by using the words 'if he were' in addition to 'as', thereby equating the agent of the first action with the agent of a second, understood, act of walking, but in a different manner. Sentence (3) does not use 'if he were'. It fails to convey the similarity of action. 'As' in (4) performs the function of equating the agents referred to by 'he' and 'director'. Thus, this is a good English sentence, whereas 'like' in (5) does not perform the same function and so that this sentence is bad. The function of 'like' in such a sentence is to establish similarity in action— as in (1) — whereas the function of 'as' is to establish identity of agents.

7.2 Translating *vat* ordained by तत्र तस्येव (P. 5.1.116)

(1) My shirt is **like that of** Suresh

is an exact equivalent of सुरेशस्य इव मम युतकम् or सुरेशवत् मम युतकम्. *Vat* in this case means 'like that of' (तस्येव).

(2) Just **as in** Gujarat, now there is a water-shortage in Maharashtra too

is an exact equivalent of गुजरातेषु इव अधुना महाराष्ट्रेषु अपि जलस्य अभावः अस्ति or गुजरातवत् अधुना महाराष्ट्रेषु अपि जलस्य अभावः अस्ति. *Vat* in this case means 'as in' (तत्र इव).

7.3 Translating *vat* ordained by तदर्हम् (P. 5.1.117)

(1) He receives king-**like** honor

is an exact equivalent of राजवत् सत्क्रियते अयम्. *Vat* in this case means 'deserved by' (तदर्हम्).

8 Inputs from sāhityaśāstra

Vat never has the meaning of *samāna*. The main import of *vat* being similarity (*sādṛśya*), we now survey three alaṅkāra*s* based on sādṛśya to see the various possible shades of similarity and the means of communicating them.

8.1 Upamā

In Sāhityadarpaṇa, similes (*upamā*) are defined as follows: साम्यं वाच्यमवैधर्म्यं वाक्यैक्य उपमा द्वयोः "Simile is the resemblance between two things expressed in a single sentence and unaccompanied with the statement of difference" (Kane 1995: १७, 89). A simile can be of two types, called *pūrṇā* and *luptā*. The former is defined as follows: सा पूर्णा यदि सामान्यधर्म औपम्यवाचि च । उपमेयं चोपमानं भवेद्वाच्यम् "The simile is fully expressed, when the common property, the word implying comparison, the object of comparison, and the standard of comparison are all expressed" (Kane 1995: १७, 90). If any one or more of these be unexpressed, there is elliptical (*luptā*) upamā. Fully expressed similes are of two types, called *śrautī* and *ārthī*. The verse defining these two types is: श्रौती यथेववाशब्दा इवार्थो

वा वतिर्यदि । आर्थी तुल्यसमानाद्यास्तुल्यार्थो यत्र वा वतिः ॥ "That (*pūrṇā*) again is Direct (*śrautī*) in which the notion of comparison is conveyed by particles, such as *yathā, iva, vā* or by the affix *vat* when it is equivalent to *iva*; it is Indirect (*ārthī*) when the notion of comparison is conveyed by attributive words such as *tulya, samāna* etc. or by the affix *vat* when employed in the sense of *tulya* (equal)" (Kane (1995:१७, 91, 92).

Yathā, *iva* and *vā* express similarity (*sādṛśya*), the relation between two things based on possession of a common property; for example, पद्ममिव मुखम्. By the employment of *iva*, a lotus (*padma*) and a face (*mukha*) are *directly* shown to be related to each other on account of their possessing some common property. The words *tulya* etc., on the other hand, are used in the sense of 'similar' (*sadṛśa* and not *sādṛśya*); e.g., पद्मेन तुल्यं मुखम् conveys that a face is is an object similar to another, a lotus. The idea of *sādṛśya* (possession of common property) is not conveyed directly, but has to be inferred by the listener.[4]

The expressive power of words like *tulya* is exhausted in being attributive to an upamāna when they qualify it. They have no further power to express sādṛśya. It is only after we reflect upon them, considering that two things cannot be comparable unless they have something in common, that we come to know, that there is some sādṛśya between them.

It follows from the above discussion that upamā is śrautī when *vat* is used in the sense of तत्र तस्येव and is ārthī when the suffix is used in the sense of तेन तुल्यं क्रिया चेद्वतिः.

8.2 Rūpaka

Kāvyaprakāśa defines metaphor (*rūpaka*) as follows: तद्रूपकमभेदो य उपमानोपमेययोः । (93) (Sharma 2000: 234). The Sāhityadarpaṇa description is रूपकं रूपितारोपाद् विषये निरपह्नवे "Metaphor consists in

4. As per Kane 1995: 91.

the representation of the subject of description, which (subject) is not concealed, as identified with another (a well-known standard)" (Kane 1995: २२, 114).

There are several similarities and dissimilarities between upamāna and upameya, but, for the sake of depicting close affinity, an identity (*abheda*) is imagined between the two in rūpaka. Both upamā and rūpaka are based on the principle of sādṛśya. However, a clear distinction is shown between upamāna and upameya in upamā, whereas an imaginary (*āhārya*) identity (*abheda*) is established between the two in rūpaka. Similarity is perceived in upamā and identity is perceived in rūpaka. Similarity is literal (*vācya*) in upamā but in rūpaka it is suggested (*vyaṅgya*).

8.3 Utprekṣā

Sāhityadarpaṇa defines utprekṣā as follows: भवेत्सम्भावनोत्प्रेक्षा प्रकृतस्य परात्मना। (Kane 1995: २९, 142).

In utprekṣā a poet sees a strong imaginary possibility (*sambhāvanā*) of something that is inexistent in the thing under consideration. Apart from sambhāvanā, being based on possession of common property (*sādṛśyamūlakatva*) remains a prerequisite for an alaṅkāra to be called *utprekṣā*; for example, लग्ना मन्ये ललिततनु ते पादयोः पद्मलक्ष्मीः। (Sharma 2000: 232).

9 *Vat* in the light of the above discussions

In the proposition 'x is y' considered in section 2, x is an embodiment of various qualities that constitute y. However when we say 'x is y' in the domain of metaphor (*rūpaka alaṅkāra*), the identity established is between two mutually independent entities e.g., the moon (*candra*) and a face (*mukha*). An actual identity between x and y is meant from the proposition 'x is y', discussed in section 2, whereas the identity established to constitute metaphor is imaginary (*kavikalpita* 'conceived by a poet'). The objective behind establishing this kind of identity of x and y is to enhance the beauty of a literary piece. Tradition[5] believes that identity of grammatical entities as proposed by Pāṇini is meant for the function of extension (*atideśa*). The cases of atideśa being intended even without using *vat*, discussed in section 6.2, also tend to substantiate this claim. The sūtra असंयोगाल्लिट् कित् (P. 1.2.5) is interpreted as असंयोगाल्लिट् किद्वत् with the help of a jñāpaka. However, the jñāpaka only prohibits the interpretation of this sūtra as a saṁjñāsūtra. The acceptance of *kit* as *kid-vat* seems to be rooted in common sense or the fact that grammarians do identify grammatical entities to show extension of properties and operations from one to the other.

The issues in question may be illustrated with some examples.[6]

1. P. 4.3.156: क्रीतवत्परिमाणात्

S. C. Vasu: "After a word denoting 'a measure', the affix expressing 'its product or part' is the same as the affix having the sense of purchased."

R. N. Sharma: "A *taddhita* affix occurs after a nominal stem which signifies some measure (*pramāṇa)* and ends in genitive in a manner similar to that of an affix with the signification of *krīta*, provided that the derivate denotes 'modification' and 'part of a whole'."

Here we see that Ramanath Sharma translates *vat* 'in a manner similar to that of' while Vasu simply translates it 'is the same as'.

2. P. 6.2.175: बहोर्नञ्वदुत्तरपदभूम्नि ।

S. C. Vasu: "A Bahuvrīhi with बहु, has the same accent as नञ्, when it denotes muchness of the object expressed by the second member."

R. N. Sharma: "The final constituent of a *bahuvrīhi* compound is accented like *naÑ* when it occurs with *bahu* 'many' used with the signification of its own multiplicity (*bahutva)*."

5 . See Kaiyaṭa's Pradīpa on Bhāṣya under P. 6.4.22 (Shastry 2006: 863).

6. The examples are given together with the translations of S. C. Vasu and R. N. Sharma.

Translations and traditional commentaries when viewed with this background, make us conclude that 'same as', apart from conveying the sense of 'actually same', can also convey the sense of 'metaphorically same'. And metaphors are suggestive of likeness as discussed in section 8.2. Figure 1 elucidates this.

From the discussion about translation of *vat* in the sense of *tulyakriyā* in section 7.1, we conclude that both 'like' and 'as if he/she/it were' are good translations of *vat* ordained by तेन तुल्यं क्रिया चेद्वतिः. However we come to know about a subtle difference between the two translations after surveying the similarity-based alaṅkāras in section 8. With the use of 'like', the sentence 'He walks **like** an old man' becomes an example of śrautī upamā, while using 'as if he were' in 'He walks **as if he were** an old man' is an example of ārthī upamā This subtle difference in translation is observed at many places. For example:

3. P. 8.1.9: एकं बहुव्रीहिवत् ।

S. C. Vasu: "When एक is repeated, it is treated like a member of a *Bahuvrīhi* compound."
R. N. Sharma: "A sequence of two, in place of one whole form of *ekam* 'one', is treated as if it is a *bahuvrīhi* compound."

4. P. 1.2.69: नपुंसकमनपुंसकेनैकवच्चास्यान्यतरस्याम् ।

S. C. Vasu: "A neuter noun, which has the same form, only differing in affix; is optionally retained, and the other is dropped, and it is like a singular number."
R. N. Sharma: "That which denotes neuter remains when it is used with that which denotes non-neuter, provided the difference is due

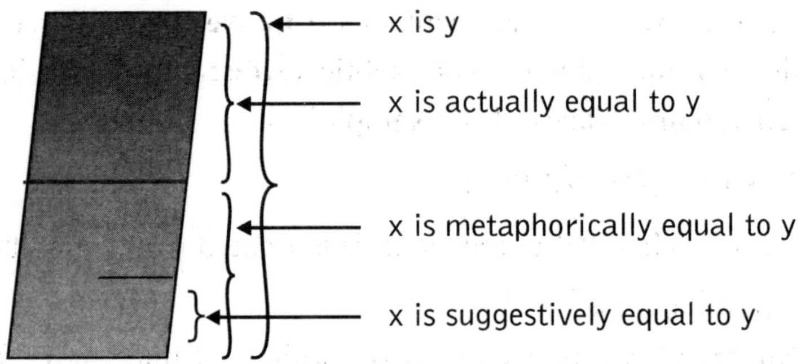
x is y
x is actually equal to y
x is metaphorically equal to y
x is suggestively equal to y

Figure: 1

only to these items. In addition, the neuter is treated optionally as denoting singular."

The sentence हरिः रामवत् गायति is clearly in the domain of the rule तेन तुल्यं क्रिया चेद्वतिः. However, the sixth case is used to indicate many non-kāraka relations as well as two kāraka relations, namely *kartṛ* and *karman*, as in रामस्य गमनम् and चक्रस्य चलनम्. The tradition tells us that the word *kriyā* from तेन तुल्यं क्रिया चेद्वतिः does not get carried over to the immediately following rule (तत्र तस्येव); by maṇḍūkapluti, it gets carried over to the rule which follows the latter, namely तदर्हम्. This helps in making *vat* by तत्र तस्येव available even in case of similarity of nonverbal relations. This also helps in limiting the scope of तदर्हम् only to deserving actions. Had *kriyā* come into the following sūtra by regular *anuvṛtti*, this rule would have included kriyā alone, and the non-kriyā which have to be taken care of by तत्र तस्येव would have been excluded. Thus, going by the given ordering of sūtras, one could argue that blocking of *kriyā* in तत्र तस्येव is for the sake of non-kriyā coming under the scope of this sūtra. Non-kriyā entities are nouns that do not reflect any action: *go, prākāra* etc. and not *gamana, gata* etc.. However, in the case of kṛdanta nominals such as *paṭhanam* or *gamanam* in sentences like रामवत् गणेशस्य गमनम् one could debate over whether (a) *kriyā* of P. 5.1.115 should carry over into P. 5.1.116, so as to include an action expressed by a kṛdantas or (b) a form with *vat* in a sentence such as this stands for non-kriyā alone. The problem with regular anuvṛtti would be that it would include kriyā expressed by finite forms (*tiṅanta*). And the problem with thinking that *vat* in the sentence cited stands for non-kriyā alone is that it includes kriyā expressed by kṛdantas. However, as tradition says, one could maintain that *non-kriyā* (absence of kriyā, as *kriyā* is blocked) means *atiṄ*. So, in sentences like रामवत् गणेशस्य गमनम् it is unclear whether *vat* here is accounted for by virtue of तेन तुल्यं क्रिया चेद्वतिः[7] or तत्र तस्येव. This also creates some differences in translating sūtras. For example:

5. P. 3.4.85: लोटो लङ्वत् ।

S. C. Vasu: "The personal endings of the Imperative are as those of the Imperfect."

R. N. Sharma: "Affix *LOT* is treated as if it were *LAṄ*."

6. P. 6.2.175: बह्वोर्नञ्वदुत्तरपदभूम्नि । (see above, 2)

A subtle difference in the meaning of the above interpretations is that direct similarity as in śrautī upamā is understood from the translation 'as that of' and indirect similarity as in ārthī upamā is understood from the translation 'as if it were'. Acceptance of the accrual of *kriyā* also apart from the non-verbal elements in P. 5.1.116 तत्र तस्येव would have two consequences:

(1) We will have to agree that domains of तेन तुल्यं क्रिय चेद्वतिः and तत्र तस्येव partly overlap. Hence the cases as above can be translated and interpreted in both the ways.

(2) It will help us validate sentences like राजप्रासादवत् गृहे भोजनम् which would otherwise be erroneous according to Pāṇini. It should be noted in this respect that Kāśikā in its comment on आद्यन्तवदेकस्मिन् (1.1.21) says the following: सप्तम्यर्थे वतिः। आदाविव अन्त इव एकस्मिन्निपि कार्यं भवति. It thus clearly supports the accrual of क्रिया also in तत्र तस्येव.

At times various commentators interpret the occurrence of *vat* in Pāṇini's sūtras according to different rules. One classic example of such a case is as follows:

7. P. 1.1.21: आद्यन्तवत् एकस्मिन् ।

7. The sentence can be arrived at with the help of तेन तुल्यं क्रिया चेद्वतिः in the following manner: रामेण तुल्यं गमनं रामवत् गमनम् गणेशस्य।

S. C. Vasu: "An operation should be performed on a single letter, as upon an initial or upon a final."
Comment:[8] आद्यन्तयोः इव एकस्मिन् व्यवहारः आद्यन्तवत् एकस्मिन् (व्यवहारः) (तत्र तस्येव).

S. D. Joshi: "When the question is of (applying a grammatical operation to) one single (phoneme), it is to be treated as if it were the initial (of a sequence) or the final (of a sequence)."
Comment: एकस्मिन् विधौ कर्तव्ये सः एकः आद्यन्ताभ्यां तुल्यम् आचर्येत । (तेन तुल्यं क्रिया चेद्वतिः).

Among Hindi translations only the one by Brahmadatta Jijnāsu has been taken into consideration in this study. A remarkable point in his translation of the sūtras in question is that all the meanings of *vat* that occur in these sūtras by virtue of different *vat*-ordaining sūtras have been tapped in his translations by merely using the phrase *ke samān* on almost at all occasions. This may be due to the power of the phrase *ke samān* in Hindi to encompass all the meanings.

Another striking point is that *vat* according to तदर्हम् does not occur anywhere in the sūtras examined. An obvious reason behind this can be the fact that the sūtra तदर्हम् does not facilitate the function of atideśa, for which *vat* has been used as the tool throughout the Aṣṭādhyāyī.

On many occasions, translators have preferred to give the consequence of a suffix *vat* rather than its translation. This makes it easier for the readers to understand the implication of the sūtra rather than the literal translation. However, a translator's understanding of *vat* in that particular sūtra cannot be understood in such instances.

10 Ambiguity and translations of *vat*

Vat poses an ambiguity for translators. A scrutiny of translations

8. In what follows, all comments are ours unless otherwise noted.

gives an insight into how translators have understood and interpreted *vat*. We try to assign a sūtra-ordained sense to each translation and interpretation of *vat*. Ambiguity or difference in interpretations seen in the translations is at the root of how scholars translate the sūtras. On the literal level one translation is convincing, while, having considered the implications, another is convincing. Considering implications and translating should be a result of the intent to make the sense of a sūtra obvious, thus making it easier for the reader to understand.

Translators end up giving different translations or interpretations because they deal with the sūtra either literally or after having considered the consequences or implications of a literal understanding. It becomes important in translating sūtras to consider whether to translate literally or to consider first the implications of a literal translation. That pretty much determines what interpretation of *vat* is reflected in a translation

11 Conclusions

Even the absence of *vat* in several instances carries out its function, atideśa, so that a unitary meaning of *vat* based on occurrences as evidence, cannot be established.

Translations of *vat* vary mainly because translators either translate literally or consider first the consequences and implications of a translation. Translations, therefore, do not really deal with the essential, literal and residual sense of *vat*. Translations vary also because of the two main different paraphrases and interpretations of *vat* which are possible, based on either P. 5.1.115 or P. 5.1.116.

If *vat* is interpreted as showing similar actions, that is, a pada-generative process (*prakriyā)*, P. 5.1.115 (तेन तुल्यं क्रिया चेद्वति:) takes precedence and if *vat* is interpreted as showing attributive similarity, then P. 5.1.116 (तत्र तस्येव) takes precedence.

References

Abhyankar, K. V. and J. M. Shukla

1977 *A Dictionary of Sanskrit Grammar.* Second edition. Gaekwad's Oriental Series 134. Baroda: Oriental Institute.

Apte, Vaman Shivaram

2004 *The Practical Sanskrit-English dictionary*. Revised and enlarged edition. Delhi: Motilal Banarasidass.

Böhtlingk, Otto

1887 *Pāṇinis Grammatik, herausgegeben übersetzt und mit verschiedenen Indices versehen.* Leipzig: Haessel. [Reprinted with foreword by Prem Singh and preface by Albrecht Wetzler, Delhi: Motilal Banarsidass, 1998]

Bronkhorst, Johannes

1980 Asiddha in the Aṣṭādhyāyī: a misunderstanding among the traditional commentators? *Journal of Indian Philosophy* 8: 69-85.

Jijnāsu, Brahmadatta.

1977-2008 *Aṣṭādhyayī-bhāṣya-prathamāvṛtti.* Three Volumes. Sonipat: Ramlal Kapoor Trust

Joshi, S. D. and Roodbergen, J. A. F.

1990 *Patañjali's Vyākaraṇa-Mahābhāṣya: Sthānivadbhāvāhnika Part I, Edited with Translation and Notes*. Pune: Bhandarkar Oriental Research Institute.

Joshi, S. D. and Roodbergen, J. A. F.

1991-2007 *The Aṣṭādhyāyī of Pāñini with Translation and Explanatory Notes.* Thirteen Volumes. New Delhi: Sahitya Akademi.

Kane, P. V.

1965 *Sāhityadarpaṇa* [*Parichedas I, II, X Arthālaṅkāras*] *with Exhaustive Notes.* Delhi: Motilal Banaridas. [Reprinted 1995]

Macdonell, Arthur. Anthony

1916 *A Vedic Grammar For Students.* London: Oxford University Press. [Indian reprint, Delhi: Motilal Banaridass, 1993]

Monier-Williams, Monier

1899 *A Sanskrit-English Dictionary Etymologically and Philologically Arranged with Special Reference to Cognate Indo-European Languages.* Oxford: Clarendon Press. [Indian reprint, Delhi: Motilal Banaridass, 2005]

Sharma, Aryendra, Khanderao Deshpande and D. G. Padhye

1969-70 *Kāśikā* (*A commentary on Pāṇin's Aṣṭādhyāyī*) *by Vāmana & Jayaditya.* Two volumes. Sanskrit Academy Series 17, 20. Hyderabad: Sanskrit Academy, Osmania University. [Reprinted, in one volume, Sanskrit Academy Series 62, 2008]

Sharma, H.

2000 *Śrīmammaṭaviracitaḥ Kāvyaprakāśaḥ Nāgeśvarīṭīkayā Samalaṅkṛtaḥ.* Varanasi: Chaukhambha Sanskrit Sansthan.

Sharma, Rama Nath

1990-2003 *The Aṣṭādhyāyī of Pāṇini ... English Translation ... with Sanskrit Text, Transliteration, Word-boundary, Anuvṛtti, Vṛtti, Explanatory Notes, Derivational History of Examples and Indices.* Five volumes. Delhi: Munshiram Manoharlal. [Volumes II-VI]

Shastri, Charudeva

1968 *Vyākaraṇamahābhāṣya* (*prathama-navāhnika*). New Delhi: Motilal Banarasidass.

Shastri, Guruprasad
2006 *Vyākaraṇamahābhāṣyam* Vol. 7. Delhi: Rashtriya Sanskrit Sansthan. [Reedition by Bal Shastri]

Tripathi, Ramsagar
1983 *Ācāryaśrīmammaṭpraṇītaḥ Kāvyaprakāśaḥ*. Delhi: Motilal Banaridass.

Vasu, Śrisa Chandra
1891 (2003a) *The Aṣṭādhyāyī of Pāñini, Edited and Translated into English*. Two Volumes. Allahabad: The Pāṇini Office. [Reprinted, Delhi: Motilal Banaridass, 2003]

1905-07 (2003b) *The Siddhanta Kaumudī of Bhattoji Dīkṣita, Edited and Translated into English*. [Reprinted, Delhi: Motilal Banaridass, 2003]

स वाचको विशेषाणां संभवाद् द्योतकोऽपि वा

सुबोध शर्मा

भगवान् पाणिनिः 'सुप्तिङन्तं पदम्'[1] इति सूत्रद्वारा प्रकृतिप्रत्ययसमुदायरूपं द्विविधं पदविभागं स्वीचकार। क्वचित् प्रकृतिमात्रस्यापि शास्त्र-प्रक्रियानिर्वाहाय पदसंज्ञां मनुते।[2] प्राचीनाचार्यास्तु चतुर्विधं पदविभागं स्वीकृतवन्तः। तथाहि – 'चत्वारि वाक्परिमिता पदानि' इति ऋग्वेदे[3], 'तद्यान्येतानि चत्वारि पदजातानि नामाख्याते चोपसर्गनिपाताश्च तानीमानि भवन्ति' इति च निरुक्ते[4] उक्तम्। अत एव च महाभाष्ये – 'चत्वारि पदजातानि नामाख्यातोपसर्गनिपाताश्च'[5] इत्युक्तम्। मीमांसाशास्त्रेऽपि 'चतुर्विधे पदे चात्र'[6] इति निर्दिष्टम्।

तत्र नामपदेन सुबन्तं गृह्यते, नमति = आख्यातार्थं प्रति विशेषणीभवतीति व्युत्पत्तेः। आख्यातपदेन च तिङन्तस्य ग्रहणं भवति, यथा – 'आख्यातमाख्यातेन क्रियासातत्ये'[7] इत्यत्र। उपसर्गपदेन च उपसर्गाः क्रियायोगे'[8] इति सूत्रेण बोधिता उपसर्गसंज्ञकाः प्रादयो गृह्यन्ते। निपातशब्देन च निपातसंज्ञकमव्ययपदं गृह्यते। पाणिनिमते निपाता अपि अव्ययत्वात् सुबन्ता एवेति तेषां न पृथग्ग्रहणम्। प्रादीनामपि 'प्रादयः'[9] इति निपातत्वादव्ययेन सुबन्तत्वमेवेति पाणिनिना द्विविधमेव पदं स्वीकृतम्।

अथ सुबन्तं तिङन्तं वा अधिकृत्य भगवान् पाणिनिः नाना सूत्राणि प्रणिनाय। निपातार्थविवेकाय च न तथा प्रणीतवान्। अतोऽत्र विषये विद्वांसः स्वस्वयुक्तिभिः निपातार्थविषये कृतपरिश्रमाः भवन्ति। निपाता द्योतका वाचका वेत्यत्र विदुषां विसंवादो भवति। अत एव च ममापि निपातार्थविमर्शाय प्रवृत्तिर्जाता।

---

1 *पा.सू.* 1.4.14

2 'नः क्ये' *पा.सू* 1.4.15, 'सिति च' *पा.सू.* 1.4.16, 'स्वादिष्वसर्वनामस्थाने' *पा.सू.* 1.4.17

3 *ऋ.वे.* 1.64.45 उद्धृ. *म.भा.पस्पशा* (1.17)

4 *नि.* 1.1.1

5 *म.भा.पस्प* (1.18)

6 *मी.द.* 1.3.9 *तन्त्रवार्त्तिके* (पृ. 306)

7 *ग.सू., पा.सू.* 2.1.72

8 *पा.सू.* 1.4.59

9 *पा.सू.* 1.4.58

निपातशब्दः 'अर्शआदिभ्योच्'[10] इत्यच्प्रत्ययान्तः = अनेकेष्वर्थेषु निपातोऽस्ति येषां ते निपाताः। निपतनं निपात इति भावघञन्तनिपातशब्दादचि सति निपातशब्दस्य निष्पत्तिः। अथवा ज्वलादित्वात् 'ज्वलिति कसन्तेभ्यो णः'[11] इति कर्तरि णप्रत्ययः = निपतन्ति अनेकेष्वर्थेष्विति निपाताः, 'उच्चावचेष्वर्थेषु निपतन्ति'[12] इति निरुक्तात्। अन्वर्थसंज्ञाविज्ञानायैव तत्र भवता भगवता पाणिनिना महती संज्ञा कृता – 'प्राग्रीश्वरान्निपाताः'[13] इति। निपतन्ति उच्चावचेषु = अनेकेषु अर्थेषु' इति निपाताः।

निपातविषये शास्त्रकाराणां विदुषां वैमत्यं भवति। केचिन् निपातानां द्योतकत्वं स्वीकुर्वन्ति। केचिच्च वाचकत्वमङ्गीकुर्वन्ति। केचिदुभयं द्योतकत्वं वाचकत्वञ्चाङ्गीकुर्वन्ति। केचिच्च केषाञ्चिन्निपातानां द्योतकत्वमेव, केषाञ्चिन्निपातानां वाचकत्वमेवेति। संग्रहग्रन्थः, महाभाष्यम्, वाक्यपदीयं वा व्याकरणशास्त्रस्याकरग्रन्थो भवति। तत्रैते सर्वे सम्भाविताः पक्षाः चर्चिताः ध्वनिताः वा सन्ति। तदुक्तम् – 'सर्ववेदपारिषदं हीदं शास्त्रं तत्र नैकः पन्थाः शक्य आस्थातुम्'।[14]

तत्र प्रथमं निपातस्य द्विधा विभागः कल्प्यते प्राद्युपसर्गरूपः तदतिरिक्तश्च। भाष्यकारो भगवान् पतञ्जलिः उपसर्गातिरिक्तनिपातानां द्योतकत्वं वाचकत्वञ्च स्वीकरोति। तथाहि – महाभाष्ये प्रारम्भे 'अथ शब्दानुशासनम्'[15] इत्यत्र 'अथेत्ययं शब्दाऽधिकारार्थः प्रयुज्यते' इत्युक्तम्। अत्र श्रीकैयटः – 'अधिकारः प्रस्तावो द्योत्यत्वेनास्य प्रयोजनमित्यर्थः। निपातानाञ्च द्योतकत्वं वाक्यपदीये निर्णीतम्'[16] इत्युवाच। अनेन निपातानां द्योतकत्वमायाति। 'अधिकारार्थः' इत्यनेन अधिकारः वाच्योऽर्थः इति नागेशः, 'परेत्वत्र वाचकत्वमेवेच्छन्ति। अधिकृतमिति च तदर्थं वदन्ति।'[17] इत्युक्तेः। उपर्युक्तविवेचनेन निपातविषये द्योतकत्वं वाचकत्वञ्चोभयमायाति। 'अव्ययं विभक्ति'[18] इति सूत्रे भाष्ये भाष्यकारः – 'इह कस्मान्न भवति – सुमद्राः सुमगधाः, सपुत्रः सच्छात्र इति। समृद्धौ साकल्य इति च प्राप्नोति। नैष दोषः। इह कश्चित् समासः पूर्वपदार्थप्रधानः, कश्चिदुत्तरपदार्थप्रधानः, कश्चिदन्यपदार्थप्रधानः, कश्चिदुभयपदार्थप्रधानः। पूर्वपदार्थप्रधानोऽव्ययीभावः,

---

[10] *पा.सू.* 5.2.127

[11] *पा.सू.* 3.1.140

[12] *नि.* 1.2.1

[13] *पा.सू.* 1.4.56

[14] *मा.भा.* 2.1.58 (2.634)

[15] *म.भा.पस्पशा.* (1.1)

[16] *म.भा.पस्पशा. प्र.टी.* (1.2)

[17] *म.भा.पस्पशा. उ.टी.* (1.3)

[18] *पा.सू.* 2.1.6

उत्तरपदार्थप्रधानस्तत्पुरुषः, अन्यपदार्थप्रधानो बहुव्रीहिः, उभयपदार्थप्रधानो द्वन्द्वः। नचात्र पूर्वपदार्थप्राधान्यं गम्यते'[19] इत्युक्त्वा अनन्तरम् – 'अथवा नेमे समासार्थाः निर्दिश्यन्ते। किं तर्हि? अव्ययार्थाः इमे निर्दिश्यन्ते। एषु अर्थेषु यदव्ययं वर्तते तत्सुबन्तेन सह समस्यते'[20] इति उक्तवान्। 'अव्ययार्थाः इमे' इत्यनेन निपातानां वाचकत्वम् आयाति।

अत्र कैयटः – 'अव्ययस्य श्रुतत्वादन्तरङ्गत्वात्तस्यैव विभक्त्यादयो विशेषणानि। तत्र यदोत्तरपदार्थावच्छिन्ना समृद्ध्यादयः प्रतिपिपादयिषिता भवन्ति तदाऽव्ययं समृद्ध्यादीनां वाचकमिति तेषां तदर्थता भवति। सुमद्रा इत्यत्र तु मद्रशब्द एव समृद्धिविशिष्टमर्थमाह, सुशब्दस्तु समृद्धिद्योतको न तु वाचकः। सपुत्र इत्यत्रापि सहशब्दस्तुल्ययोगस्य वाचकः न तु साकल्यस्य'[21] इति व्याख्याति। तदनेन स्पष्टमायाति यन्निपातानां द्योतकत्वं वाचकत्वञ्च लक्ष्यानुरोधात् स्वीक्रियते। 'नञ्'[22] इत्यत्र 'किंप्रधानोऽयं समासः? इत्युक्तम् महाभाष्ये[23]। तत्र पूर्वपदार्थापेक्षयैव उत्तरपदार्थप्रधान्यं स्यात्। अतो नञः वाचकत्वमायाति। 'अब्राह्मणम्' इत्यादौ आरोपितब्राह्मणम् इत्यर्थः। अत्र आरोपितार्थः द्योत्य एव। यदि आरोपितत्वं नञ्वाच्यं भवेत् तदा 'अब्राह्मणम्' इत्यत्र आरोपानारोपयोर्विरुद्धत्वेन बोधो न स्यात्।

उपसर्गाणान्तु द्योतकत्वमेवेति सूचितम् 'गतिर्गतौ'[24] इति सूत्रे। तथाहि – 'इहापि तर्हि न प्राप्नोति–' अभ्युद्धरति, समुदानयति, उपसमादधाति। अत्रापि नाऽभेरुदं प्रति क्रियायोगः। किं तर्हि? हरतिं प्रति क्रियायोगः। नैष दोषः। उदं प्रति क्रियायोगः। कथम्? उत् हरतिक्रियां विशिनष्टि। उदा विशिष्टाम् अभिः विशिनष्टि। तत्र 'यत् क्रियायुक्ता' इति भवत्येव संघातं प्रति क्रियायोगः। इहापि तर्हि मन्द्रसाधना क्रियाऽऽङाभिव्यज्यते – 'आयाहि मन्द्रै'रिति। ननु पूर्वं धातुरूपसर्गेण युज्यते पश्चात् साधनेनेति। नैतत् सारम्। पूर्वं धातुः साधनेन युज्यते पशचादुपसर्गेण। किं कारणम्? साधनं हि क्रियां निर्वर्तयति तामुपसर्गो विशिनष्टि[25]। अत्र प्रघट्टके – 'अभिव्यज्यते, विशिनष्टि' इत्यादिकथनेन उपसर्गाणां द्योतकता स्पष्टतयैव आयाति।

---

19 *म.भा.* 2.1.6 (2.569–570)

20 *म.भा.* 2.1.6 (2.570)

21 *म.भा.* 2.1.6 *प्र.टी.* (2.570)

22 *पा.सू.* 2.2.6

23 *म.भा.* 2.2.6 (2.666)

24 *पा.सू.* 8.1.70

25 *म.भा.* 8.1.70 (5.345–346)

एवमेव च 'सुट् कात् पूर्वः'[26] इत्यत्रापि 'धातूपसर्गयोः कार्यं यत्तदन्तरङ्गम्। कुत एतत्? पूर्वं हि धातुरूपसर्गेण युज्यते पश्चात् साधनेनेति। नैतत् सारम्। पूर्वं धातुः साधनेन युज्यते पश्चादुउपसर्गेण। साधनं हि क्रियां निर्वर्तयति तामुपसर्गो विशनष्टि'[27] इत्यादिना उपसर्गाणां द्योतकतैव सूच्यते। 'अधिपरी अनर्थकौ'[28] इत्यत्र 'अनर्थान्तरवाचिनौ अनर्थकौ, धातुनोक्तां क्रियामाहतुः तदविशिष्टं भवति' इति भाष्यम्।[29] धात्वर्थमात्रस्य द्योतकौ इत्यर्थः। 'भूवादयो धातवः'[30] इत्यत्र 'क्रियाविशेषक उपसर्गः'[31] इति वार्त्तिकव्याख्याने उपसर्गाणां क्रियाविशेषद्योतकत्वं स्पष्टमेव स्वीकृतम्। तथाहि – 'पचतीति क्रिया गम्यते, तां प्रो विशिनष्टि। . . . तिष्ठतीति व्रजिक्रियायाः निवृत्तिः, प्रतिष्ठत इति व्रजिक्रिया गम्यते। ते मन्यामहे उपसर्गकृतमेतत् येनात्र व्रजिक्रिया गम्यते। . . . बह्वर्था अपि धातवो भवन्ति।'[32] एतेन प्रघट्टकेन उपसर्गाणां द्योतकत्वमेव आयाति।

वैयाकरणधौरेयाः श्रीमन्तः कैयटमहानुभावाः निपातसामान्यस्य द्योतकत्वमङ्गीकुर्वन्ति। एते भाष्यकृद्वचनस्य 'अथेत्ययं शब्दोऽधिकारार्थः प्रयुज्यते'[33] इत्यस्य व्याख्यानं कुर्वाणाः प्रतिपादयन्ति यत् 'अधिकारार्थः' इत्यत्र अर्थशब्दः प्रयोजनपरकः। एवञ्च अधिकार = प्रस्तावः द्योत्यत्वेन प्रयोजनं यस्य सः तादृशः अर्थशब्दः प्रयुज्यते इति। एवञ्च निपातस्य अथशब्दस्य द्योतकत्वं भाष्यकृदभिप्रेतमिति एतेषामाशयः। नैतावन्मात्रं किन्तु समेषां निपातानां द्योतकत्वमङ्गीकुर्वाणा एते तत्र वाक्यपदीयकर्तुः निर्णयं संवदन्ति। तथाहि – 'निपातानां च द्योतकत्वं वाक्यपदीये निर्णीतमिति'[34]। यद्यपि निपातानां द्योतकत्वपक्ष एव कैयटेभ्यो रोचते। तथाऽपि उपसर्गातिरिक्तनिपातानां क्वचिद् वाचकत्वमपि समर्थयन्ति। 'अव्ययं विभक्तीति'[35] सूत्रे – 'अथवा नेमे समासार्थाः निर्दिश्यन्ते। किं तर्हि? अव्ययार्था इमे निर्दिश्यन्ते। एष्वर्थेषु यदव्ययं वर्तते तत्सुबन्तेन सह समस्यते'[36] इति भाष्यव्याख्यानसमये – 'तत्र यदोत्तरपदार्थावच्छिन्नाः समृद्ध्यादयः प्रतिपिपादयिषिता

---

[26] *पा.सू.* 6.1.135

[27] *म.भा.* 6.1.135 (4.4.77)

[28] *पा.सू.* 1.4.93

[29] *म.भा.* 1.4.93 (2.463)

[30] *पा.सू.* 1.3.1

[31] *म.भा.* 1.3.1। *का.वा.* 7

[32] *म.भा.* 1.3.1 (2.184–185)

[33] *म.भा.पस्पशा.* (1.1)

[34] *म.भा.पस्पशा.प्र.टी.* (1.2)

[35] *पा.सू.* 2.1.6

[36] *म.भा.* 2.1.6 (2.570)

भवन्ति, तदाव्ययं समृद्ध्यादीनां वाचकम् इति तेषां तदर्थता भवति' इत्यत्र स्पष्टमेव वाचकत्वम् उक्तवन्तः। उपसर्गाणान्तु द्योतकत्वम् एव 'भूवादयो धातवः'[37] इति सूत्रे 'क्रियाविशेषक उपसर्गः'[38] इति वार्त्तिकव्याख्यानावसरे 'इह तर्हि व्यक्तमर्थान्तरं गम्यते–तिष्ठति–प्रतिष्ठत इति। तिष्ठति इति व्रजिक्रियाया निवृत्तिः, प्रतिष्ठत इति व्रजिक्रिया गम्यते। ते मन्यामहे – 'उपसर्गकृतमेतद्येनात्र व्रजिक्रिया गम्यते' इति। प्रोऽयं दृष्टापचारः आदिकर्मणि वर्तते' इति भाष्यस्थं 'प्रोऽयमिति' प्रतीकमादाय 'अन्यत्रापि प्रयोगात्। ततश्च अन्यत्रास्य योऽर्थो द्योत्यः स एवेहापि इत्यनुमीयते। अनेकार्थत्वाद् धातूनां तिष्ठतिरेव गतिवाचीति निर्णयः'[39] इत्युक्तवन्तः। 'गतिर्गतौ'[40] इति सूत्रे 'प्रयोक्ता विशिष्टायाः क्रियायाः साधनेन सम्बन्धं प्रतिपादयितुं सोपसर्गसमुदायं प्रयुङ्क्ते। . . . परमार्थतो धतूपसर्गसङ्घात एव क्रियावाची पृथगुपदेशस्तु धातूपसर्गयोरडादिव्यवस्थार्थः। तदनेन नूनमुपसर्गाणां द्योतकत्वं सम्मतं कैयटमते। अथापि अधिकांशस्थले द्योतकत्वपक्षस्यैव समर्थनाद् द्योतकत्वमेव सर्वत्र एतन्मते सम्मतमिति भाति।

हरदत्तादिमतेऽपि द्योतकत्वमेव निपातानाम् तथा हि – 'अधिकारः प्रस्तावः = प्रारम्भः। तमथशब्दो द्योतयति।'[41] 'पूर्वप्रक्रान्तस्य वाक्यस्य अन्यथात्वद्योतनाय आकारः प्रयुज्यते।'[42] 'निवृत्तिपदार्थकोऽत्र ब्राह्मणशब्दः, सा च निवृत्तिः स्वाभाविकी नञा द्योत्यते'[43]।

श्रीमन्तो नागेशभट्टपादा अपि उपसर्गातिरिक्तनिपातानां द्योतकत्वं वाचकत्वञ्चाङ्गीकुर्वन्ति। अमी हि 'अथ शब्दानुशासनम्'[44] इत्यत्र 'निपातानां द्योतकत्वम्' इति प्रदीपप्रतीकमादाय अन्यथा व्याचक्षते – निपातानां द्योतकत्वञ्चेत्यर्थः। उपसर्गातिरिक्तनिपातानां द्योतकवाचकत्वोभयस्वीकारस्याव्ययं विभक्तीति सूत्रे भाष्ये स्पष्टत्वात्। उपसर्गाणान्तु द्योतकत्वमेवेति स्पष्टं गतिर्गताविति सूत्रे भाष्ये इति तत्रैव निरूपयिष्यामः। अत एव साक्षात् क्रियते गुरुरित्यादि संगच्छते[45]' इति। अनेन उद्योतव्याख्यानेन एतेषां मते निपातानां द्योतकत्वं वाचकत्वञ्च नूनं समर्थितं भवति। अपि च एतेषां मते अविशेषेण निपातानां

---

[37] *पा.सू.* 1.3.1

[38] *म.भा.* 1.3.1। *का.वा.* 7

[39] *म.भा.* 1.3.1 *प्र.टी.*

[40] *पा.सू.* 8.1.70.

[41] *का.वृ.प.टी.* अथ शब्दानु. (1.7)

[42] *का.वृ.प.टी.* 1.1.14 (1.133)

[43] *का.वृ.प.टी.* 2.2.6 (2.105)

[44] *म.भा.पस्पशा.* (1.1)

[45] *म.पस्पश.उ.टी.* (1.3)

वाचकत्वं द्योतकत्वञ्चोभयमपि सम्मतम्। तथाहि – 'अव्ययं विभक्ति'[46] इति सूत्रस्थप्रदीपप्रतीकमादाय 'निपातानां द्योतकत्वं, वाचकत्वञ्च, लक्ष्यानुरोधाच्च व्यवस्थेति भाव:'[47]। गतिर्गताविति सूत्रभाष्योद्योते – 'आङाभिव्यज्यत इत्यनेन द्योतकत्वपक्षं सूचयति'[48]। प्राग्रीश्वरान्निपाता:' इति सूत्रे शेखरे – 'एषां द्योतकत्वं वाचकत्वञ्च यथा कार्यं यथा प्रयोगं बोध्यमित्यन्यत्र विस्तर:'[49], 'एषां = प्रादीनां चादीनाञ्च'[50]। 'निपातानां द्योतकत्वं वाचकत्वञ्चेत्यत्रैव भाष्ये स्पष्टम्'[51] इत्यादिवचनै: श्रीमतां नागेशभट्टपादानां निपातविषये द्योतकत्वं वाचकत्वञ्चोभयमभिप्रेतम् इति स्पष्टमेव। परमलघुमञ्जूषायां निपातार्थनिर्णयावसरे एते लिखन्ति 'यद्यपि केचिच्छाब्दिका निपातानां वाचकत्वे 'शोभन: समुच्चय:' इतिवत् 'शोभनश्च' इत्यापत्ति:, 'घटस्य समुच्चय:' इतिवत् 'घटस्य च' इत्यापत्तिश्चेत्याहुस्तन्न'[52] अनेन कथनेन स्पष्टमेव चादिनिपातविषये वाचकत्वे श्रीनागेशस्य सम्मतिरायाति। 'उपसर्गाणां द्योतकत्वं तदितरनिपातानां वाचकत्वम्' इति नैय्यायिकमतं 'वैषम्ये बीजाभावात्'[53] इत्युक्त्वा खण्ड्यते तदनेनेदमेव प्रतिभाति यत् इतरनिपातां द्योतकत्वं वाचकत्वं वा लक्ष्यानुसारमस्तु इत्यत्र नाग्रह:, कश्चनापि पक्ष: समाश्रयितुं शक्यते तर्हि कथं वैषम्यं स्वीक्रियते। अनेन निपातविषये द्योतकत्वं वाचकत्वं वा समर्थितं भवति।

वैयाकरणसिद्धान्तमञ्जूषायां निपातार्थस्य अन्ते नागेश: प्रतिपादयति – 'वस्तुतस्तु निपातानां शक्तिं गृहीतवतो लक्षणाद्यज्ञानेऽपि बोधात् तच्छक्तिज्ञानकार्यकारणभाव आवश्यक:। एवं शक्तिमजानतां लक्षणाज्ञानेनैव बोधात् कार्यकारणभावोऽप्यावश्यक इति द्योतकत्वं शक्तत्वञ्चेत्युभयमपि निपातानामिति मतनिष्कर्ष:'[54]। उपसर्गाणान्तु द्योतकत्वमेव 'आङाऽभिव्यज्यते' इति 'गतिर्गतौ' इति भाष्यप्रामाण्यात्। यद्यपि एभिर्व्याख्यानै: ज्ञायते यत् उपसर्गातिरिक्तनिपातानां द्योतकत्वं वाचकत्वञ्चोभयमपि सम्मतं नागेशस्य तथापि मञ्जूषादौ भूयोभूयो द्योतकत्वपक्षस्यैव समर्थनात् मन्यामहे द्योतकत्वपक्ष एव नागेशस्याभिमत:।

---

[46] *पा.सू.* 2.1.6

[47] *म.भा.* 2.1.6 *उ.टी.* (2.570)

[48] *म.भा.* 8.1.71. *उ.टी.* (5.346)

[49] *ल.श.शे.सं.प्र.* (1.144)

[50] *ल.श.शे.सं.प्र.ज्यो.टी.*(1.114)। *ल.श.शे.ना.प्र.टी.*(पृ. 132–33) – एषां = प्रादीनां चादीनाञ्चेत्यर्थ:। . . . एतेन उपसर्गाणां द्योतकत्वं तद्भिन्ननिपातानां वाचकत्वमितिनैयायिकोक्तम् अर्द्धजरतीयानौचित्येवन सर्वेषां द्योतकत्वं वाचकत्वमिति दीक्षिताद्युक्तञ्च परास्तम्।

[51] *ल.श.शे.अव्ययीभावप्र.* (2.798)

[52] *प.ल.म.नि.नि.* (पृ. 116)

[53] *प.ल.म.नि.नि.* (पृ. 115)

[54] *वै.सि.मञ्जूषानि.नि.* (पृ. 54)

द्योत्यार्थमादायैव सर्वत्र समन्वयः कार्यः। निपातानां द्योतकत्वादेव वैयाकरणैः व्यञ्जनावृत्तिः स्वीकृतेति।

नैयायिकमतखण्डनम्

निपातार्थविषये शाब्दिकानां कृते प्रधानप्रतिवादिरूपेण नैयायिकाः प्रत्यवतिष्ठन्ते। एतन्मते उपसर्गाणां द्योतकत्वं तदितरनिपातानां तु वाचकत्वमेव भवति। एवञ्च 'अनुभूयते सुखम्' 'उपास्यते गुरुः' इत्यादौ भूधातोरेवानुभवार्थकत्वम्। अतोऽनुभवार्थे भूधातोः उपासनार्थे च आस्धातोः सकर्मकत्वात् कर्मणि लकारो न विरुध्यते। उपसर्गाणां वाचकत्वे तु अनुभवाद्यर्थस्य धात्वर्थकत्वाभावात् उपर्युक्तप्रयोगे कर्मणि लकारो नोपपद्यते। अपि च तेषां वाचकत्वे अनुगच्छतीत्यादावपि अनुभवाद्यर्थाऽनुभवानुपपत्तिश्च भवेत्। उपसर्गातिरिक्तनिपातानान्तु - 'साक्षात् प्रत्यक्षतुल्ययोः'[55] इत्याद्यमरकोषप्रामाण्यात् नूनं वाचकत्वमङ्गीकार्यमिति तेषामभिप्रायः।

अत्रेयं शङ्का जायते यत् 'साक्षात् क्रियते गुरुः' इत्यत्र कर्मणि लकारो भवति। एवञ्च कर्मणः तिङाभिहितत्वात् तत्र प्रथमा भवति। यदि तु उपसर्गेतरनिपातानां वाचकत्मेवास्थीयते तर्हि साक्षात् शब्दस्यैव साक्षात्काररूपार्थाभिधायकत्वात् कृधातोः सकर्मकत्वम् न स्यात्। यतो हि सकर्मकत्वं नाम स्वार्थफलव्यधिकरणव्यापारवाचकत्वम्। एवञ्च साक्षात्काररूपस्यार्थस्य साक्षादिति निपाताभिधेयतया तस्य कृधात्वर्थत्वाभावेन स्वार्थकत्वाऽभावः। एवञ्च 'साक्षात् क्रियते गुरुः' इत्यत्र कृधातोः सकर्मकत्वाऽभावेन कर्मणि लकारानुपपत्तेः कर्मणोऽनभिधानात् तत्र प्रथमाविभक्तेरनुपपत्तिः स्यादिति।

अत्र नैयायिकाः समादधति यत् सकर्मकत्वं नाम स्वस्वसमभिव्याहृतनिपातान्यतरार्थफलव्यधिकरणव्यापारवाचकत्वम्। एवञ्च 'साक्षात् क्रियते गुरुः' इत्यत्र साक्षात्कारार्थस्य कृधात्वर्थकत्वाऽभावेऽपि स्वसमभिव्याहृतसाक्षादिति निपातार्थकतया तादृशान्यतरार्थफलकत्वेन तद्व्यधिकरणव्यापारवाचकत्वस्य कृधातौ सत्त्वेन कर्मणि लकारस्य सूपपादत्वम्। एवञ्च कर्मण्यभिहिते प्रथमायाः सुतरामुपपत्तिर्भवति। एवञ्च उपसर्गाः द्योतकाः, द्योतकतावच्छेदकञ्चोपसर्गत्वम्। तदितरनिपाताः वाचकाः वाचकतावच्छेदकञ्च निपातत्वम् इति नैयायिकानामाशयः।

अत्रेदं विचार्यताम् - उपसर्गाणां द्योतकता उपसर्गवृत्तिधर्मावच्छेदेन वाच्यम्, स च धर्म उपसर्गत्वं निपातत्वञ्च। तत्र निपातत्वं व्यापकम्, चादिवाचकतावच्छेदकत्वेन क्लृप्तञ्चेति तदवच्छेदेनैव द्योतकत्वं वाच्यम्। तथाहि न्यायनये कार्यमात्रं प्रति अदृष्टस्य साधारणकारणत्वं स्वीक्रियते। तत्र च व्यापकत्वात् कार्यत्वमेव कार्यताच्छेदतयाङ्गीक्रियते न तु

[55] अ.को. 3.3.243

घटत्त्वादिकम्। तथा सति विनिगमनाविरहात् पटत्वादिकमादाय अनन्तकार्यकारणभावः प्रसज्यते। एवञ्च प्रकृतेऽपि समेषां निपातानामनुगतरूपेण द्योतकत्वं वाचकत्वं वाभ्युपेयम्। निपाता द्योतकाः निपातत्वात् उपसर्गवत्। अत्र जातिरूपमुपाधिरूपं वा पक्षतावच्छेदकं, संकेतसमेबन्धेन निपातपदवत्वं हेतुरिति पक्षतावच्छेदकहेत्वोर्नैक्यमिति न व्याप्त्यग्रहत्वादिदोषः। अत्रेदन्तु नाशङ्कनीयं यत् पादपूरणार्थके 'च वा ह' इत्यादौ द्योतकत्वस्यासत्त्वात्, निपातत्वस्य च सत्वाद् व्यभिचार इति, वाचकत्वाभावरूपस्य द्योतकत्वस्य साध्यत्वेन विवक्षणात्। तस्य च पादपूरणार्थके चादावपि सत्त्वेन दोषाभावात्।

अथास्य दोषस्य निरसनाय नैयायिकाः प्रतिपादयन्ति यत् – यत्र बहवः व्याप्यधर्माः व्यापकधर्मश्चैकोऽवच्छेदकत्वेन उपस्थितो भवति, तत्र गौरवात् अननुगतत्वाच्च बहूनां व्याप्यधर्माणामवच्छेदकत्वं नोचितम्। किन्त्वेकस्यैव व्यापकधर्मस्यावच्छेदकत्वं युज्यते। यत्र तु एक एव व्याप्यो धर्मः, एक एव च व्यापको धर्मः, तत्र व्याप्यधर्मस्यैवावच्छेदकत्वं स्वीक्रियते। तस्यान्यूनानतिप्रसक्तत्वात् गौरवाभावाच्च। अत एव मीमांसकैरपि द्रव्यचाक्षुषं प्रति उद्भूतरूपं कारणं तत्र च कार्यतावच्छेदकं व्याप्यं द्रव्यचाक्षुषत्वमेव न तु द्रव्यप्रत्यक्षत्वम्। किञ्च निपातत्वं पादपूरके निपातेऽपि विद्यते। तत्र च द्योतकत्वरूपस्य साध्यस्यासत्त्वेन अतिप्रसक्तत्वात् निपातस्यावच्छेदकत्वं न युज्यते। अतः 'प्रादयो द्योतका उपसर्गत्वात्' इत्यनुमानेन प्रादीनां द्योतकत्वमिति नैयायिकाः।

'निपाता द्योतका निपातत्वात्' इतयनुमानं तु न निर्दुष्टम्, उपसर्गस्योपाधेर्विद्यमानत्वाद् हेतोः सोपाधिकत्वात् व्याप्यत्वासिद्धेर्जागरुकत्वात्। यतो हि यत्र यत्र द्योतकत्वं तत्र तत्र नैयायिकमते उपसर्गत्वमिति साध्यव्यापकता यत्र यत्र निपातत्वं तत्र तत्रोपसर्गत्वमिति तु वक्तुं न शक्यते चादौ व्यभिचारादिति साधनाव्यापकतेति उपसर्गस्योपाधित्वं सुस्पष्टं प्रतिभाति।

अत्रेदं चिन्तनीयम् – प्रकर्षादिः प्रादिवाच्यः प्राद्यन्वयव्यतिरेकानुविधायिशाब्द-बुद्धिविषयत्वात्, घटशब्दान्वयव्यतिरेकानुविधायिघटपदवाच्यघटरूपार्थवत्। एवञ्च प्रजयति इत्यादौ जयादेः धातुवाच्यत्वम्, प्रकर्षादेस्तु प्रादिवाच्यत्वम्। प्रकर्षस्य स्वरूपसम्बन्धेन जयार्थेऽन्वयः नामार्थधात्वर्थयोश्च साक्षाद्भेदसम्बन्धेनान्वयस्याव्युत्पन्नतया तद्विरोधपरिहारः निपातातिरिक्तत्वनिवेशेन करणीय इति वैयाकरणाक्षेपपरिहाराय नैयायिकेनोच्यते प्रजयतीत्यादौ कथञ्चिदुपपत्तावपि 'प्रतिष्ठते' इत्यत्र प्रशब्दस्य अभावरूपोऽर्थो वाच्यः, तस्य च गमनाभावधात्वर्थं प्रति विशेष्यतयैव भानमभ्युपगम्यत इति धात्वर्थगतविशेषकत्वात् 'प्र' इत्यत्र उपसर्गत्वमेव व्याहन्यते। अतः उपसर्गाणां द्योतकता एवेति नैयायिकसिद्धान्तः।

यद्यपि द्योतकतापरपर्याया व्यञ्जनावृत्तिर्न्यायनये नाङ्गीक्रियते, तथापि एतन्मते द्योतकत्वं नाम स्वसमव्याहृतपदगतवृत्त्युद्बोधकत्वरूपम्। एवं च प्रजयतीत्यादौ धातोः प्रकर्षादिविशिष्टे

जये लक्षणा भवति। प्रपदन्तु तात्पर्यग्राहकं भवति। 'प्रतिष्ठते' इत्यत्र तु धातूनामनेकार्थत्वात् गमनार्थकत्वं तद्गतादित्वस्य च प्रशब्दद्योत्यत्वमुपपद्यते। एवञ्च न्यायनये उपसर्गाणां द्योतकत्वं तदितरनिपातानाञ्च वाचकत्वं स्थिरीभवति एवञ्च अनुभूयते सुखम्, साक्षात्क्रियते गुरुः इत्यादौ कर्मणि लकार उपपद्यत इति।

किन्तु विचार्यतां – यश्चायं परिष्कारः सकर्मकत्वस्य स्वीकृतः – स्वस्वसमभिव्याहृत – निपातान्यतरार्थफलव्यधिकरणव्यापारवाचकत्वमिति तत्र 'प्रयागात् काशीं गच्छति चैत्रे' इत्यत्र उत्तरदेशसंयोगानुकूलो यो व्यापारः तत्प्रयोज्यं यत् विभागरूपं फलं, तदाश्रयः प्रयाग इति तस्य कर्मत्ववारणाय कर्मलक्षणे व्यापारप्रयोज्यफलशालित्वमित्यत्र फले धात्वर्थत्वं निवेशनीयम्। तथा सति 'साक्षात्क्रियते गुरुः' इत्यत्र साक्षात्काररूपफलस्य निपातार्थत्वाद् धात्वर्थत्वाभावात्, तादृशधात्वर्थफलाश्रयत्वाभावात् गुरोः कर्मत्वं नोपपत्तिमञ्चति। वैयाकरणमते तु अविशेषेण निपातमात्रस्य द्योतकत्वाङ्गीकारणे साक्षात्काररूपफलस्यापि धात्वर्थतया गुरोः कर्मत्वं निर्बाधमुपपद्यत इति नैतद्दूषणम्। अतोऽविशेषेण द्योतकत्वमेव समादरणीयमिति वैयाकरणसम्प्रदायः।

द्योतकत्वे मीमांसकसम्मतिः

निपातानां द्योत्यार्थकत्वे मीमांसकानामपि सम्मतिरस्त्येव। तथाहि – भट्टपादैराकृत्यधि करणे मीमांसाभाष्ये तन्त्रवार्त्तिके[56] प्रोक्तम् –

> गौरित्येवंविधाः शब्दाः साधुत्वेन निरूपिताः।
> तेषामेवाभिधेयेऽर्थे व्यापारः क्वेति चिन्त्यते।।
>
> चतुर्विधे पदे चात्र द्विविधस्यार्थनिर्णयः।
> क्रियते संशयोत्पत्तेर्नोपसर्गनिपातयोः।।
>
> तयोरर्थाभिधाने हि व्यापारो नैव विद्यते।
> यदर्थद्योतकौ तौ तु वाचकः स विचार्यते।। इति ।

अयमाशयः – पदानां चातुर्विध्यम्–नामाखायातोपसर्गनिपातरूपं भवति। तत्र नाम्नः आख्यातस्य चेति द्विविधस्यैव पदार्थस्यार्थनिर्णयः क्रियते, तत्रैव संशयोदयात्। संशयाकारश्च–नामार्थः जातिर्व्यक्तिर्वा? धात्वर्थः व्यापारः, फलम्, तदुभयं वा? इत्येवमादिरूपः। यच्चोपसर्गरूपं पदम्, तत्र संशय एव नोदेतुमर्हति – कस्तावन्निपातार्थः? को वा उपसर्गार्थः? इत्येवंरूपः। अर्थाभिधाने उपसर्गनिपातयोः शक्तिरूपो लक्षणारूपो वा व्यापारो नैव विद्यत इति कथमिव तत्र संशयः उदीयान्नाम। संदेहापाकरणाय एव

---

56 *मी.द.* 1.3.9 *तन्त्रवार्त्तिके* (पृ. 306)

वाक्यप्रयोगनियमात्। नाम्न आख्यातस्य वा वाचकभूतस्य प्रतिपाद्यो यो विषयः, तस्यैव द्योतकत्वमनयोः निपातोपसर्गयोः विद्यत इति नामाख्यातयोरेवोक्तसंदेहापाकरणायार्थनिर्णयो मीमांसकैः प्रक्रान्तः। अत्र 'उपसर्गनिपातयोः' इति प्रयोगो ब्राह्मणवसिष्टन्यायेन कृतो बोध्यः। एवञ्च मीमांसकानां मतेऽपि निपातानां द्योतकत्वमेवेति प्रतीयते।

द्योतकत्ववादे शाकटायनमतम्

'न निर्बद्धाः उपसर्गाः अर्थान्निराहुरिति शाकटायनः'।[57] उपसर्गाः = प्रादयः, निर्बद्धाः = निर् निष्कृष्य, (नामाख्यातमध्यात्) बद्धा = पदवाक्यरूपेण रचिताः सन्तः अर्थान् न निराहुरिति शाकटायन आचार्यो मन्यते।[58] तर्हि उपसर्गा अर्थवन्तः कथमिति जिज्ञासायाम् उक्तम् – 'नामाख्यातयोस्तु कर्मोपसंयोगद्योतका भवन्ति'[59]। नामाख्यातयोरेव यत्कर्म = योऽर्थः तत्रैव = तदाश्रयमेव उपसंयोगेन = उपसर्गनिमित्तेन द्योतकाः भवन्ति।

हरिसम्मतपक्षत्रयम्

वैयाकरणानां निकाये आचार्याणां ग्रन्थेषु निपातार्थविषये त्रयः पक्षा विवेचिता दरीदृश्यन्ते। तत्र प्रथमः पक्षः निपातानां विशेषार्थद्योतकत्वमित्यायाति। यथा – 'अनुभवति' इत्यत्र उपसर्गस्यानुभवार्थद्योतकत्वम्। यदुक्तं हरिणा –

> क्वचित् सम्भविनो भेदाः केवलैरनिदर्शिताः।
> उपसर्गेण सम्बन्धे व्यज्यन्ते प्रपरादिना।।[60] इति

अत्र 'व्यज्यन्ते' इत्यनेन उपसर्गाणां धात्वर्थद्योतकत्वं नितरामायाति।

तत्र तत्रोपसर्गाणां विशेषार्थवाचकत्वमपि चर्चितमस्ति। स चायं द्वितीयः पक्षः। यथा – 'प्रतिष्ठते' इत्यत्र गतिनिवृत्तिः स्थाधातोरर्थः। प्रोपसर्गस्य च गत्यर्थोऽभिधेयः। तदुक्तं वाक्यपदीये – 'स वाचको विशेषाणाम्'[61] इति

तृतीयः पक्षस्तु – सहितौ धातूपसर्गौ सहैव विशिष्टमर्थं ब्रूतः। एवञ्च विशिष्टार्थाऽभिधाने उपसर्गाणां सहकारित्वमिति। तथाहि प्रजयतीत्यादौ प्रकर्षविशिष्टं जयं धातूपसर्गौ सहैव प्रतिपादयतः। तदिदमुक्तम् –

---

57 *नि.* 1.1.4

58 *नि.वृ.* 1.1.4 (म.म. पण्डित श्रीमुकुन्दझाशर्मकृतनिरुक्तविवृत्तिः)

59 *नि.* 1.1.4

60 *वा.प.* 2.187

61 *वा.पा.* 2.188

शक्त्याधानाय धातोर्वा सहकारी प्रयुज्यते।[62]

यद्यपि त्रयोप्येते पक्षाः शास्त्रे चर्चिता दरीदृश्यन्ते किन्तु तत्रोपसर्गाणां विशेषार्थद्योतकत्मेव सिद्धान्तितम्। एवञ्च प्रतिष्ठते इत्यत्र धातूनामनेकार्थत्वेन प्रकरणादिना अनुमानप्रयोगेण च स्थाधातोरेव गत्यर्थकत्वं भवति। प्रशब्दस्तु तादृशस्य विलक्षणार्थस्य द्योतकत्वमात्रं कुरुते। तदिदं सिद्धान्तवचनमाचार्यैः आस्थीयते –

स्थादिभिः केवलैर्यच्च गमनादि न गम्यते।
तत्रानुमानाद् द्विधात् तद्धर्मा प्रादिरुच्यते।।[63]

एवञ्च गतिनिवृत्तिः प्रसिद्धशक्त्या स्थाधातुनाऽभिधीयते इत्युक्तशक्त्या केवलेन धातुना गमनरूपोऽर्थो नाभिधीयते। किन्तु धातूनामनेकार्थत्वादनुमानप्रयोगेणाप्रसिद्धशक्त्या तस्य गतिवाचकत्वं न विरुध्यते। एवञ्चानुमानगम्यस्य एतादृशस्य धात्वर्थस्य द्योतनमात्रमुपसर्गः कुरुते। तत्र प्रथमानुमानप्रकारः – धातुरनेकार्थः, धातुत्वात् उभयवादिसम्मतानेकार्थयज्धातुवद् इति। द्वितीयानुमानप्रकारश्च – प्रशब्दो द्योतकः प्रशब्दत्वात् प्रपचतीत्यादौ दृष्टप्रशब्दवदिति। अनेन प्रकारेण पक्षत्रयमाश्रितमाचार्यैः। तथापि द्योत्यार्थे एव हरिसम्मतिः, तस्यैव भूयोभूयः समर्थनात्। इयमेव सरणिः उपसर्गेतरनिपातेऽपि विद्यते। अत्रापि त्रयः पक्षा शास्त्रे विवेचिताः सन्ति। क्वचित् निपाताऽभिसम्बन्धेन विशेषार्थद्योतकत्वमभिहितम्। कुत्रचिन्निपातानां स्वातन्त्र्येण वाचकत्वमभिहितम्। अन्यत्र च विशिष्टार्थाभिधाने उपसर्गेतरनिपातानां सहकारित्वं प्रतिपादितम्। तदिदम संकलितम् भर्तृहरिणा –

निपाता द्योतकाः केचित् पृथगर्थाभिधायिनः।
आगमा इव केऽपि स्युः सम्भूयार्थस्य वाचकाः।[64] इति।

एवं विवेचनेन इदं तावत् प्रतिभाति यत् उपसर्गाणामिव तदितरनिपातानामपि द्योतकत्वमेव भर्तृहरिपादेभ्यो रोचते।

चादयो न प्रयुज्यन्ते पदत्वे सति केवलाः।
प्रत्ययो वाचकत्वेऽपि केवलो न प्रयुज्यते।।[65]

श्रीमन्तः भट्टोजिदीक्षितमहाभागाः शब्दकौस्तुभे भूषणकारिकादौ च निपातार्थविषये पर्याप्तं विवेचितवन्तः। शब्दकौस्तुभस्य प्रारम्भे 'अथ शब्दानुशासनम्' इति महाभाष्यवाक्यस्य 'अथ' शब्दं प्रकृत्य निपातसामान्यस्यार्थनिरूपणाय सत्तर्कयुक्त्युपस्थापनपुरःसरं श्रीदीक्षितः

---

[62] *वा.प.* 2.188

[63] *वा.प.* 2.189

[64] *वा.प.* 2.192

[65] *वा.प.* 2.194

अथेति निपातस्य प्रारम्भरूपार्थद्योतकत्वं प्रतिपादयन् निपातसामान्यस्य उपसर्गवत् वाचकत्वभावं व्यवस्थापयन् द्योतकत्वं स्थिरीकरोति।

अनुभवतीत्यादौ प्रतीयमानोऽनुभवादिरूपोऽर्थः धातूनामेव, उपसर्गस्तु तत्रार्थे तात्पर्यग्राहकत्वेन द्योतको भवति। अत एव 'अनुभूयते सुखम्' इत्यादौ स्वार्थफलव्यधि करणव्यापारवाचकत्वेन कर्मणि लकारः सिद्ध्यति। एवमेव 'साक्षात्क्रियते गुरुः' इत्यादावपि साक्षात्काराद्यर्थः धातोरेव, साक्षादिति निपातस्य तु तादृशार्थद्योतकत्वमात्रम्। अत एव कर्मणि लकारादिः सिद्धयति।[66] 'राममिव पश्यामि' इत्यादावपि रामादिपदस्यैव सादृश्यविशिष्टार्थः इवशब्दस्तु तत्र तात्पर्यग्राहकतया द्योतकः। उपसर्गाणामिव तुल्ययुक्त्या तदितरनिपातानामपि द्योतकत्मेवास्थेयमिति भावः।

उपसर्गातिरिक्तनिपातानां वाचकत्वमेवेति नैयायिकोक्तं तु न समीचीनम्। वैषम्ये बीजाभावात् ततश्च व्यापकधर्मावच्छेदेन द्योतकताकल्पनमपि साधीयः, प्रमाणानां सामान्ये पक्षपातात्। तथा च उपसर्गत्वापेक्षया व्यापकं निपातत्वम्, अखण्डोपाधिरूपमस्तु, जातिरूपमस्तु, शब्दरूपं वास्तु। एतत्त्रितयपक्षेऽपि प्रादिष्विव चादिष्वपि समं विद्यते। किञ्च निपातत्वं प्रत्वादिप्रत्येकं पर्यवस्यति। अतोऽपि चादिभ्यः प्रादिषु किमपि वैलक्षण्यं न विद्यते। एवमेव उपसर्गद्योत्यार्थस्य यथा अन्यलभ्यत्वेन केवलस्योपसर्गस्याप्रयोगः तथैव केवलं तदितरनिपातानामप्यप्रयोगान्न किमपि हेतुं पश्यामो येनैकस्य द्योतकत्वमपरस्य तु वाचकत्वं प्रतिपाद्येत। तदुक्तम् –

> चादयो न प्रयुज्यन्ते पदत्वे सति केवलाः।
> प्रत्ययो वाचकत्वेऽपि केवलो न प्रयुज्यते।।[67]

यथा 'विजयते' इत्यत्र विशिष्टजये लक्षणामङ्गीकुर्वता उपसर्गस्य द्योतकता स्वीकृता, तथैव 'घटश्च' इत्यत्रापि घटशब्दस्य समुच्चितघटे लक्षणाङ्गीकर्तव्येति नैयायिकेनापि उपसर्गाणामिव तदितरनिपातानामपि द्योतकत्वमङ्गीक्रियताम्। यच्च नैयायिकैः समानाधि करणप्रातिपदि- कार्थयोरभेदातिरिक्तः सम्बन्धोऽव्युत्पन्न इति व्युत्पत्तौ निपातेतरत्वेन संकोचनमादृतं तदपि प्रमाणानुपलम्भादकिञ्चत्करम्।

किञ्च यथा समुच्चयादिशब्दप्रयोगो 'घटस्य समुच्चय' इत्येवं षष्ठी भवति तथैव चादीनां वाचकत्वाङ्गीकारे चशब्दप्रयोगेऽपि षष्ठी आपद्यते। तदर्थं शब्दशक्तिस्वभावेन चादीनां परतन्त्रत्वं स्वीकरणीयं स्यात्। द्योतकतावादिनां नये चादिद्योत्यस्य समुच्चयस्य पदार्थैकदेशत्वात् तत्र विशेषणसम्बन्ध आपादयितुं न शक्यते। 'पदार्थः पदार्थेनान्वेति न

[66] *वै.भू.सा.का.* 42–43

[67] *वा.प.* 2.194

तु पदार्थैकदेशेन' इत्युक्तेः।

वाचकतावादिनां मते अपरोपि दोषः प्रसज्यते। तथाहि रघुवंशे उक्तम् –

ततः प्रतस्थे कौवेरीं भास्वानिव रघुर्दिशम्।
शरैरूस्रैरिवोदीच्यान् उद्धरिष्यन् रसानिव।।[68]

अस्यार्थः – पश्चिमदिग्विजयानन्तरं रघुः भास्वानिव उस्रसदशैः शरैः रससदृशान् उदीच्यान् राज्ञः उद्धरिष्यन् कौबेरिम् = उदीचीं दिशं प्रतस्थे इति। एषोऽर्थ उस्रादिशब्दस्य उस्रसदृशादिरूपार्थपरत्वे सत्येव उपपद्यते। ततश्च इवेति निपातस्य तादृशार्थद्योतकत्मेव। यदि तु निपातानां वाचकत्वं स्वीक्रियते तर्हि प्रत्ययानां प्रकृत्यर्थान्वितस्वार्थबोधकत्वमिति व्युत्पत्तिविरोध आपद्यते। तथा हि – उस्रैरिति करणे तृतीया किन्तु उदग्देशीयराजोद्धरणक्रियायामुस्राणां करणत्वं नास्ति, अपितु शराणाम्। इवार्थसदृशस्य करणत्वेऽपि उस्रपदोत्तरतृतीयया तस्य बोधो न भवति, अप्रकृत्यर्थत्वात्। यतोहि तृतीयायाः प्रकृतिरुस्रशब्दः, सादृश्यञ्च न प्रकृत्यर्थः, किन्तु इवार्थः। एवञ्च वाचकत्पक्षे दूषणं भवति। उस्रादिशब्दानामुस्रादिसदृशे लक्षणाङ्गीकारे तु सादृश्यस्य प्रकृत्यर्थत्वेन नोक्तव्युत्पत्तिविरोधः।

अत्र नैयायिकाः वदन्ति – इवपदोत्तरं लुप्ततृतीयायाः अर्थः करणं, तत्र इवार्थस्यान्वयेन नोक्तव्युत्पत्तिविरोध इति। किन्तु असत्त्वार्थकस्य इव शब्दस्य कारकत्वाऽभावात् दूरापेतं करणत्वमिति 'इव' इत्यत्र तृतीयार्थः करणमित्युक्तिः कथं साधीयसी स्यात्। 'स्वयं कृतम्' इत्यादावपि तृतीयया करणरूपार्थः प्रतीयते इति वक्तुं न शक्यते उक्तयुक्तेः। किन्तु तत्र आत्मकरणार्थरूपोऽर्थः अव्ययस्यैवेति बोध्यम्, अन्यथा उस्रशब्दोत्तरश्रूयमाणतृतीयार्थान्वयस्यानुद्धारः वज्रलेपायितः स्यात्।

इदन्त्ववधेयम् – योऽयं सिद्धान्तः 'उत्तरपदार्थप्रधानस्तत्पुरुषः'[69] इति स नञ्तत्पुरुषस्थले पूर्वपदस्य नञः वाचकत्वाभावात् तदापेक्षिकस्य उत्तरपदार्थस्याभावात् सिद्धान्तभङ्गः, तदापाततः प्रतीयते। वस्तुतस्तु पूर्वपदद्योत्यार्थमादाय तदपेक्षयोत्तरपदार्थप्रसिद्ध्या तत्प्राधान्यस्य सूपपादत्वं भवति। एवञ्च द्योत्यार्थमादायैव अर्थवत्वात् निपातानां प्रातिपदिकत्वमुपपद्यते। द्योत्यार्थमादाय प्रातिपदिकत्वोपपत्तेरेव हेतोः द्योत्यार्थरहितनिपातानां प्रातिपदिकसंज्ञा विशिष्य विहिता– 'निपातस्यानर्थकस्य प्रातिपदिकसंज्ञा वक्तव्या'[70] इति। निपातानां द्योत्यार्थराहित्ये

[68] *रघु.म.का.* 4.66

[69] *म.भा.* 2.1.6 (2.570)

[70] *म.भा.* 1.2.45 (2.81)

प्रमाणम् – 'तु हि च स्म वै पादपूरणे'[71] इति कोषवचम्। कमीमिद्विति पादपूरणार्था:'[72] इति निरुक्तं च। तददिं कारिकया संकलितम् –

> नञ्समासे चापरस्य द्योत्यं प्रत्येव मुख्यता।
> द्योत्यमेवार्थमादाय जायन्ते नामतः सुपः।।[73]

वस्तुगत्या शब्दादुपस्थितस्य सामान्यार्थस्य विशेषार्थपर्यवस्थापकत्वमेव द्योतकत्वम्, न तु स्वातन्त्र्येण तदुपस्थापकत्वमिति तेनार्थवत्त्वासम्भवात् प्रातिपदिकत्वं निपातस्य न सम्भवति इति निपातेभ्य लुग्विधानं व्यर्थं सत् अव्ययेभ्यः अर्थवत्त्वाभावेऽपि सुबुत्पत्तिर्भवति इति ज्ञायते। किञ्च 'निपातस्याऽनर्थकस्य प्रातिपदिकसंज्ञा वक्तव्येति वार्त्तिकारम्भः समादृतो भाष्यकारेण अतो न दोषः। अथवा "कृत्तद्धितसमासाश्च"[74]' इति सूत्रे चकारस्यानुक्तसमुच्चयार्थकत्वेन निपातानां संग्रहात् निपातस्येत्यादिवार्त्तिकं सूत्रलभ्यार्थस्यैवानुवादसरूपम्।

अथवा 'अधिपरी अनर्थकौ'[75] इति सूत्रं निपातानामर्थवत्त्वं ज्ञापयति। तथाहि – गत्युपसर्गसंज्ञाबाधनार्थं कर्मप्रवचनीयसंज्ञा क्रियते, किन्तु अनर्थकौ इमौ इत्यनयोः क्रियायोगाभावात् बाध्ययोः संज्ञयोरप्राप्त्या तद्बाधनायारम्यमाणो विधिः व्यर्थं सज्ज्ञापयति, अर्थराहित्येऽपि = विशेषार्थकत्वाभावेऽपि निपातानामर्थवत्प्रयुक्तं कार्यं भवति इति। स्पष्टञ्चेदं प्रकृतसूत्रे भाष्ये। विशेषद्योतकत्वाभावादनर्थावित्युच्यते, धात्वर्थमात्रद्योतकत्वमस्त्येव। एवञ्च – अर्थवत्सूत्रे 'अधीते' इत्यादौ इङ्धातोरनर्थकत्वं केवलस्याप्रयोगात्। किन्तु उपसर्गविशिष्टस्यैव इङोऽर्थवत्त्वम्[76] इत्यादिहरदत्तादिभिरुक्तं तदभ्युच्चयमात्रम्। इङोऽनर्थकत्वे क्रियावाचकत्वाभावात् धातुत्वस्यैव व्याघातः स्यात्। इङ् अध्ययने इत्याद्यर्थनिर्देशश्च सार्थकत्वे प्रमाणम्, उपसर्गस्य तु द्योतकत्वमेव। एवमेव 'सर्वस्य द्वे'[77] इति सूत्रभाष्ये – "इह तर्हि 'परेर्वजने'[78] इत्यन्त्यस्याऽपि द्विवचनेन वर्ज्यमानता गम्यते"[79] इत्यत्र कैयटग्रन्थः

---

71 *अ.को.* 3.4.4

72 *निरु.* 1.3.9 'पदपूरणार्थास्ते मिताक्षरेष्वनर्थकाः कमीमिद्विति'। *श.कौ.* (1.2) 'कमीमिद्विति पादपूरणार्थाः इति निरुक्ताच्च'

73 *वै.भू.सा.का.* 46

74 *पा.सू.* 1.2.46

75 *पा.सू.* 1.4.93

76 *पा.सू.* 1.2.45 पदम, न्यास (1.339–340)

77 *पा.सू.* 8.1.1

78 *पा.सू.* 8.1.5

79 *म.भा.* 8.1.1 (5.280)

'यथाऽन्तरेण द्विर्वचनं परिर्जनार्थः प्रयुज्यते परि त्रिगर्तेभ्यः[80] इत्यादि तदप्यभ्युच्चयमात्रमेव।

उपसर्गेण धात्वर्थो बलादन्यत्र नीयते।
प्राहाराहारसंहार-विहार-परिहारवत्।।[81]

इति वृद्धोक्तिरपि निपातमात्रस्य द्योतकत्वं प्रमाणयति उपसर्गपदस्य निपातमात्रोपलक्षत्वात्, धातुपदस्य च पदान्तरोपलक्षकत्वाच्चेति भावः। एवं दीक्षितमहानुभावो विस्तरेण उपसर्गाणानमिव तदितरनिपातानामपि द्योतकत्वपक्षमेवेति द्रढीकृत्य शब्दकौस्तुभे भूषणकारिकादौ च स्थापयति।

किन्तु अन्ततो गत्वा निपातमात्रस्य वाचकत्वमिति पक्षमप्युभयत्रापि ग्रन्थे भट्टोजिदीक्षिताः अभिनन्दयन्ति। वैयाकरणभूषणकारिकायां यथा – 'निपातानां वाचकत्वमन्वयव्यतिरेकयोः।'[82] शब्दकौस्तुभे यथा – 'अस्तु वा मतान्तरम् निपाताः वाचका'[83] इति द्योतकत्वपक्षे च अस्वारस्यं व्यञ्जयन्ति। तथाहि – चन्द्र इव मुखं दृश्यते इति इवपदसमभिव्याहारे तादृशार्थः प्रतीयते। तदभावे तु न प्रतीयते इत्यन्वयव्यतिरेकाभ्यां निपातसामान्यस्य वाचकत्वमेव युज्यते। तथा च अनुमानप्रयोगः – निपाताः वाचकाः स्वसमभिहारप्रयोज्यार्थप्रतीतिकत्वात्। अत्र पक्षतावच्छेदकावच्छेदेन अनुमितिरुद्देश्या पक्षतावच्छेदकसामानाधिकरण्येण वा? आद्ये पक्षतावच्छेदकव्यापकत्वस्य हेतौ भाननियमात्, अनर्थकनिपाते निपातत्वस्य विद्यमानतया व्यभिचारः। अन्त्ये च हेत्वभावरूपोभागासिद्धस्य दुरुद्धरत्वम् इति।

तत्रेदं प्रतिसमाधानम् – सत्यम्, अवच्छेदकावच्छेदेन दोषस्यानुद्धारात् पक्षतावच्छेदक-सामानाधिकरण्येनैवानुमितिरिष्यते। तत्र च भागातिद्धिः दोषाय न कल्पत इत्युक्तानुमानेन निपातानां वाचकत्वमायाति। न च बोधकत्वरूपशक्तेः बाधः केनापि प्रमाणेन लभ्यते।

उपर्युक्तयोरन्वयव्यतिरेकयोः तात्पर्यग्राहकत्वेनापि उपपत्तिः सम्भवतीति न ताभ्यां वाचकत्वमायातमिति तु नाशङ्कनीयम्, यतो हि प्रकर्षविशिष्टस्य जयरूपार्थस्य धात्वर्थत्वम्, उपसर्गस्य तु तात्पर्यग्राहकत्वमात्रमित्येवाङ्गीकारे तुल्ययुक्त्या धातोरेव कर्तृविशिष्टभावनायां लक्षणास्वीकारेण तिङादेरपि तात्पर्यग्राहकत्वमङ्गीकरणीयं स्यात्। एवञ्च अन्वयव्यतिरेकाभ्यामभिमतं यत् तिङां वाचकत्वं तद्दुष्यते। अतुस्तुल्ययुक्त्या तिङामिव निपातानामपि वाचकत्वमेवैष्टव्यम्।

---

80 *म.भा.प्र.टी.* 8.1.1 (5.280)

81 *वै.सि.कौ.* (3.154) 'उपसर्गेण धात्वर्थो बलादन्यः प्रतीयते'इति *वै.भू.सा.नि.नि.* पृ. 377–78

82 *वै.भू.सा.का.* 47

83 *श.कौ.पस्पशा* (1.2)

यच्च वाचकत्वपक्षे धात्वर्थप्रातिपदिकार्थयोः भेदेनान्वयबोधोऽव्युत्पन्न इति समानाधिकरण- प्रातिपदिकार्थयोरभेदेनान्वय इति च व्युत्पत्तिद्वयस्य विरोध उक्तः स गत्यन्तराभावात् निपातातिरिक्तविषयत्वेनोभयत्रसंकोचात् परिहरणीयः। एवमन्येऽपि दोषाः नैयायिकरीत्यैवा- ऽपाकरणीयाः। इदन्तु नाशङ्कनीय यत् निपातानां वाचकत्वे केवलानामपि प्रयोग आपद्यते, गत्युपसर्गसंज्ञयोः 'ते प्राग्धातोः'[84] इति सूत्रेण नियमात् केषाञ्चित् केवलप्रकृतिप्रत्ययवत् उपपत्या केवलानां प्रयोगाभावात्। किञ्च 'न' इत्यादीनां कतिपयनिपातानां केवलानामपि प्रयोग इष्यते एव। तदिदं समर्थितं भर्तृहरिणाऽपि -

प्रत्ययो वाचकत्वेऽपि केवलो न प्रयुज्यते।
समुच्चयाभिधानेऽपि व्यतिरेको न विद्यते।।[85]

यच्च दूषणं वाचकत्वपक्षे – शोभनः समुच्चयः इत्यर्थे 'शोभनश्च' इत्यापत्तिरूपम्, घटस्य समुच्चयः इत्यर्थे 'घटस्य च' इत्यापत्तिरूपञ्च। तदपि निराकृतं भवति। तथा हि – एष शब्दशक्तिस्वभावो यत् निपाता नित्यपरतन्त्रा अन्यपदार्थविशेषणत्वेनैव स्वार्थम् उपस्थापयन्तीति प्रथमापत्तिर्निराकृता भवति। एवं षष्ठ्यर्थसम्बन्धबोधं प्रति भेदेनान्वयबोधं प्रति च निपातेतरजन्यायाः उपस्थितेर्हेतुत्वोपगमेन द्वितीयापत्तिर्निराकृता भवति।

एतदुक्तं भवति – नैयायिकाः उपसर्गाणां द्योतकत्वं तदितरनिपातानां वाचकत्वमित्युररीकुर्वन्ति। किन्तु ययैव युक्त्योपसर्गाणां द्योतकत्वं तैरङ्गीक्रियते तयैव युक्त्या तदितरनिपातानामपि द्योतकत्वमङ्गीकर्तुं शक्यते। किन्तु प्रकारान्तरेण सम्भावितदूषणानामुद्धारप्रयत्नेन चादिप्राद्योः कस्यचित् वैशम्यस्यासत्त्वेऽपि चादीनां वाचकत्वानङ्गीकरणं तदितरनिपातानां वाचकत्वमिति न युज्यते। अतः तुल्ययुक्त्या समेन पथा प्रादीनामिव चादीनामपि द्योतकतैवाविशेषेण स्वीकरणीयेत्येवं रीत्या दीक्षितादीनां प्रादिचाद्युभयसाधारणं द्योतकत्मेवेष्टम्। तथापि 'तुष्यतु दुर्जनः' इति न्यायेन यदि चान्वयव्यतिरेकादिना वाचकता अभ्युपगन्तव्या तर्हि सैवाऽविशेषेण निपातमात्रे अङ्गीक्रियताम्। वाचकत्पक्षेऽपि दोषाणामुद्धारो भवत्येव। अत एव उपसर्गं प्रक्रम्येदम्, 'प्रतिष्ठते' इत्यत्र 'गतिनिवृत्तिवाचकः स्थाधातुः, उपसर्गस्तदभावरूपगतिवाचकः पुण्यराजः।[86]' किन्तु केषाञ्चित् द्योतकत्वम् अन्येषान्तु वाचकत्वमिति अर्धजरतींय न समीचीनम्। तदेतत् समाकलितम् -

निपातानां वाचकत्वम् अन्वयव्यतिरेकयोः।
युक्तं वा न तु तद्युक्तं परेषां मतमेव नः।।

[84] *पा.सू.* 1.4.80

[85] *वा.प.* 2.194-195

[86] *वै.भू.सा.द.टी.* (पृ. 382)

निपातत्वं परेषां यत् तदस्माकमिति स्थितः।
व्यापकत्वाच्छक्ततायास्त्ववच्छेकमिष्यते।।[87] इति

वस्तुतस्तु – उपसर्गाणां वाचकत्वं न सम्भवति। तथा हि अन्वयव्यतिरेकाभ्यां जयादिर्धातुवाच्यः, प्रकर्षादिस्तु प्रादिवाच्यः। एवञ्च प्रतिष्ठते इत्यत्र गत्यभावस्य धात्वर्थत्वे गत्यभावाभावस्योपसर्गार्थत्वे न्यायनये तिङर्थाश्रयत्वे गत्यभावाभावस्य अप्रकृत्यर्थतया 'प्रत्ययानां प्रकृत्यार्थान्वितस्वार्थबोध – कत्वम्' इति व्युत्पत्तिविरोधान्न्यायानुपपत्तिः। आद्यगमनरूपस्य प्रस्थानार्थस्य प्रतीत्यभावापत्तिश्च स्यात्। प्रतिष्ठते इत्यत्र प्रशब्दार्थाभावस्य गमनाभाव (गतिनिवृत्ति) रूपधात्वर्थं प्रति विशेष्यतयैव भानात् प्रादेरूपसर्गत्वानापत्तिश्च वज्रलेपायिता।

किञ्च प्रादेरूपसर्गत्वं गतित्वञ्च क्रियायोग एव भवति – 'उपसर्गाः क्रियायोगे'[88] 'गतिश्च'[89] इत्युक्तेः। एवञ्च उपसर्गाणां पृथक्सत्ताभावात् धातोरेव ते तेऽर्थाः स्वीकृताः भवन्ति। उपसर्गास्तु द्योतका एव।

उपसर्गातिरिक्तनिपातास्तु केचिद् वाचकाः केचिच्च द्योतका इति प्रतीयते। वाचका यथा – नञोऽभावो वाच्यः, नञर्थाः षट्प्रकीर्तिताः, इवार्थः सादृश्यम्, अन्ययोगव्यवच्छेदादिः एवकारार्थः। सुजनः इत्यादौ यत्र क्रियावाचकासमभिव्याहारः तत्रोपसर्गत्वाभावात् प्रादीनामपि वाचकत्वमेव। अत एव 'प्रादयः'[90] इति प्रादीनां निपातसंज्ञा क्रियते। तेन 'स्वरादिनिपातमव्ययम्'[91] इति अव्ययसंज्ञा भवति। अत एव तेष्वर्थेषु वर्तमानस्य अव्ययस्याव्ययीभावसमासो भवति। निर्मक्षिकम् इत्यादौ निरित्यस्याभाववाचकता उपकृष्णमित्यादौ च उप इत्यस्य समीपवाचकता।

एवमेव 'आ नो दिवो बृहतः पर्वतात्'[92] पर्वतादर्वाक् इत्यर्थबोधः। अत्र च 'आ' इति निपातस्य वाचकत्वं विना दिगर्थकशब्दयोगाभावेन पञ्चमीविभक्तिः कथं स्यात्।[93]

वाचकताऽपि निपातानां चत्वादिरूपानुपूर्वीरूपेणैव आस्थेया, सामान्यज्ञानं न विशेषबोधोपयोगीति न्यायात्। अत एव आनुपूर्वीरूपेण जानतां निपातत्वेनाजानतामपि बोधो भवत्येव।

---

[87] *वै.भू.सा.का.* 47-48

[88] *पा.सू.* 1.4.60

[89] *पा.सू.* 1.4.61

[90] *पा.सू.* 1.4.58

[91] *पा.सू.* 1.1.37

[92] *ऋ.वे.* 5.43.11

[93] *वै.सि.ल.म.*, द्वि.भा., पृ. 89

एवञ्च सर्वेषां निपातानां द्योतकत्वम्, उपसर्गाणां द्योतकत्वं वाचकत्वञ्चोभयम्, उपसर्गाणां द्योतकत्वमेव तदितरनिपातानां वाचकत्वमेव, अविशेषेण प्रादिचाद्युभयसाधारणं द्योतकत्वमेव वाचकत्वमेव एते पक्षा उपर्युक्तव्याख्यानेन विवेचितम्।

वस्तुतस्तु प्रादिचाद्युभयसाधारणनिपातत्वावच्छेदेन द्योतकत्वं वाचकत्वं वा लक्ष्यानुसारं स्वीकरणीयमिति उपयुक्तं प्रतिभाति। तदुक्तं हरिणा –

> स वाचको विशेषाणां संभवाद् द्योतकाऽपि वा[94]

एतत् सर्वमभिप्रेत्योक्तं भर्तृहरिणा –

> निपाता द्योतकाः केचित् पृथगर्थाभिधायिनः।
> आगमा इव केऽपि स्यु सम्भूयार्थस्य वाचकाः।।[95]

इति शम्।।

संक्षिप्ताक्षरविवरणम्

अ.को.	*अमरकोषः*
का.वृ.प.टी.	*काशिकावृत्तिपदमञ्जरीटीका*
ग.सू.	*गणसूत्रम्*
नि.	*निरुक्तम्*
नि.वृ.	*निरुक्तवृत्तिः*
प.ल.म.नि.नि.	*परमलघुमञ्जूषा निपातार्थनिर्णयः*
पा.सू.	*पाणिनीयं सूत्रम् (अष्टाध्यायीसूत्रपाठः)*
म.भा.	*महाभाष्यम्*
म.भा.उ.टी.	*महाभाष्यम् उद्योतटीका*
म.भा.का.वा.	*महाभाष्यम् कात्यायनवार्त्तिकम्*
मा.भा.पस्प.	*महाभाष्यम् पस्पशाह्निकम्*
म.भा.प्र.टी.	*महाभाष्यम् प्रदीपटीका*

---

94 *वा.प.* 2.188

95 *वा.प.* 2.194

मी.द.	*मीमांसादर्शनम्*
रघु.म.का.	*रघुवंशमहाकाव्यम्*
ल.श.शे.अव्ययीभावप्र.	*लघुशब्देन्दुशेखरः अव्ययीभावप्रकरणम्*
ल.श.शे.ज्यो.टी.	*लघुशब्देन्दुशेखरः ज्योत्सनाटीका*
ल.श.शे.नागेशोक्तिप्र.टीका.	*लघुशब्देन्दुशेखरनागेशोक्तिप्रकाशटीका*
ल.श.शे.सं. प्र.	*लघुशब्देन्दुशेखरः संज्ञाप्रकरणम्*
वै.भू.सा.का.	*वैयाकरणभूषणसारकारिका*
वै.भू.सा.द.टी.	*वैयाकरणभूषणसारः दर्पणटीका*
वै.सि.कौ.	*वैयाकरणसिद्धान्तकौमुदी*
वै.सि.मञ्जूषा	*वैयाकरणसिद्धान्तलघुमञ्जूषा*
वै.सि.ल.म.द्वि.भा.	*वैयाकरणसिद्धान्तलघुमञ्जूषा* द्वितीयभागः
वै.भू.सा.नि.नि.	*वैयाकरणभूषणसारः निपातार्थनिर्णयः*
श.कौ.पस्पशा.	*शब्दकौस्तुभः पस्पशाह्निकः*

उद्धृतग्रन्थविवरणम्

अमरकोषः – चौखम्बासंस्कृतप्रतिष्ठान, दिल्ली, सन् 1985।

अष्टाध्यायीसूत्रपाठः – भार्गवपुस्तकालय, गायघाट, बनारस, सन् 1951।

काशिकावृत्तिः – (न्यासपदमञ्जरीटीकोपेता), सुधीरप्रकाशन, वाराणसी, सन् 1983 (षड् भागाः)।

निरुक्तम् – म.म. पण्डितश्रीमुकुन्दझाशर्म-कृतनिरुक्त-विवृतियुक्तम्, चौखम्बासंस्कृतप्रतिष्ठान, दिल्ली, सन् 2002।

परमलघुमञ्जूषा – महाराजसयाजिरावविश्वविद्यालयः, बड़ौदा, सन् 1961।

महाभाष्यम् – (प्रदीपोद्योतटीकासमन्वितम्), हरियाणा संस्कृत संस्थान, गुरुकुल, झज्जर (रोहतक), सन् 1962-63 (पञ्च भागाः)।

मीमांसादर्शनम् – (स्वतन्त्रवार्तिकशाबरभाष्य-समेतम्), प्रकाशकः विनायकरायः आनन्दाश्रमः, सन् 1929 (सप्त भागाः)।

रघुवंशमहाकाव्यम् – चौखम्बासंस्कृतसिरीज आफिस, वाराणसी, सन् 1961।

लघुशब्देन्दुशेखरः – शेखरदीपकोपेतः (अव्ययीभावान्तो भागः), चौखम्बासंस्कृतसिरीज आफिस, विद्याविलास प्रेस, वाराणसी, सन् 1938।

लघुशब्देन्दुशेखरः – नागेशोक्तिप्रकाशटीकोपेतः चौखम्बासंस्कृतसिरीज आफिस, वाराणसी, सन् 1991।

लघुशब्देन्दुशेखरः – षट्टीकोपेतः, वाणी विलास प्रकाशन, 2048 (भागद्वयम्)।

वैयाकरणभूषणसारः – चौखम्बासंस्कृतसिरीज आफिस, वाराणसी, सन् 1969।

वैयाकरणसिद्धान्तकौमुदी – तत्त्वबोधिनीबालमनोरमायुता, मोतिलाल बनारसीदास, सन् 1958–61 (चत्वारो भागाः)।

वैयाकरणसिद्धान्तलघुमञ्जूषा – सम्पूर्णानन्दसंस्कृतविश्वविद्यालयः, सन् 1990।

वैयाकरणसिद्धान्तलघुमञ्जूषा – द्वितीयभागाः, सम्पूर्णानन्दसंस्कृतविश्वविद्यालयः, सन् 1997।

शब्दकौस्तुभः – चौखम्बासंस्कृतसिरिज आफिस, वाराणसी, सन् 1991 (त्रयो भागाः)।

Combinations of upasargas and tiṅanta forms : lexical versus grammatical positions

George Cardona

1 Pāṇini and padakāras

1.1 Pāṇini

Pāṇini's sūtra उपसर्गादसमासेऽपि णोपदेशस्य । (**A** 8.4.14) lets *ṇ* substitute for initial *n* of a verbal base if this is a base with original *ṇ*[1] and follows an upasarga[2] with *r*, whether or not the preverb and base occur in a compound. For example, the *n-* of *nam* (*ṇama*) 'bend, bow', and *nī* (*ṇīñ*) 'guide, lead' is replaced by *ṇ-* in the derivates *-nāma* and *-nāyaka* in the compounds *praṇāma* 'bowing, reverence' and *praṇāyaka* 'leader'. Compounding a member of the upasarga class — items of the group beginning with *pra*, linked with a verb — is provided by कुगतिप्रादयः । (**A** 2.2.18), under the heading not only of **A** 2.1.22 (तत्पुरुषः ।) but also of **A** 2.1.3 (प्राक्कडारात् समासः ।) and **A** 2.1.4 ([सुप् २] सह सुपा ।), so that the second member of a compound whose first constituent is a member of the set beginning with *pra* is a pada that originally contains a nominal ending (*subanta*). Conversely, a sequence not involving a compound for **A** 8.4.14 involves a form containing a verb ending (*tiṅanta*) following an upasarga. For example, प णमति '... bows', प णयति '... leads'. Since **A** 8.4.14 explicitly allows for retroflexion whether or not a preverb and the verbal base with which it is connected occur in a compound, it follows that Pāṇini treats upasargas and following finite verb forms as distinct syntactic elements, separate padas.

In this context, consider also the following examples:

1. This *ṇ-* is unconditionally replaced by *n-*: **A** 6.1.65: णो नः (धात्वादेः ६४).

2. By A 1.4.58 (प्रादयः ।), stated under the heading A 1.4.56 (प्राग्रीश्वरान्निपाताः ।), members of the ordered set beginning with *pra* bear the class name *nipāta*. According to A 1.4.59-60 (उपसर्गाः क्रियायोगे । गतिश्च ।), if these are linked with actions — that is, with verbal bases, which signify actions — they have the class name *gati* as well as *upasarga*.

(1) अ॒पः प्र ण॑यति (TS 1.6.8.1) ‘(The Adhvaryu) brings the water’

(2) यन्त्वं रथ॑मिन्द्र ... प्र॒ णय॑सि॒ प्रान॑वद्य॒ नय॑सि (ṚV 1.129.1a-c) ‘Indra, that chariot which you lead forth … which, faultless one, you lead forth with excellence ….’

In (1), *ṇàyati* immediately follows *pra,* as does *ṇayàsi* in pāda b of (2). In both instances, the verb form begins with *ṇ-*. In the third pāda of (2), on the other hand, the verb form *ṇayàsi* is separated from its upasarga, which accordingly does not condition retroflexion. Now, in (1), the tiṅanta *ṇàyati* lacks an udātta vowel. The svarita is contextual: as provided in **A** 8.4.66: उदात्तादनुदात्तस्य स्वरितः, a svarita replaces an anudātta following an udātta. The basic form has only anudātta syllables, as shown in the padapāṭha corresponding to (1):

(1a) अ॒पः । प्रेति॑ । न॒य॒ति॒ ।

In general, the accentual properties seen in such Vedic texts hold also for the language current at Pāṇini’s time, so that he makes provision for both in common. Thus, **A** 8.1.16-18: पदस्य । पदात् । अनुदात्तं सर्वमपादादौ are headings: the first is in force prior to **A** 8.3.55 (अपदान्तस्य मूर्धन्यः ।); the second up to **A** 8.1.69 (कुत्सने च सुप्यगोत्रादौ ।); and the third sūtra is in force through the end of the first pāda of the eighth adhyāya. According to the first heading, operations stated subsequently apply to a pada, and by the second heading operations apply after a pada. Accordingly, by A 8.1.18, the whole of a pada has low-pitched vowels if it follows another pada, except where the pada in question occurs at the beginning of a verse section (*apādādau*). One sūtra that comes under this heading is **A** 8.1.28 (तिङ्ङतिङः ।): a tiṅanta is wholly anudātta if it follows a pada that terminates in an ending other than a finite verb ending. This pattern has exceptions, however. Thus, for example, if a finite verb form occurs in an utterance with the particle *hi* ‘for, because’, it is exempted from the general rule (**A** 8.1.34: हि च [न २९]), as is a tiṅanta linked with a form of *yad* in a relative sentence (**A** 8.1.66: यद्वृत्तान्नित्यम् ।). Moreover a gati (see note 2) is anudātta if it precedes a tiṅanta that has an udātta **A** 8.1.71: तिङि चोदात्तवति (गतिः ७०).

In accordance with the patterns reflected in these rules, the verb form in (1) originally has all low-pitched vowels; then the first of these is replaced by a svarita. In (2), on the other hand, *ṇayàsi* and *nayàsi* are linked to the relative pronoun *yam*, so that they are not anudātta; accordingly, the gati *pra* in (2) is low-pitched. Comparably, in (5) (§1.2), *ja̱gāmà* retains an udātta syllable in a construction with *hi*, so that the preceding gati *ā̱* is low-pitched.

As shown, the sūtras in question here apply to padas. Hence, once more, an upasarga, even if it is anudātta by virtue of preceding a tiṅanta with an udātta syllable, is a distinct pada, syntactically separate from the verb form with which it is linked.

1.2 Padakāras

Authors of padapāṭhas proceed differently. They recognize two types: (a) an upasarga precedes a tiṅanta that is sarvānudātta;[3] (b) an upasarga precedes a tiṅanta that has an udātta. In the latter case, the upasarga is anudātta.[4] Under (a), padakāras such as Śākalya, the author of the Ṛgvedapadapāṭha, treat the upasarga and tiṅanta forms as separate padas, separated by a full pause; under (b), on the other hand, the same padakāras treat the upasarga as the first member of a compound, separated from the tiṅanta by a compositional pause (*avagraha*).[5] For example:

Ṛgveda

(3)1.84.1: असा॑वि॒ सोम॑ इन्द्र ते॒ शवि॑ष्ठ धृष्ण॒वा ग॑हि ।
असा॑वि । सोम॑ः । इ॒न्द्र॒ । ते॒ । शवि॑ष्ठ । धृष्णो॒ऽइति॑ । आ । ग॒हि॒ ।

(4) 1.85.11: आ ग॑च्छन्ती॒मव॑सा चि॒त्रभा॑नवः ।
आ । ग॒च्छ॒न्ति॒ । ई॒म् । अव॑सा । चि॒त्रऽभा॑नवः ।

(5) 10.28.1: विश्वो॒ ह्य१॒॑न्यो अ॒रिरा॑ ज॒गाम॒ ममेदह॒ श्वशु॑रो ना ज॑गाम ।
विश्व॑ः । हि । अ॒न्यः । अ॒रिः । आ॒ऽज॒गाम॑ ।

3. Pāṇini provides for the tonal properties of a such a verb form by **A** 8.1.28 (§1.1).

4. Pāṇini provides for this tonal pattern by **A** 8.1.71 (§1.1).

5. As has been noted (see Whitney 1889: 399 [§1084a]), there are apparent exceptions to this procedure. In the present paper, I cannot deal with these instances, which do not affect my main thesis.

मम॑ । इत् । अह॑ । श्व॒शु॑रः । न । आ । ज॒गा॒म्॒ ।

Taittirīyasaṁhitā

(6) 1.4.39: असा॑वि॒ सोम॑ इन्द्र॒ ते॒ शवि॑ष्ठ धृष्ण॒वा ग॑हि ।
असा॑वि । सोम॑ः । इ॒न्द्र॒ । ते॒ । शवि॑ष्ठ । धृ॒ष्णो॒ । एति॑ । ग॒हि॒ ।

(7) 1.6.7.1: कस्य॒ वाह॑ दे॒वा य॒ज्ञमा॒ गच्छ॑न्ति॒ कस्य॑ वा॒ न । कस्य॑ । वा॒ । अह॑ ।
दे॒वाः । य॒ज्ञम् । आ॒गच्छ॒न्तीत्या॑-गच्छ॑न्ति । कस्य॑ । वा॒ । न ।

2 Views of modern lexicographers

In his preface to the first volume of *An Encyclopaedic Dictionary of Sanskrit on Historical Principles*, A. M. Ghatage (1976: xiii-xiv) presents an intelligent and well organized discussion of two positions with regard to entries of preverb-verb complexes in a dictionary: (a) complexes that involve finite verb forms are entered under verbal bases, but nominal compounds are treated as distinct entries; (b) preverb-verb complexes are made distinct entries, with nominal derivates included under them. Under (a), combinations like *anu bhū* and *pra bhū* come under the main entry *bhū*, but *anubhava* and *prabhava* are separate entries. Under (b), on the other hand, *anu bhū* and *pra bhū* are distinct entries, with derivates such as *anubhava*, *anubhūti*, *prabhava*, and *prabhūti* included under the respective complexes. As Ghatage points out (1976: xiva), different modern lexicographers have adopted one or the other of these positions:

> The older scholars dealing with the Dhātupāṭha and the lexicographers dealt with the roots and the preverbs along with the roots under a single dictionary entry and gave meanings and examples to illustrate them under the same head. This is the procedure we find in WESTERGAARD's Radices Linguae Sanskritae (Bonn, 1841), the dictionaries of H. H. WILSON, GOLDSTÜCKER, BÖHTLINGK-ROTH, BURNOUF, BENFEY and CAPPELLER. Others like MACDONNELL, MONIER-WILLIAMS, APTE, SCHOUPAK and others give the root with a prefix as a separate entry and

place it in the alphabetical order.[6]

Ghatage also takes up (1976: xiva) some consequences of each procedure. 'One result of this procedure [scil. (a)]', he remarks, '… is the separation of all the nominal and adjectival derivates from the verbs with prefixes and putting them in different places which obscures their interrelations and entails repetition of meanings.' A consequence of (b) is that combinations like *anu bhū*, *anubhava* and *pra bhū, prabhava* are listed separately, according to the alphabetical order of the preverbs, which '… is likely to lead to some amount of repetition and obscuration of the connection between the verb and the prefixed form, but the nominal derivates and the basic verb forms will be brought together.' Ghatage further notes that not only do semantic considerations favor procedure (b) but that '… the convenience of the user will also be served by it.'

3 Pāṇinīyas on preverb-verb combinations

3.1 Introduction

As can be seen from what I have noted (see §§1.1-1.2), comparable differences of procedure are to be seen in ancient Indian works. Here, however, the disagreements concern how combinations of upasargas and tiṅanta forms are to be treated. There is no doubt that nominal derivates such as *anubhava* constitute distinct nominal bases (*prātipadika*), compounds which, in Pāṇini's system, consist of padas containing upasargas — more technically, items called *gati* — and nominal derivates formed from verbal bases. In the early Indian context, moreover, arguments are presented for alternative positions, but, as is to be expected, these arguments do not concern how easy it is for one to use a dictionary. The arguments concern the status of items with respect to

6. Apte adopted both procedures. In his larger dictionary, he adopts (b). For example, अनुमा 'infer' is a separate entry. In *The Students' Sanskrit-English Dictionary*, however, (a) is adopted, so that the use of मा with अनु is noted under the entry for the base. I thank David Buchta for reminding me of Apte's practice in his students' dictionary.

grammatical operations.

3.2 Patañjali

In the Mahābhāṣya on A 6.1.135 (सुट् कात्पूर्वः),[7] Patañjali states[8] that it is proper to consider which operations are internally conditioned (*antaraṅga*) and which are externally conditioned (*bahiraṅga*) in the context of deriving forms such as सञ्चस्कार (*sañ caskāra*), सञ्चस्करतुः (*sañ caskaratuḥ*), सञ्चस्करुः (*sañ caskaruḥ*), in which the base *kṛ* is used with the upasarga *sam* and the augment ***suṭ*** is introduced before *-k-*.[9] Two alternative positions are entertained with respect to the linking of a verbal base with an upasarga and with a verb affix that signifies a kāraka:

I. An operation relative to the complex consisting of a verbal base and an upasarga (*dhātūpasargayoḥ*) is antaraṅga, hence takes precedence, because a verbal base is first connected with its upasarga.

II. A verb is first connected with the affix that signifies a kāraka relative to the action denoted by the base,[10] so that an operation associated with this is antaraṅga and takes precedence.

Patañjali presents arguments as follows.

A. Position I is asserted: An operation that involves a verbal base and its preverb is internally conditioned because a base is first linked with its preverb and only later with an affix that signifies a kāraka.[11]

B. The assertion is challenged: This is not correct. A dhātu is first connected with an affix signifying a kāraka. For a kāraka

7. The sūtra is a heading whereby ***suṭ***, introduced by subsequent rules, occurs before *k*.

8. युक्तमिह द्रष्टव्यम् किमन्तरङ्गं किं बहिरङ्गमिति । (Bh. IV.477)

9. The augment is provided for by A 6.1.137-138 (सम्परिभ्याम्भूषणे । समवाये च ।), according to which this is introduced when forms of *kṛ* are used with preceding *sam* and *pari,* in the sense of adorning (*bhūṣaṇe*) and of forming a conglomerate (*samavāye*).

10. Patañjali uses *sādhana*, which refers to a kāraka. This is a direct participant in an action, which contributes to bringing an action to accomplishment, so that it is directly related to an action, signified by a verbal base.

11. धातूपसर्गयोः कार्यं यत्तदन्तरङ्गम् । कुत एतत् । पूर्वं हि धातुरुपसर्गेण युज्यते पश्चात्साधनेनेति । (Bh. IV.477).

brings an action about and an upasarga qualifies it. One can speak of a qualification of a meaning by an upasarga only if the meaning in question is something that is already existent.[12] That is, one can qualify an object that actually occurs, and an action cannot occur except as it is brought about by its direct participants.[13]

C. It is true that this is the way things are. However, the relation that holds between a base and its preverb is first internalized (अभ्यन्तरं कृत्वा 'after making internal'), and then a verb is linked with an affix signifying a kāraka.[14] And it is necessary to recognize that this is so. For, what could one who maintains position II invoke as a cause to account for the fact that the base *ās* in

(8) आस्यते गुरुणा। 'The guru is sitting'

signifies an action which lacks an object,[15] and the same base takes an object in

(9) उपास्यते गुरुः। 'The guru is revered.'[16]

Patañjali thus defends position II, but with a condition: the link between a dhātu and an upasarga is internalized before the verb is

12. नैतत्सारम्। पूर्वं धातुः साधनेन युज्यते पश्चादुपसर्गेण। साधनं हि क्रियां निर्वर्त्तयति तामुपसर्गो विशिनष्टि। अभिनिर्वृत्तस्य चार्थस्योपसर्गेण विशेषः शक्यो वक्तुम्। (Bh. IV.477). On *abhinirvṛttasya* see note 13.

13. Nāgeśa brings out this point in a different manner. By *abhinirvṛttasya* ('brought about, completed'), he says, Patañjali means 'known as something to be brought to accomplishment': अभिनिर्वृत्तस्य साध्यत्वेन ज्ञातस्य। (Ud. IV.477).

14. सत्यमेवमेतत्। यस्त्वसौ धातूपसर्गयोरभिसम्बन्धस्तमभ्यन्तरं कृत्वा धातुः साधनेन युज्यते। (Bh. IV.477).

15. The base is therefore said to be *akarmaka*. Since the act in question lacks a karman, an *l*-affix (*lakāra*), in this case ***laṭ***, is introduced after the dhātu *ās* on condition that the act (*bhāva*) is to be signified (A 3.4.69: लः कर्मणि च भावे चाकर्मकेभ्यः।), and this affix is replaced by an ātmanepada ending (*ta* → *te*); see Cardona 1997: 88 (§**138**). The teacher referred to by *guru-* is the agent of the act in question; since a post-verbal affix is not introduced here to signify an agent, this nominal base is followed by a third-triplet ending signifying an agent (A 2.3.18: कर्तृकरणयोस् तृतीया।). In deriving (2), on the other hand, the *l*-affix ***laṭ*** is introduced after the verb on condition that an immediate object (*karman*) is to be signified. (9) is a passive counterpart of उपास्ते गुरुम् '… reveres his guru,' where *gurum* (← *guru-am*) includes an ending of the second triplet introduced to signify an immediate object (*karman*: A 2.3.2: कर्मणि द्वितीया।).

16. अवश्यं चैतदेवं विज्ञेयम्। यो हि मन्यते पूर्वं धातुः साधनेन युज्यते पश्चादुपसर्गेणेति तस्यास्यते गुरुणेत्यकर्मक उपास्यते गुरुरिति केन सकर्मकः स्यात्। (Bh. IV.477).

linked with a postverbal affix signifying a kāraka. This is a position that takes into consideration both the semantic differences betwen pairs such as *ās* 'sit' and *upa ās* 'venerate' and the requirements of grammatical derivation within Pāṇini's system. For deriving a sentence such as (9), *upa* and *ās* are treated as independent units included in separate padas:

(9a) उप-स् आस्-ल् गुरु-स्

However, the base *ās* incorporates the meaning 'revere', which is cosignified by the preverb *upa*. The base thus signifies an action that takes an object, so that it is followed by an L-affix —here ***laṭ*** — to signify an immediate object; this is replaced by the ending *ta* (→ *te*), before which is introduced the vikaraṇa *ya**k***.[17] It is the pada with these affixes that is then linked syntactically with the pada containing the upasarga *upa*.

Elsewhere, Patañjali explicitly says that verbal bases are polysemous and brings this point out by citing the pair *sthā* 'come to a stand, stay' : *pra sthā* 'depart'. With respect to this pair, he remarks[18] that here also *sthā* alone signifies the act of going and *sthā* alone also signifies the cessation of movement.

3.3 Nāgeśabhaṭṭa

Commenting on what Patañjali says in the passage that begins यस्त्वसौ (see §3.1C with note 14), Nāgeśa captures the issue clearly.

17. सार्वधातुके यक् । (A 3.1.67).

18. एवमिहापि तिष्ठतिरेव व्रजिक्रियामाह तिष्ठतिरेव व्रजिक्रियाया निवृत्तिम् । (Bh. 1.3.1 [II.185]). This is said in the context of an argument concerning whether one may define the term *dhātu* — which A 1.3.1 (भूवादयो धातवः ।) assigns as a name referring to bases listed in the dhātupāṭha, beginning with *bhū* — as referring to an item that signifies an action (क्रियावचनो धातुः । [Bh. II.179]). Under this view, a preverb is said to be a qualifier of an action (1.3.1 vt. 7: क्रियाविशेषक उपसर्गः ।). Earlier in the same passage Patañjali says that it is due to the upasarga that the act of going is understood when *sthā* is used with *pra*: ते मन्यामहे उपसर्गकृतमेतद्येनात्र व्रजिक्रिया गम्यत इति । He also notes that *pra* is used elsewhere, in the sense of an action's beginning: प्रोऽयं दृष्टापचार आदिकर्मणि वर्तते । In his Pradīpa, Kaiyaṭa remarks that the conclusion Patañjali intends is this: The meaning which is cosignified by *pra* elsewhere is inferred here also; since verbal bases are polysemous, *sthā* alone signifies movement. प्रोऽयमिति । अन्यत्रापि प्रयोगात् । ततश्चान्यत्र योऽर्थो द्योत्यः स एवेहापीत्यनुमीयते । अनेकार्थत्वाद्धातूनां तिष्ठतिरेव गतिवाचीति निर्णयः । (Pr. II. 185).

He remarks that what Patañjali intends to convey is the following.[19] It is certainly true that the relation with a kāraka takes precedence over a relation with a term called *upasarga*. However, it is after internalizing the meaning which you consider is manifested through the relation between a verb and its preverb — that is, making that meaning one which a verbal base itself conveys (स्वबोध्यं कृत्वा) — that two steps occur. First, since an action qua something that is brought to accomplishment requires that which brings it to this state, there is established a relation with a kāraka and the grammatical operations associated with it, namely the association of an affix with the base. Then, once there is an understanding of an action's truly being one by having the property of being brought to accomplishment, there is a relation with a term that is called *upasarga*. How else could the meaning that is to be conveyed be understood by a hearer, when it is in no way understood from the verbal base alone?

In his Laghumañjūṣā, Nāgeśa cites the passage from the Mahābhāṣya on A 6.1.135 where the two views I have summarized in §3.2 are presented and concludes with a concise summary of what he considers the Bhāṣya intends, as follows.[20] A speaker first conceives[21] of the qualified meaning — involving both a verbal base and an upasarga — that pertains to the base alone. Then, by joining the base with an affix that is introduced due to a relation with a kāraka, one has the understanding of the meaning in question as something that is to be brought to accomplishment, an action. Subsequently, in order that a hearer understand the meaning in question, the speaker links the verbal base with a term

19. यस्त्वसाविति । उपसर्गसञ्ज्ञकशब्दयोगात्पूर्वं साधनयोग इति सत्यमेव । परन्तु त्वदभिमतं धातूपसर्गसम्बन्धकृतमर्थमभ्यन्तरं कृत्वा स्वबोध्यं कृत्वा धातोः पूर्वं नियमेनाकाङ्क्षितार्थत्वात्साधनसम्बन्धः । तत्कार्यप्रत्यययोगे कृते क्रियात्वावगतावुपसर्गसञ्ज्ञकशब्दयोगः । अन्यथा केवलधातुतः सर्वत्राप्रतीयमानः सोऽर्थः कथं बुध्येतेति भावः । (Ud. IV.477-478).

20. अयं भावः । वक्ता धातोरेव विशिष्टमर्थं बुद्धौ कृत्वा साधनसम्बन्धकार्यप्रत्यययोगेन तत्र साध्यत्वावगतौ श्रोतृबोधाय क्रियायोगनिमित्तोपसर्गसञ्ज्ञकशब्दयोगं करोति । अन्यथा केवलधातुतः सर्वत्राप्रतीयमानतया श्रोतुस्तद्बोधो न स्यादिति । (LM 598).

21. बुद्धौ कृत्वा 'after putting in his thought.'

that has the technical name *upasarga*, which depends on its being related to an action.[22] He does this because this understanding would not apply for the hearer, since the meaning in question is in no way understandable from the verbal base alone.

Nāgeśa also refers to predecessors. First, he alludes to what Kaiyaṭa said in his Pradīpa on the Bhāṣya to A 1.3.1 (see note 18),[23] remarking that according to Kaiyaṭa the particular meaning involved when a dhātu is used with an upasarga pertains to the dhātu alone; the upasarga, however, serves to bring out this meaning for a hearer. Thus, he goes on to say,[24] what is meant by the formulation of the two positions I and II (see §3.2) is this: First there is the association of a verbal base's meaning with the meaning of a preverb;[25] that is, a speaker uses a verbal base to signify a certain meaning, part of which may require a preverb to be understood by a hearer. Next, before the verbal base is connected with the preverb, there is an association of this base with the operation determined by a kāraka; that is, in terms of the formation of padas which express the intended meaning and which are accounted for in Pāṇini's derivational system, a dhātu is first linked with affixes introduced to signify kārakas. Then there occurs the connection with an upasarga.

In brief, the Pāṇinian derivational sequence that accounts for (9) is as outlined above under (9a) (see §3.2).

3.4 Bhartṛhari

Nāgeśa acknowledges not only Kaiyaṭa — and through him Patañjali — but also Bhartṛhari, by citing and explaining two of his

22.Particles of the set beginning with *pra* (*prādayaḥ*) are assigned the class name *upasarga*, by **A** 1.4.59 (note 2), on condition that they bear a direct relation with an action.

23. तदुक्तं भूवादय इति सूत्रे कैयटेन अनेकार्थत्वाद्धातूनां विशिष्टोऽर्थो धातोरेव उपसर्गस्तु बोद्धारं प्रति तदर्थद्योतक इति । (LM 598).

24. एवञ्च पूर्वमुपसर्गेण योगो नाम तदर्थसम्बन्धः तत उपसर्गयोगात्पूर्वं साधनकार्ययोगः ततः उपसर्गशब्दयोग इति परिभाषाद्वयार्थः । (LM 598).

25. The meaning is cosignified (*dyotya*) by an upasarga, which functions as its cosignifier (*dyotaka)*. The actual signifier (*vācaka*) of the meaning is the verbal base itself.

kārikās.[26] The verses cited are part of a section in the Vākyapadīya where, reflecting the discussion in the Mahābhāṣya (see §3.2), Bhartṛhari presents the two viewpoints at issue and elaborates on them, as follows.

3.4.1 Position I justified

A dhātu actually is such that it combines a base and an upasarga as a unit, and it is only for the purpose of grammatical operations such as augmenting with initial *aṭ* that the two are theoretically assumed to be distinct units.[27] This viewpoint is also justified by the status of a complex *saṅgrāma* 'do battle, fight'. The augment *aṭ* is provided for a stem that incorporates *sam*, as in *asaṅgrāmayata* (3sg. impfct.).[28] Particular actions of this sort are signified from the outset by such combinations.[29] That is, Pāṇini's dhātupāṭha has an entry *saṅgrāma*,[30] in which the quasi-upasarga (see note 28) *sam* is incorporated. The particular action in question is signified from the outset by the complex, which accordingly has

26. LM 598: तदुक्तं हरिणा धातोः साधनयोगस्य भाविनः प्रक्रमाद्यथा । धातुत्वं कर्मभावश्च तथान्यदपि दृश्यताम् ॥ बुद्धिस्थादभिसम्बन्धात्तथा धातूपसर्गयोः । अभ्यन्तरीकृतो भेदः पदकाले प्रकाशते ॥ इति । (VP 2.184, 186). On these verses, see §3.4.3.

27. अडादीनां व्यवस्थार्थं पृथक्त्वेन प्रकल्पनम् । धातूपसर्गयोः शास्त्रे धातुरेव हि तादृशः ॥ (VP 2.180). See §4.

28. Patañjali gives the example असङ्ग्रामयत शूरः ('The mighty warrior fought') in the Bhāṣya on A 3.1.12: भृशादिभ्यो भुव्यच्वेर्लोपश्च हलः (Bh. III.63), where he remarks that it is necessary to say the initial augment is added to *saṅgrām-i-*, in order to account for *asaṅgrāmayata*: अवश्यं सङ्ग्रामयतेः सोपसर्गादुत्पत्तिर्वक्तव्या असङ्ग्रामयत शूर इत्येवमर्थम् । Commenting on this, Nāgeśa (Ud. III.63) notes that although *sam* in *saṅgrāma* is not truly an upasarga, one should consider that when Patañjali says *sopasargāt* ('after … with the upasarga') he means to say 'after … with a term that has the same form as the upasarga *sam*': यद्यपि सङ्ग्रामशब्दे संशब्दो नोपसर्गस्तथापि सोपसर्गादित्यस्य सोपसर्गसमानाकारादित्यर्थो बोध्यः ।

29. तथा हि सङ्ग्रामयतेः सोपसर्गाद्विधिः स्मृतः । क्रियाविशेषाः सङ्घातैः प्रक्रम्यन्ते तथाविधाः ॥ (VP 2.181).

30. सङ्ग्राम युद्धे (KṣT 10.308, DhPr. 10.296, MDhVṛ. 10.308). The base is part of the tenth set of bases in the dhātupāṭha (*curādigaṇa*), so that it takes the suffix ***ṇic*** (सत्यापपाशरूपवीणाश्लोकसेनालोमत्वचवर्मवर्णचूर्णचुरादिभ्यो णिच् । [A 3.1.25]): *saṅgrāma-i* → *saṅgrāmi-* (**A** 6.4.48: अतो लोपः [आर्धधातुके ४६]). I have cited the base as it appears in the texts noted. However, it is also accepted that a low-pitched nasalized *a* is appended as a marker to show that the base takes ātmanepada agentive endings (अनुदात्तङित आत्मनेपदम् । [**A** 1.3.12]). Accordingly, Śivarāmendrasarasvatī (RaPr. 3.1.12 [VI.67]) acknowledges the entry as *saṅgrāma a*: असङ्ग्रामयत इति । सङ्ग्राम अ इत्यकारान्तरं प्रश्लिष्यानुदात्तेत्त्वाश्रयणात्तङ् । I need not consider other details here.

the status of being a dhātu.[31]

This being so, an action already qualified by the sense understood from an upasarga enters into relations with kārakas, so that an operation that obtains between an upasarga and a dhātu is internally conditioned relative to an operation that concerns a kāraka.[32] Semantically, a meaning that is fixed for a given verb used with a preverb depends on the relation with the preverb; only after the relation between a verb and its meaning has been established, is it appropriate for another relation to apply for it.[33]

Under this view, there is a unit *upās* signifying an action which enters into relation with a kāraka such as a teacher who is the object of reverence, as expressed in (9) उपास्यते गुरुः । (§3.1).

3.4.2 Position II defended

Something is qualified, distinguished from something else, only if it is already established, an existing entity signified by terms that are capable of actual use.[34] That is, for something to be subject to qualification, it has to be an existent entity. This enters into a qualifier-qualificand relation, being signified by a term that is known to be used.[35] The items capable of coming under

31. सङ्ग्राम युद्ध इति क्रियाविशेषवाची सम्पूर्वः सङ्घात एव प्रक्रम्यते । (VPVṛ. 2.180-181 [232]). In his ṭīkā on VP 2.180 (76), Puṇyarāja says that in the case of complexes including preverbs the property of being a dhātu pertains solely to those complexes, since it is they that signify the particular acts in question: वस्तुतः पुनर्विशिष्टक्रियावचना एव त इति सोपसर्गाणामेव धातुत्वम् ।

32. कार्याणामन्तरङ्गत्वमेवं धातूपसर्गयोः । साधनैर्याति सम्बन्धं तथाभूतैव सा क्रिया ॥ (VP 2.182). By *tathābhūtā*, Bhartṛhari means that the action is such that it is signified by a base qualified by an upasarga: तस्माद्विशिष्टप्रकृतिवाच्या विशिष्टा क्रिया तथाभूतैव साध्या सती साधनसम्बन्धं प्रतिपद्यते । (VPVṛ. 2.182 [232]). Cf. VPṬī. 2.182 (77): तथाभूतैव । उपसर्गविशिष्टैव कारकसम्बन्धमुपगच्छति ।

33. उपसर्गसम्बन्धाधीना स्वार्थव्यवस्था धातूनाम् स्वार्थयोगे च सिद्धे सम्बन्धान्तरस्य सन्निधानेन भवितव्यम् । (VPVṛ. 2.182 [232]).

34. प्रयोगार्हेषु सिद्धः सन् भेत्तव्योऽर्थो विशिष्यते | (VP 2.183ab); see note 38. Puṇyarāja supplies *dhātuṣu* to be construed with *prayogārheṣu*: लब्धात्मनस्तस्या विशेष्यत्वोपपत्तेः प्रयोगार्हेषु धातुषु सिद्धः सन्नर्थो विशेष्यो भवत्युपसर्गादिभिः न तु पूर्वकाल आख्याते विशेषणयोगः । (VPṬī. 2.183 [77]).

35. इह प्रसिद्धं विशेष्यमनेकप्रकारसम्बन्धे सति दृष्टप्रयोगेण शब्देनाभिधीयमानं विशेषणविशेष्यभावं प्रतिपद्यते । (VPVṛ 2.183 [232]). For the continuation of the vṛtti, see note 39.

consideration are verbal bases in finite verb forms,[36] wherein a verbal base signifies an act as one that is to be brought to completion.[37] An act that is brought to completion requires participants that bring this about — kārakas — and these are signified by affixes attached to verb bases, e.g., *-ti* in *pac-a-ti* '... is cooking', *-te* in *āste* of *upāste* '... reveres'. Such an act thus cannot be considered existent unless it is related to a kāraka.[38] Hence, prior to such a relation, an act in process has no actual status, so that it cannot then enter into a qualifier-qualificand relation with a meaning cosignified by an upasarga. Therefore, it is the position of some that a dhātu first is linked to a term denoting a kāraka.[39]

3.4.3 Compromise justifying position I

Bhartṛhari follows Patañjali (see §3.2C) in adopting the position that the relation between the meanings connected with a dhātu and an upasarga are first internalized, though he adds two details.[40] First, he specifies that the difference that is internalized is due to the relation between a dhātu and an upasarga that is conceptual. In addition, he remarks that this difference appears explicitly[41] at the time a pada is used. That is, the particular action signified by a complex such as *upa ās* is first present conceptually, in the mind of a speaker, who uses a sentence like (9) उपास्यते गुरुः | (§3.2), where the full pada *āsyate* occurs, with the ending *te*. At the time this pada is

36. Nāgeśa (LM 599) quotes VP 2.183, then remarks that a base is capable of use after it has taken an affix: प्रयोगार्हत्वं च प्रत्ययोत्पत्त्यनन्तरम् ।

37. This contrasts with action nouns such as *pāka*, *pakti*, *pacana*, which signify an abstract action that behaves like a substance (*dravyavat*) with respect to grammatical properties and operations.

38. प्राक्च साधनसम्बन्धात् क्रिया नैवोपजायते ॥ (VP 2.183cd); see note 34.

39. साध्यत्वाच्च क्रियायाः साधनसम्बन्धान्निर्वृत्तिः । तस्मात्प्राक्साधनसम्बन्धादनुपजाता क्रिया निरात्मिका द्योतकेनोपसर्गेण सह विशेषणविशेष्यसम्बन्धं नोत्सहते प्रतिपत्तुम् । (VPVṛ. 2.183 [232]). Puṇyarāja comparably speaks of an action possibly being a qualificand only once it has gained status as an existent; see note 34.

40. बुद्धिस्थादभिसम्बन्धात्तथा धातूपसर्गयोः । अभ्यन्तरीकृताद्भेदः पदकाले प्रकाशते ॥ (VP 2.186).

41. In his vṛtti on VP 2.186 (233), Bhartṛhari says व्यक्तरूपः प्रकाशते 'appears in manifested form.'

used, together with the upasarga *upa*, the semantic difference between the meanings of *ās* and *upa ās* is manifest.

In the two kārikās which precede the above formulation,[42] Bhartṛhari draws on two parallels from grammar and one from agricultural lore.

The first grammatical parallel concerns how a verbal base is defined and given the class name *dhātu*. In the Mahābhāṣya on A 1.3.1 (भूवादयो धातवः ।), which provides that items of the ordered set starting with *bhū* are called *dhātu,* Patañjali cites an alternative formulation, according to which an item that signifies an action is assigned the name *dhātu*.[43] This presupposes that a base such as *bhū* or *ās* by itself signifies an action. However, as has been argued, one cannot speak of an actual action — qua something that is to be brought to accomplishment in time — unless it is connected with direct participants (*kāraka*, *sādhana*) that contribute to its accomplishment. Thus, stating that a dhātu by itself is an item that signifies an action presupposes from the outset (*prakramāt*) its connection with a sādhana, a connection which is to occur later.[44]

Bhartṛhari's second grammatical parallel involves **A** 3.1.7: धातोः कर्मणः समानकर्तृकादिच्छायां वा (सन् ९), which optionally introduces the affix ***san*** after a dhātu that signifies an immediate object of desiring on the part of the same agent as performs the act denoted by the base. In this case also, it is assumed that an act's being the object of wishing is manifest when a form with a derivate in *-san* is used, as

42. धातोः साधनयोगस्य भाविनः प्रक्रमाद्यथा । धातुत्वं कर्मभावश्च तथान्यदपि दृश्यताम् ॥ बीजकालेषु सम्बद्धाद्यथा लाक्षा-रसादयः । वर्णादिपरिणामेन फलानामुपकुर्वते ॥ (VP 2.184-185). *tathā* of VP 2.186 (see note 40) links with *yathā* in each of these kārikās. I leave out of consideration a detail of syntax concerning the first kārikā.

43. यदि पुनः क्रियावचनो धातुरित्येतल्लक्षणं क्रियेत । (Bh II.179). In subsequent vārttikas, Kātyāyana takes up possible objections to this formulation, which thus is known to have preceded Patañjali.

44. VPṬī. 2.184 (78): क्रियावचनो धातुरित्युक्तम् । साधनसम्बन्धाच्च प्राक्क्रियानिवृत्तेरसम्भवाद्यथा भाविसाधन-सम्बन्धसमाश्रयणेनोपक्रम एव धातुत्वं धातुसञ्ज्ञोच्यते .... Nāgeśa (LM 598) explains similarly: अस्यार्थः । यथा भाविसाधनसम्बन्धाश्रयणेन क्रियावाचित्वमाश्रित्य धातुसञ्ज्ञोच्यते ...

in *cikīrṣati* '… wishes to do, … wishes to make',[45] and is present from the outset of the derivation of a base.[46]

Bhartṛhari concludes that other technical matters (*anyad api* ('something else also') may be considered (*dṛśyatām*) similarly. That is, one may comparably assume that an action qualified by the meaning associated with an upasarga also is there from the outset.[47] As a parallel to this, Bhartṛhari brings in an example from agriculture. Seeds are soaked with substances such as lākṣā juice, and these substances then contribute to the coloring of the products of these seeds through their developing with the properties bestowed on the seeds, such as the red of lākṣā.[48]

In accordance with what has been said, some (*anye* 'others') consider that position I is proper.[49]

3.5 Conclusion

Both Patañjali and Bhartṛhari consider two opposed positions and end by adopting a compromise. An upasarga is considered to be linked first with a verbal base, since it serves to qualify the act

45. ← *cikīrṣa-**laṭ***, with the base *cikīrṣa-* ← *kṛ-sa-*.

46. In his vṛtti on VP 2.184, Bhartṛhari emphasizes that a primary base such as *kṛ* is abstracted, through reasoning by anvaya and vyatireka from complexes that are given in actual usage. This process of abstraction results in constituents and constituent meanings. A base thus abstracted is assumed to signify an action, although an action is not actually manifest except as dependent on a kāraka. Comparably, from a complex such as *cikīrṣati*, a base *cikīrṣa* is abstracted, and from this one abstracts also the primitive base *kṛ*, assuming that it now denotes an act that is the object of desiring. VPVṛ 2.184 (233): प्रसिद्धप्रयोगे समुदायेऽन्वयव्यतिरेकाभ्यां कार्यार्थमवयवेष्ववयवार्थेषु च प्रयुज्यमानेषु केवलायाः प्रकृतेरपोद्धृताया एव साधनाधीनप्रादुर्भावं क्रियारूपमाश्रित्य यथैव क्रियावचनत्वाद्धातुसञ्ज्ञा विधीयते यथा च धातोः कर्मण इति कर्मव्यपदेशाश्रया सन उत्पत्तिरन्वाख्यायते तथा विशेषणविशेष्यभावोऽपि व्यवतिष्ठते । The printed edition has प्रसिद्धप्रयोगं समुदायान्वयव्यतिरेका°, which Ashok Aklujkar has emended to प्रसिद्धप्रयोगे समुदायेऽन्वयव्यतिरेका° in his electronic version. It is also possible to emend to प्रसिद्धप्रयोगात्समुदायादन्वयव्यतिरेका° on syntactic grounds. In the present discussion, it is neither possible nor necessary to take up details of this issue.

47. This is stated by Puṇyarāja: (VPṬī. 2.184 [78]): भाविसम्बन्धादुपक्रम एव विशिष्टक्रियावचनत्वं दृश्यताम् को दोषः ।

48. See VP 2.185 (note 42). Cf. BĀUŚ 4.3.7 (p. 247): बीजभावनाय पुष्पफलादीनां गुणान्तरोत्पत्तिदर्शनात् ।, SDS 49.15-16: यथा वा लाक्षारसावसिक्तानां कार्पासबीजादीनामङ्कुरादिपारम्पर्येण कार्पासादौ रक्तिमनियमः ।

49. तस्मात्पूर्वं धातुरुपसर्गेण युज्यत इत्यपरे मन्यन्ते । (VPVṛ. 2.184 [233]).

signified by that base. On the other hand, a base has first to be linked with an affix denoting a kāraka that contributes to the accomplishment of the action signified by that base, since an action, qua one that is brought to accomplishment, cannot have any status in the absence of a kāraka. The compromise position which is adopted starts with a semantic relation: an action is semantically qualified by a meaning which is conveyed by a preverb used with it. However, this relation is incorporated as a meaning of a base itself, a meaning which then appears (*prakāśate*) explicitly with the use of a preverb, which serves as a cosignifier that brings out the meaning in question.

Nāgeśa links the compromise clearly with the contrast between speaker and hearer. A speaker uses a form like *upāste*, with the preverb *upa*, so that a hearer may understand the meaning conveyed, which is attributed to the base *ās* itself.

4 Technical reasons for adopting the compromise

Bhartṛhari begins his discussion of the issues in question (see §3.4.1 with note 27) by remarking that a dhātu and a related upasarga are theoretically considered separate in order to allow for the proper distribution of *aṭ* and other grammatical elements.

4.1 Augmenting

According to **A** 6.4.71-72: लुङ्लङ्लृङ्क्ष्वडुदात्तः । आडजादीनाम् (अङ्गस्य १), the augment *aṭ* is added as the initial element of a stem followed by endings that have replaced *l*-affixes ***luṅ***, ***laṅ***, ***lṛṅ***, but the augment is *āṭ* for stems beginning with a vowel. For example: *bhū* 'be, become': *abhūt* (3sg. aor. ← *abhū-s-t* ← *bhū-**luṅ***) 'has been, has become', *abhavat* (3sg. impfct. ← *abhū-a-t* ← *bhū-**laṅ***) 'was, became', *abhaviṣyat* (3sg. condit. ← *abhū-isya-t* ← *bhū-**lṛṅ***) 'would have been, would have become'; *anu bhū* 'experience': *anv abhūt, anv abhavat, anv abhaviṣyat*; *īkṣ* 'look': *aikṣiṣṭa* (← *āīkṣ-s-ta* ← *īkṣ-**luṅ***), *aikṣata* (← *āīkṣ-a-ta* ← *īkṣ-**laṅ***), *aikṣiṣyata* (← *āīkṣ-isya-ta* ← *īkṣ-**lṛṅ***); *pari īkṣ* 'examine': *pary aikṣiṣṭa, pary aikṣata, pary aikṣiṣyata.*

If position I were accepted not merely from the semantic viewpoint but also for the derivational process, one would recognize *anubhū* and *parīkṣ* as complex units. This would allow deriving incorrect forms like **ānubhūt, *ānubhavat, *ānubhaviṣyat*; **aparīkṣiṣṭa, *aparīkṣata, *aparīkṣiṣyata* instead of the forms shown above.

4.2 Perfect forms

Forms called 'perfect' in western terminology are derived, with iteration of a syllable of a verbal base, from posited forms that have the *l*-suffix ***liṭ***.[50] If a base begins with a heavy syllable containing one of the vowels denoted by *ic*, excepting *ṛcch* 'go', however, *ām* is introduced and ***liṭ*** is dropped.[51] For example: *bhū*: *babhūva* (← *bhū-**liṭ***) 'was, became'; *anu bhū*: *anu babhūva*; *īkṣ*: *īkṣāñ cakre* (← *īkṣ-**liṭ** kṛ-**liṭ***); *pari īkṣ*: *parīkṣāñ cakre* (← *pari īkṣām-**liṭ*** ...).

If position I were accepted for the derivational process, one would allow deriving **anunubhūva* (← *anubhū-**liṭ***). Further, since the initial of *parīkṣ* is not *ī*, one would allow **paparīkṣe* (← *parīkṣ-**liṭ***).

4.3 Some denominatives

There is also a group of derived bases, formed with the suffix ***kyaṅ***, meaning 'become …', in which this suffix is added to items of a set that includes *bhṛśa* 'intense'.[52] This rule serves to form derivates found in complexes such as *su manāyate* '… is, becomes benevolent', corresponding to which, on the evidence of

50. लिटि धातोरनभ्यासस्य । (A 6.1.8). This is one of a group of sūtras stated under the heading of A 6.1.1-2: एकाचो द्वे प्रथमस्य । अजादेर्द्वितीयस्य । In general the first syllable of a unit is iterated, but if this begins with a vowel, its second syllable undergoes this operation. For example, the second syllable of *e-dhi-dhi-sa* is iterated: *edidhiṣate* 'wishes to thrive', where the unit ending in the desiderative suffix *sa**n*** is subject to iteration; see below. It is not necessary to discuss here details of derivation, including whether part of a base is iterated or undergoes replacement.

51. A 3.1.36: इजादेश्च गुरुमतोऽनृच्छः (आम् लिटि ३५), 2.4.81: आमः (लेः ८०, लुक् ५८). Details of derivation need not be discussed here.

52. A 3.1.12: भृशादिभ्यो भुव्यच्वेर्लोपश्च हलः (क्यङ् ११).

Kātyāyana and Patañjali, the imperfect is *sv amanāyata*, with the augment *aṭ* added to *manā-ya.*[53] If ***kyaṅ*** followed an undivided unit *sumanas,*[54] the augment would be added to *sumanāya-,* so that **asumanāyata* would wrongly be derived. Comparably, if the absolutive suffix ***ktvā***[55] is added to *manāya*, and then a compound is formed with the preverb,[56] the suffix is replaced by ***lyap***:[57] *sumanāya-ya → sumanāyya.*[58] If, however, *sumanas* is treated as a single unit followed by ***kyaṅ***, *sumanāya-* of *sumanāya-itvā* is not a compound, so that augmented *itvā* is now not subject to replacement. Consequently, the grammar would allow **sumanāyitvā* instead of *sumanāyya.* Again, supposing that the desiderative suffix ***san*** (**A** 3.1.7, see §3.4.3) followed *abhimanāya-* 'yearn for, be delighted', the second syllable of *abhimanāya-isa* would be subject to iteration,[59] resulting in **abibhimānayiṣa* (3sg. pres. **abibhimānayiṣate*). On the other hand, the desired form *abhi mimānayiṣa* (*abhi mimānayiṣate*) is derived if *mānaya* is separate from *abhi*.

This begs the question: why then is the quasi-preverb of *saṅgrāma* not treated as separate unit? If *saṅgrāma* were treated in the same way as *sumanāya* or *abhimanāya*, one would allow **samagrāmayata* instead of *asaṅgrāmayata.* Patañjali himself reconciles the two situations by saying that Pāṇini includes *saṅgrāma* in his dhātupāṭha (see note 30) in order to provide for a

53. In the Bhāṣya on A 3.1.12, while discussing vt. 6 (सोपसर्गादिति चेदटि दोषः ।), Patañjali quotes this form as well as the absolutive *sumanāyya* and the desiderative *abhimimanāyiṣate*: सोपसर्गादिति चेदटि दोषो भवति स्वमनायतेति । अत्यल्पमिदमुच्यते अटि दोषो भवतीति । अड्ल्यब्द्विर्वचनेष्विति वक्तव्यम् । अट्युदाहृतम् । ल्यपि सुमनाय्य । द्विर्वचने अभिमिमनायिषते । (Bh. III.62). In his sixth vārttika, Kātyāyana only brings up the problem involving ***aṭ***.

54. *sumanas-ya → sumana-ya → sumanā-ya* (**A** 7.4.25: अकृत्सार्वधातुकयोर्दीर्घः ।).

55. A 3.4.21: समानकर्तृकयोः पूर्वकाले (क्त्वा १८). *ktvā* gets the initial augment ***iṭ***: आर्धधातुकस्येड् वलादेः (**A** 7.2.35).

56. **A** 2.2.18; see §1.1.

57. समासेऽनञ्पूर्वे क्त्वो ल्यप् (**A** 7.1.37).

58. A 6.4.48: अतो लोपः (आर्धधातुके ४६).

59. सन्यङोः (**A** 6.1.9). This sūtra comes under the heading of A 6.1.1-2 (see note 50), so that the first or second syllable of a base ending in ***san*** is subject to iteration.

restriction: of denominative verbal bases with a quasi-preverb, only *saṅgrāma-i* has the status of a unit verb after which an affix is introduced.[60]

5 Pāṇini's position

As I have pointed out (§1.1), Pāṇini treats sequences of upasargas and related tiṅanta forms as separate padas, even if the upasarga has no udātta syllable. This is compatible with position II, that a dhātu first enters into relation with an affix denoting a kāraka (see §§3.2-3.4). As noted, moreover, this position fits within Pāṇini's formal derivational system. There is additional evidence in support of the conclusion that Pāṇini adopted the view that a verbal base signifies not only the meanings attributable to it when used without any preverb but also meanings particular to complexes with preverbs, so that the latter serve as cosignifiers of meanings considered to be directly signified by the verbs with which they are linked.

5.1 Multiple meanings given in sūtras for single bases

Consider first a series of sūtras which provide that ātmanepada or parasmaipada endings replace *l*-suffixes following verbal bases.

गन्धनावक्षेपणसेवनसाहसिक्यप्रतियत्नप्रकथनोपयोगेषु कृञः (A 1.3.32)[61] provides for ātmanepada affixes after *kṛ* used in a series of meanings: reveal or point out a fault in someone which that person does not wish to have known, so that it harms him or her (*gandhana*); threaten, abuse (*avakṣepaṇa* ['throw down']); serve, follow (*sevana*); act with boldness, violently (*sāhasikya*); add a quality to something (*pratiyatna*); relate, tell (*prakathana*); employing for the sake of merit, to fulfill a desire (*upayoga*). For example:

(10) द्यामिवाह्वयमानं तमवोचद् भूधरं कपिः । उपकुर्वन्तमत्यर्थं प्रकुर्वाणोऽनुजीविवत् ॥ कुलभार्यां प्रकुर्वाणमहं द्रष्टुं दशाननम् । यामि त्वरावान् शैलेन्द्र मा कस्यचिदुपस्कृथाः ॥ यो

60. अवश्यं सङ्ग्रामयतेः सोपसर्गादुत्पत्तिर्वक्तव्या असङ्ग्रामयत शूर इत्येवमर्थम् । तन्नियमार्थं भविष्यति सङ्ग्रामयतेरेव सोपसर्गान्नान्यस्मात्सोपसर्गादिति । (Bh. 3.1.12 [III.63]). It is not necessary to deal here with the details of the argument involved.

61. *ātmanepadam* of अनुदात्तङित आत्मनेपदम् । (A 1.3.12) is understood to recur in this and the following rules.

ऽपचक्रे वनात्सीताम्° 'The monkey (Hanumat) addressed the mountain (Menaka), that appeared to challenge the sky, as he favored him greatly, acting towards him in a devoted manner, as though he were his servant, (saying): I am going in haste to see Rāvaṇa, who is approaching with daring the wife of a noble family, o great mountain, who abused Sītā in the forest; do not add (further greatness to) me (through your hospitality).' (BhK 8.18-20a)

The participles *prakurvāṇaḥ* 'serving', *prakurvāṇam* 'approaching in a daring manner', and the perfect *apa cakre* 'abused' illustrate usages provided for by **A** 1.3.32.[62]

According to सम्माननोत्सञ्जनाचार्यकरणज्ञानभृतिविगणनव्ययेषु नियः (**A** 1.3.36), ātmanepada affixes follow *nī* ('lead, guide to') used in the following senses: honoring (*sammānana*); elevating (*utsañjana*); act of a teacher (*ācāryakaraṇa*); knowing, learning (*jñāna*); supporting with wages (*bhṛti*); pay off what is due (*vigaṇana*); expend (*vyaya*). The forms *vineṣye* 'I will expend, give up' and *udāneṣye* 'I will elevate' illustrate such usage in

(11) विनेष्ये वा प्रियान् प्राणानुदानेष्येऽथवा यशः ॥ 'I will either expend my own life or, (doing away with Rāvaṇa,) I will elevate my fame.' (BhK 8.21cd)

अपह्नवे ज्ञः (**A** 1.3.44) provides that ātmanepada affixes replace an *l*-suffix after *jñā* in the sense 'hide, deny'. For example, in

(12) आत्मानमपजानानः शशमात्रोऽनयद्दिनम् । '(Hanumat) passed the day concealing himself, the size of a rabbit.' (BhK 8.26ab)

apajānānaḥ contains the participle *jānāna-*, with the ātmanepada

62. In rendering 'abused Sītā in the forest', I follow Jayamaṅgala, who glosses *apacakre* with *abhibabhūva* 'overcame' and notes that the ātmanepada ending is used relative to the meaning 'abuse'. He also remarks that *vanāt* is used to refer to the forest as a place where Rāvaṇa committed the act, the ablative being to signify an immediate object signified by an understood absolute *upagamya* 'after coming to'. This accords with what Kātyāyana said in 2.3.28 vt. 1 (पञ्चमीविधाने ल्यब्लोपे कर्मण्युपसङ्ख्यानम् ।), according to which provision is to be made for the use of a fifth-triplet ending signifying an immediate object when an absolutive with ***lyap*** is understood although not used. BhKJ 8.20: यः सीतामपचक्रे अभिबभूव । अवक्षेपणे तङ् । वनादिति वनमुपगम्य । ल्यब्लोपे कर्मणि पञ्चमी ।

suffix *śānac*[63] replacing *laṭ*.

As can be seen, the particular meanings in question require the use of specific preverbs with verbal bases. Indeed, the Kāśikā remarks that *jñā* occurs in the meaning 'deny' only when it is used with a preverb, not by itself.[64] Yet, in the sūtras cited here, and in other rules of the same section, Pāṇini simply speaks of *kṛ*, *nī*, *jñā* and other verbs used in certain meanings. This is compatible with the stand that the meanings in question are treated as signified by the verbal bases themselves, but require accompanying preverbs as cosignifiers.

5.2 Entries in the dhātupāṭha

How particular entries appear in the dhātupāṭha also accords with the position that a dhātu alone is considered to signify meanings which may require accompanying preverbs as cosignifiers.

Consider first the entry अनो रुध कामे । (KṣT 4.65, DhPr. 4.63, MDhVṛ. 4.69). This appears as shown in all editions of the texts in question. However, as Bruno Liebich noted,[65] all the manuscripts available to him read अनु रुध कामे, which he emended in accordance with two other entries, namely आङः शसि इच्छायाम् । (KṣT 1.417) and आङः शासु इच्छायाम् । (KṣT 2.15). That is, the last two entries have the ablative form of the upasarga *āṅ*. This usage requires that *ā śas* and *ā śās* not be treated as involving lexical units *āśas* and *āśās*. Instead, they show that the bases *śas* and *śās*, which alone receive the class name *dhātu* by **A** 1.3.1 (see note 18), are listed and that they are said to be preceded by the upasarga *āṅ*. The Mādhavīyadhātuvṛtti also has आङः शसि इच्छायाम् । (MDhVṛ. 1.407) and आङः शासु इच्छायाम् । (MDhVṛ. 2.15). Similarly, the dhātupāṭha accompanying Candragomin's Cāndravyākaraṇa has अनो रुध कामे । (4.112), आङः शन्सु इच्छायाम्। (1.460), and आङः शासु इच्छायाम् । (2.42).[66]

63. A 3.2.126: लक्षणहेत्वोः क्रियायाः (लटः शतृशानचौ १२४). The participial form *jānāna-s* compounds with *apa-s* by **A** 2.2.18 (§ 1.1).

64. अपह्नवोऽपह्नुतिः अपलापः । सोपसर्गश्चापह्नवे वर्तते न केवलः । (Kāś. 1.3.44).

65. Liebich 1930: 129 n. 4: '*alle Hss*. anu; *vgl.* I, 660, II, 12.'

66. Liebich 1902: 25*, 15*; B. J. Doshi 1967: 113.

On the other hand, although the Dhātupradīpa has अनो रुध कामे ।, it also has आङ् शासि इच्छायाम् । (DhPr. 1.403) and आङ् शासु इच्छायाम् । (DhPr. 2.12) instead of आङः शसि इच्छायाम् । and आङः शासु इच्छायाम् ।. This does not mean, nevertheless, that Maitreya Rakṣita considered the entries to be single lexical units *āśas* and *āśās*. On the contrary, it is clear from what he himself says that this is not so. He remarks that *śās**u*** has the marker *u* for two reasons, one of which concerns us here: the marking is made so that the suffix ***ktvā*** following this verb be subject to optional augmenting with *iṭ*[67] and cites the absolutives *āśāsitvā, āśāstvā*. Now, these forms would be appropriate if *āśās*- found here were not a compound. For ***ktvā*** is regularly replaced by ***lyap*** in a compound (**A** 7.1.37, see note 57); and if this replacement did apply, the augment *iṭ* would not come into play, since this is added to ārdhadhātuka affixes beginning with consonants other than *y* (**A** 7.2.35, see note 55). Accordingly, Maitreya remarks that the marker in *śās**u*** is meant to indicate that this item is not followed by ***lyap*** in Vedic usage; the non-replacement of ***ktvā*** by this is accounted for by a particular rule providing that in Vedic usage ***ktvā*** also occurs in compounds.[68]

From this, one must conclude that even where the entry does not have an ablative form of the upasarga, the compilers of the dhātupāṭha did not understand that an entry like आङ् शासु इच्छायाम् involves a single lexical unit *āśās* for Pāṇini's bhāṣā.

This accords with Pāṇini's derivational procedures.[69]

67. **A** 7.2.56: उदितो वा (क्त्वि ५५, इट् ३५) provides that the absolutive suffix ***ktvā*** optionally receives the initial augment *iṭ* if it follows a base marked with *u*.

68. क्त्वापि छन्दसि (**A** 7.1.38). DhPr. 2.12: उकारोऽस्य ... उदितो वेति विशेषणार्थश्च । क्त्वाप्रत्ययस्य च प्रयोगश्छन्दस्येव सम्भवति । तत्र ल्यपोऽभावः फलम् । क्त्वापि छन्दसीत्यनादेशः । (DhPr. 2.12). In his comments on KṣT 2.15, Kṣīrasvāmin also cites *āśāstvā, āśāsitvā* and refers to **A** 7.2.56: उदितो वा आशास्त्वा आशासित्वा ।

69. I am grateful to Saroja Bhate, Hideyo Ogawa and Dipti Tripathi for reading a draft of my paper and making typographical corrections.

References and Abbreviations

[The mode of reference for citations is indicated in square brackets.]

A — *Aṣṭādhyāyī* [adhyāya, pāda, sūtra]

Abhyankar, Vasudev Shastri

1978 — *Sarva-darśana-saṁgraha of Sāyaṇa-Mādhava Edited with an Original Commentary in Sanskrit by the Late Mahāmahopādhyāya Vasudev Shastri Abhyankar*. Third edition, seen through the press by T. G. Mainkar. Government Oriental Series Class A, No. 1. Poona: Bhandarkar Oriental Research Institute.

BĀUŚ — Śaṅkara's bhāṣya on the *Bṛhadāraṇyakopaniṣad.* See Bhagavat, Hari Raghunath.

Bh. — *Mahābhāṣya* [volume, page]. See Vedavrata.

Bhagavat, Hari Raghunath

1928 — *Works of Shankaracharya in Original Sanskrit, Vol. II, Part II: The Upanishadbashya* (*Bṛihadaranya-kopanishad*). Poona: Ashtekar & Co.

Bhandari, Madhava Shastri et al.

1925 — *Vaiyākaraṇa Siddhānta Laghumañjūshā by M.M. Srī Nāgesha Bhaṭṭa with two Commentaries called 'Kunjikā' of Shri Durbalāchārya and 'Kalā' of Bālam Bhaṭṭa* ... Two volumes continuously paginated. Chowkhamba Sanskrit Series 44. Benares: Chowkhamba. Reprinted 1989.

BhK — *Bhaṭṭikāvya.* See Joshi and Paṇśīkar.

BhKJ — Jayamaṅgala's *Jayamaṅgalā* commentary on the *Bhaṭṭikāvya.*

Cardona, George

1997 — *Pāṇini, his Work and its Traditions, vol. I: Background and Introduction.* Second edition. Delhi: Motilal Banarsidass.

Chakravarti, Srish Chandra

1918 *The Dhātu-Pradeepa by Maitreya-Rakshita, Edited with Annotations ....* Savitārāya-Smṛtisaṁrakṣaṇa-Granthamālā 2. Rajshahi: The Varendra Research Society. Revised edition by Yudhiṣṭhira Mīmāṁsaka, 1986: धातुप्रदीपः मैत्रेयरक्षितविरचितः [पाणिनीय-धातुपाठस्य प्राच्यपाठस्य व्याख्यारूपः] सम्पादकः श्रीशचन्द्रचक्रवर्ती भट्टाचार्यः परिष्कर्त्ता युधिष्ठरो मीमांसकः. Bahalgarh (Sonipat-Haryana): Ramlal Kapoor Trust.

DhPr. *Dhātupradīpa* [gaṇa, serial number]. See Chakravarti, Srish Chandra.

Doshi, Bechardas Jivraj

1967 आचार्यचन्द्रगोमिप्रणीतं चान्द्रव्याकरणम्. राजस्थानपुरातन ग्रन्थमाला ३९. Jodhpur: Rajasthan Oriental Research Institute.

Dwarikadas Shastri

1964 *The Mādhavīyā Dhātuvṛitti [A Treatise on Sanskrit Roots Based on the Dhātupāṭha of Pāṇini] by Sāyaṇācārya.* Prāchya Bhāratī Series 1. Varanasi: Prāchya Bhāratī Prakāshana.

Ghatage, A. M.

1976 *An Encyclopaedic Dictionary of Sanskrit on Historical Principles.* Volume I. Poona: Deccan College Postgraduate and Research Institute.

Joshi, Vināyak Nārayaṇ Shāstrī and Wāsudev Laxmaṇ Shāstrī Paṇśīkar

1928 *The Bhaṭṭikāvya of Bhaṭṭi with the Commentary (Jayamangalā) of Jayamangala.* Seventh edition. Bombay: Nirṇaya Sāgar Press.

Kāś. *Kāśikāvṛtti.* See Sharma, Aryendra, Khanderao Deshpande and D. G. Padhye.

KṣT *Kṣīrataraṅgiṇī* [gaṇa, serial number]. See Yudhiṣṭhira Mīmāṁsaka.

Liebich, Bruno

1902 *Cāndra-Vyākaraṇa, die Grammatik des*

Candragomin: Sūtra, Uṇādi, Dhātupāṭha. Abhandlungen für die Kunde des Morgenlandes XI.4. Leipzig: Brockhaus.

1930 *Kṣīrataraṅgiṇī, Kṣīrasvāmin's Kommentar zu Panini's Dhātupāṭha, zum ersten Mal herausgegeben ... mit fünf Anhängen.* Indische Forschungen 8/9. Breslau: M. & H. Marcus.

LM *Vaiyākaraṇasiddhāntalaghumañjūṣā* [page]. See Bhandari, Madhava Shastri et al.

MDhVṛ. *Mādhavīyadhātuvṛtti* [gaṇa, serial number]. See Dwarikadas Shastri.

Narasimhacharya, M. S.

1973-83 *Commentaires sur le Mahābhāṣya de Patañjali et le Pradīpa de Kaiyaṭa, Mahābhāṣya Pradīpa Vyākhyānāni.* Ten volumes. Publications de l'Institut Français d'Indologie 51,1-51,10. Pondichéry: Institut Français d'Indologie.

Pr. *Mahābhāṣyapradīpa* [volume, page]. See Vedavrata.

RaPr. *Ratnaprakāśa* [volume, page]. See Narasimhacharcya, M. S.

Rau, Wilhelm

1977 *Bhartṛharis Vākyapadīya, Die Mūlakārikās nach den Handschriften herausgegeben und mit einem Pāda-Index versehen.* Abhandlungen für die Kunde des Morgenlandes Band XLII, 4. Wiesbaden: Steiner.

ṚV *Ṛgveda.* See Sontakke, N. S. et al.

SDS *Sarvadarśanasaṅgraha.* See Abhyankar, Kashinath Vasudev.

Sharma, Aryendra, Khanderao Deshpande and D. G. Padhye

1969-70 *Kāśikā, A Commentary on Pāṇini's Grammar by Vāmana & Jayāditya.* Two volumes. Sanskrit

Academy Series 17, 20. Hyderabad: Sanskrit Academy, Osmania University. Reprinted in one volume, 2008.

Sontakke, N. S. and T. N. Dharmadhikari
1970-2010 *Taittirīya Saṁhitā with the Padapāṭha and the Commentaries of Bhaṭṭa Bhāskara Miśra and Sāyaṇācārya*. Four volumes in eight parts. Poona:/ Pune: Vaidika Saṁśodhana Maṇḍala.

Sontakke, N. S. et al.
1933-51 *Ṛgveda-Saṁhitā with the Commentary of Sāyaṇāchārya*. Five volumes. Poona: Vaidic Samshodhan Mandal.

Subramania Iyer, K. A.
1983 *Vākyapadīya of Bhartṛhari* (*An ancient Treatise on the Philosophy of Sanskrit Grammar*) *Containing the Ṭīkā of Puṇyarāja and the Ancient Vṛtti, Edited ... with a Foreword by Ashok Aklujkar, Kāṇḍa II*. Delhi: Motilal Banarsidass.

TS *Taittirīyasaṁhitā. S*ee Sontakke, N. S. and T. N. Dharmadhikari.

Ud. *Mahābhāṣyapradīpoddyota* [volume, page]. See Vedavrata.

Vedavrata
1962-63 श्रीभगवत्पतञ्जलिविरचितं व्याकरण-महाभाष्यम् [श्रीकैय्यटकृतप्रदीपेन नागोजी-भट्टकृतेन भाष्यप्रदीपोद्द्योतेन च विभूषितम्] Five volumes. Gurukul Jhajjar (Rohtak): Harayāṇā-Sāhitya-Saṁsthānam.

VP *Vākyapadīya* [kāṇḍa, kārikā]. See Rau, Wilhelm.

VPVṛ. *Vākyapadīyavṛtti* [kāṇḍa, kārikā, page]. See Subramania Iyer.

VPṬī. *Vākyapadīyaṭīkā* [kāṇḍa, kārikā, page]. See Subramania Iyer.

Whitney, William Dwight
1889 *Sanskrit Grammar Including both the Classical*

Language and the older Dialects of Veda and Brahmana. Second edition. Leipzig: Breitkopf & Härtel. Eighth issue of the second edition. Cambridge, Massashusetts: Harvard University Press; reprinted 1964. Indian reprint, 1962, 1969, Delhi: Motilal Banarsidass.

Yudhiṣṭhira Mīmāṁsaka

saṁ. 2014 क्षीरतरङ्गिणी क्षीरस्वामिविरचिता पाणिनीयधातुपाठस्य पश्चिमोत्तरशाखाया व्याख्या. Ram Lal Kapoor Trust Series 25. Amritsar: Ram Lal Kapoor Trust.

Bhartṛhari on three types of linguistic unit-meaning relations*

Hideyo Ogawa

0 Introduction

In VP 1.24–26 Bhartṛhari mentions two types of linguistic unit-meaning relations (*śabdārthasambandha*): capacity (*yogyatā*) and cause-and-effect relation (*kāryakāraṇabhāva*)[1] and discusses these types in the Sambandhasamuddeśa (VP 3.3.29, 32).[2] These two types of relations form two of the eight topics to be covered by the Vākyapadīya. It is important to note, however, that, in addition to these types, Bhartṛhari accepts another type also: 'this-is-that' relation *so 'yam iti sambandhaḥ* (Vṛtti on VP 1.23 [59.1]). This relation consists in identity (*abheda*) between a linguistic unit and its meaning, or what Helārāja and Puṇyarāja call *adhyāsa* 'super-imposition'. Helārāja is acutely aware that Bhartṛhari approaches the linguistic unit-meaning relation from three different angles.

* The present paper is one of the outcomes of the seminar on the second kāṇḍa of the Vākyapadīya, conducted by Professor Ashok Aklujkar, Kyoto, October 2003–February 2004. I would like to express my heartfelt gratitude to Prof. Aklujkar for providing me with the text of the Vṛtti on the second kāṇḍa of the Vākyapadīya, critically edited, though unpublished, by him.

1. VP1.24–26: *apoddhārapadārthā ye ye cārthāḥ sthitalakṣaṇāḥ / anvākhyeyāś ca ye śabdā ye cāpi pratipādakāḥ // kāryakāraṇabhāvena yogyabhāvena ca sthitāḥ / dharme ye pratyaye cāṅgaṁ sambandhāḥ sādhvasādhuṣu // te liṅgaiś ca svaśabdaiś ca śāstre 'sminn upavarṇitāḥ / smṛtyartham anugamyante kecid eva yathāgamam //* The eight topics are as follows. Two types of meanings: meanings as they really are and abstracted meanings; two types of linguistic units: linguistic units to be explained and those which serve to explain the former; two types of relations: a causal relation and the relation of capacity; two types of results: merit, acquired by using a correct speech form, and an understanding of a meaning, brought about even by using an incorrect speech form. See Cardona 1999: 92.

2. VP 3.3.29: *indriyāṇāṁ svaviṣayeṣv anādir yogyatā yathā / anādir arthaiḥ śabdānāṁ sambandho yogyatā tathā //* See §4.2.1. VP 3.3.32: *śabdaḥ kāraṇaṁ arthasya sa hi tenopajanyate / tathā ca buddhiviṣayād arthāc chabdaḥ pratīyate //* See §1.3.

Obviously, he tries to link the three types of relations together when he says the following:

Prakāśa on VP 3.3.1 (123.4–5): *ata eva dvividhaḥ sambandhapadārtho vyavatiṣṭhate yogyatā kāryakāraṇabhāvaś ca / adhyāsas tu dvayor api paramārtha eva na pṛthag-rūpaḥ //*

"For this very reason, the entity 'relation' (*sambandha*) is posited [for a linguistic unit and its meaning] in two different manners: as *yogyatā* and as *kāryakāraṇabhāva*. Both have superimposition for their ultimate [basis]; this superimposition is not separated [from these two types of relations]."

We see here that Helārāja treats superimposition as the primary relation (*mukhyasambandha*) between linguistic unit and meaning.[3]

In this paper I shall consider: (1) why Bhartṛhari, who holds that there can obtain the above-mentioned three types of relations between linguistic unit and meaning, specifies only the capacity and the causal relation as the relation between linguistic unit and meaning; and (2) how the superimposition relation is related to the other two types. I shall thereby show that, contrary to a recent claim, Helārāja's understanding of the linguistic unit-meaning relation is well founded on Bhartṛhari's theory about it.[4] A clue for

3. Prakāśa on VP 3.3.2 (126.15–17): *evaṁ ca kṛtvā tātparyadṛśādhyāsa eva yogyatāyāṁ kāryakāraṇabhāve ca phalataḥ sambandho 'vatiṣṭhata iti sa eva mukhyaḥ /* ("Viewed in this light, in the final analysis in the relation of capacity and that of cause and effect superimposition is virtually established to be the relation [between linguistic unit and meaning]; therefore the very superimposition is a primary relation.")

4. Houben 1995: 157–162 discusses the *adhyāsa* relation, observing: "It is to be noted, that superimposition (*adhyāsa*) is according to Helārāja nothing less than the ultimate reality with regard to the two types of relation which are explicitly discussed by Bhartṛhari, namely the 'suitability' (*yogyatā*) relation and the causal relation (*kāryakāraṇabhāva*) (3.3.29, 32). If this was Bhartṛhari's conviction too, why didn't he say so in the Samuddeśa devoted to relation? From Helārāja's explanations one has to conclude that *adhyāsa* concerns the relation between individual word and individual word meaning, so if it was the main relation it should have been discussed in this Samuddeśa. As we will see

answering the first question is Pāṇinīyas' view of relation and a hint about the second question is given in the Vṛtti passage: *asyedaṁbhāve sati śabdārthayoḥ so 'yam iti [yaḥ] sambandhaḥ* (Vṛtti on VP 1.23 [59.1]). We must say that strangely no light has been thrown to the above-mentioned questions so far.

1 *śabdasya arthaḥ*; *arthasya śabdaḥ*

Between linguistic unit (*śabda*) and meaning (*artha*) there is a relation (*sambandha*). Thus one is allowed to have the utterances *śabdasya arthaḥ* 'the meaning *of* a linguistic unit' and *arthasya śabdaḥ* 'the linguistic unit *of* a meaning'. In these utterances the sixth triplet ending -*ṅas* (*śabda*-*ṅas*, *artha*-*ṅas*), whose introduction to the nominal bases *śabda*- and *artha*- is explained by A 2.3.50 *ṣaṣṭhī śeṣe*, denotes a relation.[5]

later on, there are indeed some kārikās (39–51) which can be interpreted as a support for Helārāja's mentioning of *adhyāsa*, although there is no indication that it would be the main relation, underlying the two other types." Houben 1995: 162 concludes his consideration of the *adhyāsa* relation by saying: "To conclude: (1) A commitment to the *adhyāsa* relation (in two different ways)—whether or not one holds it to be in accordance with the gist of Bhartṛhari's preferred theories—is much more prominent in Puṇyarāja's and Helārāja's commentary than in the VP itself. (2) Helārāja's *adhyāsa* remains in the context of individual words and word meanings, and may be supported, perhaps, by 39–51. Otherwise, little support is found for Helārāja's *adhyāsa*. (3) Puṇyarāja emphasizes *adhyāsa* too, likewise with little support in the kārikās themselves. His *adhyāsa* is quite different from Helārāja's because it concerns only the sentence and sentence meaning." VP 3.3.39–51 deals with the metaphorical, secondary, existence of a meaning (*upacārasattā*). According to Bhartṛhari, the existence of a cognition of a meaning is superimposed on the meaning, so that the meaning in question assumes existence. This superimposition has nothing to do with the *adhyāsa* relation between linguistic unit and meaning. It is a matter of course that "there is no indication that it [*adhyāsa*] would be the main relation, underlying the two other types." Thus in Houben's view it must follow that 'little support is found for Helārāja's *adhyāsa*'. But this is not the case. Furthermore, it is not appropriate to distinguish between Helārāja's *adhyāsa* and Puṇyarāja's. It is highly unlikely that Helārāja did not know of VP 2.40: *so 'yam abhisambandho buddhyā prakramyate yadā / vākyārthasya tadaiko 'pi varṇaḥ pratyāyakaḥ kvacit //*. According to this kārikā, the *adhyāsa* relation serves to establish the signifier-significand relation between any type of linguistic unit and any type of meaning. On this kārikā, see §8.

5. On A 2.3.50, see PWT **251**.

1.1 *kriyākārakapūrvaka*

In Pāṇinīyas' view, a relation is preceded by an action-kāraka relation (*kriyākārakapūrvaka*) and it is expressed either with an action being explicitly mentioned or not. Bhartṛhari says:

> VP 3.7.156: *sambandhaḥ kārakebhyo 'nyaḥ kriyākāraka-pūrvakaḥ / śrutāyām aśrutāyāṁ vā kriyāyāṁ so 'bhidhīyate //*
> "A relation is something different from the [six] kārakas and is preceded by an action-kāraka relation. It is denoted [by a sixth triplet ending], whether or not an action is explicitly mentioned."[6]

Examples are (1) *putro mātuḥ smarati* 'The son remembers his mother' and (2) *rājñaḥ puruṣaḥ* 'servant of the king'. (1) contains the verb form *smarati* which explicitly denotes the action of remembering and (2) contains no verb form. In (1) the sixth triplet ending *-ṅas* in *mātuḥ*, whose occurrence is accounted for by A 2.3.52 *adhīgarthadayeśāṁ karmaṇi*, denotes that relation of the mother with the act of remembering which is preceded by an action-object (*karman*) relation between the act and the mother as in *putro mātaraṁ smarati* 'The son remembers his mother'. In (2), on the other hand, the sixth triplet ending *-ṅas* in *rājñaḥ*, whose occurrence is accounted for by A 2.3.50, denotes the possession-possessor relation (*svasvāmibhāva*), which presupposes that the king and the servant take part in the same main action as certain kārakas as in the utterance *rājā puruṣāya dadāti* 'the king gives [something] to the servant', where the king serves as agent (*kartṛ*) and the servant as recipient (*sampradāna*) with respect to the action of giving (*dānakriyā*).[7] For Pāṇinīyas, any relation among substances (*dravya*), which are denoted by nominals, results from their being related to a shared action.[8] Thus we must assume that

6. For a full account of VP 3.7.156, see Cardona 2007.

7. Prakāśa on VP 3.7.156 (355.6): *rājā hi puruṣāya dadāti yatas tato rājñaḥ puruṣa iti svasvāmibhāvo 'vatiṣṭhati /*

8. See Cardona 2007: 19. The concept of a substance here is what is explained in VP 3.4.3: *vastūpalakṣaṇaṁ yatra sarvanāma prayujyate / dravyam ity ucyate*

the relation between linguistic unit and meaning as expressed by the utterances *śabdasya arthaḥ* and *arthasya śabdaḥ* is preceded by an action-kāraka relation.

1.2 *karaṇa*: *karman*

Bhartṛhari specifies what the action which a linguistic unit and a meaning conjointly bring to accomplishment is.

> VP 2.405: *kriyāvyavetaḥ sambandho dṛṣṭaḥ karaṇakarmaṇoḥ / abhidhāniyamas tasmād abhidhānābhidheyayoḥ //*
> "It is observed that an instrument (*karaṇa*) and an object (*karman*) are related to each other through the intermediary of an action. Therefore, [the relation of] that by which [a meaning] is denoted (*abhidhāna*) and that which is to be denoted by it (*abhidheya*) is regulated by the action of denoting (*abhidhā*).[9]"

Bhartṛhari here takes into consideration the following utterance:

> [1] *devadattaḥ śabdena artham abhidhatte* 'Devadatta expresses a meaning by using a linguistic unit'.

In this utterance the linguistic unit serves as instrument and the meaning as object. To express the linguistic unit as an agent as in *asiś chinatti* 'The sword cuts' for *asinā chinatti devadattaḥ* 'Devadatta cuts with a sword', one has the following utterances.

> [2] *śabdaḥ artham abhidhatte* 'A linguistic unit denotes a meaning'.
>
> [2'] *śabdaḥ artham vakti* 'A linguistic unit signifies a meaning'.[10]

We may accordingly say that a linguistic unit and a meaning are related to each other through the intermediary of the action denoted

so 'rtho bhedyatvena vivakṣitaḥ // ("That, with reference to which a pronominal that refers to an entity is used, is called a substance; this meaning is something that is intended to be conveyed as something to be differentiated.")

9. That the relation in question is regulated by the act of denoting means that whenever this relation is present, the act of denoting is also present.

10. One may have the following utterance also: [1'] *devadattaḥ śabdena artham vakti* 'Devadatta expresses a meaning by using a linguistic unit'. See VP 2.403 (§6.1), where it is stated that a linguistic unit and a meaning are related to each other through the act of expressing (*ukti*).

by *abhi-dhā* or *vac* (expressing, denoting, signifying, conveying) and that the relation between them is preceded by the relation of the linguistic unit, serving as instrument, to the action and that of the meaning, serving as object, to the same action.

Another question arises: What is the action denoted by such verbs? In his Vṛtti on the kārikā Bhartṛhari ingeniously answers this question in accordance with Pāṇiniīyas' view of an action as leading to a fruit (*phala*).[11] Bhartṛhari says:

> [A] Vṛtti on VP 2.405 (303.3–9): (a) *iha kārakāṇāṁ <u>niśrayaṇīparvaṇām</u>*[12] *iva sākṣāt sambandho nāsti* / (b) *kriyāyāṁ tv ekasyāṁ sannipatitāni tannibandhanāni kriyāvyavahitaṁ sambandham anubhavanti* / (c) *tatrābhidhānaṁ śabdaḥ karaṇam abhidheyo 'rthaḥ karma* / (d) *<u>karaṇakarmaṇoś ca kriyām antareṇa na praklṛptiḥ</u>*[13] / (e) *phalavatī ca kriyaiva nānyasyārthasya phalavattā* / (f) *tad yathā kaṇatuṣavipramokṣaviśiṣṭe taṇḍulajanmany ulūkhalamusalayoḥ karaṇādhikaraṇayor vrīhīṇāṁ ca karmaṇām udyamananipātanarūpo 'vahantiḥ <u>phalaprasavanimittaṁ</u>*[14] (g) *tathābhidhānābhidheyayor <u>api niyataṁ</u>*[15] *sampratyayākhyaṁ phalaṁ prakalpayitavyam* //
>
> "(a) In our view, there is no direct relation among kārakas, as [there is not] among the rungs of a ladder (*niśrayaṇīparvan*).[16]

11. As in *devadattas taṇḍulān pacati* 'Devadatta is cooking rice' the verb *pac* can denote actions performed by the principal agent Devadatta, such as putting a pot on the stove, so in [1] and [1'] (see note 10) the verb *dhā* preceded by the upasarga *abhi* and the verb *vac* can denote actions performed by the principal agent Devadatta, a speaker, such as applying (*viniyoga*) and directing (*praṇidhi*). See §6. On the denotation of kārakas' own activities by a verb, see Cardona 1974: 237.

12. Iyer: *niśreṇīparvaṇām*.

13. Aklujkar: *karaṇakarmaṇoś ca [na] kriyām antareṇa praklṛptiḥ*.

14. Iyer: *phalaprasavānimittaṁ*.

15. Aklujkar: *tathābhidhānābhidheyayor a[bhidhā]niyataṁ*.

16. Vṛtti on VP 2.197 (237.15–16): *kriyā hi dvayor arthayor upaśleṣikā niśrayaṇīparvasambandhanakāṣṭhavad upagrāhikā* / ("Indeed, an action, uniting two entities, helps them to be related to each other, just as [two vertical] pieces of

(b) When kārakas assemble (*saṁnipatita*) for the purpose of bringing a single action to accomplishment, however, they enjoy, on the basis of the action, a relation, which obtains through the intermediary of that action.
(c) There [in the case of the relation between linguistic unit and meaning], that by which [a meaning] is denoted (*abhidhāna*), a linguistic unit, is an instrument and that which is denoted by it (*abhidheya*), a meaning, is an object.
(d) And it is not in order for a certain thing to be an instrument or an object without an action.
(e) Furthermore, an action alone brings forth fruit (*phalavatī*) and nothing else.
(f) For example, [in the situation expressed by the utterance *vrīhīn avahanti* '... beat (out) the [unhusked] rice', the arising of polished rice (*taṇḍulajanman*), which is qualified by the removing husks from grain (*kaṇatuṣavipramokṣa*), is related to a wooden mortar (*ulūkhala*) which serves as locus (*adhikaraṇa*), a pestle (*musala*) which serves as instrument, and the unhusked rice (*vrīhi*) which serves as object. In this case, the action of beating (*avahanti*) constituted by lifting and letting fall [the instrument] (*udyamana-nipātanarūpa*) is the cause of producing the fruit [in the form of the arising of polished rice].
(g) Similarly, [with reference to the action of denoting which is] related to that by which [a meaning] is denoted and to that which is to be denoted by it, too, it is to be assumed that this action produces a specific (*niyata*) fruit which is called the understanding [of a meaning] (*sampratyaya*).[17]"

wood which connect the rungs of a ladder.") This statement is parallel to the following Bhāṣya passage. MBh on A 2.1.34–35 (I.386.22–387.1): *kārakāṇāṁ kriyayā sāmarthyaṁ bhavati na teṣām anyonyena / tadyathā niśrayaṇyā dvābhyāṁ kāṣṭhābhyāṁ sāmarthyaṁ na teṣām anyonyena /* See Cardona 2007: note 42.
17. Vt. 2 on A 1.1.68: *na vā śabdapūrvako hy arthe saṁpratyayas tasmād*

The point made in [A](a)–(b) is that kārakas are related to one another through the intermediary of an action, which has already been shown in §1.1. In [A](c) it is explicitly stated that a linguistic unit and a meaning respectively function as instrument and as object with respect to one and the same action of denoting. Let us note [A](e)–(g). Bhartṛhari says the following. An action bears fruit (*phalavat*).[18] Just as in *vrīhīn avahanti* the action of beating produces the fruit of the arising of polished rice, so in [1] the action of denoting produces the fruit of the understanding of a meaning. A parallel argument is found in the Mahābhāṣyadīpikā.[19] According to Bhartṛhari, the result of the action of denoting is: an understanding of a meaning (*sampratyaya*), the conveying of a meaning (*pratyāyana*), a cognition of a meaning (*tadavabodha*). The action denoted by *abhi-dhā*, we may say, consists in the activity that leads to these fruits. Thus [2] can be paraphrased as follows:

> [3] *śabdaḥ arthasampratyayam* (*arthāvabodham*) *janayati* 'A linguistic unit brings about the understanding of a meaning'.

arthanivṛttiḥ // MBh on A 1.1.68 (I.176.5–6): *śabdapūrvako hy arthe saṁpratyayaḥ / śabdapūrvako hy arthasya saṁpratyayaḥ /* A hearer understands a meaning after hearing a linguistic unit. It is likely that Bhartṛhari has the present vārttika in mind in using the term *sampratyaya* here.

18. An action is a composite of component actions, which leads to a result. When Bhartṛhari states the following kārikā, he takes this for granted. VP 3.8.15: *anantaraṁ phalaṁ yasyāḥ kalpate tāṁ kriyāṁ viduḥ / pradhānabhūtāṁ tādarthyād anyāsāṁ tu tadākhyatā //* According to Bhartṛhari, in the view of some, a component action immediately after which a certain result comes about is called *kriyā* 'action' and other preceding component actions are secondarily called so on account of the relation such that the latter are meant for the former.

19. MBhD IV.1.24.24–25.1: *arthapratyāyanaṁ bodhaḥ / tatra pratyāyyo 'rthaḥ / pratyāyanaṁ phalam / śabdaḥ karaṇam / śabdārthayoḥ karmakaraṇayoḥ asati kriyārthe sambandhābhāvāt kriyābhyupagantavyā / yathā ca dhānyānāṁ vrīhīṇām avahanane muśalodyamananipātanābhyāṁ vyavahitena sambandho bhavati tataś ca kaṇamokṣatuṣavipramokṣaḥ phalaṁ nirvartate / evam ihāpi śabdo dravyabhūtaḥ karaṇam / arthaḥ karma pratyāyyate / tadavabodhaḥ phalam / tat phalaṁ kriyāyāḥ /* See also Vṛtti on VP 2.403 ([J](b) [§6.2]).

[3'] *śabdaḥ artham sampratyāyayati* (*avabodhayati*) 'A linguistic unit makes understood a meaning'.

1.3 **arthaḥ śabdena upajanyate*

[3] reminds us of VP 3.3.32, in which Bhartṛhari assumes that the action of bringing about connects a linguistic unit and a meaning. The kārikā is as follows:

VP 3.3.32: *śabdaḥ kāraṇam arthasya sa hi tenopajanyate / tathā ca buddhiviṣayād arthāc chabdaḥ pratīyate //*
"A linguistic unit is the cause of a meaning. For a meaning is brought about by a linguistic unit. In addition, a linguistic unit is understood from a meaning which is in the domain of the mind (*buddhiviṣaya*)."

A linguistic unit is understood by a hearer when it is uttered, brought about, by a speaker. Here Bhartṛhari assumes that one may have the following utterances:

[4] *śabdaḥ artham janayati* 'A linguistic unit brings about a meaning'.

[5] *arthaḥ śabdam janayati* 'A meaning brings about a linguistic unit'.

It goes without saying that [4] is pertinent to the situation where from hearing a linguistic unit there arises the understanding of a meaning to a hearer of the linguistic unit and that [5] the situation where a speaker utters a linguistic unit to convey to a hearer the meaning which the speaker has in mind.[20] The question of how a causal relation obtains between linguistic unit and meaning shall be discussed in detail later.[21]

1.4 As shown above (§1.1), a linguistic unit and a meaning are related to each other through the intermediary of the act denoted by *abhi-dhā* or *vac* and the act of bringing about. This is how it is

20. Prakāśa on VP 3.3.32 (145.13–15): *śrotṛbuddhyupārūḍhasyārthasya śabdaḥ kāraṇaṁ janakatvāt / śabdārtho hy artho bahīrūpatayāvasīyamānaḥ / tathā cānyac ca vaktṛbuddhiniveśino 'rthāt kāraṇabhūtāt śabdaḥ śrutiviṣayam anuprāptaḥ pratīyata ity artho 'pi śabdasya kāraṇam /*

21. See §3.

established that, between linguistic unit and meaning, there obtain the relation of what denotes and what is to be denoted (*abhidheyābhidhānabhāva*) or that of signifier and significand (*vācyavācakabhāva*) and that of cause and effect (*janyajanakabhāva, kāryakāraṇabhāva*).

2 *artha*: *svarūpa*, *bāhyārtha*, *jñāna*

To be sure, there are the above-mentioned relations between linguistic unit and meaning, but we are now confronted with the question of what is meant by the term *artha* 'meaning'. As [3] and [4] suggest, this term may have different senses, since what a linguistic unit brings about is the understanding of an artha in [3] and it is just an artha in [4]. Thus we have to consider the following kārikā, in which Bhartṛhari mentions a threefold meaning that is related to a single linguistic unit.

> VP 3.3.1: *jñānaṁ prayoktur bāhyo 'rthaḥ svarūpaṁ ca pratīyate / śabdair uccaritais teṣāṁ sambandhaḥ samavasthitaḥ //*
>
> "A speaker's cognition (*prayoktur jñānam*), an external object (*bāhyo 'rthaḥ*), and a linguistic unit's own form (*svarūpa*) are understood from linguistic units which have been uttered. The relation of those things with the linguistic units is fixed [in both the things and the linguistic units]."

The meaning (*artha*) which is deemed to be related to a linguistic unit is threefold: a cognition (*jñāna*), an external object (*bāhyārtha*), and the linguistic unit's own form (*śabdasvarūpa*). How is the linguistic unit related to these meanings?

It may be useful in this connection to consider what Helārāja says in commenting on the present kārikā. He makes the following points:[22]

22. Prakāśa on VP 3.3.1 (122.5–123.7): *prayogeṇābhijvalitaiḥ śabdais tritayam avagamyate—ātmīyaṁ rūpam arthaś ca phalasādhanaḥ prayoktur abhiprāyaś ca / ... svarūpe prathamaṁ pratipattir ... / tato 'dhyastasvarūpe 'rthakriyākāriṇīty ābhyām arthasvarūpābhyāṁ śabdasya vācyavācakasambandhaḥ /*

1. From a manifested (*abhijvalita*) linguistic unit[23] three factors are understood: the linguistic unit's own form; an external object, which brings forth fruit or causal efficacy (*arthakriyā*) and on which the linguistic unit's own form is superimposed (*adhyastasvarūpa*); and a speaker's intention (*prayoktrabhiprāya*).
2. Between a linguistic unit and an external object and between the linguistic unit and its own form, the signifier-significand relation (*vācyavācakasambandha*) obtains.
3. Between a speaker's intention and a linguistic unit, the cause-effect relation obtains.
4. Between what a speaker has in mind (*vaktrabhiprāyārūḍha*) and a linguistic unit, the cause-effect relation obtains.[24]

prayoktrabhiprāyeṇa tu saha kāryakāraṇabhāvaḥ / ... vaktrabhiprāyārūḍhasyaiva śabdārthatve tatra kāryakāraṇasambandham āha / ... yathā cehopacārasattāsamāviṣṭaṁ vastu śabdārthaṁ vakṣyati tathā kāryakāraṇabhāvo 'pi sambandhaḥ /

23. See Vṛtti on VP 1.25 ([D] [§3.2]), where the expression *nādābhivyakta* 'manifested by the sequential utterance of sounds' is employed.

24. See §3.2. Helārāja cites from Dharmakīrti's Pramāṇavārttika, Pramāṇasiddhi chapter, to support this point. PV II.2: *vaktṛvyāpāraviṣayo yo 'rtho buddhau prakāśate / prāmāṇyaṁ tatra śabdasya nārthatattvanibandhanam //* According to Dharmakīrti, the meaning which a speaker intends to convey appears in a hearer's cognition; a linguistic unit is a valid means of cognition with respect only to the intended meaning and not to reality. In commenting on VP 3.3.1, Helārāja says the following. Bhartṛhari, accepting that what a speaker has in mind is a meaning of a linguistic unit, states that a linguistic unit has a causal relation to something a speaker has in mind. This is to include incidentally (*upasaṁgrahārtham*) the view of those (Buddhists) who accept that an external object is not the meaning of a linguistic unit, since the science of grammar is an associate of all schools of thought. Prakāśa on VP 3.3.1 (123.14–15): *sarvapārṣadaṁ punar idaṁ śāstram iti ye bāhyasyārthasya śabdavācyatvaṁ necchanti tanmatopasaṅgrahārthaṁ vaktrabhiprāyārūḍhasyaiva śabdārthatve tatra kāryakāraṇasambandham āha /* This remark of Helārāja's is somewhat misleading. From his remark we should not understand that Pāṇinīyas do not hold what a speaker has in mind to be the meaning of a linguistic unit or that the concept of the causal relation between linguistic unit and meaning is not rooted in the Pāṇinian tradition. As shall be shown further on, Bhartṛhari builds up the theory on the linguistic unit-meaning relation by means of considering closely what a speaker and a hearer have in mind in actual communication. When

5. Between a linguistic unit and an entity which is endowed with metaphorical existence (*upacārasattāsamāviṣṭavastu*), the cause-effect relation obtains. This existence consists in the image of an object (*arthākāra*) which appears in the mind (*buddhisamārūḍhārthākārarūpā sattā*).[25]

Point 1 shows that Bhartṛhari means a speaker's intention by 'a speaker's cognition' (*prayoktur jñānam*). Point 5 shows that the cognition related to a linguistic unit is not restricted to a speaker's and that a hearer's cognition is also related to the same linguistic unit. Thus [4] and [5] may be respectively paraphrased as follows:

[6] *śabdaḥ jñānam janayati* 'A linguistic unit brings about a cognition.'

[7] *jñānam śabdam janayati* 'A cognition brings about a linguistic unit'.

In this connection it is important to note that [7] is a paraphrase of the following utterance:

[7'] *buddhiviṣayārthaḥ śabdam janayati* 'A meaning in the domain of the mind brings about a linguistic unit'.[26]

Helārāja says the above, he must intend to imply that Bhartṛhari's argument that there is a causal relation between linguistic unit and meaning results in including the Buddhists' view.

25. VP 3.3.39: *vyapadeśe padārthānām anyā sattaupacārikī / sarvāvasthāsu sarveṣām ātmarūpasya darśikā //* ("By virtue of verbal expression, [external] entities (*padārtha*) have a different existence, which is something metaphorical and which, of all entities in all states, presents their own images.") Prakāśa on VP 3.3.39 (150.11–13): *vyapadeśe vyapadeśanimittaṁ śabdena pratyāyane padapratyāyyānām arthānāṁ bāhyānāṁ vastūnāṁ bāhyavilakṣaṇā sattā buddhyopacaritā bāhyārthasattāyā hi anyā buddhisamārūḍhārthākārarūpā sattā /*

26. See VP 3.3.32 (§1.3).

Patañjali uses the term *buddhiviṣaya* to refer to something mental.[27] According to Helārāja, by the term *jñāna* in the present kārikā Bhartṛhari means what appears in a speaker's intention (*vaktrabhiprāyārūḍha*) [point 4] and the image of an object which appears in a hearer's mind (*buddhisamārūḍhārthākāra*) [point 5]. Accordingly, [6] and [7] must be respectively paraphrased as follows:

[8] *śabdaḥ arthākārajñānam janayati* 'A linguistic unit brings about a cognition with the image of an object'.

[9] *arthākārajñānam śabdam janayati* 'A cognition with the image of an object brings about a linguistic unit'.

Bhartṛhari thoroughly discusses how the image of an object takes part in a verbal cognition, which shall be considered in dealing with the causal relation between linguistic unit and meaning.[28]

Concerning a speaker's intention, there is a point to make clear. As shown in VP 3.3.1, what is understood from a linguistic unit must be a meaning of the linguistic unit.[29] In Bhartṛhari's view, a mere intention of a speaker, which is something understood through inference (*anumāna*), should not be considered to be a

27. MBh on A 3.1.26 (II.36.17–18): *te 'pi hi teṣām utpattiprabhṛty ā vināśād ṛddhīr vyācakṣāṇāḥ sato buddhiviṣayān prakāśayanti /* Patañjali says: Narrators of the story of the slaying of Kaṁsa, when speaking of his flourishing from birth to death, illuminates in the mind of the audience him, who is existent as something in the domain of their minds. The point made by Patañjali is stated by Bhartṛhari in VP 3.7.5, as follows: *śabdopahitarūpāṁś ca buddher viṣayatāṁ gatān / pratyakṣam iva kaṁsādīn sādhanatvena manyate //* ("And besides, [a narrator of the story of the slaying of Kaṁsa and the like] considers [them] to be a sādhana, whose forms [i.e., images] have been created by linguistic units and who have entered the domain of his mind, as if the narrator perceived them.") Paddhati on Vṛtti to VP 1.23 (61.28): *sato buddhiviṣayān iti / buddhiviṣayān sata iti / buddhisthān sata ity arthaḥ /*

28. See §3.

29. Evidently, in VP 3.3.1 Bhartṛhari presupposes Pāṇinīyas' definition of 'meaning' (*artha*), which is given in VP 2.330: *yasminn uccarite śabde yadā yo 'rthaḥ pratīyate / tam āhur arthaṁ tasyaiva nānyad arthasya lakṣaṇam //* ("When a linguistic unit is uttered, a thing (*artha*) is understood. [Others (Grammarians)] call the thing the meaning (*artha*) of the very linguistic unit. There is no other definition of 'meaning'.") According to this definition, a meaning is what is understood from a linguistic unit when it is uttered.

meaning.[30] To understand what a speaker intends to convey is one thing and to understand that a speaker has the intention to convey something is another. Not to speak, what a speaker intends to convey by uttering a linguistic unit must be considered to be a meaning of the linguistic unit.

Point 2 shows that [2] is paraphrased as follows:

[10] *śabdaḥ bāhyārtham abhidhatte* 'A linguistic unit denotes an external object'.

[11] *śabdaḥ svarūpam abhidhatte* 'A linguistic unit denotes its own form'.

We need not take a linguistic unit's own form into consideration here since it is the most internal, non-deviating, meaning of a linguistic unit and hence it necessarily takes part in a verbal cognition.[31] Regarding [10] questions arise. As shown by [3], [10] is paraphrased as follows:

30. VP3.14.198: *śabdād arthāḥ pratāyante sa bhedānāṁ vidhāyakaḥ / anumānaṁ vivakṣāyāḥ śabdād anyan na vidyate //* ("[Different] meanings unfold from [different] linguistic units. Linguistic units create differences [with regard to a single entity]. There is no other means of inferring (*anumāna*) a speaker's intention than the linguistic unit.") A speaker utters a linguistic unit which is capable of conveying the meaning the speaker intends to convey. With reference to the same woman, if the word *dāra* (m.) is used by a speaker, a hearer understands that the speaker of this word has the intention to convey the woman as qualified by the property of being a male; if the word *bhāryā* (f.) is used by a speaker, a hearer understands that the speaker of this word has the intention to convey the woman as qualified by the property of being a female. Prakāśa on VP 3.14.198 (247.24): *dāraśabdaḥ striyaṁ puṁstvaviśeṣaṇām ācaṣṭe / bhāryāśabdaḥ strītvaviśiṣṭām /*

31. VP 3.3.2: *pratipattur bhavaty arthe jñāne vā saṁśayaḥ kvacit / svarūpeṣūpalabhyeṣu vyabhicāro na vidyate //* ("In some cases a hearer entertains a doubt as to an external object or its cognition. When linguistic units' own forms are perceived, there is no deviation in their understanding.") A hearer (*pratipattṛ*), who has not learned the relation between linguistic unit and meaning or who has heard a homonym such as *akṣa* 'axis, cart, die, etc.', conceives a doubt: On the basis of the cognition of what did a speaker utter a linguistic unit? Even such a hearer can understand the linguistic unit's own form. Prakāśa on VP 3.3.2 (127.13–16): *apravṛttasaṅketasya arthe tadviṣaye jñāne sandeho jāyate na tu śrute svarūpe / arthāparijñānāc ca kim ayaṁ veda vaktety ayam api vaktṛjñānaviṣayaḥ sandeho jāyata evāpravṛttasaṅketasyāpy akṣādisāmānyaśabdād eva cākṣādau sandeho na tu svarūpa iti siddham /*

[12] *śabdaḥ bāhyārthāsampratyayam janayati* 'A linguistic unit brings about the understanding of an external object'.

What is the understanding of an external object? How is this understanding linked with the cognition with the image of an object? These questions are also fully discussed by Bhartṛhari in his Vṛtti in dealing with the causal relation between linguistic unit and meaning.

3 *kāryakāraṇabhāva*

In the Vṛtti on VP 1.23 and 1.25 Bhartṛhari gives a detailed account of the causal relation between linguistic unit and meaning.

3.1 Vṛtti on VP 1.23 *arthasarūpapratyavabhāsa*

VP 1.23 states that the Pāṇinian tradition declares that the relation between linguistic unit and meaning is permanent (*nitya*).[32] In the Vṛtti on this kārikā Bhartṛhari mentions three types of relations, to which I referred earlier in §0.

[B] Vṛtti on VP 1.23 (60.2–61.2): *arthasarūpapratyavabhāsānāṁ vā pratyayānāṁ bāhyeṣv artheṣu pratyastānām akṣaranimittākṣarakalpanāvad arthavad evaikaviṣayatve*[33] *'bhyupagamyamāne nityam avicchinnapāramparyaḥ kāryakāraṇabhāvaḥ śabdārthayoḥ sambandhaḥ /*

"(a) Alternatively, [there obtains a causal relation between linguistic unit and meaning.]

(b) [From a linguistic unit there arise] cognitions (*pratyaya*) in which a form similar to an [external] object appears (*arthasarūpapratyavabhāsa*).[34]

(c) [In this case] they are superimposed (*pratyasta*) on external objects (*bāhyeṣv artheṣu*).[35]

32. VP 1.23: *nityāḥ śabdārthasaṁbandhās tatrāmnātā maharṣibhiḥ / sūtrāṇāṁ sānutantrāṇāṁ bhāṣyāṇāṁ ca praṇetṛbhiḥ //*

33. Aklujkar: *arthatve.*

34. Paddhati on Vṛtti to VP 1.23 (61.10): *arthena bāhyena samānarūpapratyavabhāso yeṣāṁ pratyayānām /*

35. Paddhati on Vṛtti to VP 1.23 (61.11–13): *yadā te pratyayās teṣu bāhyeṣv artheṣu pratyastā buddhyāropitā bāhyam evedaṁ vastv iti paricchidyamānāḥ kiñcitsādṛśyāt pratyastā bhavanti, yatas taddarśanāt tadadhyavasāyaḥ /*

> (d) [Consequently] it is always (*nityam*)[36] accepted that they have objects identical with the external objects (*tadeka-viṣayatva*) as if they had for their objects the external objects (*arthavat*).
> (e) This is comparable to the case where written symbols (*lipyakṣara*) which have as their causes [true articulated] sounds (*akṣaranimitta*) are spoken of as sounds (*akṣara-vyavahāra*).[37]
> (f) This being the case, there obtains a causal relation [whose understanding is conditioned by convention (*samayopādhi*)]; this relation comes down in uninterrupted transmission [and hence is permanent].[38]"

According to Vṛṣabha, when there arise cognitions in which a form similar to an external object appears, they are superimposed on external objects because of some similarity in form; and, when this superimposition takes place, one determines that the entity one has in mind is nothing other than an external object (*bāhyam evedaṁ vastu*), since the cognition that this is X (*taddarśana*; *darśana*, see [D] [§3.2]) leads to the determination such that X is an external object (*tadadhyavasāya*).

36. Paddhati on Vṛtti on VP 1.23 (61.16): *nityam iti / sadaivaiṣām arthākāra-pratyayajananam /* Vṛṣabha says that whenever meaningful linguistic units are uttered, they bring about cognitions in which an image of an object appears. This is the reason that the cognitions appear as if they had for their objects external objects. The form of an object which appears in such cognitions is determined to be an external object. See Vṛtti on VP 1.25 ([C](b) [§3.2]).

37. Paddhati on Vṛtti to VP 1.23 (61.13–14): *yathākṣaranimitteṣu lipyakṣareṣu anakṣareṣv apy akṣaravyavahāraḥ tadekatvavyavasāyaś ca lipidarśane 'kṣarāvabodhāt tathā tadrūpe 'pi pratyaye 'rthavyavahāra iti /* According to Vṛṣabha, one speaks of written symbols, which are in reality not articulated sounds, as articulated sounds and as identical with them since on seeing the written symbols one understands them to be articulated sounds; in the same manner, one speaks of a cognition, in which a form similar to an external object appears, as the external object.

38. The phrase *samayopādhiḥ* is construed with the phrase *kāryakāraṇabhāvaḥ*. According to Vṛṣabha, only one who has learned the causal relation between a linguistic unit and a meaning can have the understanding of the meaning from the linguistic unit. In this sense *samaya* 'convention' may be said to function as a co-operator (*sahakārin*). Paddhati on Vṛtti to VP 1.23 (61.17): *atrāpi samayopādhir iti sambandhanīyam / tena sahakāriṇā saha kāryajananāt /* Here the term *samaya* means the observation of the usage of elders (*vyavahāradarśana*).

The present Vṛtti explains the causal relation between linguistic unit and meaning from a hearer's point of view. [B](b) says that the cognition that arises from a linguistic unit has a form similar to an external object (*arthasarūpa*). This cognition is superimposed on the external object ([B](c)). When this superimposition takes place, the cognition appears as if it had for its object the external object because it has an object identical with the external object ([B](d)). According to Vṛṣabha, this amounts to saying that the form (*rūpa*) or image (*ākāra*) which appears in the cognition is determined to be the external object.[39] The form which appears in the cognition is assumed to be the external object, just as a written symbol is assumed to be an articulated sound itself ([B](e)). This implies that when a hearer understands something from a linguistic unit, the hearer understands it as if it existed in the external world.[40]

3.2 Vṛtti on VP 1.25 *arthākāra*

VP 1.25 is one of the set of kārikās (VP 1.24–26) which mentions the eight topics to be dealt with in the Vākyapadīya.[41] In the kārikā in question Bhartṛhari mentions the two types of relations between linguistic unit and meaning, *yogyatā* 'capacity' and *kāryakāraṇa-bhāva* 'causal relation'. The following Vṛtti passages explain the causal relation.

In connection with the relation of capacity, Vṛṣabha says (Paddhati on VP 1.23 [60.20–21]): *samayo vyavahāradarśanam / sa upādhir asyā yogyatāyāḥ / bhūyastvena vyavahāraṁ dṛṣṭavataḥ sa yogyatāpratipattinibandhanam /* Helārāja also says the same thing. Prakāśa on VP 3.3.31 (144.25): *vṛddhavyava-hāraparamparāparaparyāyāt samayāt ... /* One learns the relation between linguistic unit and meaning from the usage of elders.

39. According to Vṛṣabha, the point made by the present Vṛtti passage is: From a linguistic unit there arises a cognition with an image of an object, which image is determined to be an external object; in this case the linguistic unit is a cause and the cognition is an effect. Paddhati on Vṛtti to VP 1.23 (61.14–15): *śabdād dhi sārthākārā buddhir utpadyate taṁ tv ākāram ayaṁ bāhyatvena manyate iti kāryakāraṇalakṣaṇaḥ sambandhaḥ /*

40. Similarly, a speaker speaks of a thing as if it existed in the external world. See note 27.

41. See note 1.

To begin with, Bhartṛhari explains that a linguistic unit is the cause of a meaning, as follows:

[C] Vṛtti on VP 1.25 (71.4–5): *arthākāranirbhāsamātrānugatasya pratyayasyārtheṣu pratyastarūpasyārthatvenādhyavasāye tasyārthātmanaḥ śabdo nimittam /*

"(a) A cognition (*pratyaya*) is accompanied by images of objects (*arthākāra*), which are something appearing in the cognition (*nirbhāsa*) and which appear as if they were parts (*mātrā*) of the cognition.

(b) The cognition is determined to be external objects (*arthatvenādhyavasāyaḥ*) because its forms are superimposed on external objects.

(c) When this determination takes place, a linguistic unit is the cause (*nimitta*) of that cognition which is identical with the external objects (*tasyārthātmanaḥ*)."

[C](a) clearly says that, in a cognition arising from a linguistic unit, there appears an image of an object, which appears as if it were part of the cognition. [C](b) says the same thing as [B](c)–(d). We notice that for Bhartṛhari there is no ontological distinction between a cognition and the image appearing in the cognition.[42] As shown in [C](c), when a cognition has the image which is identified with an external object on account of the determination of the image as the external object, the cognition itself is said to be identical with the external object.[43]

Bhartṛhari goes on to explain that a meaning is the cause of a linguistic unit.

[D] Vṛtti on VP 1.25 (71.5–6): *tathārthāvagrahadarśanaṁ so 'yam iti śabdārthayoḥ sambandhaprasiddher nādābhi-*

42. Paddhati on Vṛtti to VP 1.25 (71.16–17): *arthākārair nirbhāsair avayava* [read: *avayavair*] *ivānusyūtasya pratyayasya / artheṣu iti / teṣāṁ bāhyārthatvenādhyavasāyāt te tatra pratyastā ucyante /*

43. Paddhati on Vṛtti to VP 1.25 (71.17–18): *arthatvena iti / vastutvena / tasyārthātmano buddhiniviṣṭasya śabdo nimittakāraṇam /* What enters into a cognition (*buddhiniviṣṭa*) is something mental (*buddhistha*) and hence a mental image of an external object.

> *vyaktasyāntaḥkaraṇasanniveśinaḥ śabdasya pravṛttau kāraṇam* /
>
> "(a) And likewise,[44] a cognition which determines an object (*arthāvagrahadarśana*) is the cause of the occurrence of the linguistic unit which enters into the internal organ (*antaḥkaraṇasanniveśin*) [i.e., a linguistic unit enjoying mental existence (*buddhistha*)][45] and which is manifested by the sequential utterance of sounds (*nādābhivyakta*).
>
> (b) For the relation of 'this-is-that' is established between linguistic unit and meaning."

According to Vṛṣabha, what Bhartṛhari means by *arthāvagraha-darśana* 'a cognition which determines an object' is a cognition with an image of an object (*arthākāraḥ pratyayaḥ*).[46] It is important to note here that the linguistic unit which is deemed to be the cause of a meaning is something mental which is to be manifested by the sequential utterance of sounds.[47] This is an indication that a meaning brings about a linguistic unit within the mind of a speaker. Vṛṣabha describes this: the cognition with the image of a linguistic unit arises from the cognition with the image of an object.[48]

44. Paddhati on Vṛtti to VP 1.25 (71.18–19): *evaṁ kāryakāraṇalakṣaṇaṁ sambandham abhidhāyātraivābhedalakṣaṇam antarbhāvayiṣyann āha tathā iti* / It is important to note here that Vṛṣabha states that [D] is meant for including the relation of identity in the causal relation. See §6.3.

45. Paddhati on Vṛtti to VP 1.25 (71.21): *antaḥkaraṇasanniveśinaḥ iti / buddhi-sthasya* /

46. Paddhati on Vṛtti to VP 1.25 (71.19–20): *arthāvagraho 'rthaparicchedaḥ tadātmakadarśanam arthākāraḥ pratyayaḥ* /

47. In VP 1.47 Bhartṛhari says that a linguistic unit which appears in a speaker's cognition (*buddhistha*) is the cause of a linguistic unit which is actually heard (*śruti*). See note 96.

48. Paddhati on Vṛtti to VP 1.25 (71.21–22): *yato 'rthākārāyā buddheḥ śabdā-kārā buddhir utpadyate* / Vṛṣabha says that a cognition with a mental image of a linguistic unit (*śabdākāra*) arises from a cognition with a mental image of an external object (*arthākāra*). In this case it is said that an external object is a cause while a linguistic unit is an effect; namely that a causal relation obtains between the two. Note that in his Paddhati on Vṛtti to VP 1.23 Vṛṣabha states that a cognition with an image of an object arises from a linguistic unit. See note 39. We may say that the relation of identity between linguistic unit and

More significantly, Bhartṛhari states that what establishes such a causal relation is the relation of 'this-is-that' ([D](b)). In his view, it is on the basis of the relation of 'this-is-that' that the image of an object brings about that of a linguistic unit. According to Vṛṣabha, the relation of 'this-is-that', which is characterized by identity (*abhedalakṣaṇa*), is included in the causal relation.[49] Naturally, it is conceivable that the relation of 'this-is-that' accounts for the fact that the cognition with the image of an object arises from the cognition with the image of a linguistic unit within the mind of a hearer. These points shall be considered in dealing with the relation of 'this-is-that' between linguistic unit and meaning.[50]

3.3 We are now able to see that Bhartṛhari views the causal relation between linguistic unit and meaning as follows:

[13] *śabdākārajñānam bāhyārthajñānam janayati*

[14] *bāhyārthajñānam śabdākārajñānam janayati*

[13] means: A cognition with the image of a linguistic unit brings about a cognition with that image of an object which is determined to be an external object. [14], on the other hand, means: A cognition with that image of an object which is determined to be an external object brings about a cognition with the image of a linguistic unit. [13] applies in a hearer and [14] in a speaker.

Three points are now ascertained: First, Pāṇinīyas hold that a cognition has an image (*ākāra*, *rūpa*). In a verbal cognition there appear the images of an object and a linguistic unit, which are precisely what is in the domain of the mind (*buddhistha*, *buddhiviṣaya*). When Pāṇinīyas say that a cognition is a meaning, they

meaning establishes the causal relation between them. See §6.3.

49. Vṛṣabha, commenting on VP 1.25 (64.15–16), says the following: *kāryakāraṇabhāvena iti / sambandhasya dvaividhyam / abhedalakṣaṇasyāsya kāryakāraṇabhāve 'ntarbhāvaṁ vakṣyati /* See note 44 and §6.3. It is important to note here that Vṛṣabha states that the relation between linguistic unit and meaning is twofold. Such an account presupposes that the relation spoken of as the one between linguistic unit and meaning is of the type *tasyedam* 'this-of-that'. See §1 and §5.1.

50. See §5.2 and §6.3.

intend to imply that the image of an object which appears in the cognition is also a meaning (*arthasya buddhirūpatā*).[51] Secondly, the expression *bāhyārthajñāna* means 'a cognition where there appears the image of an object which is determined to be an external object'. To speak of the action denoted by *abhi-dhā*, this action must consist in the activity leading to the understanding of something as if it were an external object. It goes without saying that it is because the occurrence of a verbal cognition is independent of the existence of an external object (*bāhyasattā*, *mukhyasattā*) that *bāhyārthajñāna* has to be interpreted in the above-described manner. Thirdly, the relation of 'this-is-that' plays a crucial role in determining the causal relation between linguistic unit and meaning.

4 *yogyatā*

There is no point in simply saying that there are the relation of what denotes and what is to be denoted (or that of signifier and significand) and that of cause and effect between linguistic unit and meaning. For this may be seen from observation of everyday interaction. It is evident that in the exposition of the causal relation in the Vṛtti Bhartṛhari spends himself on the task of analyzing a verbal cognition which arises from a linguistic unit and a verbal cognition which lets a speaker utter a linguistic unit. In the case of the relation of capacity, on the other hand, he imposes on himself the task of showing that this relation is permanent in his Vākyapadīya and Vṛtti. For Bhartṛhari's theory of kāraka necessarily leads him to positing the relation of capacity between linguistic unit and meaning.

4.1 *sāmarthya*

As said in §1.2, Bhartṛhari, assuming that [1] is generally used in everyday speech, observes that a linguistic unit and a meaning respectively function as instrument and as object with respect to

51. To support this point Bhartṛhari cites the Bhāṣya passage under A 3.1.26, quoted in note 27. In his Paddhati on Vṛtti to VP 1.23 (61.18) Vṛṣabha says: *buddhirūpatāṁ cārthasyāgamena pratipādayati* /.

the action denoted by *abhi-dhā*. It is well known that in the Sādhanasamuddeśa of his Vākyapadīya Bhartṛhari defines a sādhana 'what brings an action to accomplishment', or a kāraka, as follows:

VP 3.7.1: *svāśraye samavetānāṁ tadvad evāśrayāntare / kriyāṇām abhiniṣpattau sāmarthyaṁ sādhanaṁ viduḥ //*

"[Pāṇinīyas] recognize that a sādhana is the capacity with respect to bringing about actions that reside in a locus of [the capacity] itself or, in a like manner, in another locus."

In his Mahābhāṣyadīpikā, Bhartṛhari treats a linguistic unit in [1] as a substance (*dravya*).[52] Patañjali holds that a kāraka is a substance or a quality (*guṇa*) and Bhartṛhari calls the quality as a capacity (*sāmarthya*). The substance bears this quality.[53] Thus it must follow that in [1] a linguistic unit has the capacity to function as instrument with respect to the act denoted by *abhi-dhā* and that a meaning has the capacity to function as object with respect to the very same act. Vṛṣabha explicitly states that what Bhartṛhari means by *yogyatā* in the context of the relation between linguistic unit and meaning is none other than the capacity.[54] On the assumption that *abhi-dhā* signifies the act of denoting, accordingly, we may say that a linguistic unit and a meaning respectively have the capacities to denote and to be denoted. In cutting wood, one who wishes to cut the wood employs as an instrument a thing which is capable of cutting it, such as an ax. Similarly, Devadatta utters a specific linguistic unit which is capable of denoting a specific meaning. The specific linguistic unit has the capacity to denote the specific meaning. The wood, on the other hand, is capable of being cut by the ax: what is not capable of being cut cannot be cut. Similarly, the specific meaning has the capacity to be denoted by the specific linguistic unit. Thus the relation of what denotes and

52. MBhD IV.1.24.28: *śabdo dravyabhūtaḥ karaṇam /* See note 19.

53. See Cardona 1974: 275–278.

54. Vṛṣabha explicitly states that what is meant by the term *yogyatā* is *sāmarthya* 'capacity', which is a synonym of the term *śakti*. Paddhati on Vṛtti to VP 1.23 (60.14): *yogyatā iti / sāmarthyam /* On Bhartṛhari's concept of 'capacity', see Ogawa 2009.

what is to be denoted consists in a composite of the linguistic unit's capacity to denote the specific meaning and the specific meaning's capacity to be denoted by the linguistic unit. This is the relation of capacity between the specific linguistic unit and the specific meaning.

4.2 *prakāśyaprakāśakabhāva*

In the Vṛtti on VP 1.23 and 1.25 Bhartṛhari explains the relation of capacity, assuming that [3'] can be paraphrased as follows:

> [15] *śabdaḥ artham prakāśayati* 'A linguistic unit makes known a meaning.'
>
> [16] *arthaḥ śabdena prakāśyate* 'A meaning is made known by a linguistic unit'.

In these utterances, of course, a linguistic unit is intended to be conveyed as an agent with respect to the act of making known. According to Bhartṛhari, a linguistic unit has a capacity to make known a meaning (*prakāśakabhāva*, i.e., *prakāśakatva*) and a meaning has a capacity to be made known by a linguistic unit (*prakāśyabhāva*, i.e., *prakāśyatva*). Now let us consider relevant Vṛtti passages.

4.2.1 Vṛtti on VP 1.23 *samayopādhi*

As said earlier in §3.1, VP 1.23 talks about the permanence of the relation between linguistic unit and meaning. Of the relation of capacity Bhartṛhari says:

> [E] Vṛtti on VP 1.23 (60.1–2): *indriyaviṣayavad vā prakāśyaprakāśakabhāvena samayopādhir yogyatā śabdārthayoḥ sambandhaḥ /*
>
> "(a) Alternatively,[55] as between sense organs (*indriya*) and their objects (*viṣaya*), a relation such that one is capable of making known and the other is capable of being made known (*prakāśyaprakāśakabhāva*) holds between a linguistic unit and its meaning.

55. Under VP 1.23 Bhartṛhari mentions three types of relations between linguistic unit and meaning in the order of the relation of 'this-is-that', that of capacity, and that of cause and effect.

(b) This relation of capacity, [whose understanding is] conditioned by convention (*samayopādhi*), [is permanent]."

[E](a) shows that, like a sense organ and its object, a linguistic unit and its meaning have the relation of capacity, which consists in the relation of what makes known and what is to be made known (*prakāśyaprakāśakabhāva*). As said above, the relation of capacity in question must therefore consist in a composite of the capacity to make known and the capacity to be made known.[56]

[E](b) says that the relation of capacity between a linguistic unit and its meaning is that whose understanding is conditioned by convention (*samayopādhi*). The point is this: Just as the visual organ, even if it has the capacity to make known color, does not function to make known the latter requiring an assisting factor in the form of light, so a linguistic unit, even if it has the capacity to make known its own meaning, does not function to make known the latter unless it expects an assisting factor in the form of convention.[57] Accordingly, the undesirable consequence does not follow that as, for all persons, the visual organ makes known its object, so, even for a person who has not learned the relation between a linguistic unit and its meaning, the linguistic unit makes known the meaning.[58]

The present Vṛtti passage is, in passing, a parallel to the following kārikā:

56. Paddhati on Vṛtti to VP 1.23 (60.14–16): *prakāśyaprakāśakabhāvena iti / śabdasya prakāśakatvam arthasya prakāśyatvam / etad dvayaṁ saṁhatyaikaḥ sambandhaḥ na punaḥ pratyekaṁ śabdārthayor yogyatayā pṛthak sambandhābhidhānam /* Vṛṣabha comments: A linguistic unit has the property of making known (*prakāśakatva*), while a meaning has the property of being made known (*prakāśyatva*). These two properties jointly form a single relation, but each of these is not separately spoken of as a relation.

57. Paddhati on VP 1.23 (60.21–23): *tatra yathaiva cakṣurādayaḥ satyām api rūpaprakāśanayogyatāyāṁ nānapekṣitālokasahāyā rūpaṁ prakāśayanti tathā śabdāḥ satyām apy arthaprakāśanayogyatāyāṁ samayasahāyā iti /*

58. Paddhati on VP 1.23 (60.18–19): *yathaiva tarhi indriyaṁ svayogyatayā viṣayaṁ sarvasya prakāśayati tathā śabdo 'nirjñātasambandhasyāpi prakāśayed ity āha samayopādhiḥ iti /*

VP 3.3.29: *indriyāṇāṁ svaviṣayeṣv anādir yogyatā yathā / anādir arthaiḥ śabdānāṁ sambandho yogyatā tathā //*
"Sense organs have a beginningless relation of capacity with their own objects [such that the former have the capacity to make known the latter and the latter have the capacity to be made known by the former]. Similarly, linguistic units have a beginningless relation of capacity with their meanings [such that the former have the capacity to make known the latter and the latter have the capacity to be made known by the former]."

4.2.2 Vṛtti on VP 1.25 *sādhubhāva*

In the Vṛtti on VP 1.25 Bhartṛhari elaborates on the points he has made in the Vṛtti on VP 1.23.

[F] Vṛtti on VP 1.25 (71.7–9): (a)–(c) *indriyaviṣayavat tu prakāśyaprakāśakabhāvena viśiṣṭānāṁ śabdānāṁ viśiṣṭeṣv artheṣu nityam akartṛvyāpārasādhyam avyabhicarita-prasiddhasādhubhāvānāṁ vācakānāṁ* <u>*śabdānāṁ*</u>[59] *vācyeṣu yogyatvam* (d) *aprasiddhasambandhānāṁ prathamaprati-pādane samayopādhikam /*

"(a) Just as sense organs and their objects have the relation of capacity such that the former have the capacity to make known the latter and the latter have the capacity to be made known by the former, on the other hand, so also do specific linguistic units (*viśiṣṭa-śabda*) and their specific meanings (*viśiṣṭa-artha*);

(b) the relation of capacity is not something that could be brought about through the function of a creator (*akartṛ-vyāpārasādhya*).

(c) In this case, the specific linguistic units, whose correctness (*sādhubhāva*) [with respect to the specific meanings] has been established as always (*nityam*) not deviating from them, are the signifiers (*vācaka*) of the specific meanings

59. Aklujkar omits this.

and the specific meanings are the significands (*vācya*) of such specific linguistic units.

(d) Insofar as those for whom the relations between linguistic units and meanings have not been established are [observed to be] taught the relations for the first time, [the relation of capacity is] that whose understanding is] conditioned by convention."

The points made in [F](a), (b), and (d) have already been stated in Vṛtti on VP 1.23. Let us note [F](c). According to Vṛṣabha, Bhartṛhari here takes into consideration the following cases:

[17] *gośabdaḥ sāsnādimadartham prakāśayati* 'The word *go* makes known an object with a dewlap and so on'.

[18] *goṇīśabdaḥ sāsnādimadartham prakāśayati* 'The word *goṇī* makes known an object with a dewlap and so on'.

[19] *goṇīśabdaḥ āvapanaviśeṣārtham prakāśayati* 'The word *goṇī* makes known a specific vessel (*āvapana*)'.

The form *goṇī* is an incorrect speech form with respect to the object with a dewlap and so on which is understood from this form and a correct speech form with respect to the specific vessel which is also understood from this form.[60] It is open to question whether or not an incorrect speech form is a direct signifier of a meaning.[61] Therefore, Bhartṛhari here confines himself to dealing with the relation of capacity between a correct speech form and its meaning. If the view is accepted that an incorrect speech form

60. Paddhati on Vṛtti to VP 1.25 (72.6–9): *avyabhicarita iti / avyabhicaritaḥ prasiddhaḥ sādhubhāvo yeṣām iti / ye nityaṁ sādhutām aparityajantaḥ prasiddhāḥ / yathā gavādayaḥ / etac cābhidheyāvyabhicārāt / na hi gośabdaḥ svam arthaṁ jahāti / hāne punar asādhutaiva / yathā goṇīśabdasyāvapanārthaparityāge gotvena sāsnādimati pravṛttasya /*

61. That is why in the Vṛtti passages succeeding the above-cited passages Bhartṛhari states that there are two views regarding this question: the direct signifier view (*pratyakṣapakṣa*) and the indirect signifier view (*anumānapakṣa*). Vṛtti on VP 1.25 (72.2–3): *viśiṣṭapratyayotpattau ca pratyakṣapakṣeṇa vyavasthāṁ prakalpayati / anumānapakṣeṇa tu sambandhisambandhād akṣinikocādivad apabhraṁśāḥ pratyayaviśeṣeṣv aṅgabhāvam upagacchantīti /* See VP 1.180–181 and VP 3.3.30. Cardona 1999: §4 considers the question in some detail.

conveys a meaning by calling to mind a correct speech form, the incorrect speech form cannot be said to have the capacity to convey the meaning.

5 *so 'yam iti sambandhaḥ*

In [D] we have seen that the relation of 'this-is-that' between linguistic unit and meaning determines the causal relation between them.[62] We are now in a position to consider the relation of 'this-is-that' between linguistic unit and meaning. In the following, let us consider this relation.

5.1 *tasyedam*; *so 'yam*

Generally speaking, the relation of 'this-is-that' is to establish the relation of identity between two different entities. Before moving on to the main task, it is desirable to see what this relation is. Patañjali says the following:

> MBh on A 4.1.48 (II.218.13–19): *nāvaśyam ayam evābhisambandho bhavati tasyedam iti / ayam apy abhisambandho 'sti so 'yam iti / kathaṁ punar atasmin sa ity etad bhavati / caturbhiḥ prakārair atasmin sa ity etad bhavati tātsthyāt tāddharmyāt tatsāmīpyāt tatsāhacaryād iti /*
>
> "It is not necessarily the case that there is only a relation (*abhisambandha*) designated by the expression *tasyedam* 'this of that'. There is also a relation designated by the expression *so 'yam* 'this is that'.
>
> [Question] But how is a thing (Y) which is not *that* (X) spoken of as *that*?
>
> [Answer] In a fourfold manner Y which is not X is spoken of as X: due to Y being located in X (*tātsthyāt*); Y having a property of X (*tāddharmyāt*); Y being in proximity to X (*tatsāmīpyāt*); Y being accompanied by X (*tatsāhacaryāt*)."

According to Patañjali, on the assumption that Y is not X, the extended usage *Y is X* is brought into play on the basis of the identity relation between X and Y which is not a primary one but

62. See §3.2.

something superimposed.[63] Thus the relation designated by an expression of the type *so 'yam* 'this-is-that' here in the context of the relation between linguistic unit and meaning is the relation of identity which is superimposed on a linguistic unit and a meaning that are two different entities and that originally have the relation designated by an expression of the type *tasyedam* 'this-of-that'.

5.2 Vṛtti on VP 1.23 *asyedaṁbhāva*

Now we have to consider the following passage in the Vṛtti on VP 1.23:

> [G] Vṛtti on VP 1.23 (59.1–3): (a) *asyedaṁbhāve sati śabdārthayoḥ so 'yam iti yaḥ sambandhaḥ* (b) *so 'rthādeśanasya kartum aśakyatvād autpattikaḥ svabhāvasiddhaḥ* (c) *na kenacit kartrā kañcit pratipattāraṁ praty ajñātapūrvaḥ tatprathamaṁ kṛta iti* / (d) *tasmād anādir nityamprāptāvicchedaḥ*[64] *śabdārthayoḥ sambandhaḥ* /
>
> "(a) When there is the occurrence (*bhāva*) of *asyedam*, there is the relation of 'this-is-that' between linguistic unit and meaning.
>
> (b) This relation is eternal (*autpattika*) and something established by nature (*svabhāvasiddha*) [in a linguistic unit and its meaning], since one cannot teach meanings.[65]
>
> (c) It is not the case that the relation, which had not previously been known by some hearer, was created by some creator for the first time for the sake of the hearer.
>
> (d) Therefore, the relation between linguistic unit and meaning is beginningless, ever-present (*nitya*[*m*]*prāpta*), and without interruption (*aviccheda*)."

63. Pradīpa on MBh to A 4.1.48 (III.503): *caturbhir iti / āropyate tādrūpyaṁ na tu mukhyam ity arthaḥ /*

64. Aklujkar: *nityam aprāptavicchedaḥ*.

65. Patañjali gives three reasons for not teaching meanings: for the sake of brevity (*laghvartha*) to avoid the fault of infinite regress, because of impossibility (*asambhava*) owing to polysemy, and the existence of items whose meanings are not perceptible. See MBh on A 2.1.1 (I.363.7–28).

[G](b)–(d) are devoted to explaining that the relation of 'this-is-that' between linguistic unit and meaning is permanent. According to Bhartṛhari, permanence discussed by Pāṇinīyas in the context of their linguistic theory consists in the uninterrupted tradition of usage (*vyavasthānityatā*), or the uninterrupted transmission of verbal activities from generation to generation (*vyavahāra-nityatā*).[66]

We must note [G](a). According to Vṛṣabha, the compound word *asyedaṁbhāva* may be paraphrased as *asyedam ity arthasya bhāvaḥ* 'the occurrence of a thing spoken of as *asyedam*' or *asyedam iti śabdasya bhāvaḥ* 'the occurrence of the utterance *asyedam*'.[67] The thing *asyedam* or the thing referred to by the phrase *asyedam* is *sārūpya* 'the state of having this essential feature' or a cognition as its effect (*kārya*). The cognition is such that this has this for its signifier (*asyedaṁ vācakam*); this has this for its significand (*asyedaṁ vācyam*).[68] It is to be noted in passing that *sārūpya* as 'the state of having this essential feature' is, in the words of Patañjali, *tāddharmya.*[69]

In addition, the locative absolute *asyedaṁbhāve sati* 'there

66. VP 1.28: *nityatve kṛtakatve vā teṣām ādir na vidyate / prāṇinām iva sā caiṣā vyavasthānityatocyate //* Bhartṛhari says: Linguistic units, permanent or produced, have no beginning just as animate things' acquisition of bodies; being beginningless is called the permanence in the form of the uninterrupted tradition of usage. The permanence said of the causal relation and the capacity relation is also this permanence.

67. Paddhati on Vṛtti to VP 1.23 (59.12–14): *asyedam iti sārūpyaṁ jñānaṁ vā [/] tad abhidheyatvenāsyedaṁśabdenocyate / tasya bhāva iti samāsaḥ / anukaraṇaṁ vā / asyedam ity etasya śabdasya bhāva iti / kva cāsya bhāvaḥ / yatra tadartho 'sti /*

68. Paddhati on Vṛtti to VP 1.23 (59.10–12): *asyedaṁ rūpam api [/] yatra sārūpyaṁ tatrābhedena sarvasya sarveṇeti / pratipattinibandhanaṁ vā sārūpyam, tac ca svata eva vyavasthitam, asyedaṁ vācakam asyedaṁ vācyam iti jñānena kāryeṇa pratīyate /*

69. When the behavior observed in Brahmadatta is observed in a certain ascetic, the ascetic is spoken of as Brahmadatta. This is an instance of the extended usage based on *tāddharmya,* given by Patañjali. MBh on A 4.1.48 (II.218.16–18): *tāddharmyāt / jaṭinaṁ yāntaṁ brahmadatta ity āha / brahmadatte yāni kāryāṇi jaṭiny api tāni kriyanta ity ato jaṭī brahmadatta ity ucyate /*

being the occurrence of *asyedam*' signifies the domain (*viṣaya*) in which the relation of 'this-is-that', which Vṛṣabha characterizes as identity (*abheda*), occurs.[70] Furthermore, *so 'yam iti* refers to the cognition 'this is that' (*so 'yam iti jñānam*) and by *so 'yam iti* is meant the object of this cognition, that is, the non-difference in essence (*abhinnarūpatā*). The relation of identity consists in this non-difference in essence.[71] Thus [G](a) means the following:

1. *sārūpyasya bhāve sati śabdārthayoḥ so 'yam iti [yaḥ] sambandhaḥ*
   'When there is the occurrence of the state of having this essential feature (*rūpa*), there is the relation of 'this-is-that', the relation of identity, between linguistic unit and meaning';
2. *asyedaṁ vācakam asyedaṁ vācyam iti jñānasya bhāve sati śabdārthayoḥ so 'yam iti [yaḥ] sambandhaḥ*
   'When there is the occurrence of the cognition: this has this for its signifier (*asyedaṁ vācakam*); this has this for its significand (*asyedaṁ vācyam*), there is the relation of 'this-is-that', the relation of identity, between linguistic unit and meaning'.

A linguistic unit and a meaning are different entities. There is in reality no identity relation between them. Thus the essential feature of a meaning is not found in a linguistic unit nor is the essential feature of the linguistic unit found in the meaning. These two essential features are respectively brought about in the linguistic unit and in the meaning on the basis of superimposition. Consequently it follows that interpretation 1 means that the identity relation between linguistic unit and meaning is established on the basis of superimposition.

A linguistic unit (L) has its own essential feature and a mean-

70. Paddhati on Vṛtti to VP 1.23 (59.10): *asyedaṁbhāve ity abhedalakṣaṇasambandhasya viṣayakathanam /*

71. Paddhati on Vṛtti to VP 1.23 (59.15–16): *so 'yam iti / svarūpakathanam / so 'yam iti jñānena viṣayanirdeśaḥ / abhinnarūpateti yāvat /*

ing (M) also has its own essential feature. If L, losing its own essential feature, has the essential feature of M, it follows that L is M; and, if M, losing its own essential feature, has the essential feature of L, it follows that M is L. This is what is meant by the term *sārūpya*.[72]

The identity relation between a linguistic unit (L) and a meaning (M) warrants the following:

(1) On condition that the essential feature of M is superimposed on L and L is identified with M, M is understood when L is understood;

(2) on condition that the essential feature of L is superimposed on M and M is identified with L, L is understood when M is understood.

We have to note that insofar as the identity between linguistic unit and meaning is a relation, it must reside both in a linguistic unit and in a meaning.[73] According to Vṛṣabha, (1) explains the case in which a linguistic unit serves as the cause of a meaning.[74] When the essential feature of a specific meaning is transferred to,[75] or superimposed on, a specific linguistic unit so that the specific linguistic unit may have the essential feature of the specific meaning and the specific linguistic unit may be identified with the specific meaning, the specific linguistic unit, when grasped, is grasped only as something to which the image of a certain object

72. Of course, in reality it is impossible for L (or M) to lose its essential feature and get a different essential feature. To be strict, L (or M) appears as if it did so. See [H](e) (§5.3).

73. Paddhati on Vṛtti to VP 1.23 (59.16–17): *sārūpyasyobhayagatatve 'pi ... /*

74. In this case, according to Vṛṣabha, the linguistic unit has the essential feature which is identical with that of the meaning, having the identity relation with the meaning. This identity relation in the direction of the meaning is the cause of understanding the meaning when the linguistic unit is understood. And besides, when the linguistic unit has the identity relation with the meaning, it is said to have the relation in the form of the non-abandoning of the meaning (*atyāga*). Paddhati on Vṛtti to VP 1.23 (59.19–20): *sā ceyam abhinnarūpatā śabde 'rthasya pratipattihetutvāt / atyāgo 'rthena vā sambandha ity uktaḥ /*

75. Paddhati on Vṛtti to VP 1.23 (59.16–17): *śabde prakāśakatvabhāvatvāt arthasya rūpasaṁkrāntiḥ ... /*

(*arthākāra*) has been transferred.[76] Thus this linguistic unit becomes what makes known the meaning. Vṛṣabha says that when the linguistic unit has the essential feature of the meaning, one has: 'This linguistic unit denotes this meaning'.[77] This is accounted for by the second interpretation.

As Vṛṣabha states, there is a causal relation between the relation of 'this-is-that' between linguistic unit and meaning and the cognition 'This has this for its signifier'; 'This has this for its significand'. The former is the cause of the latter. The cognition in question shows that there is the signifier-significand relation between the linguistic unit and the meaning and hence that there obtain a causal relation and a capacity relation between them. Thus it follows that the relation of 'this-is-that' between linguistic unit and meaning underlies those two types of relations between them.

5.3 Vṛtti on VP 1.48: *arthe niveśitaḥ*

In VP 1.48 Bhartṛhari states that, before being uttered by a speaker to convey a specific meaning, a linguistic unit has been determined by the mind of the speaker and has entered into the specific meaning and that this linguistic unit is manifested by the sequential utterance of sounds produced by the articulatory organs.[78] These points have already been suggested by [D].[79] A question is precisely what makes it possible that one utters a specific linguistic unit to

76. Paddhati on Vṛtti to VP 1.23 (59.18–19): *śabdo gṛhyamāṇaḥ saṁkrāntārthākāra eva gṛhyate /*

77. Paddhati on Vṛtti to VP 1.23 (59.20–21): *kas tarhi śabdasyārthe vyāpāraḥ / ayam ucyate so 'rtham abhidhatta iti /*

78. VP 1.48: *vitarkitaḥ purā buddhyā kvacid arthe niveśitaḥ / karaṇebhyo vivṛttena dhvaninā so 'nugṛhyate //* Paddhati on VP 1.48 (105.10): *dhvaninā nādena / anugṛhyate abhivyajyate /* In the Vṛtti Bhartṛhari uses the terms *śabdatattva*, *dhvani*, and *nāda*. The atomic sound *dhvani* and the audible sound *nāda* are the appearance of the Word Principle (*śabdatattva*) in a form different from the one in which the Principle in itself is (*vivṛtta*). There is no need to go into details about this issue.

79. See §3.2.

convey a specific meaning. Under the Vṛtti on the present kārikā Bhartṛhari says the following:

[H] Vṛtti on VP 1.48 (105.3–6): (a) *iha śabdārthayoḥ so 'yam iti sambandhānugame kriyamāṇe yac chabdarūpam arthe samāropayitum iṣyate* (b) *yasmin vārtharūpam upayogena vyāveśaṁ labhate* (c) *tat pūrvaṁ buddhinirūpaṇayā kṛtasaṁsparśam* (d) *abhidheyātmani prāpyamāṇaṁ yathābhiprāyaṁ* (e) *rūpaviparyāseneva rūpāntaropagrāhi svarūpaṁ niveśayati* /

"(a) In our view (*iha*), when the relation of 'this-is-that' between a linguistic unit and a meaning is taught (*sambandhānugama*),[80] the form of the linguistic unit (*śabdarūpa*) [i.e., the image of the linguistic unit] is desired to be superimposed on [the form of] the meaning;

(b) or, the form of the meaning [i.e., the image of the meaning] (*artharūpa*)[81] attains entering (*vyāveśa*) into the form of the linguistic unit through the function (*upayoga*) [of superimposing itself on the form of the linguistic unit].[82]

(c) [In the case where a speaker utters the linguistic unit to

80. Paddhati on Vṛtti to VP 1.48 (105.12): *sambandhānugame iti / sambandhavyutpādane /* When one learns a relation through an utterance of the type 'this-is-that', such as *ayaṁ devadattaḥ* 'This is Devadatta', a linguistic unit used in the utterance, such as *devadatta*, is *anuvācaka* or a signifier in a secondary sense. For the linguistic unit is not established as a signifier with respect to a thing referred to by 'this' until the relation with the thing is established. This secondary signifier functions as a *dyotaka* or the revealer of the meaning. Paddhati on Vṛtti to VP 1.48 (105.11): *śabdārthayoḥ iti / vācyānuvācakatayāpy ubhayor api sambandho 'nugantavyaḥ /* In the Saṁgraha quoted in the Vṛtti on VP 1.44 (101.2–3) it is stated: *upādāno dyotaka ity eke so 'yam iti vyapadeśena sambandhopayogasya śakyatvād iti /* ("Some say the following: [When] *upādāna*[*śabda*] [i.e., a signifier] is not connected with its meaning as its signifier, it is something that brings out the meaning (*dyotaka*). For, such an *upādāna*[*śabda*] can be employed for [teaching identity] relation through an expression of the type 'this-is-that' (*so 'yam iti vyapadeśaḥ*).") On *upādānaśabda*, see §5.1.

81. Paddhati on Vṛtti to VP 1.48 (105.16): *artharūpam arthākāraḥ /*

82. Paddhati on Vṛtti to VP 1.48 (105.116–17): *upayogena iti / vyāpāreṇa svarūpasamāropaṇākhyena /*

convey the meaning,] before the utterance of the linguistic unit [the following has taken place].[83] The form of the linguistic unit[84] has already been connected with the determination by [the speaker's] cognition [i.e., it has already been determined by the cognition];[85]

(d) the form of the linguistic unit has itself (*svarūpa*) enter into the [meaning] itself which is to be denoted by the linguistic unit (*abhidheyātman*) in order that it may be obtained in the meaning according to the speaker's intention.

(e) [In this case,] the form of the linguistic unit appears as if it seized a different essential feature by means of changing its own essential feature (*rūpaviparyāsa*) [since it appears as if it abandoned the essential feature of the linguistic unit and got the essential feature of the meaning].[86]"

In VP 1.48 Bhartṛhari makes clear what is essential for a speaker to utter a linguistic unit. There are two things to be done by a speaker before the utterance of a linguistic unit: (1) the determination of a linguistic unit to be uttered; (2) the learning of the relation between the linguistic unit and its meaning to be conveyed by it. It is a matter of course that the determination of a linguistic unit precedes

83. Paddhati on Vṛtti to VP 1.48 (105.19): *pūrvam iti / uccāraṇāt /*

84. Paddhati on Vṛtti to VP 1.48 (105.18–19): *tad iti / śabdarūpam / pūrvatra hi pakṣadvaye 'pi yacchabdena śabdo 'bhihitaḥ /* Vṛṣabha suggests reading *yac chabdarūpam* in [H](a) as *yacchabdarūpam* 'the form of a certain linguistic unit' (← *yacchabdasya rūpam*) and interprets *tat* in [H](c) as referring to the form of a linguistic unit (*śabdarūpa*). Here Vṛṣabha seems to think that a linguistic unit is not distinguished from its form or image appearing in a verbal cognition.

85. Paddhati on Vṛtti to VP 1.48 (105.20–21): *buddhyādinirūpyamāṇas tadviṣayabhāvāpatteḥ spṛṣṭa ity ucyate /* Vṛtti on VP 1.54 (113.3–4): *...prayoktā śabdaviśeṣaviṣayaṁ prayatnam abhipadyamānaḥ pratiśabdaṁ paritaḥ paricchinnāñ śabdātmanaḥ saṁspṛśann iva manaḥ praṇidhatte /* Here Bhartṛhari says: a speaker, making an effort to articulate a specific linguistic unit, puts the speaker's mind to the linguistic unit to think as if the speaker touched a linguistic unit per se, determined to be differentiated in every respect from other linguistic units.

86. Paddhati on VP 1.48 (105.25): *śabdarūpam apahāyārtharūpāpatteḥ /*

its utterance ([H](c)). This determination is none other than the determination of the linguistic unit's own form.[87] Thus in [H] Bhartṛhari devotes himself to explaining how the relation between linguistic unit and meaning is taught and how one learns it.[88]

Now we have to note the point made in [H](a)–(b) that when the relation of 'this-is-that' between linguistic unit and meaning is taught, either of the following takes place for one who learns the relation:

(A) The form of the linguistic unit is superimposed on that of the meaning, that is, the form of the linguistic unit enters into that of the meaning;[89]

(B) the form of the meaning enters into that of the linguistic unit, that is, the form of the meaning is superimposed on that of the linguistic unit.[90]

The relation of 'this-is-that' may be learned in two manners: (A) is relevant to the case in which one who does not know a linguistic unit with respect to a meaning has to learn the identity relation of the meaning to the linguistic unit, while (B) the case in which one who does not know a meaning with respect to a linguistic unit has to learn the identity relation of the linguistic unit to the meaning. However, it is to be noted, once one has learned the relation in question, one can let the form of the linguistic unit merge with that of the meaning and vice versa because of the relation consisting in the relation of identity.

87. Paddhati on Vṛtti to VP 1.54 (113.11–12): *śabdoccāraṇāya prayatnam ārabhamāṇaḥ prathamataḥ śabdarūpaṁ buddhyā nirūpayati tad iti rūpeṇa /*

88. [H](d) explains the expression *arthe niveśitaḥ* '[the linguistic unit] has entered into a certain meaning' in VP 1.48. Vṛṣabha comments on this expression (105.9): *etena vyutpannasambandhatām āha.* According to Vṛṣabha, the linguistic unit which has entered into a meaning is the one whose identity relation with the meaning has been learned.

89. See note 108.

90. Paddhati on Vṛtti to VP 1.48 (105.17–18): *pūrvatra śabdādhyāropo 'rthe sampraty artharūpādhyāropaḥ śabda iti /* According to Vṛṣabha, as to (A) the following must hold: the form of the linguistic unit enters into that of the meaning.

Let us note [H](d)–(e). First of all, it is extremely important to note Bhartṛhari's concept of 'identification' (*vyāveśa* 'entering', *sanniveśayati* 'has something enter into something else').[91] According to him, the following holds:

> If X is superimposed on Y, then X enters into Y or X is identified with Y, so that X appears as if it got the essential feature of Y.

There are two points to note: First, the identification is a mental process, so that Bhartṛhari brings in the concept of a mental image (*rūpa*, i.e., *ākāra*) here. Secondly, the superimposition of X on Y is different from that of the essential feature/property of X on Y. In the former superimposition X is transferred to Y, so that X is identified with Y.[92] In the latter, on the other hand, the essential feature/property of X is transferred to Y, so that Y is treated as X.[93]

Now, with reference to the linguistic unit whose relation of 'this-is-that', the relation of identity, to a specific meaning has been established through (A) or (B), before its utterance there can be two ways of setting it and its meaning in the identity relation: (1) by means of identifying the linguistic unit with the meaning or (2) by means of identifying the meaning with the linguistic unit. [H](d)–(e) explains the case in which (1) takes place. The point is: The linguistic unit, entering into the meaning in question, identified with the meaning, and appearing as if it acquired the essential feature of the meaning, receives the meaning as its significand and becomes a signifier only of the meaning.[94] This accounts for the fact that a speaker utters the linguistic unit which serves as the

91. I find it difficult to render *-viś* and its derivates into English. It is well known that they are commonly used to describe the situation where a certain person is possessed by a demon or a devil.
92. This is also found in the superimposition of a cognition or an image of an object on an external object. See [B](c) (§3.1) and [C](b) (§3.2).
93. This superimposition is found in (1) and (2) in §5.2.
94. On the case where a meaning enters into a linguistic unit and is identified with the latter, see [K](b) (§6.2).

signifier of the meaning the speaker intends to convey and not of other meanings.

5.4 *upādānaśabda*

We have seen that the relation between linguistic unit and meaning which is to be taught and learned is the relation of 'this-is-that' between them. For one who has not learned this relation, the linguistic unit as its relatum cannot function as a signifier of the meaning as its relatum. We have to say that the relation of 'this-is-that' between linguistic unit and meaning determines a specific linguistic unit being a signifier with respect to a specific meaning. This idea, interestingly, is reflected in the concept of *upādānaśabda*.

In [D] and VP 1.48 it has been shown that a speaker utters a linguistic unit which the speaker has in mind. In VP 1.44 Bhartṛhari rightly observes that two kinds of linguistic units, between which a causal relation holds, are recognized in a speaker uttering a sound to convey a meaning:[95] according to VP 1.47, one is a linguistic unit which appears in the mind (*buddhistha*), a mental linguistic unit, and the other a linguistic unit which is actually heard (*śruti*).[96] In VP 1.44 Bhartṛhari uses the term *upādānaśabda* to distinguish meaningful sounds (*vācaka*) from mere sounds such as the gurgling of a river (*nadīghoṣa*).[97]

In the Vṛtti on VP 1.44 Bhartṛhari explains the term

95. VP 1.44: *dvāv upādānaśabdeṣu śabdau śabdavido viduḥ / eko nimittaṁ śabdānām aparo 'rthe prayujyate //* ("Experts in language recognize two linguistic elements in *upādānaśabda*s: one is the cause of linguistic elements [which are directly heard] and the other is conducive to [a hearer understanding] a meaning.") On this kārikā, see Cardona 2012: 100–101.

96. VP 1.47: *araṇisthaṁ yathā jyotiḥ prakāśāntarakāraṇam / tadvac chabdo 'pi buddhisthaḥ śrutīnāṁ kāraṇam pṛthak //* ("Just as the fire in a fire stick is the cause of another, kindled fire, so also a linguistic unit which is in the mind [of a speaker] is the cause of linguistic units which are actually heard and which are different from the former.")

97. Paddhati on VP 1.44 (100.21–22): *śabdaśabdasya nadīghoṣādāv api darśanād avacchinatti upādānaśabdeṣu iti / upādāno vācakaḥ, ... /*

upādānaśabda, making clear what happens when material sounds are understood to be meaningful.[98] Bhartṛhari says:

Vṛtti on VP 1.44 (100.6): *upādīyate yenārthaḥ svarūpe 'dhyāropyate tadbhāvam ivāpādyate*[99] *sa upādānaśabdaḥ* /

The linguistic unit termed *upādānaśabda* has three characteristics which are closely related to one another:

1. *upādīyate yenārthaḥ saḥ*:
upādānaśabda is that by which a meaning is taken.[100]
2. *yenārthaḥ svarūpe 'dhyāropyate saḥ*:
upādānaśabda is that by which a meaning is superimposed on its own form (*svarūpa*).[101]
3. *yena [ātmā] tadbhāvam ivāpādyate saḥ*:[102]

98. The Vṛtti in question (101.4) gives a different interpretation of this term: a linguistic unit to be taken as a whole (*upādeyo vā samudāya upādānaḥ*). This interpretation need not be considered here.
99. Aklujkar: *ivāpadyate*.
100. Paddhati on Vṛtti to VP 1.44 (100.25): *upādīyate iti / svīkriyate / karaṇasādhanam āha [yena iti] /*
101. This superimposition consists in the transfer of the image of an object to a linguistic unit's own form. Paddhati on Vṛtti to VP 1.44 (100.25–26): *svarūpe iti / śabdasvarūpe 'rthākārasankrāntir adhyāropaḥ /*
102. The reflexive pronoun *ātman* is to be supplied. Bhaṭṭikāvya 8.83: *kiṁ vilāpayase* 'Why do you let yourself talk?' = *kim ātmānaṁ vilāpayase* ← *tvam vilapasi*. Mallinātha comments: *kim atyarthaṁ vilāpayase vividhaṁ bhāṣayase ātmānam iti śeṣaḥ /* Bhaṭṭi gives this instance to explain A 1.4.52 *gatibuddhipratyavasānārthaśabdakarmākarmakāṇāṁ aṇikartā sa ṇau* (specifically, a verb that denotes an activity whose object is a sound [*śabdakarma*]). On this sūtra, see PWT **267**. The verb *pad* preceded by *ā* is the one which denotes a movement (*gatyartha*).

It is patent, I think, that in order to account for the form *tadbhāvam* (*tadbhāva*, acc. sg. m.) the causative form *āpādyate* (*ā-pad-**ṇic***, 3rd sg. pres. pass.) is to be assumed. The relative pronoun *yena* refers to an *upādānaśabda* as a prompter-agent (*prayojaka, hetu*). We may assume the following sentence: *yo ātmānaṁ tadbhāvam ivāpādayati saḥ* (*āpādayati*, 3rd sg. pres. act.). The demonstrative pronoun *tad-* refers to *artha*. Paddhati on Vṛtti to VP 1.44 (100.27): *tadbhāvam iti / artharūpatāṁ vihāya svabhāvataḥ svata evāpadyata ity ucyate /*

Another interpretation is also possible. 3'. *yena tad bhāvam ivāpādyate saḥ*: In this reading the relative pronoun *yena* refers to that to which the image of an object has been transferred (*pratisaṁkrāntārthākāra*), a mental linguistic *upādānaśabda* is that which appears (*iva*) to cause itself to attain the state of being the meaning.

Characteristic 1 clearly shows that what is called *upādānaśabda* is a signifier (*vācaka*) and not a mere sound such as the gurgling of a river. Characteristic 2 accords with what is stated in [H](b). Characteristic 3 shows that what is called *upādānaśabda* is that which is superimposed on the meaning, which accords with what is stated in [H](a).[103] All this shows that, in Bhartṛhari's view, a linguistic unit is what has a meaning, that on which the meaning is superimposed, and that which is superimposed on the meaning. This implies that, for one who has not learned the relation of 'this-is-that' between a linguistic unit and a meaning, the linguistic unit cannot work as a signifier of the meaning.[104] Here too we see that the relation of 'this-is-that' between a linguistic unit and a meaning

unit (*buddhisthaśabda*) or the image of the linguistic unit (*śabdākāra*). This is defined as *upādānaśabda*. The demonstrative *tad* (nom. sg. n.) refers to *svarūpa*. What is meant is that a speaker (*prayoktṛ*) causes the internal linguistic unit, *upādānaśabda*, to cause its own form to be heard. Paddhati on Vṛtti to VP 1.44 (101.7–8): *pratisaṁkrāntārthākāreṇa śabdam uccārayan prayoktā prayojaka iti ṇicā āpādyate iti paṭhanti /* According to Vṛṣabha, a speaker of a linguistic unit causes this mental linguistic unit to cause the linguistic unit to be heard/to arise.

103. According to Vṛṣabha, the superimposition of a linguistic unit on a meaning is of the nature different from that of a cot on the baby lying on the bed as in *mañcāḥ krośanti* 'The cots are crying'. Vṛṣabha says that the essential feature of a meaning which a linguistic unit appears as if it got is like a reflection in a mirror (*pratibimbakalpa*). The mirror can show both itself and the reflection. Similarly, in reality the linguistic unit does not abandons its own essential feature, so that it can convey two distinct entities: its form and its meaning. This is the reason that Bhartṛhari uses the word *iva* 'as if'. In the case of the superimposition in *mañcāḥ krośanti*, on the other hand, the cot should abandon its own essential feature; otherwise, the verb form *krośanti* '… are crying' could not be employed. Paddhati on Vṛtti to VP 1.44 (100.26–101.1): *na ca yathā mañca-puruṣayor adhyāropas tathā ity āha / tadbhāvam iti / artharūpatāṁ vihāya svabhāvataḥ svata evāpadyata ity ucyate / tasya ca rūpasya pratibimbakalpa-tvād ivaśabdopādānam / ataś ca śabdasvarūpavad arthākāram api pradarśayan pratipādayatīty ucyate /*

104. Paddhati on Vṛtti to VP 1.44 (101.15–16): *nāvyutpanne saṁvyavahārād abhede śabdasya vācakatvam /*

is essential to determining the linguistic unit to be the signifier of the meaning.

5.5 *śaktyavaccheda*

In §4 we have seen that there is the capacity relation between a linguistic unit and its meaning. According to Bhartṛhari, the establishment of the identity relation between them serves to restrict their capacities. Let us consider the following Vṛtti:

[I] Vṛtti on VP 1.68 (126.3–5): (a) *svarūpādhyāropacikīrṣāyāṁ bāhyeṣv arthātmasu* <u>*śabdārthānāṁ*</u>[105] *svarūpeṇādhiṣṭhāna-bhūtenārthavattvāt prathamā vidhīyate* / (b) *so 'yam iti ca sañjñinā śaktyavacchedalakṣaṇaḥ sambandho niyamyate / tad yathā / gaur vāhīkaḥ siṁho māṇavaka iti* /

"(a) Of the meanings of a linguistic unit, when the form of the linguistic unit is desired to be superimposed on external (*bāhya*) [i.e., other] meanings themselves [as in *ayaṁ devadattaḥ* 'This is Devadatta'], a first triplet ending (*prathamā*) is introduced [after the linguistic unit, which is a nominal base (*prātipadika*)], because of the meaningfulness (*arthavattva*) based on the linguistic unit's own form, which is its fundamental significand (*adhiṣṭhāna*).[106]

(b) By means of providing [a name with] a thing to be named by it (*sañjñin*) through an utterance of the type 'this-is-that', the relation [of the name-word with its meanings] is restricted [to a specific meaning], since the relation [of the name-word with the specific meaning] is characterized by exclusion of other denoting powers (*śaktyavaccheda*). This is comparable to the case where the utterances *gaur*

105. Aklujkar: *śabdānāṁ*.

106. In *devadattaḥ* (*devadatta-**su***), the nominal base *devadatta* is assigned the name *prātipadika* by A 1.2.45 *arthavadadhātur apratyayaḥ prātipadikam*, which provides that a meaningful element (*arthavat*) other than a verb, an affix, or an item that ends in an affix is called *prātipadika*, and the first triplet ending ***su*** is introduced after *devadatta* by A 2.3.46 *prātipadikārthaliṅgaparimāṇavacana-mātre prathamā*, which provides that when nothing more than a base meaning and a gender, a measure, or a umber is to be denoted, a first triplet ending is introduced. On these sūtras, see PWT **48** and **156**, respectively.

vāhīkaḥ 'The inhabitant of the Vāhīka country is an ox' and *siṁho māṇavakaḥ* 'The boy is a lion' are used."

In the name-giving utterance *ayaṁ devadattaḥ*, which is the kind of utterance that teaches the linguistic unit-meaning relation (*sambandhavyutpādanavākya*),[107] the nominal base *devadatta* is meaningful (*arthavat*) because it denotes its own form. In this utterance, the speaker of the utterance intends to superimpose a

107. Vṛṣabha says that the utterances given below are *sambandhavyutpādanavākyas*. Paddhati on Vṛtti to VP 1.68 (126.21): *sarvathā sambandhavyutpādanavākyam /* According to Helārāja, there are different utterances to teach the relation between linguistic unit and meaning. (1) *ayaṁ gauḥ* 'This is an ox'; (2) *ayam arthaḥ* 'This is the meaning'; (3) *ghaṭaśabdasyāyam arthaḥ* 'This is the meaning of the linguistic unit *ghaṭa* 'pot''; (4) *yadā gaur ity ucyate tadāyaṁ sāsnādimān artho boddhavyaḥ* 'When the linguistic unit *go* is uttered, this meaning, a thing with a dewlap and so forth, is to be understood'. (1), which may be paraphrased as *yo 'yam arthaḥ sa gośabdaḥ* 'That, which is this meaning, is the linguistic unit *go*', and (2), which may be paraphrased as *yo 'yaṁ śabdaḥ so 'rthaḥ* 'That, which is this linguistic unit, is the meaning, are found in everyday speech. From these utterances one has a cognition in which a linguistic unit and its meaning appear as identical with each other (*śabdārthayor abhedāvabhāsanam*). Therefore, it is determined that a linguistic unit denotes its meaning only if it denotes its own form. (3) and (4) are used to explain the relation. In these utterances the term 'this' (*ayam*) refers to the meaning grasped as identical with the linguistic unit in question (*śabdābheda*) and not to a mere meaning. Prakāśa on VP 3.3.2 (123.10–16): *ayaṁ gaur ayam artha iti śabdārthayor abhedāvabhāsanāt svarūpam abhidadhad eva śabdo 'rtham abhidhatta iti niścīyate / svarūpāvivekenaiva hy arthaparāmarśo 'bhidhānam ucyate / vṛddhavyavahārāt tathaiva sambandhavyutpatteḥ / tathā hi ayaṁ gaur iti saṅketaḥ kriyate [/] bhedenaiva ghaṭaśabdasyāyam artha iti tu vyākhyātṛbhūmir na vyavahāradaśā / atrāpi cāyam iti śabdābheda eva / yadā gaur ity ucyate tadāyaṁ sāsnādimān artho boddhavya ity apy ayam ity abhedenaiva parāmarśe saṅketapravṛttiḥ /*

It is interesting to note that Helārāja explains, by using the term *anupraveśa* 'entering into', the reason that in (1) there occurs the cognition in which the linguistic unit and the meaning appear as identical with each other. He says that from (1) the linguistic unit's own form is grasped precisely as what enters into the meaning which is the chief qualificand (*pradhānabhūtaviśeṣya*) of the verbal cognition arising from (1). Prakāśa on VP 3.3.2 (125.3–6): *tad yathā śuklaḥ paṭo 'yam iti śuklaguṇacchuraṇayā sakṛd eva viśeṣyapaṭapratyavamarśaḥ / na hy atra śuklaguṇasya pṛthakparāmarśaḥ / evaṁ ghaṭo 'yam iti pradhānabhūtaviśeṣyānupraveśenaiva ghaṭasvarūpaparāmarśa ity ekaiveyaṁ śabdanātmikā pratītiḥ śabdārthayoḥ /*

linguistic unit's own form on a meaning other than the form so as to have the form enter into the meaning.[108]

Let us note [I](b). The exclusion of other denoting powers can be explained as follows. Linguistic unit L1 has more than one power to denote a meaning: it can denote meanings M1, M2, M3; and M1 has more than one power to be denoted by a linguistic unit: it can be denoted by linguistic units L1, L2, L3. In L1 different denoting powers are intermixed (*saṅkīrṇa*) and in M1 different powers to be denoted. Once the utterance to identify L1 with M1 is made, L1's power to denote M2 and M3 are excluded (*vyavaccheda*) and its power to denote a meaning is restricted to M1 (*niyama*). The same is said of M1's power to be denoted.[109] Consider the following utterances:

A. *gaur vāhīkaḥ* 'The inhabitant of the Vāhīka country is an ox'.

B. *gām adhyāpayet* 'One should teach the ox'.

The word *go* in B refers to the inhabitant of the Vāhīka country who is spoken of as an ox in A. Now in A the inhabitant of the Vāhīka country is a thing named by the word *go*. The word *go* is a name (*sañjñā*) for the inhabitant. The word *go* has the powers or capacities (*yogyatā*, *sāmarthya*) to signify both a thing with a dewlap and the inhabitant of the Vāhīka country. In A the word *vāhīka*, which refers to a person who is to get the name *go*, excludes the power of the word *go* to signify a thing with a dewlap

108. Paddhati on Vṛtti to VP 1.68 (126.9): *ayaṁ devadatta iti śabdarūpaṁ yadā tasmin sañjñini niveśayitum icchati /* In the utterance *ayaṁ devadattaḥ* one who teaches the relation of 'this-is-that' between a certain entity to be named and the name *devadatta* wishes to have the form *devadatta* enter into the entity. According to Vṛṣabha, when there takes place the superimposition of the form *devadatta* on the entity, the form enters into the latter. See §5.3.

109. Paddhati on Vṛtti to VP 1.68 (126.16–20): *kiṁsvabhāva ity āha śaktyavacchedalakṣaṇaḥ [iti] / sa puruṣas tāṁ śaktiṁ tadviṣayatayā niyacchati / pratyayārthapratipādikā (pratyāyyārthapratipādikā?) [na] bahvyo 'saṅkīrṇāḥ śaktayaḥ / tatra puruṣas tadanyāḥ śaktīr avacchidyaikāṁ śaktiṁ vyavahāryatāṁ nayatīti niyamaḥ / arthāntarapratipādanaśaktiṁ vāpāsya tadviṣayaiva śaktiḥ prabodhyata iti / niyamaś cārthāntarebhyo vyāvartanāt / so 'yam īdṛśo niyamaḥ /*

and restricts a denoting power of this word to the inhabitant.[110] Thus the identification of a linguistic unit and a meaning, given by an utterance of the type 'this-is-that', serves to specify the relation of capacity between them. A linguistic unit has more than one capacity to convey a meaning and a meaning also has more than one capacity to be conveyed by a linguistic unit. When the relation of 'this-is-that' is established between the linguistic unit and the meaning, the restriction on the linguistic unit's capacity to convey a meaning is made: This is capable of conveying only this meaning; and, at the same time the restriction on the meaning's capacity to be conveyed by a linguistic unit is made: This is capable of being conveyed only by this linguistic unit.

The same point as in [I](b) is made in VP 2.369.

VP 2.369: *vṛddhyādīnāṁ ca śāstre 'smiñ chaktyavaccheda-lakṣaṇaḥ / akṛtrimo hi sambandho viśeṣaṇaviśeṣyavat //*

"Indeed, in this science of grammar also, the non-artificial relation of names like *vṛddhi* with the named consists in excluding their other powers to signify other meanings. This relation is like the relation of qualifier-qualificand."

To explain the point referring to the Vṛtti:[111] The quality blue (*nīla*) has the power to qualify any substance (*viśeṣaṇaśakti*) and the substance lotus (*utpala*) has the power to be qualified by any quality (*viśeṣyaśakti*). When the utterance *nīlam utpalam* 'blue lotus' is used, the power of the quality blue to qualify any sub-

110. Paddhati on Vṛtti to VP 1.68 (126.22–25): *yadā sarve śabdā guṇasamudāye vartante iti pakṣaḥ tadāyaṁ gośabdaḥ sarvān jātyādīn āha / tatra yadā vāhīka-śabdena śaktyavacchede jātyādinivṛttyā viśiṣṭārthābhidhāyitvaṁ gośabdasya tadā puruṣeṇa sañjñāśabdānāṁ śaktyavaccheda iti /* On the view that a linguistic item denotes a collection of qualities (*guṇasamudāya*), see MBh on A 2.2.6 (I.411.15) and Wezler 1985.

111. Vṛtti on VP 2.369 (292.3–7): *śāstre 'pi vṛddhir ityevamādīnāṁ sañjñānāṁ sarvasañjñiviṣayā śaktir ādaicprabhṛtiṣv avacchidyate / ādaicprabhṛtīnām api sarvasañjñāviṣayā śaktir vṛddhyādiṣv avacchidyate / tad yathā nīlam iti sarvā-śrayaviśeṣaṇaśaktir utpalādiviṣayā parigṛhyate / utpalādīnām api sarva-viśeṣaṇaviṣayā viśeṣyaśaktir nīlādiṣu niyamyate / tasmāc chāstre 'pi lokavat pravṛttir iti //*

stance is restricted to the substance lotus and the power of the substance lotus to be qualified by any quality is restricted to the quality blue. The same is said of the name *vṛddhi* and what is named by this name. The term *vṛddhi* is capable of being the names of all things and what is named by this term is capable of being named by any word. When, in grammar, the name-named relation (*sañjñāsañjñisambandha*) between *vṛddhi* and *ādaic* is established by formulating A1.1.1: *vṛddhir ādaic*, the power of the term *vṛddhi* to convey any thing is restricted to a set of sounds referred to by the term *ādaic* and the power of the set of sounds to be conveyed by any term is restricted to the term.

It is clear from the above that when the relation of 'this-is-that' is established between a specific linguistic unit and a specific meaning, the specific linguistic unit's capacity to denote a meaning is restricted to the specific meaning and the specific meaning's capacity to be denoted by a linguistic unit is restricted to the specific linguistic unit, through the exclusion of other capacities.

6 A speaker's acts: *abhidhā*, *ukti*, *praṇidhi*, *viniyoga*

In §1, it has been shown that a linguistic unit and its meaning are related to each other through the intermediary of the act denoted by *abhi-dhā* and that this act consists in an activity leading to a result, the understanding of the meaning. Bhartṛhari discusses what activity a speaker, an principal agent, performs in bringing such an act to accomplishment conjointly with other kārakas, a linguistic unit as an instrument and a meaning as an object. According to Bhartṛhari, the activity carried out by a speaker is *viniyoga* 'the activity of applying [a linguistic unit to a meaning]' or *praṇidhi* 'the activity of directing [a linguistic unit to a meaning]'. These activities can be performed by the speaker only if the speaker has learned the relation of 'this-is-that' between the linguistic unit and the meaning.

It is to be noted in passing that Bhartṛhari accepts that there are three cases in which a linguistic unit is uttered: to commit it to memory (*abhyāsa*); to teach its own form: to convey a meaning other than its own form. In the last case a speaker has to perform the above-mentioned activities.[112]

6.1 *praṇidhi* 1

In his Mahābhāṣyadīpikā, Bhartṛhari, discussing speech acts, says that *praṇidhi* is a speaker's activity in the situation expressed by an utterance like [1].

> MBhD IV.I.25.1–2: *kā punaḥ sā kriyā / ucyate / praṇidhiḥ prayoktuḥ śabdān prerayatas tadviṣayaḥ / praṇidhiś cetaso vṛttir ayaṁ yogya etam arthaṁ pratyāyayitum iti / sā kriyā /*
> "[Question] But what is the action [of a speaker]? An answer is: The action is the activity of directing (*praṇidhi*) linguistic units (*tadviṣayaḥ*) [to meanings], performed by the speaker who sets the linguistic units into play. The activity of directing is the function of [the speaker's] mind, performed] as 'This [linguistic unit] is capable of conveying this meaning' (*ayaṁ yogya etam arthaṁ pratyāyayitum*). That is the action."

The important point to note is that saying a speaker directs a linguistic unit to a meaning amounts to saying the speaker has the understanding that the linguistic unit is capable of conveying the meaning, namely the understanding of the capacity relation between them. This understanding must be the same as the one the speaker has already acquired in learning the relation of 'this-is-that' between the linguistic unit and the meaning. By calling the

112. In the Mahābhāṣyadīpikā, Bhartṛhari contrasts *viniyoga* with *abhyāsa* 'repeated recitation' and *parapratipādana* 'teaching a linguistic unit to others'. MBhD IV.I.25.9–10: *tathā brāhmaṇaśabdā abhyāsakāle 'narthakāḥ parapratipādane svarūpapadārthakāḥ evaṁ paṭhaivaṁ paṭheti / viniyogakāle 'rthavantaḥ /* The words in the Brāhmaṇas are meaningless when being committed to memory; they refer to their own forms when the way of reciting them is taught to others; they are meaningful when being applied to their meanings. The point made in the cited passages of the Mahābhāṣyadīpikā is stated in VP 2.407: *āmnāyaśabdān abhyāse kecid āhur anarthakān / svarūpamātravṛttīṁś ca pareṣāṁ pratipādane //*

relation to mind, the speaker can have such an understanding. This point will be made clear in the Vākyapadīya and the Vṛtti.

6.2 VP 2.403 *viniyoga*

In VP 2.403 Bhartṛhari brings in the concept of *viniyoga* as an activity to be performed by a speaker.

> VP 2.403: *viniyogād ṛte śabdo na svārthasya prakāśakaḥ / arthābhidhānasambandham uktidvāraṁ pracakṣate //*
>
> "A linguistic unit does not make known its own meaning unless it is applied to the meaning. They say that a meaning and that by which it is denoted are related to each other through the act of expressing (*ukti*)."

Clearly Bhartṛhari here bears in mind an utterance such as the following:

> [17] *devadattaḥ śabdena artham vakti* 'Devadatta expresses a meaning by using a linguistic unit'.

According to Bhartṛhari, in the situation expressed by this utterance Devadatta performs the activity of applying a linguistic unit to a meaning (*viniyoga*). Bhartṛhari comments as follows:

> [J] Vṛtti on VP 2.403 (302.13–18): (a) *iha kecid ācāryāḥ śabdajātim arthasambandhinaṁ*[113] *manyante kecic chabdavyaktim* / (b) *anyeṣāṁ tu jātisādhanā vyaktisādhanā vā kriyā sampratyayaphalā* / (c) *atrānenāyaṁ*[114] *vaktavya ity ubhayor vācyavācakayoḥ parigrahaṁ kṛtvā buddhisthaḥ śabdo buddhisthe yatra viniyujyate pravaṇīkriyate* (d) *saty apy anekārthatve tatrāsya sāmarthyam avacchidyate* / (e) *yāsau*[115] *śabdagatoktiḥ sā sambandham āvirbhāvayati* / (f) *sā hi*[116] *yogyatā tāvad avacchidyate yāvad uktyānugṛhītā praṇatim ivāpāditā bhavati //*
>
> "(a) Here in our system some teachers hold the view that the universal of a linguistic unit (*śabdajāti*) is related to

113. Aklujkar: *arthasambandhinīṁ*.
114. Aklujkar: *tatrānenāyaṁ*.
115. Iyer: *yāsau tatra*.
116. Aklujkar: *[ta]sya hi*.

[the universal of] a meaning [without the intermediary of an action]; some hold the view that an individual linguistic unit (*śabdavyakti*) is related to an [individual] meaning [without the intermediary of an action].
(b) But, in the view of others, an action, whose sādhanas[117] are universals or individuals, brings about the understanding [of a meaning] (*sampratyayaphalā*).
(c) In this view, after receiving both, [the meaning] to be signified (*vācya*) and [the linguistic unit] signifying it (*vācaka*), a speaker applies the linguistic unit the speaker has in mind (*buddhistha-śabda*) to [the meaning] the speaker has in mind (*buddhistha-*[*artha*]), that is, the speaker directs the former towards the latter (*pravaṇīkriyate*), as 'This [meaning] is capable of being signified by this [linguistic unit] (*anenāyaṁ vaktavyaḥ*)'.
(d) Although the linguistic unit in question has more than one meaning (*anekārthatva*), the capacity (*sāmarthya*) of this linguistic unit to signify a meaning is restricted to the meaning in question by excluding its other capacities to signify other meanings (*avacchidyate*).
(e) [This is why] the very activity of expressing (*ukti*) [which consists in the speaker's activity of applying a linguistic unit to a meaning], related to the linguistic unit, manifests the relation [of capacity between the linguistic unit and the meaning].
(f) For, [the linguistic unit's] capacity (*yogyatā*) [to signify a meaning is restricted [to the meaning in question by excluding its other capacities to signify other meanings], insofar as the capacity, by the help of [the speaker's activity of] expressing (*uktyānugṛhītā*), appears to have acquired an inclination (*praṇati*) [towards the meaning]."

117. That is, a kāraka, which brings an action to accomplishment. See §4.1.

First of all, [J](a)–(b) are interesting in that Bhartṛhari points out that, as to the relation between linguistic unit and meaning, there are three views: (1) the universal of a linguistic unit is related to the universal of a meaning without the intermediary of an action; (2) an individual linguistic unit is related to an individual meaning without the intermediary of an action; (3) the relation is established through the intermediary of an action. As shown in §1, Bhartṛhari takes an approach to the relation according to the third view.

Now Bhartṛhari here considers the speaker's act of expressing (*ukti*) to consist in the activity of applying a linguistic unit, which the speaker has in mind, to a meaning, which also the speaker has in mind. Accordingly, [17] must be paraphrased as follows:

[18] *devadattaḥ śabdam arthe viniyunakti* 'Devadatta applies a linguistic unit to a meaning'

Let us note [J](c). The term *viniyujyate* is glossed with the term *pravaṇīkriyate*. To apply the specific linguistic unit to the specific meaning is to direct the former towards the latter, which is none other than what is meant by the term *praṇidhi*. Thus what is stated in [J](c) is the same as in the Mahābhāṣyadīpikā passage cited above.[118] A speaker, who has learned the relation of 'this-is-that' between the specific linguistic unit and the specific meaning, can have both the image of the specific linguistic unit and that of the specific meaning (*ubhayor vācyavācakayoḥ parigrahaḥ*) and apply the former to the latter as 'This meaning is capable of being conveyed by this linguistic unit'.

In this connection, it is important to note what Bhartṛhari states concerning the application of a linguistic unit to a meaning in his Mahābhāṣyadīpikā. He says:

MBhD IV.I.25.10–11: *tatra yāsau viniyogakāle parigṛhītārthavato 'rtheṣu prapattiḥ sa sambandhaḥ /*

"In that case [where the words in the Brāhmaṇas become meaningful at the time of their application], that which lets

118. See §6.1.

the linguistic unit with the meaning taken at the time of its application go towards meanings is a relation."[119]

The point is that a speaker can apply a linguistic unit to a meaning on the basis of their relation, which the speaker has learned. Without reflecting upon the learned relation, one cannot achieve verbal communications.

The point made in [J](d) is the same as in [I](b).[120] The establishment of the relation of 'this-is-that' between a specific linguistic unit and a specific meaning results in restricting their capacities.

[J](e) says that the speaker's activity of applying the specific linguistic unit to the specific meaning manifests the relation of capacity such that the specific meaning is capable of being signified by the specific linguistic unit and the latter is capable of signifying the former. As shown in §4, the relation of capacity between a linguistic unit and a meaning is ever-present and begininngless and its understanding is conditioned by 'convention'. [J](f) gives the reason for the point in [J](e). When the speaker applies the specific linguistic unit to the specific meaning, the specific linguistic unit appears as if it acquired the capacity to signify the specific meaning. But actually the specific linguistic unit's capacity to signify a meaning is only restricted to the specific meaning.

The important point to note in VP 2.403 is that when the speaker applies the specific linguistic unit to the specific meaning, the former becomes the signifier of the latter. This point is made clearer in VP 2.404.

6.2 VP 2.404 *praṇidhi* 2

In VP 2.404 the term *viniyoga* is rephrased by *praṇihita*, *saṁnihita*:

119. Bronkhorst 1987: 84: "Here the approach of [the word,] which has meaning, towards the meanings, grasped at the time of application [of the word], is the connection [between word and meaning]." I have taken the word *prapatti* (← *pra-pad-**ktin*** [A 3.3.94 *striyāṁ ktin*], *pra-pad* 'enter upon, go to') as a karaṇasādhana ('that by which something is entered upon, gone to').

120. See §5.5.

VP 2.404: *yathā praṇihitaṁ cakṣur darśanāyopakalpate / tathābhisaṁhitaḥ śabdo bhavaty arthasya vācakaḥ //*
"Just as the visual organ, when directed towards an object, brings about the perception of the object, so a linguistic unit, when directed towards a meaning, becomes the signifier of the meaning."

This kārikā shows that [17] can be paraphrased as:

[19] *devadattaḥ śabdam arthe praṇidhatte (abhisaṁdhatte)*
'Devadatta directs a linguistic unit to a meaning'.

On the present kārikā Bhartṛhari comments as follows:

[K] Vṛtti on VP 2.404 (302.21–23): (a) *tatra cakṣur yathā sarvadṛśyopalabdhiviṣayābhir yogyatābhir yuktaṁ yatra yatra saṅkalpena praṇidhīyate tatra tatropalabdhiṁ karoti* (b) *tathā śabdo 'py anekārthapratyāyanayogyo yam arthaṁ praty abhisaṁhito bhavati tam upasaṅgṛhṇāti svātmani sanniveśayati prakāśayati //*

"(a) In that case [it is proper to say the following]. The visual organ, which is endowed with capacities (*yogyatā*) that are exercised in the domain of the perception of all things to be seen (*sarvadṛśyopalabdhi*), brings about the perception (*upalabdhi*) of whatever it is intentionally (*saṅkalpena*) directed towards.

(b) Similarly, a linguistic unit, which is capable of conveying more than one meaning (*artha*), accepts (*upasaṁgṛhṇāti*), causes to enter into itself (*svātmani saṁniveśayati*), makes known (*prakāśayati*), the meaning towards which it is directed [by the speaker] (*abhisaṁhita*)."[121]

It is shown that the application of a linguistic unit to a meaning is the directing of the linguistic unit to the meaning (*praṇidhi*, *abhisaṁdhi*). What is stated in [K](b) is the same as in the Mahā-

121. MBhD IV.I.25.3–6: *yathā saty eva cakṣuṣi sati ca rūpe na cakṣur apraṇihitam anadhiṣṭhitaṁ manasā viṣayālocane samarthaṁ bhavaty evaṁ śabdo vyavasthito 'rthe 'pi prayoktuḥ praṇidhānam antareṇa pratyāyane asamarthaḥ ity etat prayogagrahaṇenācaṣṭe /*

bhāṣyadīpikā (§6.1) and [J](c). Moreover, [J](c) reminds us of [H](c)–(e). When a speaker directs a specific linguistic unit to a specific meaning as 'This meaning is capable of being signified by this linguistic unit', on the basis of the relation of 'this-is-that' between the specific linguistic unit and the specific meaning, the specific linguistic unit must be what accepts the specific meaning, what has the specific meaning enter into itself, and hence what makes known the specific meaning.[122] The specific linguistic unit is an *upādānaśabda* with respect to the specific meaning.[123]

The above-described operations are only the recurrence of what the speaker performed at the time of learning the relation between the linguistic unit and the meaning.[124] Importantly, the activity of applying a linguistic unit to a meaning or directing the former to the latter is none other than that of re-relating the former to the latter by means of establishing the relation of 'this-is-that' between them. Bhartṛhari says that when the application or directing of a linguistic unit to a meaning takes place, the meaning enters into the linguistic unit (*śabdo ... arthaṁ ... svātmani sanniveśayati*). As shown earlier,[125] this implies that the meaning is identified with the linguistic unit and the relation of identity is established between them. It must be recalled here that in VP 1.48 Bhartṛhari says that a mental linguistic unit which has entered into a mental meaning (*arthe niveśitaḥ śabdaḥ*) is manifested by the sequential utterance of sounds. When the linguistic unit enters into the meaning, the former is identified with the latter.[126]

122. For one who has learned the relation of 'this-is-that' between linguistic unit and meaning, two ways of superimposing can take place. See §5.3.
123. See §5.4.
124. See [G](b) in §5.3.
125. See §5.3.
126. When commenting on VP 2.403–404 Puṇyarāja does not refer to the points made by Bhartṛhari in the Vṛtti. Puṇyarāja, in introducing VP 2.404, says the following. Ṭīkā on VP 2.404 (161.17–19): *atha kiṁ svābhāvikaḥ śabdārthasambandho 'thedṛśīṁ daśām upeto yad amī śabdā vaktṛviniyogamukhaprekṣaṇasaṁbandhāḥ / hantaivaṁvādinā bhavatā vibhūṣitaiva vaiyākaraṇadhurety āśaṅkyaitatsamarthanārtham āha /* ("Now a question arises: Is the relation

6.3 We can see from what has been said in the present section why Vṛṣabha says that the relation of identity between linguistic unit and meaning is included in the causal relation between them.[127] In a speaker's cognition, the following holds on the basis of the relation of 'this-is-that' between a linguistic unit (L) and a meaning (M): when the image of L appears, that of M appears; when the image of L does not appear, that of M does not appear: when the image of M appears, that of L appears; when the image of M does not appear, that of L does not appear. A speaker may identify M with L and L with M. In a hearer's cognition, on the other hand, the following holds on the basis of the same relation: when the image of L appears, that of M appears; when the image of L does not appear, that of M does not appear.[128] This is how the relation of

between linguistic unit and meaning something established by itself (*svābhāvika*), or does it have a state such that those linguistic units are related to their meanings by virtue of a speaker keeping the meanings in view by means of applying the former to the latter? O you, by advancing the latter view, have wrongly ornamented the doctrine (lit. load) of grammarians. To sweep away the suspicion that these two views are contradictory to each other and establish the point in VP 2.403, Bhartṛhari states VP 2.404.") Iyer 1977: 172 interprets this introductory remark: "The fact that conscious and deliberate application of a word to a meaning is necessary does not make the relation between word and meaning man-made. It is eternal." As shown above, in the Vṛtti on the kārikās in question Bhartṛhari does not problematize the speaker's activity of applying or directing from the angle as noted by Puṇyarāja. Puṇyarāja here misses the point that the relation between linguistic unit and meaning, whose understanding is conditioned by convention, must be learned. See §4.2.1. It is very likely that Puṇyarāja has not read the Vṛtti on the kārikās.

127. See notes 44 and 49.

128. From a hearer's point of view, Helārāja says the following. Prakāśa on VP 3.3.2 (126.7–9): *ata eva ca svābhiprāyānusāreṇa śrotrā vaktṛjñānasyānumānāt svayaṁ śabdasvarūpādhyastam artham avabuddhya tathaiva vaktary anumānam ucitam ity abhedenaiva ghaṭaśabdādhyastaṁ prayoktṛjñānam avasīyate /* On hearing a linguistic unit a hearer by himself/herself understands the meaning which is superimposed on the linguistic unit's own form. The hearer infers that a speaker's cognition is superimposed on the same form for establishing the identity between the linguistic unit in question and the meaning in question. Bhartṛhari may say that the hearer infers that the image of the meaning, which appears in the speaker's cognition, is superimposed on the image of the linguistic unit's own form by the speaker.

'this-is-that' determines the causal relation. In this connection it is highly important to note that Helārāja observes the following: The fact that the causal relation between linguistic unit and meaning is bidirectional shows that it is of a different kind from that between fire and smoke and that there is the relation of identity, characterized by superimposition, between them.[129] Of course, when it is said that there obtains a relation between linguistic unit and meaning, there must obtain a capacity relation as well as a causal relation between them. It is because of the relation of 'this-is-that' not only that, of a linguistic unit and a meaning, when one is understood, the other is understood, but also that the capacity relation between them is manifested. The identification of a specific linguistic unit and a specific meaning results in the restriction on the linguistic unit and the meaning which are to be related to each other on the assumptions that any linguistic unit can be related to any meaning and that any meaning can be related to any linguistic unit.

7 VP 3.3.3 *tattvam apy ato vyapadiśyate*

We have been dealing with the three types of relations between linguistic unit and meaning. We are now in a good position to consider the third kārikā of the Sambandhasamuddeśa, which has admitted of different interpretations.

> VP 3.3.3: *asyāyaṁ vācako vācya iti ṣaṣṭhyā pratīyate / yogaḥ śabdārthayos tattvam apy ato vyapadiśyate //*[130]
>
> Iyer 1971: 79–80: "That this word is expressive of that meaning, that this meaning is the expressed meaning of that word, such a relation between word and meaning is under-

129. Prakāśa on VP 3.3.32 (145.15–17): *evaṁ cobhayathā kāryakāraṇabhāvavarṇanād dhūmāgnivailakṣaṇyena śabdārthayor abhedena saṁbandho 'dhyāsalakṣaṇaḥ pratipādito bhavati /* Cardona 1981: 97 points out that when X occurs, Y occurs; when X is absent, Y is absent; when Y occurs, X occurs; when Y is absent, X is absent—if all these hold, the identity between X and Y is established.

130. Iyer reads pāda d: *tattvam ity ato vyapadiśyate.* I have followed Rau's reading.

> stood from the genitive suffix. That is why they are understood as identical."
>
> Houben 1995: 170: "'This is the signifier of this, [and this] is the signified [of this],' thus the connection of word and thing-meant is known through the sixth nominal ending (genitive). On this ground, the real nature (*tattvam*, sc. of word and thing-meant) is also indicated."

Helārāja explains the phrase *tattvam apy ato vyapadiśyate* in two manners:

> Prakāśa on VP 3.3.3 (128.3–5): *ata eva ca svābhāvikāt sambandhāc chabdārthayos tattvaṁ gaur ayam artha ity abhedena vyavahriyata ity arthaḥ / yadi vā ataḥ ṣaṣṭhyāḥ sakāśāt tattvaṁ svarūpaṁ sambandhasyocyate //*
>
> "(1) What is meant is this: In addition (*api* = *ca*), on the basis of this natural relation (*ataḥ* = *svābhāvikāt sambandhāt*) the identity (*tattva*) between linguistic unit and meaning is expressed (*vyapadiśyate* = *vyavahriyate*), that is, they are expressed as identical with each other (*abhedena*) as in *gaur ayam arthaḥ* 'This meaning is an *ox*'.
>
> (2) Another alternative interpretation: From this sixth triplet ending (*ataḥ* = *ṣaṣṭhyāḥ sakāśāt*),[131] the essence (*tattva* = *svarūpa*) of a relation is spoken (*vyapadiśyate* = *ucyate*)."

We have the following utterances:

> [20] *asya arthasya ayam śabdaḥ vācakaḥ* 'This linguistic unit is the signifier of this meaning'.
>
> [21] *asya śabdasya ayam arthaḥ vācyaḥ* 'This meaning is the significand of this linguistic unit'.

From the sixth triplet ending in these utterances it is understood that there is the signifier-significand relation (*vācyavācakabhāva*) between the specific linguistic unit and the specific meaning. But there is little point in simply arguing this. This is comparable to the case in which one argues that the possessor-possession relation

131. The expression *ataḥ* is paraphrased as *ṣaṣṭhyāḥ sakāśāt*. This paraphrase shows that *ataḥ* is equivalent to *asyāḥ ṣaṣṭhyāḥ* 'from this sixth triplet ending'.

is understood from the sixth triplet ending in the utterance *rājñaḥ puruṣaḥ*.

In connection with the present kārikā it must be recalled that in the Vṛtti on VP 1.23 Bhartṛhari states: *asyedaṁbhāve sati śadārthayoḥ so 'yam iti [yaḥ] sambandhaḥ* ([F](a))[132] and that this passage can be interpreted as follows. When one has the cognition: 'This has this for its signifier' (*asyedaṁ vācakam*); 'This has this for its significand (*asyedaṁ vācyam*)', it is known from this cognition that there is the identity relation between the specific linguistic unit and the specific meaning. The identity relation is the cause of the cognition. If we take into consideration this interpretation of the above-mentioned Vṛtti passage, we may take VP 3.3.3 as meant for introducing the identity relation between linguistic unit and meaning and as implying that the identity relation is the relation underlying the relation understood from the sixth triplet ending in [20] and [21], the causal relation and the capacity relation. Accordingly, the present kārikā can be interpreted as follows:

> "[Since] from the sixth triplet ending in the utterances *asyāyaṁ vācakaḥ* 'this is a signifier of this' and *asyāyaṁ vācyaḥ* 'this is a significand of this' the relation (*yoga*) between linguistic unit and meaning is understood, therefore (*ataḥ*) they are also said to be identical with each other (*tattva*)."

Helārāja's first interpretation accords with Bhartṛhari's theory on the relation between linguistic unit and meaning. Helārāja gives the second interpretation by taking into consideration VP 3.3.4, which argues that nominals such as *sambandha* cannot touch on the essence of a relation, which is denoted by a sixth triplet ending.[133] In my opinion, VP 3.3.1–3 make a set. In VP 3.3.1[134]

132. See §5.2.

133. VP 3.3.4: *nābhidhānaṁ svadharmeṇa sambandhasyāsti vācakam / atyantaparatantratvād rūpaṁ nāsyāpadiśyate //* ("There is no nominal to denote a relation in terms of its own property. Because it is absolutely dependent, its

Bhartṛhari mentions three relata of a single linguistic unit and points out that the relation between the linguistic unit and the three items is permanent; in VP 3.3.2[135] he states that, unlike the other relata, the linguistic unit's own form is invariably understood from the linguistic unit; in VP 3.3.3 he states that the understanding of a relation in utterances like [20] and [21] indicates that, as an underlying relation of the relation, there is the relation of identity. We may take the set of kārikās in this way. Bhartṛhari need not elaborate on the relation of identity which underlies the relation as understood in [20]–[21] in the Sambandhasamuddeśa, since it is a kind of meta-relation.

8 Conclusion

Bhartṛhari's contribution is that he considered speech acts within the framework of Pāṇini's kāraka theory. A linguistic unit and a meaning are related to each other through the intermediary of the action denoted by *abhi-dhā* or *vac*. A linguistic unit and its meaning serve respectively as instrument and as object with respect to such an action. This shows that, as substances, a linguistic unit and a meaning have respectively the capacities to function as instrument and as object with respect to the action in question. Thus it naturally follows, on the assumption that the action is that of denoting, that the linguistic unit has the capacity to denote the meaning, that the meaning has the capacity to be denoted by the linguistic unit and hence that there is the capacity relation between the linguistic unit and the meaning.

In addition, the action in question leads to the fruit of the understanding of the meaning. From hearing the linguistic unit a hearer can understand the meaning and a speaker utters the linguistic unit in order to convey the meaning to the hearer. We can easily see that there obtains a causal relation between the linguistic unit

form cannot be referred to by its own word.") On the interpretation of this kārikā, see Cardona 1999: 122.

134. See §2.

135. See note 31.

and the meaning in two ways: from the points of view of a speaker and a hearer. But Bhartṛhari goes further into details. He explains the very core of the causal relation between linguistic unit and meaning in terms of the relation between a linguistic unit in the domain of the mind (*buddhisthaśabda*) and a meaning in the domain of the mind (*buddhisthārtha*). In the case of a speaker, the speaker, before uttering a linguistic unit, has the cognition in which the image of the meaning to be conveyed appears. How is this image of the meaning linked with the image of the linguistic unit? In the case of a hearer, the hearer, by hearing a linguistic unit, has the cognition in which the image of the linguistic unit appears. How is this image of the linguistic unit linked with the image of the meaning? Bhartṛhari answers these questions by pointing out that there is the relation of 'this-is-that', the relation of identity, between the linguistic unit and the meaning. This relation must be taught and learned. One learns the relation in two manners: by means of superimposing the linguistic unit on the meaning to attain the linguistic unit's identity with the meaning; by means of superimposing the meaning on the linguistic unit to attain the meaning's identity with the linguistic unit. The relation of 'this-is-that' allows the two ways of superimposition to occur. Thus this relation makes it possible that the image of the meaning and that of the linguistic unit are linked with each other: when the image of the meaning occurs, the image of the linguistic unit occurs; when the image of the meaning is absent, the image of the linguistic unit is absent: when the image of the linguistic unit occurs, the image of the meaning occurs; when the image of the linguistic unit is absent, the image of the meaning is absent. All this clearly shows that the relation of 'this-is-that' between linguistic unit and meaning underlies the causal relation between them. In this sense, we may include, as Vṛṣabha does, the former in the latter.

What is more, the establishment of the relation of 'this-is-that' between a linguistic unit and a meaning leads to making restrictions on their capacities. On the basis of this establishment, the linguistic unit's capacity to convey a meaning is restricted to the specific meaning, while the meaning's capacity to be conveyed by a linguistic unit is restricted to the specific linguistic unit. In the former the linguistic unit's other capacities to convey other meanings are excluded, while in the latter the meaning's other capacities to be conveyed by other linguistic units are excluded. Thus the relation of 'this-is-that' between a linguistic unit and a meaning serves to manifest that this specific linguistic unit is capable of conveying this specific meaning and that this specific meaning is capable of being conveyed by this specific linguistic unit. This is the way the relation of 'this-is-that' between linguistic unit and meaning underlies the capacity relation between them. It is presupposed that there is a relation between a linguistic unit in general and a meaning in general.

Bhartṛhari characterizes the activity performed by a speaker in speech acts, as directing a linguistic unit to a meaning or as applying the former to the latter. Such an activity of a speaker is to re-establish the relation of 'this-is-that' between the linguistic unit and the meaning in order for the former to become the signifier of the latter.

To summarize the main points Bhartṛhari makes about the relation of 'this-is-that' between a linguistic unit and a meaning: First, this relation is taught and learned through an utterance of the type *so 'yam* 'this-is-that'. Secondly, the relation is established by the identification of the linguistic unit and the meaning. Once the relation is established, the linguistic unit and the meaning appear respectively as identical with the meaning and the linguistic unit. Thirdly, the identification comes to the restriction on the linguistic units and meanings which can be related to each other.

All this gives the answer to the second question mentioned earlier in §0. Therefore we may be justified in arguing that Helārāja's understanding of the relation between linguistic unit and meaning is thoroughly founded on Bhartṛhari's theory on it.

The first question I raised in §0 has to be answered. The

answer is simple. The Pāṇinīyas' view of a relation is formed on the basis of their kāraka theory. This is the reason that Bhartṛhari specifies only the two types of relations as the relation between linguistic unit and meaning, which is established in view of the action denoted by *abhi-dhā* or *vac*. It is quite reasonable that Bhartṛhari discusses only the two types in the Sambandhasamuddeśa. For this samuddeśa deals with relations of the type *tasyedam* 'this-of-that'.

Readers may have wondered why I constantly use the expression 'linguistic unit' for the term *śabda*. The reason is also simple. In VP 2.40 Bhartṛhari says:

> VP 2.40: *so 'yam ity abhisambandho buddhyā prakramyate yadā / vākyārthasya tadaiko 'pi varṇaḥ pratyāyako kvacit //*
> "In some cases, when, with a sentence meaning, the identity relation in the form 'this is that' is intended to be established by the mind, even a single phoneme becomes a conveyer of the sentence meaning."

In Bhartṛhari's view, even a single phoneme can become a signifier of a sentence meaning if the relation of 'this-is-that' between the phoneme and the sentence meaning is established. This implies that in his view any type of linguistic unit, a phoneme, a word, or a sentence, can be meaningful with respect to a given meaning if the identification of the linguistic unit and the meaning is established. We must be fully aware that, in Bhartṛhari's theory of the relation of linguistic unit and meaning, much significance is attached to the relation of 'this-is-that' between them. In the theory this relation plays a central role.

References and Abbreviations

A Pāṇini's *Aṣṭādhyāyī*.

Abhyankar, Kashinath Vasudev

1962–72 *The Vyākaraṇa-mahābhāṣya of Patañjali, edited by F. Kielhorn, third edition, revised and furnished with additional readings, references and select critical notes by K. V. Abhyankar*. Three volumes. Poona: Bhandarkar Oriental Research Institute. [1: 1962; 2: 1965; 3: 1972]

Bhaṭṭikāvya Bhaṭṭi's *Bhaṭṭikāvya*. See Kamalāśaṅkara Prāṇaśaṅkara Trivedī 1898.

Bronkhorst, Johannes

1987 *Mahābhāṣyadīpikā of Bhartṛhari, Fascicule IV: Āhnika I*. Post-Graduate and Research Department Series 28. Poona: Bhandarkar Oriental Research Institute.

Cardona, George

1974 Pāṇini's *kārakas*: Agency, animation and identity. *Journal of Indian Philosophy* 2: 231–306.

1981 On reasoning from anvaya and vyatireka in early Advaita, in Dalsukh Malvania and Nagin J. Shah (eds.), *Studies in Indian Philosophy: A Memorial Volume in Honour of Pandit Sukhlalji Sanghavi*, Ahmedabad: L. D. Institute of Indology, pp. 79–104.

1997 *Pāṇini, His Work and Its Traditions. Volume I: Background and Introduction*. Second edition. Delhi: Motilal Banarsidass.

1999 Approaching the *Vākyapadīya*. *Journal of the American Oriental Society* 119.1: 88–125.

2007 *Pānini and Pāṇinīyas on Śeṣa Relations* (*First Kunjunni Raja Memorial Lecture*). Aluva: Kunjunni Raja Academy of Indological Research.

2012 A note on Vākyapadīya 1.45/46: *ātmabhedas tayoḥ kecid ...*, in Chikafumi Watanabe, Michele Desmarais, and Yoshichika Honda (eds.), *Saṁskṛta-sādhutā: Goodness of Sanskrit; Studies in Honour of Professor Ashok Aklujkar*, New Delhi: D.K. Printworld, pp. 100–109.

Houben, Jan E. M.

1995 *The Saṃbandha-samuddeśa (Chapter on Relation) and Bhartṛhari's Philosophy of Language: A Study of Bhartṛhari Saṁbandha-samuddeśa in the context of the Vākyapadīya with a translation of Helārāja's commentary Prakīrṇa-prakāśa.* Gonda Indological Studies, Vol. II. Groningen: Egbert Forstein.

Kamalāśaṅkara Prāṇaśaṅkara Trivedī

1898 *The Bhaṭṭi-kāvya or Rāvaṇavadha Composed by Śrī Bhaṭṭi, Edited with the Commentary of Mallinātha.* Two volumes. Bombay Sanskrit Series LVI–LVII. Bombay: Government Central Book Depôt.

MBh. Patañjali's *Vyākaraṇamahābhāṣya.* See Vedavrata 1962–63, Abhyankar 1962–72. [References to volumes, pages, and lines of Abhyankar 1962–72.]

MBhD Bhartṛhari's *Mahābhāṣyadīpikā.* See Bronkhorst 1987. [References to pages and lines.]

Ogawa, Hideyo

2009 On Bhartṛhari's notion of 'power' (śakti), in Mithilesh Chaturvedi (ed.), *Bhartṛhari: Language, Thought and Reality (Proceedings of the International Seminar Delhi, December 12–14, 2003)*, Delhi: Motilal Banarsidass, pp. 225–252.

Paddhati Vṛṣabhadeva's *Paddhati.* See Subramania Iyer 1966.

Pradīpa Kaiyaṭa's *Pradīpa.* See Vedavrata 1962–63. [References to volumes and pages]

Prakāśa Helārāja's *Prakāśa*. See Subramania Iyer 1963, 1973. [References to kārikā, pages, and lines]

PV Dharmakīrti's *Pramāṇavārttika*. See Ram Chandra Pandeya 1989.

PWT See Cardona 1997.

Ram Chandra Pandeya

1989 *The Pramāṇavārttikam of Ācārya Dharmakīrti, with the Commentaries Svopajñavṛtti of the Author and Pramāṇavārttikavṛtti of Manorathanandin*. Delhi: Motilal Banarsidass.

Rau, Wilhelm

1977 *Bhartṛharis Vākyapadīya: Die Mūlakārikās nach den Handschriften herausgegeben und mit einem Pāda-Index versehen*. Abhandlungen für die Kunde des Morgenlandes XLII, 4. Wiesbaden: Franz Steiner Verlag.

Subramania Iyer, K. A.

1963 *Vākyapadīya of Bhartṛhari with the Commentary of Helārāja, Kāṇḍa III, Part 1*. Deccan College Monograph Series 21. Poona: Deccan College.

1966 *Vākyapadīya of Bhartṛhari with the Commentaries Vṛtti and Paddhati of Vṛṣabhadeva*. Deccan College Monograph Series 32. Poona: Deccan College.

1971 *The Vākyapadīya of Bhartṛhari, Chapter III, pt.1: English Translation*. Deccan College Building Centenary & Silver Jubilee Series 71. Poona: Deccan College.

1973 *Vākyapadīya of Bhartṛhari with the Commentary of Helārāja, Kāṇḍa III, Part II*. Poona: Deccan College.

1977 *The Vākyapadīya of Bhartṛhari, Kāṇḍa II: English Translation with Exegetical Notes*. Delhi: Motilal Banarsidass.

1983 *The Vākyapadīya of Bhartṛhari (An Ancient Treatise on the Philosophy of Sanskrit Grammar), Containing the Ṭīkā of Puṇyarāja and the Ancient Vṛtti, Kāṇḍa II, with a Foreword by Ashok Aklujkar.* Delhi: Motilal Banarsidass.

Ṭīkā Puṇyarāja's *Ṭīkā.* See Subramania Iyer 1983. [References to kārikās, pages, and lines]

Vedavrata

1962–63 *Śrībhagavatpatañjaliviracitaṁ Vyākaraṇamahābhāṣyam (Śrīkaiyaṭakṛtapradīpena nāgojībhaṭṭakṛtena bhāṣyapradīpoddyotena ca vibhūṣitam).* Five volumess. Gurukul Jhajjar (Rohatak): Hairyāṇā-Sāhitya-Saṁsthānam.

VP Bhartṛhari's *Vākyapadīya.* See Rau, Subramania Iyer. [References to kārikās as numbered in Rau 1977]

vt. *Vārttika* of Kātyāyana. Vedavrata 1962–63, Abhyankar 1962–72.

Vṛtti *Vākyapadīya Vṛtti.* See Subramania Iyer 1966, 1983. [References to kārikās, pages, and lines]

Wezler, Albrecht

1985 A note on Mahābhāṣya II 366.26: *guṇasaṃdrāvo dravyam* (Stuides on Mallavādin's *Dvādaśāranayacakra* II), in *Essays in Honour of Dr. Shozen Kumoi on His Seventieth Birthday*, Kyoto: Heirakuji Shoten, pp. 1–33.

Just a cavil or not: an example of outsiders' dispute on the Aṣṭādhyāyī

Yuki Tomonari

0 Introduction[1]

As is well known, the tradition of Pāṇinian grammar (*pāṇinīyavyākaraṇa*) accepts as a fundamental tenet that when the meaning of a sūtra of the Aṣṭādhyāyī is not clear and a doubt occurs, what should be reliable then is an explanation (*vyākhyāna*) given by Pāṇinian grammarians themselves. Through the very explanation, we will be assured that the meaning of the sūtra is certain and undoubted. This principle is expressed in the paribhāṣā *vyākhyānato viśeṣapratipattir na hi sandehād alakṣaṇam.*[2]

Pāṇinian grammarians' explanations, among which Patañjali's Mahābhāṣya is of the highest fame and importance, cover those problems thoroughly, and as the result of succeeding grammarians' great efforts found in the traditional commentaries on the Aṣṭādhyāyī and so on, it seems that there is no longer any more scope for further dispute about Aṣṭādhyāyī sūtras.

On the other hand, it does not seem to be well known that there exist some works of non-grammarians which include a series of disputes directly pointing out some problematic issues in the Aṣṭādhyāyī. For instance, Prabhākara Miśra's Bṛhatī on MS 1.3.24–29 has a series of criticisms of the Aṣṭādhyāyī as an opponent's statement or a pūrvapakṣa. Jayanta Bhaṭṭa's Nyāyamañjarī also introduces a series of parallel or very similar arguments in the closing portion of its sixth āhnika. Studies on the

1. The author would like to express his gratitude here to all the venerable participants in the vyākaraṇa session of the 15th WSC, who gave many beneficial suggestions and information to him. He cannot say that all the advice has been utilized for this paper, but this is due to nothing but his inability to do so. This work was supported by Grant-in-Aid for JSPS Fellows.

2. Apparently, this phrase appeared for the first time in the Mahābhāṣya, and was regarded as the first paribhāṣā by Nāgeśa Bhaṭṭa in his Paribhāṣenduśekhara.

works of Pāṇinian grammarians are numerous; however, the arguments treated by these two non-grammarians[3] do not seem previously to have been referred to often, although they deserve consideration, since they give us much suggestive information about how Pāṇinian grammar was accepted in their era.[4]

In this paper, I will first confirm some basic information concerning these arguments, then examine them by comparing actual texts to make the nature of the arguments clear, and, finally, consider some problems we may meet with in those disputes.

1 Basic information

1.1 Background of the dispute

The section to which Jaimini's Mīmāṁsāsūtra 1.3.24–29 belong is known to us by two names: *sādhupada(prayukty)adhikaraṇa* and *vyākaraṇādhikaraṇa*. Presumably, these sūtras and the Bhāṣya by Śabara Svāmin on them have as their main concern the distinction between correct words (*sādhuśabda/śabda*) and incorrect words (*asādhuśabda/apaśabda*), and the restriction on the usage (*prayoga*) of these two kinds of words (*vyavasthā/niyama*). The first name is based on this characteristic of the section. The name *vyākaraṇādhikaraṇa*, on the other hand, seems to be based on the content of the commentaries written by Kumārila Bhaṭṭa and Prabhākara Miśra, the Tantravārttika and Bṛhatī. Both

3. According to Raghavan (1960), Jayanta Bhaṭṭa was one of the commentators or vṛttikāras on the Aṣṭādhyāyī, though his vṛtti is now not accessible.

4. Jha 1911 seems to be the only study to take the pertinent Bṛhatī arguments in its scope, but a summary of the argument is replaced by the arguments found in the Tantravārttika. On the related āhnika of the Nyāyamañjarī, only Bronkhorst 2008 is available except for two translations, namely Bhattacaryya 1978 and Shah 1975–92. Examining the Nyāyamañjarī's paragraph on an enumeration of word forms whose derivations present difficulties, Bronkhorst (2008) discusses a Cārvāka Udbhaṭa, who is supposed to have been a Pāṇinian grammarian with non-orthodox tendency because he did not accept the authority of the Mahābhāṣya.

commentaries explicitly use the word *vyākaraṇa*, which is not found in the sūtras and the Bhāṣya.[5]

Although both the Tantravārttika and the Bṛhatī argue on the topic of grammar with lengthy prima facie arguments (*pūrvapakṣa*),[6] their contents are quite different from each other. Kumārila's opponent puts his major emphasis on the purpose (*prayojana*) of Pāṇinian grammar,[7] while Prabhākara's directly discusses some problematic issues in Aṣṭādhyāyī sūtras.

The Bṛhatī's pūrvapakṣa part begins with a question: "Then, if it is the case that vyākaraṇasmṛti has no basis, in what manner is it suspected that the Veda has no authority?"[8] *Mūla* ('basis') is a keyword in this pāda of the Mīmāṁsāsūtra. As far as the sūtra and Bhāṣya discuss, it seems that the purpose of this adhikaraṇa was to establish a distinction and restriction between the two sorts of words on the basis of a certain śāstra. However, for Kumārila and Prabhākara, this was not enough, so that the śāstra, that is, Pāṇinian grammar itself, must have been taken into consideration as a basis of the distinction and restriction. In spite of this, the pūrvapakṣin in the Bṛhatī declares his opinion rather boldly[9] and commences to discuss sūtras of the Aṣṭādhyāyī. We will deal with

5. The word *śāstra* in 1.3.24: *prayogotpattyaśāstratvāc chabdeṣu na vyavasthā syāt* could nevertheless possibly refer to vyākaraṇa. The Bhāṣya and Tantravārttika were both translated by Professor Ganganatha Jha. See Jha 1933–36 and 1983. Joshi and Roodbergen 1986 gives a helpful summary of the Tantravārttika's argument in each related part of the Mahābhāṣya.

6. For example, in the Tantravārttika, more than one hundred forty verses with several prose paragraphs are devoted to the pūrvapakṣa, and approximately eighty verses to the uttarapakṣa. The Bṛhatī's pūrvapakṣa extends to twenty-six pages, while its uttarapakṣa is less than four pages long.

7. See Ramachandrudu 1994.

8. B 117.10–11: *kathaṁ punar vyākaraṇasmṛter nirmūlatve sati vedasyāprāmāṇyam āśaṇkyate*.

9. B 119.6–7: *āstāṁ tāvan mūlacintā śabdānuśāsanaṁ tāvad aniyatārtham* "Leave the consideration of the basis aside. From the beginning, grammar (*śabdānuśāsana*) does not have any definite meaning"

his argument later, but now, let us see the corresponding argument in the Nyāyamañjarī.

The sixth āhnika of this work is situated in the concluding section of the first half of the entire work. The first half of this Kashmirian scholar's masterpiece mainly discusses the four means of gaining correct knowledge (*pramāṇa*) admitted in the Nyāya-school: perception (*pratyakṣa*), inference (*anumāna*), comparison (*upamāna*), and verbal testimony (*śabda*). Among these, the Nyāyamañjarī devotes four āhnikas to establish the status as a pramāṇa of śabda. The sixth āhnika is thus the conclusion of the śabda section also. This āhnika can be divided into two parts, of which the first mainly concerns the process of verbal understanding in daily life, while the second is "a long section dealing with grammar as an instrument for Vedic interpretation."[10]

In the Nyāyamañjarī, the critic's main concern is how — by what means — one can interpret sentences from the Vedas, which convey meanings not knowable through perception or inference, and decide what such sentences enjoin one to do. Taking a simple Vedic sentence *agnihotraṁ juhuyāt svargakāmaḥ* as an example, the critic raises a question: which kind of knowledge (*kā pramā*) enables the hearer to decide that this sentence urges him only to perform the agnihotra, but not to eat dog flesh?[11] At this point, Pāṇinian grammar, counted as one of the six vedāṅgas and praised as the most fruitful one,[12] comes to be criticized. In the pūrvapakṣin's opinion, the Aṣṭādhyāyī itself contains a lot of problems so that no one can use it to interpret the Vedas.

10. Bronkhorst 2008 :293. The pūrvapakṣa part runs continuously for twenty-seven pages, while its uttarapakṣa accounts for sixteen pages in Mysore edition.

11. NM 220.4–12: *svayaṁ rāgādimān nārthaṁ vetti cet tasya nānyataḥ/ na vedayati vedo 'pi vedārthasya kuto gatiḥ// …. tenāgnihotraṁ juhuyāt svargakāma iti śrutau/ khādec chvamāṁsam ity eṣa nārtha ity atra kā pramā//* These ślokas are quoted from Pramāṇavārttika, a work of the famous Buddhist logician Dharmakīrti.

12. See MBh I.1.18–20: *āgamaḥ khalv api/ brāhmaṇena niṣkāraṇo dharmaḥ ṣaḍaṅgo vedo 'dhyeyo jñeya iti/ pradhānaṁ ca ṣaṭsv aṅgeṣu vyākaraṇam/ pradhāne ca kṛto yatnaḥ phalavān bhavati//*

Disputing some of Pāṇini's sūtras, the pūrvapakṣin attempts to show that the Aṣṭādhyāyī is unreliable when one needs to decide the meaning of unclear words in the Vedas. If this system of grammar could not be reliable, those Vedic words would not be understood, and the Veda would lose its authority (*prāmāṇya*). This logic is shared by pūrvapakṣins both in the Bṛhatī and the Nyāyamañjarī.

1.2 On the pūrvapakṣin

Was there any existent opponent or was he merely imagined by Prabhākara or Jayanta? On this account, we have hardly anything on which we could depend in either the Bṛhatī or the Nyāyamañjarī.[13] Whether he existed or not, Jayanta's uttarapakṣa describes the pūrvapakṣin as a "discord-causing and cavilling roguish scholar (*viplavakāravaitaṇḍika-paṇḍitataskara*).[14] The compound used shows us an unwelcome character of the censurable scholar,[15] who perhaps had been on Jayanta's mind.

To learn more characteristics of the critic, we have these two concluding ślokas:[16]

> "He who is under the influence of bad stars or is cowed down with the fear of royal punishment or has been cursed by his parents embraces the study of grammar of a classical language."

13. Certainly, the Nyāyamañjarī's pūrvapakṣa quotes several verses of Dharmakīrti, and this Buddhist logician advocated the uselessness of vyākaraṇa as an instrument for Vedic interpretation; however, the dispute concerning sūtras of the Aṣṭādhyāyī is not found in his work; the Bṛhatī with its commentary keeps silent about who is regarded as the opponent here.

14. NM 259.9–11: *na ca teṣām api doṣotprekṣaṇasambhavād anavasthā nipuṇa-darśitamārge viplavakāravaitaṇḍikapaṇḍitataskarāvakāśānupapatteḥ/*

15. Cf. A 2.1.53: *kutsitāni kutsanaiḥ.*

16. NM 246.13–17: *duṣṭagrahagṛhīto vā bhīto vā rājadaṇḍataḥ/ pitṛbhyām abhiśapto vā kuryād vyākaraṇe śramam// ... vṛttiḥ sūtraṃ tilā māṣāḥ kaṭaṇḍī kodravodanaḥ/ ajaḍāya pradātavyaṃ jaḍīkaraṇam uttamam//* Translation by Bhattacharyya (1978: 895).

> "In order to blunt the edge of one's sharp intellect Pāṇini's grammar and its commentary known as vṛtti should be prescribed for his study, and sesame, a kind of pulses, wood apples[17] and boiled rice prepared from a particular kind of rice should be prescribed for his food since these are the best instruments of benumbing keen intellect."

Their exact meaning and true origin are not sure, but one thing is obvious, that both verses attempt — ironically — to keep the hearer from studying Pāṇinian grammar. With these verses, we may sense the pūrvapakṣin's antipathy to Pāṇinian grammar.

2 The dispute about the Aṣṭādhyāyī

2.1 Criticized sūtras

Before we look into the actual argument, let us take a brief glance at the list of sūtras mainly criticized in the Bṛhatī and Nyāyamañjarī. In the order of their appearance, these are: A 1.3.1: *bhūvādayo dhātavaḥ,* 1.4.24: *dhruvam apāye 'pādānam,* 1.4.32: *karmaṇā yam abhipraiti sa sampradānam,* 1.4.42: *sādhakatamaṁ karaṇam,* 1.4.45: *ādhāro 'dhikaraṇam,* 1.4.49: *kartur īpsitatamaṁ karma,* 1.4.54: *svatantraḥ kartā,* 1.4.55: *tatprayojako hetuś ca,* 2.1.1: *samarthaḥ padavidhiḥ,* 4.1.82: *samarthānāṁ prathamād vā,* 1.2.45: *arthavad adhātur apratyayaḥ prātipadikam,* 1.2.46: *kṛttaddhitasamāsāś ca.* Ten of the twelve sūtras criticized are sañjñāsūtras, in which technical terms (*sañjñā)* are defined.

2.2 Text comparison

Now, let us compare the Bṛhatī and Nyāyamañjari texts concerning the dispute. The texts are divided into small sections according to their content and arranged showing corresponding arguments in the two works.[18] Note the resemblance between two texts, especially the phrases I have underlined.

17. The word *kaṭaṇḍī* used here is obscure. NMGBh 177.9 says: ***kaḍa(ṭa)ndī kodravodana*** *iti / kaḍa(ṭa)ndī vaiśeṣikabhāṣyaviśeṣaḥ/* (boldface and variant reading in brackets by the editor). For more detail, see NMGBh: 177, n.3, Introduction 9.

18. Numbers in brackets are for future reference. Aṣṭādhyāyī sūtras are shown in boldface; I have changed punctuation and sandhi.

On A 1.3.1: B 120.11–124.10/NM 238.11–239.10

B	NM
[B1.1]: .... *dhātoḥ pare pratyayā bhavanti iti,*[a] *....ko nāmāyaṁ dhātuḥ? nanu* ***bhūvādayo dhātavaḥ*** *iti kāṁścic chabdān kayācit paripāṭyā paṭhitvā, dhātava iti sañjñā kṛtā, atas tayā sañjñayā ye sañjñino lakṣyante, tebhyaḥ pare pratyayā bhavantīti, kiṁ nopapadyate?*[b]	[NM1.1]: ... *dhātoḥ pare pratyayā bhavantīti lakṣaṇaṁ kurvatā vaktavyam kaḥ punar ayaṁ dhātur nāmeti/ nanu* ***bhūvādayo dhātavaḥ*** *ity uktam eva tatsvarūpam, kecana śabdāḥ kayācit paripāṭyā paṭhitāḥ, te dhātusañjñayā lakṣyante, tebhyaḥ pare tiṅaḥ kṛtaś ca pratyayā bhavantīti / satyam uktam etat, kintv evaṁ pāṭhe kṛte ʾpi na dhātusvarūpanirṇaya upavarṇito bhavati /*
[B1.2]: *gaṇḍatītyādīnām api sādhutvaṁ prāpnoti/*[c] *ghataṁ bhūyata iti ca/ sattādīnām api tārtīyapratyayaprasaṅgaḥ/ anārṣaḥ pāṭha iti cet, bhavatv apy ayaṁ parihāraḥ, gaṇḍatyādīnāṁ punar aprayoga eva/*[d]	[NM1.2]: *tathā ca gaṇḍatīty api prāpnoti, dhātos tiṅpratyayavidhānāt/ .... adhātor api ghaṭabhūyacchabdarūpāt pare tiṅpratyayā bhaveyuḥ/*
[B1.3]: *atha kriyāvacano dhātur ity ucyate, na, bhavati tiṣṭhatītyādīnām aprayogaḥ, gaṇḍateś cānarthakaḥ pāṭhaḥ/ ....*	[NM1.3]: *kriyāvacano dhātur iti cet, bhavati, tisthati ity evamādīnām adhātutvaṁ prāpnoti, gaṇḍeś cānarthakah pāṭhaḥ/*
[B1.4]: *pāṭhakriyāvacanābhyāṁ niyama iti cet, tatrāpi samuditaṁ vyastam iti vaktavyam/ samuditapakṣe gaṇḍatibhavatyādīnāṁ tathaiva vyudāsaḥ/ pratyekam iti cet, pacatyādīnāṁ pāṭhānarthakyam/ āgamayatyādīnāṁ nivṛttyartham iti*[e] *cet, ubhayaṁ tarhy āśritam, evaṁ sati bhavatyādiṣu sa eva doṣaḥ/ ...*	[NM1.4]: *ubhayaṁ tarhi dhātulakṣaṇam, pāṭhaḥ, kriyāvacanatā ceti, na bhavitum arhati/ tad api hi vyastaṁ vā lakṣaṇam, samastaṁ vā/ vyastapakṣe pratyekam abhihite, doṣas tadavastha eva/ samastapakṣe ʾpi bhavatyādau kriyāvacanatvasya dvitīyalakṣaṇasya cābhāvād adhātutvam eva syād iti/ ...*[f]

[a]It is noteworthy that the finite verb form *bhavanti* is used here instead of the optative *syuḥ*.

[b] On the following arguments, cf. MBh I.253–261, esp. vārttikas.1, 3, 5, 12.

[c] In the Dhātupāṭha in the Mādhavīyā Dhātuvṛtti, the root *gaḍI* appears twice in the first gaṇa: 1.55 and 1.247. On 1.55: *gaḍI vadanaikadeśe*, the commentary has handed down an opinion of another commentator, Kāśyapa: *atyādayaḥ pañcaite na tiṅviṣayāḥ*. Here, *atyādayaḥ* refers to *atI*, *adI*, *idI*, *bidI*, and *gaḍI*.

[d] This argument is very interesting, for it indicates that before Prabhākara's date, there was a debate over the authorship of meaning entries in the Dhātupāṭha. On this issue, see Cardona (1984).

[e] Keeping in mind vārttika 12 ad A 1.3.1 (*bhūvādipāṭhaḥ prātipadikāṇapayatyādinivṛttyarthaḥ*), *āṇapayati*, a vernacular form of *ājñapayati* is preferable here.

[f] I have transferred some arguments that follow to [NM8.1] and [NM8.2] for the sake of comparison. See [NM8.1] and [NM8.2].

To understand the relationship between these two arguments, Cakradhara's Nyāyamañjarīgranthibhaṅga is helpful. According to Cakradhara, at least one passage, *ghaṭaṁbhūyata iti ca* has its origin in the Bṛhatī, and Jayanta commented on this very phrase.[19]

On A 1.4.24: B 125.4–126.3/NM 240.2–9

[B2.1]: *tathā kārakaniyamāsiddhiḥ/* ***dhruvam apāye 'pādānam iti*** *dhruvatayāpādānam uktam/ dhruvasya kārakatvam eva nopapadyate/ meṣān meṣo 'pasarpati iti*[a] *kārakam, meṣād iti kasyāḥ kriyāyāḥ kārakam etat? yasya hi yasyāṁ kriyāyāṁ vyāpāro vidyate sa tasyāṁ kārakam, na ca dhruvasya vyāpāra upalabhyate/*	[NM2.1]: *tathā kārakānuśāsanam api duḥstham/* ***dhruvam apāye 'pādānam ity*** *ucyate, tatra dhruvasya vṛkṣādeḥ, vṛkṣāt patito devadattaḥ iti patanakriyāyām acalataḥ kṛśam api na kārakatvam utpaśyāmaḥ/ kriyāyogi hi kārakam, sā ca vṛkṣe nopalabhyata iti/*
[B2.2]: .... *sārthād dhīnaḥ, rathāt patitaḥ iti sārtharathayoḥ kriyopalabhyate iti, nāsti kriyā sārthasya rathasya ca, api tu gamanarūpā, na ca kriyāntare vyāpṛtaṁ kriyāntare kārakaṁ bhavati, na ca gameḥ kartā pacatīty asyāvasīyate/ tasmān niṣkriyaṁ kārakam iti vadato vyāpṛtād anyat sarvaṁ sarvatra kārakaṁ syāt/....*	[NM2.2]: *sārthād dhīnaḥ, rathāt patitaḥ iti sārtharathayoḥ kriyopalabhyate, na vṛkṣavan niścalatvam iti cet, satyam, sva- rasapravṛttā tayor asti kriyā, hāne yāne ca pādapanirviśeṣāv eva sārtharathau, na ca yad ekasyāṁ kriyāyāṁ kārakam, tat sarvāsu kriyāsu kārakaṁ bhavati, atiprasaṅgāt/*

[a] Cf. Vākyapadīya 3.7.140-141. For *apādāna*, cf. MBh ad A 1.4.23 as well as MBh ad A 1.4.24.

19. NMGBh 173.11–15: *ghaṭaṁ bhūyata iti ca iti prābhākarī ṭīkā sādhu-śabdādhikaraṇe tatra ghaṭaṁbhūyata [iti] phakkikāṁ vyākhyātum āha —* ***ghaṭa ceṣṭāyām*** *ityādinā/ ghaṭaś ca am ca bhūś ca yaś ca taś ca ghaṭaṁbhūyat/ tasmād ghaṭaṁbhūyato 'pi prāpnoti prātipadikebhyo 'pi ghaṭādibhyaḥ pratyayās tiṅādayaḥ prāpnuvantīty arthaḥ/* (underline, boldface, and bracketed text in original). The phrase *ghaṭaṁ bhūyate* is obscure. According to Cakradhara, Jayanta seems to understand this phrase as a samāhāra dvandva compound *ghaṭaṁbhūyat*. Śālikanātha regards this as a sentence *ghaṭaṁ bhūyate*. See Ṛjuvimalāpañcikā 121.13–20.

On A 1.4.32: B 126.4–127.7/NM 240.11–19

[B3]: .... ***karmaṇā yam abhipraiti sa sampradānam*** *iti/ karmaṇā ced abhipreyate, na kārakam/ kartrā hi karmaṇā yo 'bhipreyate sa sampradānam ity udāharaṇād vidmaḥ upādhyāyāya gāṁ dadātīīti/ kartṛvyāpārānuniṣpādivyāpāraṁ ca kārakam, yaḥ punar abhipreyate, na tasyābhiprayaṇe vyāpāraḥ/ tena tam iti karmakaraṇanirdeśāt phalaṁ karma bhavati, na kārakam, yajer iva svargaḥ/ nanu ca karmaṇā yam abhipraitīti kārakaṁ karma parigṛhyate, sutarām akārakatvam/ na hi kārakasambandhitayā kārakavyapadeśo bhavati, karoti iti kārakaśabdavyutpādanāt/* .... *kriyāsambandhitayā ca [kārakatve]*[a] *viśeṣānuśāsanaṁ na sidhyati, ṣaṣṭhī ca sarvakārakāṇāṁ prāpnoti, svargasya ca yāgakārakatvaprasaṅgaḥ, prayājādīnāṁ ca darśapūrṇamāsayoḥ/*[b]	[NM3]: ***karmaṇā yam abhipraiti sa sampradānam*** *iti, atra karmaśabdaḥ kriyāvacano vā syād, īpsitatamakārakavācī vā/ ādye pakṣe kriyayā sarvakārakāṇy abhipreyanta iti kriyāsu kārakāṇi sampradānatāṁ pratipadyeran/ na copadhyāya-sya kiñcid abhiprīyamāṇasya vyāpāram utpaśyāma ity asāv akārakam eva tatra syāt/ pratigrahas tu kriyāntaram eva/ tatra coktaṁ kriyayā cābhipreyamāṇaṁ phalaṁ bhavati, na kārakam iti vakṣyāmaḥ/*[c] *dvitīyas tu pakṣaḥ, karmaṇā kārakeṇa gavādinā yam abhipraitīti sutarāṁ saṅkaṭaḥ/ kriyāsambandhitayā hi kārakaṁ kārakaṁ bhavati, na kārakasambandhitayā, karotīti kārakam iti vyutpatteḥ/*

[a] The bracketed addition is supplied by the editor.

[b] It may be noteworthy that the opponent uses Mīmāṁsaka-like terminology, such as: *yajer iva svargaḥ*, *svargasya ca yāgakārakatvaprasaṅgaḥ*, *prayājādīnāṁ ca darśapūrṇamāsayoḥ*. Even so, is it possible for a Mīmāṁsaka to appear in such an anti-Vedic context?

c See [NM6.2].

On A 1.4.42: B 127.7–128.6/NM 241.2–6

[B4]: *yad api* ***sādhakatamaṁ karaṇam*** *ity ucyate, kiṁ tat sādhakatamam iti,* .... *prācuryāt iti cet, yasya hi ā phalaniṣpatteḥ punaḥ punaḥ vyāpāraḥ, kasya vā nāstīti*	[NM4]: ***sādhakatamaṁ karaṇam*** *iti tamabarthānavadhāraṇād anupapannam/* .... *prācuryeṇa hi pradhānasampattiparyantavyāpārayogitvam ityādi sarvasādhāraṇam* ....

On A 1.4.45: B 128.7–129.7/NM 241.9–242.2

[B5.1]: ***ādhāro 'dhikaraṇam*** *iti cānuśāsanam/ kasyādhāratvam? yatrādhīyate sa ādhāra iti, yadi tāvat kriyā, sarvakārakāṇām adhikaraṇatvaprasaṅgaḥ/*	[NM5.1]: ***ādhāro 'dhikaraṇam*** *iti yad ucyate, tatra vaktavyaṁ kasyādhāra iti/ kriyāyāḥ, kārakasya vā/ yadi kriyādhāratvam adhikaraṇalakṣaṇam, aśeṣakārakāṇām adhikaraṇasañjñā prasajyeta, kriyāyogāviśeṣāt/*

[B5.2]: *atha yatra karma tad adhikaraṇam iti cet, same pacati iti na prāpnoti, apsu pacati iti prāpnotīti, kaṭe bhuṅkte iti cāpabhraṁśaḥ/ kartur hi tad adhikaraṇaṁ na kriyāyāḥ, nāpi karmaṇaḥ/*	[NM5.2]: *atha yatra sthālyādau karmāśritaṁ taṇḍulādi tad adhikaraṇam, same deśe pacati iti na syāt, apsu pacati iti syāt, kaṭe sthito bhuṅkte iti cāpabhraṁśo bhavet/ kartur hi tad adhikaraṇam, na karmaṇaḥ/....*
[B5.3]: *sarvakārakavyavasthānaṁ yatreti cet, sthālyām odanaṁ pacatīti na prāpno- ti/ adhikaraṇasya vā 'kārakatvaprasa- ṅgaḥ/ na hy adhikaraṇam adhikaraṇavya- vasthitam iti śakyate vaktum/ sambandhi- tayā sarvakārakādhikaraṇatā vā 'dhikara- ṇatve hetur uktaḥ/*[a]	[NM5.3]: *yadi tu sakalakārakādhāratvam adhikaraṇalakṣaṇam, sthālyām odanaṁ pacati iti na syāt, sakalakārakānadhikaraṇatvāt/ sthālyā adhikaraṇasya cākārakatvaprasaktiḥ/ na hy adhikaraṇam adhikaraṇāśritaṁ bhavati/*
[B5.4]: *nirvyāpāratvaṁ ca kālādiṣūktam/*	[NM5.4]: .... *kālādīnām avyāpāratvād akārakatvam eva bhavet/....*

[a] See [B3].

On A 1.4.49: B 129.7–130.6/NM 242.4–243.4

[B6.1]:.... ***kartur īpsitatamaṁ** karma iti, ko 'yam ātiśāyinakaḥ? sarvaṁ kriyārtham īpsitatamam/*	[NM6.1]: ***kartur īpsitatamaṁ karma** iti, sādhakatamavad ihāpi na vācako 'yam atiśāyanaḥ, sarvakārakāṇāṁ kriyārthitayā kartur īpsitatamatvāt/*
[B6.2]: *athāyam abhiprāyaḥ, yadarthā kriyā tat tamapābhidhīyate, prāptam akārakatvam/ uktaṁ hi sampradānasūtre/*[a]	[NM6.2]: *atha yadarthā kriyā tadarthaṁ kartur īpsitatam, tadarthaṁ tv anyat iti tatra tamappratyaya ity ucyate/ tarhi tasya kārakatvam eva na yuktam/ kriyāsampādakaṁ hi kārakam ucyate, na kriyāsampādyam/ kriyāsampādyaṁ tu phalaṁ bhavati, na kārakam/....*

[a] See [B3].

On A 1.4.54–55: B 130.6–132.3/NM 243.6–244.5

[B7.1]: *tathā **svatantraḥ kartā** iti, kim idaṁ svātantryam? yadīcchātaḥ pravṛttiḥ, jāyate, mriyate, kūlaṁ patati ity akartṛtā prāpnoti/ tataś cāsādhutāprasaṅgaḥ śabdasya/*	[NM7.1]: ***svatantraḥ kartā** iti, kim idaṁ svātantryaṁ kriyāsampādyam? yadicchātaḥ pravartanam iti cet, kūlaṁ patati iti caitanyaśūnyatayā kūlasyecchānupalambhād akartṛtvaṁ bhavet/*
[B7.2]: *atha tadvyāpārādhīnaṁ kārakāntaraṁ manyase, keyaṁ tadadhīnatā? yasmin sati yo niṣpadyate tat tadadhīnam, prāptaṁ tarhi sarvakārakāṇāṁ kartṛtvam itaretarādhīnatvāt/ na kenacid vinā kasyacit niṣpattim upalabhāmahe/ yasya hi yena vinā vyāpāraniṣpattiḥ na tena tad apekṣate, parasparāpekṣaś ca kāraka-grāmaḥ*	[NM7.2]: *atha yadvyāpārādhīnaḥ kārakāntaravyāpāraḥ sa kartā ity ucyate, sarvakārakanirvartyatvāt kriyāyāḥ, na vidmaḥ kiṁvyāpārādhīnaḥ, kasya vyāpāra iti, samagrakāraka-grāmasya parasparāpekṣatvāt/....*

[B7.3]: *dhātūpāttavyāpāraḥ kartā iti cet, na vidmaḥ kasya dhātūpātta iti, sarveṣāṁ sambandhitayāvagamāt/*	[NM7.3]: *atha dhātunā 'bhidhīyamāna-vyāpāraḥ kartā iti, tatrāpi na vidmaḥ kasya dhātunā 'bhihito vyāpāraḥ, sakala- kārakavācitvāt paceḥ/* ....
[B7.4]: *tatprayojako hetuś ca iti, prayojyenaiva vyākhyātam/*....	[NM7.4]: *tatprayojako hetuś ca iti, prayojyenaiva vyākhyātam/*....

On tiṅ-suffixes: B 134.6–135.6/NM 239.9–19[20]

[B8.1]: *evaṁ kṛtpratyayā api vyākhyātāḥ/ tiṅpratyayā api kālādyupādhayah, na tadvacanāḥ/*	[NM8.1]: *evaṁ dhātoḥ prakṛter anirṇītatvāt, kutaḥ pare tiṇaś ca kṛtaś ca pratyayā utpadyeran/ kiñca kecana tiṅpratyayāḥ kālādyupādhayaḥ, na tadvacanāḥ/* ....
[B8.2]: *kena coktaṁ kālādayo nocyanta iti? uktaṁ bhagavatā bhāṣyakāreṇa bhūte dhātvartha iti/* [a] *na ca dhātvarthenaiva dhātvarthanirūpaṇaṁ śakyam/ tathā liṅā- dayo 'pi vidhyādyarthānirūpaṇāt/ kathaṁ punar vidhyāder anirūpaṇam? upapadā-rthavaśatvād bhedasya/ na svato bhedaḥ śakyate 'vagantum/*	[NM8.2]: *ucyatāṁ tarhi tiṅbhiḥ kālādaya iti cet, na, bhāṣyavirodhāt/ uktaṁ hi bhagavatā bhāṣyakāreṇa bhūte dhātvartha iti/ na ca dhātvarthenaiva dhātvartho vyavasthāpayituṁ śakyate/ liṅādayaś ca sutarām anadhigamyamānaviṣayāḥ/ te hi vidhyādāv arthe vidhīyante/ sa ca vidhirūpo 'rthaḥ svarūpataś copādhitaś ca na śakyo nirṇetum iti/*

[a] Cf. MBh II.111.2–5.

On A 2.1.1, A 4.1.82: B 135.6–136.6/NM 244.9–17

[B9.1]: *tathā taddhitasamāsau samarthavacanā[t] durnirūpau/ kim idaṁ samarthavacanād iti,* ***samarthānāṁ prathamād vā***, ***samarthaḥ padavidhiḥ*** *iti cānuśāsa- nam/ ekārthānvayitā ca sāmarthyam, tallakṣaṇatvārthaṁ ca samāsa-viśeṣābhidhānaṁ taddhitaviśeṣābhi-dhānaṁ ca, tena ca tau lakṣyete itītaretarāśrayam/*	[NM9.1]: *kiñca yad api taddhitasamāsānuśāsanaṁ tat sāmarthyaniyamapūrvakam,* ***samarthānāṁ prathamād vā***, ***sama- rthaḥ padavidhiḥ iti*** *paribhāṣāṇāt/ tad atrāpi vaktavyam sāmarthyaṁ nāma kim ucyata iti/ ekārthānvayitvam iti cet, tat kuto 'vagamyate? taddhitasamāsaprayogapratipattibhyām eveti cet, tarhi tābhyāṁ sāmarthyāvagamaḥ, sāmarthye sati tayoḥ pravṛttir itītaretarāśrayam/*

20. [NM8.1] and [NM8.2] actually do not appear after [NM7.4] but after [NM1.4]. Although the order of appearance is not the same as in the Bṛhatī, the content is almost the same. Operations concerning verb endings (*tiṅpratyaya*) depend on the meaning of a verbal root (*dhātu*) and particular kārakas, so that the criticism is appropriate. However, so long as the referent of *dhātu* is undetermined, it is not known after what the endings should occur. Therefore there is nothing logically strange if the argument is placed after [NM1.4].

[B9.2]: *asamarthānāṁ tāvat samāsaḥ, aśrāddhabojī, dadhighaṭaḥ, gorathaḥ iti/ samarthāc cānutpattis taddhitasya, aṅgulyā khanati, vṛkṣamūlād āgataḥ iti/*	[NM9.2]: *api ca sāmarthyam antareṇāpikvacit prayuṇjate samāsam, aśrāddhabhojī, dadhighaṭaḥ, gorathaḥ iti/ tathā saty api sāmarthye taddhita-prayogaṁ pariharanti, aṅgulyā khanati, vṛkṣamūlād āgataḥ iti āṅgulikaḥ, vārkṣamūlaḥ iti na vaktāro bhavantīti etad apy asamañjasam anuśāsanam/*

On A 1.2.45–46: B 137.1–139.1/NM 244.19–245.7

[B10.1]: *tathā* ***arthavad adhātur apratyayaḥ prātipadikam*** *iti, ... vākyasya tarhi prātipadikasañjñā prāpnoti/ samāsagrahanaṁ tanni-vṛttyartham iti cet, adhātur apratyaya ity anarthakam, tasyāpi samāsa-grahaṇān nivṛttiḥ/*	[NM10.1]: *tathā* ***arthavad adhātur apratyayaḥ prātipadikam*** *iti sañjñālakṣaṇam ativyāpakam, vākyasyāpi prātipadikasañjñāprasaṅgāt/ atha* ***kṛttaddhitasamāsāś ca*** *iti sūtrāntare samāsagrahaṇaṁ vidhiśeṣatvena varṇyamānaṁ taditarapratiṣedhaphalaṁ bhavati iti, tato vākyanivṛttiḥ setsyati/ yady evam, adhātur apratyayaḥ iti na vaktavyam, dhātupratyayayor api tata eva pratiṣedhasiddheḥ/*
[B10.2]: *ekārthatve sati nirvartakaṁ nārthāntare iti cet, tad ayuktam, samāsasyāpy arthāntarābhyupagamād vāvacanānarthakyena/ ....*	[NM10.2]: *atha ekārthatayā samānaśīlasya vākyasyaiva pratiṣedhe prabhavati samāsagrahaṇam, na dhātupratyayayoḥ iti, tad api durāśāmātram, vākyasamāsayor api vāvacanānarthakyakathanena pārthagarthyavyavasthāpanād iti/....*

As one can easily grasp from above, the disputes in both the Bṛhatī and the Nyāyamañjarī resemble each other to a high degree. The question arises: did Jayanta make his pūrvapakṣa with the Bṛhatī's argument in mind? In the light of the Nyāyamañjarī-granthibhaṅga, at least one phrase has a direct connection with the Bṛhatī. However, taking into consideration Jayanta's own words in the first āhnika,[21] there would be no surprise if he did paraphrase some of the disputes found in the Bṛhatī's pūrvapakṣa as a part of his own pūrvapakṣa.[22]

2.3 Characteristics of the dispute

The technical terms (*sañjñā*) we have considered above play

21. NM I.3.3–4: *kuto vā nūtanaṁ vastu vayam utprekṣituṁ kṣamāḥ/ vacovinyāsavaicitryamātram atra vicāryatām//*

22. In the sixth āhnika, we can also find close connection to the Tantravārttika. See Ramachandrudu 1994.

significant roles in Pāṇinian grammar because they are closely connected with morphological and semantic aspects of this grammar. This means that it can be fatal to the system of Pāṇinian grammar to point out any doubtful points in the sūtras in question.

In advance of examining characteristics of the dispute, let me briefly confirm what we can say about the nature of sañjñās. The distinction made by Pāṇinian grammarians between long terms (*mahāsañjñā*) and artificial terms (*kṛtrimasañjñā*)) is noteworthy. Sañjñāsūtras that define artificial terms are quite simple. In such sūtras, the sañjñā itself and what is defined with the sañjñā — such as a certain word form, a list of word forms, a certain syllabic condition, etc. — are shown plainly, so that there is little possibility of any doubt. In the case of sañjñāsūtras that define mahāsañjñās, however, the situation is complicated. There exist problems caused by uncertainty regarding what is defined with the mahāsañjñā. Furthermore, because of their length, such terms are not fully compatible with the system of Pāṇinian grammar, in which pithy expression with an extremely small number of syllables is preferred, so that, as a result, some special explanations are needed.

For example, in A 1.4.23: *kārake*, which precedes the sections defining the particular kāraka-members, the term *kāraka* itself appears, although we cannot find out any other words to be defined at a glance. In order to solve these problems in A 1.4.23, the Mahābhāṣya suggests that the use of a long term (*mahatī sañjñā*) make it known that the term has literal meaning (*anvarthasañjñā*):

> "The sūtra *kārake* brings about the mahāsañjñā, and every sañjñā has nothing smaller or shorter than it. [Q] Why is it so? [A] Because technical terms are brought about for brevity. A mahāsañjñā is used here for the purpose of letting us understand a term whose meaning is literal: a

> kāraka is that which brings about (an action)."[23]

This grammarian's explanation is good because it resolves both problems. In spite of this, the explanation given arouses a new suspicion about the sūtra in question. Let us see a typical example of the criticism. On A 1.4.24, the critic states in [NM2.1]:

> "The grammarian says that an apādāna is a kāraka that is a fixed point in separation. Then, in expressions such as 'Devadatta fell from a tree,' we hardly find any nature of kāraka in the tree, which never moves in Devadatta's action of falling. Indeed, the nature of a kāraka is something connected with action, and no action of the tree is perceived."

Certainly, this criticism reveals the points which might be problematic if we understand the term *kāraka* in A 1.4.23 literally and interpret the next sūtra, A 1.4.24, straightforwardly.

However, was it possible for Pāṇinian grammarians to overlook such an easily predictable problem? In fact, further attention to the discussions in the Mahābhāṣya suggests how we can interpret the sūtra, keeping the literal meaning of the term and avoiding the problem.[24] As shown above, the critic continues to attack other sūtras that also contain unclear expressions like *karmaṇā* in A 1.4.32 ([B3], [NM3]) or the suffix *-tamaP* in A 1.4.42 ([B4], [NM4]), 49 ([B6.1–2], [NM6.1–2]), although those problems had already been predicted and argued by Pāṇinian grammarians.[25]

3 Considerations and conclusion

As regards to the characteristic of these arguments, it can be pointed out that those criticisms could be examples of criticisms of Aṣṭādhyāyī sūtras, but not criticisms of the Pāṇinian system of

23. MBh I.324.7–9: *kāraka iti mahatī sañjñā kriyate/ sañjñā ca nāma yato na laghīyaḥ/ kuta etat/ laghvarthaṁ hi sañjñākaraṇam/ tatra mahatyāḥ sañjñāyāḥ karaṇa etat prayojanam anvarthasañjñā yathā vijñāyeta/ karotīti kārakam iti/*

24. See MBh I.324.13–326.17.

25. For the Pāṇinian interpretation of A 1.3.1: *bhūvādayo dhātavaḥ*, see Ogawa 2005.

grammar, despite the pūrvapakṣins' intention.[26] From this point of view, we can easily understand the reason why the siddhānta sections in the Bṛhatī and Nyāyamañjarī that answer to the criticism are very concise, as follows:

> "The explanation for these problems has been answered by interpreters in a certain manner. Would you accept the explanation they gave as it is? Indeed, their explanation is also smaraṇa."[27]
>
> "As for critics saying in many ways that the system of Pāṇini has uncertainty in the teaching of dhātu, prātipadika, and each kāraka-member, however, this criticism had also been solved by wise men. Moreover no infinite chain of wise men is needed for the possibility of mistake. Because, no room for discord-causing and cavilling, roguish scholars can be left in a path guided by the precise-minded."[28]

At this point, the second qualifier in the compound *viplavakāravaitaṇḍikapaṇḍitataskara*, *vaitaṇḍika*, deserves consideration. The word *vaitaṇḍika* is derived from *vitaṇḍā*, which is enumerated as the term for one of the sixteen categories in the Nyāya-school.[29] Explaining its definition, Jayanta describes a vaitaṇḍika as one who does nothing but dispute others' thought and

26. It was the fault of pūrvapakṣins that they did not examine enough what was argued in Mahābhāṣya and so on. At this point, it is interesting that the critics' ignorance of — or rather indifference to — the tradition of Pāṇinian grammar seems to match that of non-orthodox Pāṇinian grammarians, as indicated by Bronkhorst (2008). The criticism might have come from critics' indifference to the tradition of Pāṇinian grammar, but to siddhāntins it seemed merely to be a result of pūrvapakṣins' ignorance.

27. B 145.5–7: *tadvyākhyānaṁ kathañcit samāhitaṁ vyākhyātṛbhiḥ/ yathā samāhitaṁ kathañcit tathaiva parigṛhyatām/ tad api hi smaraṇam eva/*

28. NM 259.9–12: *yad api pāṇinitantre dhātuprātipadikakārakādyanuśāsana-visaṁṣṭhulatvam anekaśākham ākhyāpitaṁ, tad api nipuṇamatibhiḥ pratisamāhitam eva/ na ca teṣām api doṣotprekṣaṇasambhavād anavasthā, nipuṇadarśitamārge viplavakāravaitaṇḍikapaṇḍitataskarāvakāśānupapatteḥ/*

29. Nyāyasūtra 1.1.1: *pramāṇaprameyasaṁśayaprayojanadṛṣṭānta-siddhāntāvayavatarkanirṇayavādajalpavitaṇḍāhetvābhāsacchalajāti-nigrahasthānānāṁ tattvajñānān niśśreyasādhigamaḥ.*

does not have his own opinion.[30] In this sense, what we have examined above is a cavil or vitaṇḍā. No matter how reasonable an argument might be as a serious criticism of the Aṣṭādhyāyī, as long as the pūrvapakṣins do not give any alternative opinion of their own, it is just a cavil.[31]

30. See NM 602.13–603.14 on Nyāyasūtra 1.2.3: *sa pratipakṣasthāpanāhīno vitaṇḍā.*

31. But in a broader context, they have clearly declared that their aim is to negate the authority of the Vedas. In addition to this, we may guess a "discord-causing" characteristic of the Bṛhatī's pūrvapakṣins. See the ironical use of the word namaḥ in B 127.6 and the word *pramāṇam* in B 132.2. Prabhākara also states (B 141.3–4): *ākṛtigaṇābhidhānaṁ ca śāstrato niyamasya mātṛkā/ bahulagrahaṇaṁ ca śāstrato 'niyamasya ḍiṇḍimaḥ/* Even if they are mere cavils, some of the criticisms might deserve further consideration in the future. For example, on the problem of the verb gaṇḍati in [B1.2] and [NM1.2], we need to examine the actual usage of this verb.

References and abbreviations

A *Aṣṭādhyāyī* of Pāṇini.

Abhyankar, K. V.

1962–72 *The Vyākaraṇa=Mahābhāṣya of Patañjali Edited by F. Kielhorn, revised and furnished with additional readings, reference, and select critical notes, third edition.* Poona: Bhandarkar Oriental Research Institute. [Reissued: 1985 (vol.1, 4th ed.), 1965 (vol. 2, 3rd ed.), 1982 (Vol. 3, 3rd ed.)]

B *Bṛhatī* of Prabhākara. See Subramania Śāstrī, S.

Bhāṣya *Bhāṣya* of Śabara Svāmin. See Subramania Śāstrī, S.

Bhattacharyya, Janaki Vallabha.

1978 *Jayanta Bhaṭṭa's Nyāya-mañjarī: The Compendium of Indian Speculative Logic.* Vol.1. Delhi: Motilal Banarasidass.

Bronkhorst, Johannes

2008 Udbhaṭa, a grammarian and a Cārvāka, in Mrinal Kaul and Ashok Akuljkar (eds.), *Linguistic Traditions of Kashmir: Essays in Memory of Paṇḍit Dinanath Yaksha*, New Delhi: D.K. Printworld, pp. 281–299.

Cardona, George

1984 On the Mahābhāṣya evidence for a Pāṇinīya Dhātupāṭha without meaning entries, in S. D. Joshi (ed.). *Amṛtadhārā: Professor R.M. Dandekar Felicitation Volume*, Delhi: Ajanta Publications, pp. 79–84.

Dwarikadass Shastri

1964 *The Mādhavīyā Dhātuvṛitti* [*A Treatise on Sanskrit Roots Based on the Dhātupāṭha of Pāṇini*] *by*

Sāyaṇācārya. Prāchya Bhāratī Series 1. Varanasi: Prāchya Bhāratī Prakāshana.

Jha, Ganganatha.

1911 *The Prābhākara School of Pūrva Mīmāmsā*. Delhi: Motiral Banarasidass. [Reprinted 1978]

1933–36 *Shabara-bhāṣya: Translated into English* .... Three volumes. Gaekwad's Oriental Series 66, 70, 73. Baroda: Oriental Institute.

1983 *Kumārila Bhaṭṭa Tantravārttika: A Comentary on Śabara's Bhāṣya on the Pūrvamīmāṁsā Sūtras of Jaimini*. Two volumes. Delhi: Sri Satguru Publications. [second edition]

Joshi, S.D. and Roodbergen, J.A.F.

1986 *Patañjali's Vyākaraṇa-Mahābhāṣya Paspaśāhnika: Introduction, Text, Translation and Notes*. Publications of the Centre of Advanced Study in Sanskrit Class C. Pune: University of Poona.

Mādhavīyā Dhātuvṛtti See Dwarikadas Shastri.

MBh *Mahābhāṣya* of Patañjali. See Abhyankar, K. V.

MS *Mīmāṁsāsūtra*. See Subramania Śāstrī, S.; Subbāśāstrī.

Mīmāṁsāsūtra See B.

NM *Nyāyamanjarī* of Jayantabhaṭṭa. See Varadacharya, K.S.

NMGBh *Nyāyamanjarīgranthibhaṅga*. of Cakradhara. See Shah, Nagin J.

Nyāyasūtra See See Varadacharya, K.S.

Ogawa, Hideyo

2005 *Process and Language*: A *Study of the Mahābhāṣya ad A1.3.1 bhūvādayo dhātavaḥ*. Delhi: Motilal Banarsidas.

Raghavan, V.
1960 Why was Jayantabhatta known as the Vrttikara?, in H. L. Hariyappa and M. M. Patkar (eds.), *Professor P. K. Gode Commemoration Volume*, Poona Oriental Series 93-3, Poona: Oriental Book Agency, pp.173–174.

Ramachandrudu, P. Sri
1994 Kumārila Bhaṭṭa on the prayojana of vyākaraṇa, in R. C. Dwivedi (ed.), *Studies in Mīmāṁsā: Dr. Mandan Mishra Felicitation Volume*, Delhi: Motilal Banarasidass, pp. 243–255.

Ṛjuvimalāpañcikā See Subramania Śāstrī, S.

Shah, Nagin J.
1972 *Cakradhara's Nyāyamañjarī-Granthibhaṅga*. L. D. Series 35. Ahmedabad: L. D. Institute of Indology.
1975–92 *Nyāyamaṅjarī, Gujarātībhāṣāṇuvādasahitā*. Five volumes. L. D. Series 48, 67, 97, 108. Ahmedabad: L. D. Institute of Indology.

Subbāśāstri
1929-33 *Śrījaiminipraṇīt*[*aṁ*] *Mīmāṁsādarśan*[*am*] ... *Śrīkumārilabhaṭṭaviracitantravārtikākhyavyākhyās ahitaśābarabhāṣysasamet*[*am*]. Five volumes. Ānandāśrama Sanskrit Series 97. Poona: Ānandāśrama.

Subramania Iyer, K. A.
1963 *Vākyapadīya of Bhartṛhari with the commentary of Helārāja, kāṇḍa III*, Pt. 1. Deccan College Monograph Series 21. Poona: Deccan College. [Reprinted 1994]

Subramania Śāstrī, S.
1962 *The Bṛhatī of Prabhākara Miśra* [*on the Mīmāṁsā*

Sūtrabhāṣya of Śabara] *with the Ṛjuvimalā Pañcikā of Śālikanāth* (*Adhyāya I Pādas 2, 3, 4 and Adhyāya II complete*). Madras University Sanskrit Series 24. Madras: University of Madras.

TV *Tantravārttika* of Kumārila. See Subbāśāstrī.

Vākyapadīya See Subramania Iyer, K. A.

Varadacharya, K.S.

1969-83 *Nyāyamanjarī of JayantabhaṭṭaWith Ṭippaṇī — Nyāyasaurabha by the Editor*. Two volumes. Oriental Research Institute Series 116, 139. Mysore: Oriental Research Institute.

vārttika See MBh.

सारस्वतव्याकरणे प्रक्रियासारल्यम् : सुबन्तसन्दर्भे

वेदमित्र आर्य

'युगे-युगे व्याकरणान्तराणि' अत एव सम्प्रति संस्कृतभाषायाः साधुत्वप्रतिपादनाय लोके बहवः व्याकरणसम्प्रदायाः दृश्यन्ते। तेषु श्रीतत्त्वविधनामके वैष्णवग्रन्थे नवविध व्याकरणानि उल्लिखितानि।

> ऐन्द्रं चान्द्रं काशकृत्स्नं कौमारं शाकटायनम्।
> सारस्वतं चापिशलं शाकलं पाणिनीयकम्।।[1]

एतेषु व्याकरणेषु सारस्वतव्याकरणस्य महत्त्वं सर्वविदितमेव। पञ्चाशदधिकैकादशवैक्रमाब्दे (1150 वि०सं०) लोकानुग्रहकांक्षिणा अनुभूतिस्वरूपाचार्येण चरमे वयसि बालानां सुखबोधाय अनायासेन च व्याकरणकलाज्ञानाय सारस्वतनामकं व्याकरणं व्यरचि।

अनुभूतिस्वरूपाचार्यस्य विषये प्राचीनविद्वद्वर्यैरेषा किम्वदन्त्यपि प्रस्तूयते यत् पुरा कदाचिदनुभूतिस्वरूपाचार्यस्य मुखारविन्दात् वार्द्धक्येन दन्तविहीनतया च 'पुंसु' इत्यस्य प्रसङ्गे 'पुंक्षु' इत्ययमपशब्दः न्यसरत्। तदानीं तत्र स्थिताः सर्वे वैयाकरणविद्वान्सः तदीयाशुद्धशब्दमाकर्ण्य उपजहसुः। उपहासानन्तरमनुभूतिस्वरूपाचार्याः स्वोच्चारितस्य अशुद्धशब्दस्य साधुत्वं प्रतिपादयितुं गृहमागत्य सरस्वतीं देवीं प्रार्थयामासुः। प्रसन्ना सती सा देवी तस्मै सूत्राणां सप्तशतीं ददौ। तानि सूत्राण्याधृत्य महानुभावा अनुभूतिस्वरूपाचार्याः यद् व्याकरणं रचयामासुः तदेव सारस्वतव्याकरणमिति नाम्ना प्रसिद्धम्। सारस्वतव्याकरणं द्विधा विभक्तम् – पूर्वार्द्धमुत्तरार्द्धञ्च। तत्र पूर्वार्द्धे सुबन्तप्रकरणे स्वरान्ताः पुँल्लिङ्गाः, स्वरान्ताः स्त्रीलिङ्गाः, स्वरान्ताः नपुंसकलिङ्गाः, हसान्ताः पुँल्लिङ्गाः, हसान्ताः स्त्रीलिङ्गाः, हसान्ताः नपुंसकलिङ्गाः, युस्मदस्मद्प्रक्रियाश्च विद्यन्ते। पाणिनीयव्याकरणवत् सारस्वतेऽपि प्रातिपदिकेभ्यो विहिताः एकविंशतिः प्रत्ययाः समानमेव। परन्तु तत्र 'सु' इत्यस्य स्थाने 'सि' 'औट्' इत्यस्य स्थाने च 'औ' इति पाणिनितो भेदो वर्तते।

आचार्येण सारस्वते पाणिन्यपेक्षया कुत्रचित् स्पष्टनिर्देशेन प्रक्रियालाघवं कृतं, क्वचिच्च स्वदर्शनानुगुणं यथेच्छं प्रक्रियापरिवर्त्तनं विहितम्। तान्येव परिवर्तनानि अस्य व्याकरणस्य पाणिनितो वैशिष्ट्यम्। परिवर्तनेषु तेषु सुबन्तमधिकृत्य अत्र शब्दविदाम् पुरस्तात् प्रस्तूयते। तत्र प्रथमतः प्रक्रियायां स्पष्टनिर्देशमधिकृत्य वर्ण्यते। तथाहि –

---

[1] पण्डितयुधिष्ठिरमीमांसकेन विरचिते संस्कृत-व्याकरणशास्त्रेतिहासे, प्रथमे भागे, पृ० 62 ।

(क) स्पष्टनिर्देशपूर्वकं प्रक्रियासारल्यम्-

1. द्वये-द्वयाः

इत्यत्र 'संख्याया अवयवे तयप्'[2] इत्यनेन सूत्रेण अवयवार्थे संख्यावाचिनः उभशब्दात् तयप्प्रत्ययं विधाय तस्य स्थान अयजादेशे कृते 'उभय' इति रूपं सिध्यति। पदमञ्जरीकारमते स्थानिवद्भावेन उभयशब्दस्तयबन्तः।[3] अतः जसि परतः 'प्रथमचरमतयाल्पार्धकतिपयनेमाश्च'[4] इत्यनेन सूत्रेण विकल्पेन उभयशब्दस्य सर्वनामसंज्ञा यथा भवति तथैव द्वयशब्दस्यापि भवति। ततश्च 'द्वये-द्वयाः' इति रूपद्वयं सिध्यति।

अनुभूतिस्वरूपाचार्येण तु 'तयायडौ संख्याया अवयवे'[5] इति सूत्रेण साक्षादेव अयट्प्रत्ययं विधाय 'प्रथमचरमतयायडल्पार्द्धकतिपयनेमानां जसी वा'[6] इत्यनेन सूत्रेण अयट्प्रत्ययान्तद्वयशब्दस्य जसः स्थाने विकल्पेन ईकारादेशं कृत्वा 'द्वये-द्वयाः' इति रूपद्वयं साधितम्।

अत्र सारस्वते साक्षान्निर्देशेन प्रक्रियालाघवं सारल्यञ्च प्रस्फुटमेव। चान्द्र[7]-हैम[8]-सरस्वतीकण्ठाभरणेषु[9] व्याकरणेष्वपि अयडिति प्रत्ययान्तरं स्वीकृतम्।

2. हे अस्थे-हे अस्थि

पाणिनीयप्रक्रियायां सम्बोधने 'हे अस्थि-सु' इति स्थिते सोर्लुकि[10] सति 'हे अस्थि' इति रूपं सिध्यति। अत्र 'इकोऽचि विभक्तौ'[11] इति सूत्रे अचिग्रहणसामर्थ्यात् 'न लुमताङ्गस्य'[12] इति सूत्रस्य अनित्यत्वं ज्ञाप्यते भाष्यकारेण।[13] अतः क्वचित् लुमतालुप्ते

---

[2] *अष्टा०* 5.2.42 ।

[3] उभाववयवावस्य 'उभादुदात्तो नित्यम्' (*अष्टा०* 5.2.44) इति तयपोऽयजादेशः। स्थानिवद्भावाद्भवत्यं तयबन्तः। – *पदमञ्जरी,* 1.1.33 ।

[4] *अष्टा०* 1.1.33 ।

[5] *सा०व्या०* 19/50 पू० ।

[6] *सा०व्या०* 7/32 पू० ।

[7] प्रथमचरमतयायाल्पार्धनेमकतिपयात्। – *चा०व्या०* 2.1.14

[8] नेमार्धप्रथमचरमतयायाल्पकतिपयस्य वा। – *सि०हैम०* 1.4.10

[9] प्रथमचरमतयायाल्पार्धनेमकतिपयेभ्यः। – *स०क०* 3.1.172

[10] स्वमोर्नपुंसकात्। – *अष्टा०* 7.1.23

[11] *अष्टा०* 7.1.73 ।

[12] *अष्टा०* 1.1.63 ।

[13] न लुमताङ्गस्येति प्रत्ययलक्षणस्य प्रतिषेधः। एवं तर्हि सिद्धे सति यदज्ग्रहणं करोति तज्ज्ञापयत्याचार्यो भवतीह कश्चिदन्योऽपि प्रकारः प्रत्यय लक्षणं नामेति। – *म०भा०* 7.1.73, प्रतिभाप्रकाशनसंस्करणे सप्तमे भागे, पृ० 69 ।

सत्यपि प्रत्ययलक्षणकार्यं भवतीत्यायाति। तेन प्रत्ययलक्षणेन 'अस्थि ø' इत्यत्र सम्बुद्धौ परतः गुणे[14] सति 'हे अस्थे' इति रूपं सिध्यति। एवं पाणिनीयप्रक्रियायां व्याख्यानेनैव ज्ञातव्यं भवति यदाचार्यपाणिनिना सम्बोधने रूपद्वमिष्यते।

अनुभूतिस्वरूपाचार्यस्तु अत्र सारल्यार्थं स्पष्टरूपेण इकारोकार-ऋकारान्तानां धौ परतः वैकल्पिकं गुणं विधाय रूपद्वयं (हे अस्थि/हे अस्थे इति) साधयति।[15]

3. अनेन-अनयोः

अत्र पाणिनीयप्रक्रियायां 'इदम्-टा' 'इदम्-ओस्' इति स्थितौ 'अनाप्यकः'[16] इत्यनेन सूत्रेण आब्विभक्तौ परतः 'इदम्' इत्यस्य इद्रूपस्य स्थाने अन् विधीयते। 'अनाप्यकः' इत्यस्मिन् सूत्रे आब्ग्रहणेन प्रत्याहारो गृह्यते वृत्तिकारमते।[17] तत्रापि 'टा' 'ओस्' इति विभक्तिद्वयमेव गृह्यते पारिशेष्यात्। ङेभ्यामादीनां विभक्तीनां ग्रहणं तु न भवति तत्रान्यकार्याणां विधानात्। एवं प्रकारेण अत्र 'टा' 'ओस्' इत्यनयोरेव विभक्त्योः परत इदमोऽनादेशो भवति। ततश्च 'अनेन, अनयोः' इति रूपद्वयं सिध्यति। एवं पाणिनीयपरम्परायां पारिशेष्यन्यायादेव इदं सर्वं सेत्स्यति। सारस्वते पुनः प्रतिपत्तिलाघवाय इदमः स्थाने साक्षादेव 'टा' 'ओस्' इत्येतयोः विभक्त्योः परतः अन विधीयते।[18] अतः नात्र पारिशेष्यन्यायोऽपेक्ष्यते। एवं पाणिनीयेतरमलयगिरि[19]-मुग्धबोध[20] सरस्वतीकण्ठाभरणेषु[21] व्याकरणेष्वपि साक्षादेव 'टा' 'ओस्' विभक्त्योः परत अन् विहितः।

4. अष्टाभिः-अष्टभिः

अत्र पाणिनीयप्रक्रियायां 'अष्टन्-भिस्' इति स्थिते 'अष्टन आ विभक्तौ'[22] इत्यनेन सूत्रेण 'अष्टन्' इत्यस्याङ्गस्य आकारादेशो भवति विभक्तौ परतः। 'अष्टनो दीर्घात्' इति पाणिनीये सूत्रे दीर्घ-ग्रहणेन 'अष्टाभ्य औश्' इत्यत्र च आत्वपूर्वकनिर्देशेन ज्ञायते यत् आचार्यपाणिनिना 'अष्टन आ विभक्तौ' इत्यस्मिन् सूत्रे आत्वविकल्पमिष्यते।[23]

[14] ह्रस्वस्य गुणः। – *अष्टा०* 7.3.108

[15] य्वृणां नपुंसके धौ वा गुणो वक्तव्यः। – *सा०व्या०वा०* 9/8 पू०

[16] *अष्टा०* 7.2.112 ।

[17] आपीति प्रत्याहारः तृतीयैकवचनात्प्रभृति सुपः पकारेण। – *काशिका*, 7.2.112

[18] अन टौसोः। – *सा०व्या०* 10/29 पू०

[19] टाओसि अनः। – *मलय०ना०* 4/65

[20] टौसीदमोऽनकोऽनः। – *मु०बो०* 205

[21] टौसोरनः। – *स०क०* 6.4.79

[22] *अष्टा०* 7.2.84 ।

[23] विकल्पेनायमाकारो भवति, एतज्ज्ञापितम् 'अष्टनो दीर्घात्' (6.1.172) इति दीर्घग्रहणात्, 'अष्टाभ्य औश्' (7.1.21) इति च कृतात्वस्य निर्देशात्। तेनाष्टभिः, अष्टभ्य इत्यपि भवति। – *काशिका०* 7.2.84

एवं ज्ञापिते सति अष्टन्नित्यस्याङ्गस्य आत्वं विकल्प्यते, तेन अष्टाभिः अष्टभिरिति रूपद्वयं भवति। सारस्वतव्याकरणे तु सारल्यार्थं स्पष्टरूपेण सूत्रे एव वाग्रहणं कृतम्।[24] तेन अष्टाभिः अष्टभिरिति रूपद्वयं सिध्यति। अत्रापि साक्षादेव वाग्रहणेन अष्टनः आत्वविकल्पप्रक्रियायां प्रतिपत्तिलाघवं भवति। हैम[25]-मलयगिरि[26]-सरस्वतीकण्ठाभरणेषु[27] व्याकरणेष्वपि साक्षादेव आत्वविकल्पं निर्दिश्यते।

इत्थञ्चोपर्युक्तेषूदाहरणेषु पाणिन्यपेक्षया सारस्वतव्याकरणे स्पष्टनिर्देशेन प्रक्रियासारल्यं विस्पष्टं दृग्गोचरीभवति। उपर्युक्तेषु निदर्शनेषु स्पष्टनिर्देशो निरूपितः।

(ख) प्रक्रियालाघवेन सारल्यम्

इदानीं प्रक्रियालाघवमाधृत्य सारल्यं प्रतिपाद्यते। तत्र इमान्युदाहरणानि प्रदर्श्यन्ते –

1. **देवः** – अत्र सारस्वतव्याकरणे सकाररेफयोर्विसर्जनीयादेशो भवत्यधातोः रसे पदान्ते च परतः।[28] यथा – 'देव-सि' इत्यत्र अनुबन्धलोपे सकारस्य च विसर्गे सति 'देवः' रूपं सिध्यति। पाणिनीयप्रक्रियायां तु 'सु' इत्यस्य रेफः,[29] रेफस्य च विसर्गे[30] सति 'देवः' इति रूपं सिध्यति। पाणिनीयेतर चान्द्र[31]-जैनेन्द्र[32]-शाकटायन[33]-सरस्वतीकण्ठाभरणेषु[34] व्याकरणेष्वपि रेफस्य स्थाने विसर्गो विधीयते। अत्रोपर्युक्तव्याकरणापेक्षया अनुभूतिस्वरूपाचार्येण लाघवार्थं सारल्यार्थञ्च सकारस्यैव विसर्जनीयो विहितः।

2. **हरयः** – अत्र सारस्वतव्याकरणे इकारान्तस्य उकारान्तस्य च जसि परे एकारः ओकारश्च भवति।[35] यथा – 'हरि-जस्' इत्यत्र हरेः इकारस्य एकारे,

---

[24] वासु। – *सा०व्या०* 10/26 पू०

[25] वाऽष्टन आः स्यादौ। – *सि०हैम०* 1.4.52

[26] अष्टनः आ। – *मलय०ना०* 4/13

[27] अष्टनो वा सुप्यात्। – *स०क०* 6.4.53

[28] स्रोर्विसर्गः। – *सा०व्या०* 7/4 पू०

[29] ससजुषो रुः। – *अष्टा०* 8.2.66

[30] खरवसानयोर्विसर्जनीयः – *अष्टा०* 8.3.15

[31] विरामे विसर्जनीयः। – *चा०व्या०* 6.4.20

[32] विरामे विसर्जनीयः। – *जै०व्या०* 5.4.19

[33] रः पदान्ते विसर्जनीयः। – *शा०व्या०* 1.2.67

[34] विरामे विसर्जनीयः। – *स०क०* 7.4.20

[35] एओ जसि। – *सा०व्या०* 7/37 पू०

एकारस्य अयादेशे[36] च कृते 'हरयः' इति रूपं सिध्यति। जैनेन्द्र[37]-पाणिनीय[38]-सरस्वतीकण्ठाभरणेषु[39] व्याकरणेषु गुणविधानपूर्वकं रूपं साध्यते। अत्रानुभूतिस्वरूपाचार्येण गुणविधानापेक्षया इकारोकारयोः स्थाने स्पष्टतः एकारौकारौ विहितौ प्रतिपत्तिलाघवाय। यतो हि पाणिनीयव्याकरणे गुण-विधानाय 'स्थानेऽन्तरतमः'[40] इति परिभाषाश्रयणीया।

3. **हरौ** - सारस्वतेऽत्र इदुद्भ्यामुत्तरस्य ङेः स्थाने औ भवति स च डित्।[41] यथा – 'हरि-ङि' इत्यत्र ङेः स्थाने औकारादेशे, डित्त्वात् 'डिति टेः'[42] इत्यनेन टिलेपे च सति 'हरौ' इति रूपं सिध्यति। पाणिनीयप्रक्रियायां 'अच्च घेः'[43] इत्यनेन सूत्रेण घिसंज्ञकादुत्तरस्य ङेरौकारादेशे, घेरकारादेशे, 'वृद्धिरेचि'[44] इत्यनेन सूत्रेण वृद्ध्येकादेशे च सति रूपं सिध्यति। अत्र पाणिनीये घेरकारादेशापेक्षया अनुभूतिस्वरूपाचार्यस्य डित्विधानपूर्वकटिलोपप्रक्रियायां प्रतिपत्तिलाघवो वर्तते। यतो हि पाणिनीयप्रक्रियायां घेरकारादेशस्य पश्चाद्वृद्ध्येकादेशे कृत एव इष्टं रूपं सिध्यति। तत्र च गौरवं वर्तते।

4. **सखा** - सारस्वतव्याकरणे सखिशब्दस्य अधेः सेर्डा भवतीत्युक्तम्।[45] यथा – 'सखि-सि' इत्यत्र सेः स्थाने डादेशे डित्त्वात् टिलोपे[46] सति 'सखा' इति रूपं सिध्यति। पाणिनीयप्रक्रियायां तु अनङादेशे,[47] उपधादीर्घे,[48] सुलोपे,[49] नलोपे[50]

---

[36] ए अय्। – *सा०व्या०* 3/8 पू०

[37] जसि। – *जै०व्या०* 5.2.104

[38] जसि च। – *अष्टा०* 7.3.109

[39] जसि च। – *स०क०* 7.2.147

[40] *अष्टा०* 1.1.50 ।

[41] ङेरौ डित्। – *सा०व्या०* 7/42 पू०

[42] *सा०व्या०* 7/43 पू० ।

[43] *अष्टा०* 7.3.119 ।

[44] *अष्टा०* 6.1.88 ।

[45] सेर्डाऽधेः। – *सा०व्या०* 7/44 पू०

[46] डिति टेः। – *सा०व्या०* 7/43

[47] अनङ् सौ। – *अष्टा०* 7.1.93

[48] सर्वनामस्थाने चासम्बुद्धौ। – *अष्टा०* 6.4.8

[49] हल्ङ्याब्भ्यो दीर्घात्सुतिस्यपृक्तं हल्। – *अष्टा०* 6.1.68

[50] नलोपः प्रातिपदिकान्तस्य। – *अष्टा०* 8.2.7

च सति 'सखा' इति रूपं निष्पद्यते। पाणिनीयेतरचान्द्र[51]-जैनेन्द्र[52]-सरस्वतीकण्ठाभरणेषु[53] व्याकरणेष्वपि अनङादेशं विधाय रूपं साध्यते। अत्रोपर्युक्त-व्याकरणप्रयुक्तानङादेशप्रक्रियापेक्षया डादेशप्रक्रिया संक्षिप्ता सरला च वर्तते।

5. **सखायौ** – अनुभूतिस्वरूपाचार्यस्य मते सखिशब्दस्यैकारादेशो भवति धिवर्जितेषु पञ्चसु परेषु।[54] यथा – 'सखि-औ' इति स्थिते खकारोत्तरवर्त्तिन इकारस्य ऐकारादेशे, आयादेशे[55] च सति 'सखायौ' इति रूपं सिध्यति। पाणिनीयप्रक्रियायां तु सखि शब्दात् परं सर्वनामस्थानसंज्ञकं 'सु' णिद् भवति,[56] णित्त्वाच्च वृद्धौ[57] आयादेशे[58] च सति 'सखायौ' इति रूपं सिध्यति। पाणिनीयेतरजैनेन्द्रव्याकरणेऽपि[59] णित्त्वाश्रयणं कृतम्। अत्र पाणिनिजैनेन्द्राभ्यां णित्त्वमाश्रितम् अनुभूतिस्वरूपेण तु नाश्रितम्। तत्र स्पष्टमेव प्रक्रियालाघवम्।

6. **पिता** - सारस्वतव्याकरणे ऋकारान्तात्परस्य सेः स्थान आकारादेशो भवति स च डित्।[60] यथा - 'पितृ-सि' इति स्थिते सेः स्थाने आकारादेशे डित्त्वात् टिलोपे[61] च सति 'पिता' इति रूपं सिध्यति। पाणिनीयप्रक्रियायां अनङादेशे,[62] उपधादीर्घे,[63] सुलोपे,[64] नकारलोपे[65] च सति 'पिता' इति रूपं सिध्यति। पाणिनीयेतरचान्द्र[66]-जैनेन्द्र[67]-सरस्वतीकण्ठाभरणेषु[68] व्याकरणेष्वपि

---

[51] ऋदुशनस्पुरुदंसोऽनेहसां चानङ् सौ। – *चा०व्या०* 5.4.45

[52] अनङ् सौ। – *जै०व्या०* 5.1.70

[53] ऋदुशनस्पुरुदंसोऽनेहसां चानङ् सौ। – *स०क०* 6.4.44

[54] ऐ सख्युः। – *सा०व्या०* 7/45 पू०

[55] ऐ आय्। – *सा०व्या०* 3/8 पू०

[56] सख्युरसम्बुद्धौ। – *अष्टा०* 7.1.92

[57] अचोञ्णिति। – *अष्टा०* 7.2.115

[58] एचोऽयवायावः। – *अष्टा०* 6.1.78

[59] सख्युरकौ। – *जै०व्या०* 5.1.69

[60] सेरा। – *सा2०व्या०* 7/57 पू०

[61] डिति टेः। – *सा०व्या०* 7/43

[62] ऋदुशनस्पुरुदंसोऽनेहसां च। – *अष्टा०* 7.1.94

[63] सर्वनामस्थाने चासम्बुद्धौ। – *अष्टा०* 6.4.8

[64] हल्ङ्याब्भ्यो दीर्घात्सुतिस्यपृक्तं हल्। – *अष्टा०* 6.1.68

[65] नलोपः प्रातिपदिकान्तस्य। – *अष्टा०* 8.2.7

[66] ऋदुशनस्पुरु०. . . .। – *चा०व्या०* 5.4.45

[67] ऋदुशनस्पुरु०. . . . । – *जै०व्या०* 5.1.71

[68] ऋदुशनस्पुरु०. . . . । – *स०क०* 6.4.44

अनङादेशपूर्वकमेव रूपं निष्पाद्यते। अत्र अनङादेशापेक्षया अनुभूतिस्वरूपाचार्यस्य डित्पूर्वकटिलोपप्रक्रिया लाघवार्थं सारल्यार्थञ्च वर्तते।

7. **पितरौ** – सारस्वतप्रक्रियायां ऋकारस्यार् भवति पञ्चसु स्यादिषु परेषु।[69] यथा – 'पितृ–औ' इत्यत्र ऋकारस्यारादेशे 'पितरौ' इति रूपं सिध्यति। पाणिनीयप्रक्रियायां तु गुणे,[70] रपरत्वे[71] च कृते 'पितरौ' इति रूपं भवति। पाणिनीयेतरसरस्वतीकण्ठा– भरणव्याकरणेऽपि[72] गुणप्रक्रियया एव रूपं साधयन्ति। अत्र पाणिनिभोजदेवयोः गुणप्रक्रियापेक्षया अनुभूतिस्वरूपाचार्यस्य साक्षादेव 'अर्' विधानं लाघवपरम् वर्तते।

8. **गौः** – सारस्वतप्रक्रियायामत्र ओकारस्यौकारादेशो भवति पञ्चसु परेषु।[73] यथा – 'गो–सि' इत्यत्र ओकारस्य औकारे सकारस्य च विसर्गे[74] सति 'गौः' इति रूपं सिध्यति। पाणिनीयप्रक्रियायां तु गोशब्दात् परं 'सु' इत्ययं णित्[75] क्रियते, णित्त्वाच्च वृद्धौ[76] सत्यां 'गौः' इति रूपं सिध्यति। जैनेन्द्रेऽपि[77] णित्त्वाश्रयेणैव वृद्धिपूर्वकं रूपं साध्यते। अत्र पाणिनिजैनेन्द्रयोर्णित्वाश्रितवृद्ध्यपेक्षया अनुभूतिस्वरूपाचार्यस्य साक्षादौकारविधानम् प्रक्रियालाघवाय वर्तते।

9. **अन्यत्** – सारस्वतप्रक्रियायां अन्यादेर्गणात्परयोः स्यमोः श्तुर्भवति।[78] यथा – 'अन्य–सि' इत्यत्र सेः स्थाने 'श्तु' सर्वादेशो भवति। ततश्च 'अन्यत्' इति रूपं सिध्यति। पाणिनीयप्रक्रियायां सोः स्थान अद्‌डादेशे[79] टिलोपे[80] च सति रूपं सिध्यति। अत्रानुभूतिस्वरूपाचार्येण अद्‌डादेशापेक्षया श्त्वादेशः प्रतिपत्तिलाघवार्थं क्रियते। यतो हि अद्‌डादेशे कृते टिलोपमपि अपेक्ष्यते पाणिनीयप्रक्रियायाम्।

---

[69] अर् पञ्चसु। – *सा०व्या०* 7/58 पू०

[70] ऋतो ङिसर्वनामस्थानयोः। – *अष्टा०* 7.3.110

[71] उरण् रपरः। – *अष्टा०* 1.1.51

[72] ऋतो ङिसुटोर्गुणः। – *स०क०* 7.2.61

[73] ओरौ। – *सा०व्या०* 7/64 पू०

[74] स्रोर्विसर्गः। – *सा०व्या०* 7/4 पू०

[75] गोतो णित्। – *अष्टा०* 7.1.90

[76] अचोञ्णिति। – *अष्टा०* 7.2.115

[77] गोर्णित्। – *जै०व्या०* 5.1.67

[78] श्त्वन्यादेः। – *सा०व्या०* 9/6 पू०

[79] अद्‌ड् डतरादिभ्यः पञ्चभ्यः। – *अष्टा०* 7.1.25

[80] डित्यभस्याप्यनुबन्धकरणसामर्थ्यात्। – *म०भा०वा०* 6.4.143

10. **शुनः** - सारस्वतप्रक्रियायां श्वादेर्वकारस्य उत्वं भवति शसादौ स्वरे परे।[81] यथा – 'श्वन्-शस्' इत्यत्र वकारस्य उत्वे अनुबन्धलोपे विसर्गे[82] च सति 'शुनः' इति रूपं सिध्यति। पाणिनीये व्याकरणे 'श्वन्' इत्येतस्याङ्गस्य सम्प्रसारणे[83] कृते रूपं सिध्यति। अत्रानुभूतिस्वरूपाचार्येण पाणिनीयसम्प्रसारणप्रक्रियापेक्षया स्पष्टरूपेण वकारस्य उत्वं लाघवार्थं विधीयते। यतो हि सम्प्रसारणे कृते 'सम्प्रसारणाच्च'[84] इति सूत्रमपि अपेक्ष्यते पाणिनीयव्याकरणे।

11. **अद्भिः** - सारस्वतप्रक्रियायामत्राबादीनां भकारे परे दत्वं भवति।[85] यथा – 'अप्-भिस्' इत्यत्र पकारस्य दकारे विसर्गे च सति 'अद्भिः' इति रूपं सिध्यति। पाणिनीयप्रक्रियायां तु 'अपो भि'[86] इत्यनेन पकारस्य तकारे, 'झलां जशोऽन्ते'[87] इत्यनेन च तकारस्य दकारे कृते रूपं सिध्यति। अत्र सारस्वतप्रक्रियायां पाणिन्यपेक्षया स्पष्टतः पकारस्य दकारविधानेन प्रक्रियालाघवं भवति।

12. **त्वम्-अहम्** – अत्र सारस्वतप्रक्रियायां सिसहितयोर्युष्मदस्मदोस्त्वमहमित्येतावादेशौ भवतो यथासंख्येन।[88] यथा – 'युष्मद्-सि' 'अस्मद्-सि' इत्यत्र सिसहितस्य युष्मदः स्थाने 'त्वम्' इत्यादेशे, सिसहितस्य अस्मदश्च स्थाने 'अहम्' इत्यादेशे कृते त्वमहमिति रूपे सिध्यतः।

पाणिनीयप्रक्रियायां तु युष्मद्-सु, अस्मद्-सु इत्यत्र 'ङेप्रथमयोरम्'[89] इत्यनेन सोरमादेशे, 'त्वाहौ सौ'[90] इत्यनेन यथासंख्यं त्व, अह, इत्यादेशयोः कृतयोः त्व अद्-अम्, अह अद्-अम् इति स्थिते 'अतो गुणे'[91] इत्यनेन पररूपे, 'शेषे लोपः'[92] इत्यनेनाङ्गान्त्यस्य दकारस्य लोपे त्व-अम्, अह-अम् इति स्थिते

---

[81] श्वादेर्व उः। – *सा०व्या०* 10/15 पू०

[82] सोर्विसर्गः। – *सा०व्या०* 7/4 पू०

[83] श्वयुवमघोनामतद्धिते। – *अष्टा०* 6.4.133

[84] *अष्टा०* 6.1.104 ।

[85] भि दपाम्। – *सा०व्या०* 11/8 पू०

[86] *अष्टा०* 7.4.48 ।

[87] *अष्टा०* 8.2.39 ।

[88] त्वमहं सिना। – *सा०व्या०* 13/1 पू०

[89] *अष्टा०* 7.1.28 ।

[90] *अष्टा०* 7.2.94 ।

[91] *अष्टा०* 6.1.94 ।

[92] *अष्टा०* 7.2.90 ।

'अमि पूर्वः'[93] इत्यनेन च पूर्वरूपे कृते त्वमहमिति रूपे सिध्यतः। अत्र पाणिन्यपेक्षया अनुभूतिस्वरूपाचार्यस्य सिसहितयोर्युष्मदस्मदोः स्थाने त्वमहमादेशप्रक्रिया संक्षिप्ता सरला च वर्त्तते।

13. **यूयम्-वयम्** - सारस्वतप्रक्रियायां जसा सहितयोर्युष्मदस्मदोर्यूयं वयमित्येतावादेशौ भवतः।[94] यथा – 'युष्मद्-जस्' 'अस्मद्-जस्' इत्यत्र जस्सहितयोर्युष्मदस्मदोः स्थाने यूयं वयमित्यनयोरादेशयोः कृतयोः यूयं वयमिति रूपे सिध्यतः। पाणिनीयप्रक्रियायां युष्मद्-जस्, अस्मद्-जस् इत्यत्र 'ङेप्रथमयोरम्'[95] इत्यनेन अमादेशे, 'यूयवयौ जसि'[96] इत्यनेन यथासंख्यं यूयवयादेशयोः कृतयोः यूय अद्-अम्, वय अद्-अम् इति स्थिते 'अतो गुणे',[97] इत्यनेन पररूपे, 'शेषे लोपः'[98] इत्यनेनाङ्गान्त्यस्य दकारस्य लोपे, पूर्वरूपे[99] च कृते यूयं वयमिति रूपे सिध्यतः।

14. **तुभ्यम्-मह्यम्** - अत्र सारस्वतप्रक्रियायां ङेसहितयोर्युष्मदस्मदोः स्थाने यथासंख्यं तुभ्यं मह्यमित्यनयोरादेशयोः कृतयोः[100] तुभ्यं मह्यमिति रूपे सिध्यतः। पाणिनीयप्रक्रियायां युष्मद्-ङे, अस्मद्-ङे, इत्यत्र 'ङेप्रथमयोरम्'[101] इत्यनेन अमादेशे 'तुभ्यमह्यौ ङयि'[102] इत्यनेन यथासंख्यं तुभ्यमह्यादेशयोः कृतयोः, तुभ्य-अद्-अम्, मह्य अद्-अम् इति स्थिते पररूपे,[103] दकारस्य लोपे,[104] पूर्वरूपे[105] च सति तुभ्यं मह्यमिति रूपे सिध्यतः।

15. **तव-मम** - अत्रापि सारस्वतप्रक्रियायां ङस्सहितयोर्युष्मदस्मदोः स्थाने यथासंख्यं

---

[93] *अष्टा०* 6.1.107 ।

[94] यूयं वयं जसा। – *सा०व्या०* 13/4 पू०

[95] *अष्टा०* 7.1.28 ।

[96] *अष्टा०* 7.2.93 ।

[97] *अष्टा०* 6.1.94 ।

[98] *अष्टा०* 7.2.90 ।

[99] अमि पूर्वः। – *अष्टा०* 6.1.107

[100] तुभ्यं मह्यं ङया। – *सा०व्या०* 13/8 पू०

[101] *अष्टा०* 7.1.28 ।

[102] *अष्टा०* 7.2.95 ।

[103] अतो गुणे। – *अष्टा०* 6.1.94

[104] शेषे लोपः। – *अष्टा०* 7.2.90

[105] अमि पूर्वः। – *अष्टा०* 6.1.107

> तवममयोरादेशयोः कृतयोः[106] तव ममेति रूपे सिध्यतः। पाणिनीयप्रक्रियायां युष्मद्-ङस्, अस्मद्-ङस् इत्यत्र 'युष्मदस्मद्भ्यां ङसोऽश्'[107] इत्यनेन अशादेशे, 'तवममौ ङसि'[108] इत्यनेन तवममादेशयोः च तव अद्-अश्, मम अद्-अश् इति स्थिते 'अतो गुणे'[109] इत्यनेन पररूपे, 'शेषे लोपः'[110] इत्यनेन टिलोप पक्षे[111] अद् भागस्य लोपे तव ममेति रूपे सिध्यतः।

उपर्युक्ते युष्मदस्मदोः प्रसङ्गे अनुभूतिस्वरूपाचार्येण पाणिनीयदीर्घप्रक्रियापेक्षया प्रकृतिप्रत्यययोरुभयोः स्थान आदेशप्रक्रियामाध्यमेन महल्लाघवं सारल्यञ्चं विहितम्।

निष्कर्षः

संस्कृतव्याकरणस्य सुमहत्परम्परायामशेषशेमुषीसम्पन्नाचार्यपाणिनेरुत्तरकालं नैके वैयाकरणाः प्रादुरभवन्। तेष्वनुभूतिस्वरूपाचार्योऽन्यतमः। अनेन विदुषा तात्कालिकसमाजप्रभावेन लघुतामिच्छद्भ्यो व्याकरणाध्येतृभ्यः पाणिन्यादिव्याकरणापेक्षया लघुतरव्याकरणग्रन्थो व्यरचि। येन ग्रन्थेन स्वल्पश्रमेणैव अल्पेन च कालेन सहजतया व्याकरणावबोधो यथा स्यात्। तथैवायमाचार्यः सारस्वतव्याकरण-नाम्नि स्वग्रन्थारम्भे प्रतिजानीते –

> प्रणम्य परमात्मानं बालधीवृद्धिसिद्धये।
> सारस्वतीमृजुं कुर्वे प्रक्रियां नातिविस्तराम्।।

अत एव तत्र तत्र सारस्वतव्याकरणे पाणिन्यपेक्षया लाघवं सारल्यञ्चावलोक्यते। यद्यपि वैज्ञानिकी पाणिनीयप्रक्रिया, पुनरपि सारस्वतव्याकरणप्रणेता अनुभूतिस्वरूपाचार्यः लघुतां सरलतां च अक्षिलक्ष्यीकरोति। तस्मादेव सुबन्तप्रसङ्गे क्वचिद् वाग्रहणेन कुत्रचित् गुणादि संज्ञापेक्षया साक्षात् संज्ञिवर्णविधानेन कदाचिच्च प्रकृतिप्रत्यययोरुभयोः स्थाने सर्वादेशं कृत्वा प्रक्रियालाघवं विहितम्। येन कोमलमतयो बाला अपि अनायासेनैव व्याकरणज्ञानं प्राप्नुयुः।

सन्दर्भ-ग्रन्थसूची

अष्टाध्यायी – आचार्यपाणिनिप्रणीतः *अष्टाध्यायीसूत्रपाठः*, सम्पा० पण्डितब्रह्मदत्तजिज्ञासु, बहालगढ़ सोनीपत, रामलाल कपूर ट्रस्ट, ई०सन् 1956 ।

---

[106] तवमम ङसा। – *सा०व्या०* 13/11 पू०

[107] *अष्टा०* 7.1.27 ।

[108] *अष्टा०* 7.2.96 ।

[109] *अष्टा०* 6.1.94 ।

[110] *अष्टा०* 7.2.90 ।

[111] केचित्तु शेषे लोपं टिलोपमिच्छन्ति। – *काशिका* 7.2.90

काशिका – श्रीवामनजयादित्यविरचिता *पाणिनीयाष्टाध्यायीसूत्रवृत्तिः*, सम्पा० विजयपालो विद्यावारिधिः, बहालगढ़, सोनीपत, रामलाल कपूर ट्रस्ट, ई०सन् 1956 ।

चान्द्रव्याकरणम् – चन्द्रगोमिना प्रणीतम् *चान्द्रव्याकरणम्*, सम्पा० क्षितीश चन्द्र चटर्जी, पूना, डेक्कन कॉलेज, ई०सन्, 1953–61 ।

जैनेन्द्रव्याकरणम् – पूज्यपाददेवनन्दिविरचितं *जैनेन्द्रव्याकरणं* तस्य टीका आचार्याभयनन्दिप्रणीता जैनेन्द्रमहावृत्तिः, सम्पा० पण्डितशम्भुनाथ त्रिपाठी, सहायक पण्डितमहजादेव चतुर्वेदी, काशी, भारतीय ज्ञानपीठ, ई०सन् 1956 ।

पदमञ्जरी – श्रीहदत्तमिश्रविरचिता पदमञ्जरी (वामनजयादित्यविरचितायाः काशिकाया व्याख्या) सम्पादकौ डॉ० पुल्लेल श्री रामचन्द्रुडु, विठ्ठलदेवुनि सुन्दरशर्मा, दौ भागौ, हैदराबाद, संस्कृत परिषत्, उस्मानियाविश्वविद्यालय, ई०सन् 1969–85 ।

मलयगिरिशब्दानुशासनम्– आचार्यश्रीमलयगिरिविरचितं *शब्दानुशासनं* स्वोपज्ञवृत्तियुतम्। सम्पा० पण्डितबेचरदास जीवराज दोशी, अहमदाबाद, लालभाई दलपतभाई भारतीय संस्कृति विद्यामन्दिर, ई०सन्, 1967 ।

महाभाष्यम् – श्रीमद्भगवत्पतञ्जलिमुनिविरचितं *व्याकरणमहाभाष्यम्* महामहोपाध्याय-श्रीनागोजिभट्टविरचितमहाभाष्य-प्रदीपोद्द्योतोद्भासितेन महामहोपाध्यायश्रीकैयटोपाध्याय विरचितेन प्रदीपेन विराजितम्, सम्पा० श्रीगुरुप्रसाद शास्त्री, नवभागाः, दिल्ली, प्रतिभा प्रकाशन, ई०सन् 1938, प्रथमसंस्करणम् ।

मुग्धबोधव्याकरणम् – महामहोपाध्यायेन श्रीमतावोपदेवेन विरचितम् श्रीमददुर्गादासविद्यावागीश – श्रीरामतर्क वागीश-कृत टीकासमेतम्। पण्डितकुलपतिना वि, ए उपाधिधारिणा श्री जीवानन्दविद्यासागरभट्टाचार्य्येण संस्कृतं प्रकाशितञ्च। वाराणसी, चौखम्बा विद्याभवन, ई०सन् 1994 ।

शाकटायनव्याकरणम् – पाल्यकीर्तिशाकटायनप्रणीतं *शाकटायनव्याकरणम्*, अमोघवृत्तिसहितम्, सम्पा० शम्भुनाथ त्रिपाठी, दिल्ली, भारतीयज्ञानपीठ प्रकाशन, ई०सन्० 1971 ।

सरस्वतीकण्ठाभरणम् – श्रीभोजदेवप्रणीतं *सरस्वतीकण्ठाभरणं* श्री नारायणदण्डनाथविरचितया हृदयहारिण्याख्यया वृत्त्या समेतम्, के० साम्बशिवशास्त्रिणा संशोधितम्। अनन्तशयनसंस्कृतग्रन्थावलिः। त्रिवेन्द्रम्, महोन्नतमहामहिमश्रीचित्रावतारमहाराजशासनेन राजकीयमुद्रणयन्त्रालये तद्ध्यक्षेण मुद्रयित्वा प्रकाशितम्। ई०सन्० 1935 ।

सारस्वतव्याकरणम् – अनुभूतिस्वरूपाचार्यप्रणीतं *सारस्वतव्याकरणं* श्रीचन्द्रकीर्तिसूतिप्रणीतचन्द्रकीर्तिनाम्न्यासुबोधिकया व्याख्यया, श्रीवासुदेवभट्टविरचित-प्रसादाख्यटीकया च समन्वितम् . . . यास्क श्रीनवकिशोरशास्त्रिणा निर्मितया मनोरमया विवृत्या समुद्भासितम्। द्वौभागौ। काशीसंस्कृतग्रन्थमाला 111, वाराणसी, चौखम्भा संस्कृत संस्थान, ई०सन् 1985 ।

सिद्धहैमशब्दानुशासनम् – कालिकालसर्वज्ञ श्रीहेमचन्द्राचार्यविरचितं *श्रीसिद्धहेमचन्द्रशब्दानुशासनम्*तत्त्वप्रकाशिकाख्या बृहद्वृत्त्या समन्वितम् सम्पा० – व्याकरणाचार्य पन्न्यासश्रीहेमचन्द्रविजयो गणिः, द्वौ भागौ। मुंबई, श्री अमृतजैनसाहित्यवर्धकसभा, ई०सन्० 1972 ।

ऐतिहासिकग्रन्थः

मीमांसक, युधिष्ठिर, *संस्कृत-व्याकरणशास्त्र का इतिहास*, बहालगढ़, सोनीपत, रामलाल कपूर ट्रस्ट, ई०सन्, 1950 ।

संकेताक्षरसूची

अष्टा०	–	*अष्टाध्यायी*
चा०व्या०	–	*चान्द्रव्याकरणम्*
जै०व्या०	–	*जैनेन्द्रव्याकरणम्*
पू०	–	पूर्वार्द्धम्
पृ०	–	पृष्ठम्
म०भा०	–	*महाभाष्यम्*
म०भा०वा०	–	*महाभाष्यवार्तिकम्*
मलय०	–	*मलयगिरिशब्दानुशासनम्*
मलय०ना०	–	*मलयगिरिशब्दानुशासनम्-नाम*
मु०बो०	–	*मुग्धबोध*
शा०व्या०	–	*शाकटायनव्याकरणम्*
स०क०	–	*सरस्वतीकण्ठाभरणम्*
सा०व्या०	–	*सारस्वतव्याकरणम्*
सा०व्या०वा०	–	*सारस्वतव्याकरणवार्तिकम्*
सि०हैम०	–	*सिद्धहैमशब्दानुशासनम्*

शिवराजविजयस्य शाब्दिकदृष्ट्या समीक्षणम्

डॉ. परमानन्द झा

अवतरणम्

संस्कृतसाहित्यजगति इदम्प्रथमतया आधुनिकीम् उपन्यासविधाम् अवतारयन् प्रायेण सर्वत्र विचित्रशैलीविजृम्भितः श्रीमद्व्यासाम्बिकादत्तविरचितः शिवराजविजयो नाम वैयाकरणानां बहूपकारको गद्यप्रबन्धः। पदे पदे सुविशिष्टानां सन्धिसुबन्ताव्ययकारकीयाणां सस्त्रीप्रत्ययसमस्तानां सतद्धितानां पूर्वोत्तरतिङन्तकृदन्तानां पदानामिह विहिताः प्रत्यग्रप्रयोगाः प्रसह्य प्रेक्षावतां चेतांसि चमत्कुर्वन्ति। साहित्येन सह बहुतरेतरशास्त्रोपकारित्वमवेक्ष्यैव अर्वाचीनैः शिक्षाविद्भिर्ग्रन्थोऽयं देशे विदेशेषु च प्रायः सकलेषूच्चावचेषु संस्कृतशिक्षापाठ्यक्रमेष्वङ्गत्वेनाङ्गीकृतः। प्रबन्धस्यास्य त्रीनपि विरामानविरामं पर्यालोचयतो मे शाब्दिकदृशा नैके चामत्कारिकाः, कतिपये चिन्त्याश्च प्रयोगाश्चक्षुष्पथमारूढाः, यानधिकृत्य सविस्तरो विचारः, परमावश्यकः परिष्कारश्चात्र प्रकरणशः प्रस्तूयते।

सन्धयः

शिवराजविजयकारः काव्येऽस्मिन् प्रायशः सकलान् सन्धीन् यथावसरमञ्जसा प्रयुञ्जानोऽपि केषाञ्चित् सांहितिककार्याणां प्रकामप्रियो दृश्यते। स्वरसन्धिषु पित्रनुमतिं[1], नोमिति[2], चोमिति[3]–इत्यत्र यण्[4]–पररूप[5]–कार्ययोः विशिष्टं निदर्शनमवाप्यते।

व्यञ्जनसन्धिषु वंश्यांश्च[6], जनांश्च[7], अस्मांस्ताडय[8], विनिन्दकांस्तस्य[9], परांस्तोषयितुम्[10]

---

[1] *शिवराजविजयः* (*शि.वि.*), निश्वासः 9, पृष्ठम् 69
अत्र सम्पूर्णेऽपि निबन्धे उपन्यासस्यास्य वाराणसीस्थेन व्यासप्रकाशनेन 1983तमे वर्षे प्रकाशितं संस्करणम् उपयुज्यते।

[2] *शि.वि.* 8.233

[3] तत्रैव 8.252

[4] इको यणचि (*पा.सू.* 6.7.77)।

[5] ओमाङोश्च (*पा.सू.* 6.1.95)।

[6] *शि.वि.* 1.23

[7] तत्रैव 1.27

[8] तत्रैव 1.28

[9] तत्रैव 1.73

[10] *शि.वि.* 5.8

इत्यादिषु नश्छव्यप्रशान्[11] इतिसूत्रविहितस्य रुत्वविधेरुपयोगे कविः सातिशयमभिरुचिं दर्शयति। तच्छुभमात्मनः[12], उच्छलच्छोणित-[13], मच्छिबिरम्[14] इत्यादिषु च्छत्वस्य, प्रणमन्नुवाच[15], विदन्नपि[16], तस्मिन्नेव[17] इत्यादिषु नुडागमस्य[18], तद्धस्तात्-[19] इत्यादौ पूर्वसवर्णस्य[20] चापि विशिष्टाः प्रयोगाः कविना प्रदर्शिताः। विसर्गसन्धिषु स्वादिसन्धिषु च पुनः पुना रोदितुम्[21], अस्माभी राज्यात्[22], सन्धी राजधर्मः[23] इत्यादिषु रेफलोपस्य[24], शाखात उत्तार्य[25], युद्ध उत्तिष्ठेत्[26], सिंहदुर्ग एव[27], मार्ग एव[28], इत्यादिषु यलोपस्य[29] च विशिष्टाः प्रयोगाः प्रेक्षणपथमवतरन्ति। पुनराह[30] इतीमं प्रयोगं प्रस्तुवता कविना रुत्वसम्बन्धिनो रेफस्यैव यत्व[31] लोप[32] योरौचित्यं स्मारितम्[33]।

य एते[34] इत्यत्र कविना प्रदर्शितो यलोप[35]स्तु चिन्त्य एव, ये इति प्रकरणात्

---

[11] *पा.सू.* 8.3.7
[12] *शि.वि.* 2.100
[13] तत्रैव 3.152
[14] तत्रैव 9.95
[15] तत्रैव 2.58
[16] तत्रैव 2.70, 6.62
[17] तत्रैव 2.103
[18] ङमो ह्रस्वादचि ङमुण् नित्यम् (*पा.सू.* 8.3.32)।
[19] *शि.वि.* 5.2, 8.226
[20] *पा.सू.* 8.4.62
[21] *शि.वि.* 1.18
[22] तत्रैव 6.81
[23] तत्रैव 9.95
[24] रो रि (*पा.सू.* 8.3.14)।
[25] *शि.वि.* 3.158
[26] तत्रैव 5.9
[27] तत्रैव 5.29
[28] तत्रैव 6.49
[29] लोपः शाकल्यस्य (8.3.19)।
[30] *शि.वि.* 9.39
[31] भोभगोअघोअपूर्वस्य योऽशि (*पा.सू.* 8.3.17)।
[32] लोपः शाकल्यस्य (*पा.सू.* 8.3.19)।
[33] अतो रोः॰ (*पा.सू.* 6.1.113) इत्यत्र 'रोः' इत्यस्य फलमेतत्।
[34] *शि.वि.* 7.122
[35] लोपः शाकल्यस्य (*पा.सू.* 8.3.19)।

स्त्रीलिङ्गपरस्य एदन्तद्विवचनस्य[36] प्रगृह्यसंज्ञा[37]प्रयुक्तेन प्रकृतिभावेन[38] अयादेशलोपकार्ययो[39]रशक्यत्वात्।

सुबन्ताः

अल्पेऽपि[40], विश्वेषाम्[41], विश्वस्मिन्[42], निर्जरसाम्[43], सेनानीः[44], सेनान्यम्[45], दक्षिणस्याम्[46], उत्तरस्याम्[47], पथः[48], पथा[49], पथिषु[50], अध्वा[51], यूनाम्[52], मघवा[53], योगिराजः[54], योगिराट्[55]- इत्यादिषु सुबन्तपदप्रयोगेषु सर्वनामीभूतान्यविश्व-निर्जरसेनानी-दक्षिणोत्तरा-पथिन्-अध्वन्-युवन्-मघवन्-योगिराजादीनां शब्दानां विशिष्टानि रूपाणि समवलोक्यन्ते। एनम्[56], एनाम्[57], नगरमेनद्[58]-इत्यादिषु इदम्शब्दस्य अन्वादेशविषयनिबन्ध

---

[36] अत्र प्रसङ्गे सुन्दर्योः पूर्वपरामर्शको यच्छब्दः।

[37] ईदूदेद्द्विवचनं प्रगृह्यम् (*पा.सू.* 1.1.11)।

[38] प्लुतप्रगृह्या अचि नित्यम् (*पा.सू.* 6.1.125)।

[39] एचोऽयवायावः (*पा.सू.* 6.1.78), लोपः० (*पा.सू.* 8.3.19)।

[40] *शि.वि.* 4.193

[41] तत्रैव 1.5, 2.81

[42] तत्रैव 12.304

[43] तत्रैव 10.131

[44] तत्रैव 7.190

[45] तत्रैव 7.182

[46] तत्रैव 3.157

[47] तत्रैव 3.157

[48] तत्रैव 1.4

[49] तत्रैव 3.157

[50] तत्रैव 11.225

[51] तत्रैव 3.145

[52] तत्रैव 4.188

[53] तत्रैव 4.168

[54] तत्रैव 1.12

[55] तत्रैव 1.13

[56] तत्रैव 2.54, 7.145, 10.129

[57] तत्रैव 3.45, 4.194

[58] *शि.वि.* 7.159

नानि एन[59]-एनदादेश[60] घटितानि विशिष्टानि सुबन्तरूपाणि काव्येऽस्मिन् कविः प्रकाशमानयति। जानेऽहं वां[61], नौ वादयति[62], नौ विना[63], न यूयं वां[64], नौ चेतः[65] इत्यादिषु युष्मदस्मदोः वांनौ-आदेशयो[66] विशिष्टानि वाक्योदाहरणानि कविना प्रदर्शितानि। एवमेव अददत्[67], बिभ्यत्[68], अभिदधत्[69], विदधत्[70], परिजहद्[71] इत्यादिषु नाभ्यस्ताच्छतुः[72] इतिसूत्रविहितो नुम्भावाभावः कविना सुतरां स्मारितः[73]। निपतद्वारिबिन्दुनी नयने[74], माधुर्यवर्षिणी अक्षिणी[75], तेजस्वीनि अपत्यानि[76] इत्यादिषु प्रयोगेषु कविना क्लीबत्वप्रयुक्तो नुम्विधिः[77] साधु निदर्श्यते।

सेनानीनाम्[78] इति प्रयोगस्तु चिन्त्य एव, एरनेकाचोऽसंयोगपूर्वस्येति[79] यण्शास्त्रस्य जागरूकत्वात् सेनान्याम् इति रूपस्यैव समुचितत्वात्। विश्वस्मिन्नपि विश्वस्मिन्[80] इत्यत्र

---

59 द्वितीयाटौस्वेनः (*पा.सू.* 2.4.34)।

60 अन्वादेशे नपुंसके एनद् वक्तव्यः (*सि.कौ.*, हलन्तनपुंसकलिङ्गप्रकरणे) । एनदिति नपुंसकैकवचने (2.4.34 *वा.*)।

61 *शि.वि.* 3.120

62 तत्रैव 3.129

63 *शि.वि.* 3.136

64 तत्रैव 3.146, 3.159

65 तत्रैव 3.148

66 युष्मदस्मदोः षष्ठीचतुर्थीद्वितीयास्थयोर्वांनावौ (*पा.सू.* 8.1.20)।

67 *शि.वि.* 2.51

68 तत्रैव 6.99

69 तत्रैव 6.115

70 तत्रैव 8.113, 8.220

71 तत्रैव 4.168

72 *पा.सू.* 7.1.78

73 एषु उदाहरणेषु उभे अभ्यस्तम् (*पा.सू.* 6.1.5) इति अभ्यस्तसंज्ञा।

74 *शि.वि.* 1.23

75 तत्रैव 4.123

76 तत्रैव 4.176

77 नपुंसकस्य झलचः (*पा.सू.* 7.1.72)।

78 *शि.वि.* 2.78

79 *पा.सू.* 6.4.82

80 *शि.वि.* 12.304

संसारवाचिनि द्वितीयस्मिन् विश्वशब्दे सर्वनामत्वप्रयुक्तः स्मिन्नादेशोऽपि नैवोचितः, सर्वादिगणे सर्वसाहचर्यात् सर्ववाचकस्यैव विश्वशब्दस्य सर्वनामतायाः शाब्दिकाचार्यैः स्थिरीकृतत्वात्[81]। वाचममुमाकर्ण्य[82] इत्यत्र अमुम् इति स्थाने अमूम् इत्येतद् दीर्घरूपमेव प्रयोज्यम्, अदसोऽसेर्दादु दो मः[83] इत्यत्र उ इति ह्रस्वदीर्घयोः समाहारद्वन्द्वाद् अदस्शब्दस्य स्त्रीलिङ्गे तादृशस्य दीर्घरूपस्यान्तरतम्याद् विधानात्। वृद्धोऽसौ[84], अदोऽपि वचः[85] इत्यनयोर्वाक्ययोरपि वृद्धोऽयम्, इदमपि वचः इतीमे इदम्शब्दरूपे एव सङ्गते,

> इदमस्तु सन्निकृष्टं, समीपतरवर्ति चैतदो रूपम्।
> अदसस्तु विप्रकृष्टं, तदिति परोक्षं विजानीयात्।।[86]

इति वचनात् प्रस्तुते सन्निकर्षप्रसङ्गे अदसः प्रयोगस्य अनुचितत्वात्। तदवलम्ब्य[87], तदालम्ब्य[88] इति प्रयोगयोरपि स्थाने क्रमात् तं ताम् इत्येते पुम्स्त्रीलिङ्गविशिष्टे तच्छब्दरूपे एव प्रयोज्ये, तयोः प्रस्तुते प्रकरणे क्रमशः वंशशृङ्खलाशब्दयोः पूर्वपरामर्शित्वात्। त्रिंशद् वा वीरान् सह नीत्वा[89] इत्यत्रापि त्रिंशतं वीरान्–इत्येष एव प्रयोगः आप्तसम्मतः,

> यल्लिङ्गं, यद् वचनं, या च विभक्तिर्विशेष्यस्य।
> तल्लिङ्गं, तद् वचनं, सा च विभक्तिर्विशेषणस्यापि।।[90]

इति नियमाद् वीरान् इति द्वितीयान्तविशेष्यपदानुरूपं त्रिंशच्छदादपि तादृश्याः द्वितीयाविभक्तेरावश्यकत्वात्।

---

[81] द्रष्टव्यम् – *महाभाष्यम्* – सर्वादीनि सर्वनामानि (*पा.सू.* 1.1.27) इति सूत्रोपरि।

[82] *शि.वि.* 12.288

[83] *पा.सू.* 8.2.80

[84] *शि.वि.* 9.37

[85] तत्रैव 12.307

[86] प्रौढमनोरमायां हलन्तपुंलिङ्गप्रकरणे इदम्शब्दव्याख्याप्रसङ्गे उदधृतं पद्यम्।

[87] *शि.वि.* 11.187

[88] तत्रैव 11.187

[89] तत्रैव 9.37

[90] प्राचीनोक्तिरियम्, मूलं मृग्यम्।

स्त्रीप्रत्यया:

स्त्रीप्रत्ययेषु लज्जमाना[91], स्मयमाना[92], ईक्षमाणा[93]–इत्यादिषु कविना टाप्प्रत्ययस्य[94] निदर्शनानि प्रस्तूयन्ते। लोचनरोचिका[95] इत्यादिषु टापि परे इत्वविधेः[96], तारकापटलम्[97] इत्यादिषु तदभावस्य[98] चोदाहरणानि कविः प्रस्तौति। अनुभवन्ती[99], पश्यन्ती[100], पर्यटन्ती[101], प्रवहन्ती[102], दहन्ती[103], ध्यायन्ती[104] इत्येतेषु उगितश्चेति[105] विहितस्य ङीपो मालिकेव कविना काव्येऽस्मिन् प्रकाशमानीताऽस्ति। सहैव, रुदती[106], निश्वसती[107], निघ्नती[108], बिभ्रती[109], चिन्वती[110], तिरस्कुर्वती[111], कृन्तती[112], इत्यादिषु कविना व्यासेन शतृप्रत्ययस्यावर्णान्तधातुभ्यः परं विहितत्वाभावाद् नुम्भावाभावः[113] सुतरां स्मारितः।

---

[91] *शि.वि.* 8.209

[92] तत्रैव 8.209

[93] तत्रैव 8.219

[94] अजाद्यतष्टाप् (*पा.सू.* 4.1.4)।

[95] *शि.वि.* 4.169

[96] प्रत्ययस्थात् कात् पूर्वस्यात इदाप्यसुपः (*पा.सू.* 7.3.44)।

[97] *शि.वि.* 10.146

[98] तारका ज्योतिषि (सि.कौ. न यासयोः (*पा.सू.* 7.3.45) इति सूत्रे) इति नियमात्।

[99] *शि.वि.* 7.155

[100] तत्रैव 12.322

[101] तत्रैव 10.116

[102] तत्रैव 11.254

[103] तत्रैव 4.164

[104] *शि.वि.* 12.272

[105] तत्रैव 4.181

[106] तत्रैव 7.149

[107] तत्रैव 5.152

[108] तत्रैव 7.179

[109] तत्रैव 10.116

[110] तत्रैव 10.116

[111] तत्रैव 11.192

[112] तत्रैव 4.188

[113] तत्रैव 7.139

एवमेव पाणिगृहीती[114], त्वादृशी[115], तालफलस्तनी[116], शतपदी[117] इत्यादिषु स्थलेषु विशिष्टैः ततत्सूत्रै[118] र्विहितानां स्त्रीप्रत्ययानां कविना कृताः सहजप्रयोगाः शाब्दिकानां चेतांसि हठादावर्जयन्ति। शृण्वन्ती[119], उच्छ्वसन्ती[120], लिहन्ती[121] इत्येतेषु स्थलेषु नुम्विशिष्टाः प्रयोगास्तु चिन्त्या एव, नुम्विधायकैः शास्त्रैः आच्छीनद्योर्नुम्[122] इतिसूत्रनिर्देशेन अवर्णान्तात् एव धातुभ्यः (विकरणविशिष्टेभ्यः) नुम्विधानात्। एवमेव चौरायाम्[123], विजित्वरया[124] इत्यनयोष्टाप्प्रत्ययावपि नोचितौ, तत्र क्रमात् ताच्छीलिके णेऽपि[125], टिड्ढाणञ् . . . क्वरपः[126] इत्येतन्नियमद्वयेन ङीब्विधानात्।

कारकाणि

कविर्व्यासो विभिन्नानां सविशेषाणां कारकोपपदविभक्तीनां प्रयोगेऽपि प्रस्तुते गद्यबन्धे पुष्कलं पाटवमुपदर्शयति। तथाहि –

कुशलवार्ताः आलप्य[127], अस्मान् स्निह्यति[128], भवन्तमाशिषो ब्रुवन्ति[129], महाराजस्तव पाणिं मां ग्राहयिष्यति[130], राजमाता कुशलमावेदनीया[131], बन्धुवियोगदुःखं स्मारित इव[132]

---

114 *शि.वि.* 12.350

115 तत्रैव 11.207

116 तत्रैव 11.203

117 तत्रैव 3.148

118 यथा पाणिगृहीती भार्यायाम् (*वा.*) इत्यादिभिरित्यर्थः।

119 *शि.वि.* 12.322

120 तत्रैव 8.261

121 तत्रैव 9.76

122 *पा.सू.* 7.1.80

123 *शि.वि.* 3.52

124 तत्रैव 4.179

125 कार्मस्ताच्छील्ये (*पा.सू.* 6.4.172) इति सूत्रे एवं तर्हि सिद्धे सति यन्निपातनं करोति तज्ज्ञापयत्याचार्यस्ताच्छीलिके णेऽण्कृतानि भवन्तीति भाष्यम् ।

126 *पा.सू.* 4.1.15

127 *शि.वि.* 4.193

128 तत्रैव 10.149

129 तत्रैव 6.94

130 तत्रैव 12.275

131 तत्रैव 12.276

132 तत्रैव 3.116

इत्यादिषु स्थलेषु कविना द्वितीयाविभक्तेर्विशिष्टाः प्रयोगाः समुपस्थापिताः सन्ति।

श्रीमन्तं द्वेष्टि[133], द्रुह्यन्ति भवन्तम्[134] इत्यनयोः स्थलयोः प्रयुक्ता द्वितीया तु चिन्त्यैव प्रतिभाति, क्रुधद्रुहेर्ष्या[135] इत्यादिसूत्रनियमाच्छ्रीमद्-भवच्छब्दाभ्यां चतुर्थ्याः औचित्यात्। एवमेव मम परितो गच्छताम्[136], नगरस्यास्य परितः[137] इत्यनयोः स्थलयोः कविना प्रयुक्ता षष्ठी असंगता भाति, अभितःपरितःसमयानिकषाहाप्रतियोगेऽपि[138] इतिवार्तिकनियमाद् मां परितः, नगरं परितः इतिप्रयोगयोरेव समुचितत्वात्।

आकृत्या सुन्दरः वर्णेन गौरः जटाभिस्तापसः[139] धैर्येण समम्[140], मन्द्रेण स्वरेण[141], अलं बाह्यालापशतैः[142] इत्येतेषु स्थलेषु विशिष्टास्तृतीयान्तप्रयोगाः कवेर्नितरां निभालनीयाः।

तेन साक्षात्कारः[143] इत्यत्र तु तस्येति षष्ठी एवोचिता, कर्तृकर्मणोः कृती[144]तिशास्त्रस्य जागरूकत्वात्। एवमेव अवलोकयन्तु सर्वैः[145] इत्यत्रापि सर्वे इत्येवोचितं, तिङाऽभिहिते कर्तरि प्रथमायाः विधानात्[146]। लज्जया विरज्य[147] इति स्थानेऽपि लज्जाया इति पञ्चम्येव प्रयोक्तुमुचिता प्रतिभाति, विभागे सति अवधिभूतात् पञ्चम्याः विधानात्[148]।

---

133 *शि.वि.* 6.102

134 तत्रैव 11.210

135 *पा.सू.* 1.4.37

136 *शि.वि.* 7.121

137 तत्रैव 11.187

138 कर्मणि द्वितीया (*पा.सू.* 2.3.2) इति सूत्रे समयानिकषाहायोगेषूपसंख्यानम् (*वा.* 1) इति वार्तिकम्, तत्र च भाष्यम् - अपर आह - द्वितीयाविधानेऽभितःपरितःसमयानिकषाऽध्यधिधिग्योगेषूपसंख्यानम् इति।

139 *शि.वि.* 1.6

140 तत्रैव 1.26

141 तत्रैव 2.62

142 तत्रैव 7.138

143 तत्रैव 4.170

144 *पा.सु.* 2.3.65

145 *शि.वि.* 7.186

146 प्रथमानन्तरम् अनभिहिते (*पा.सू.* 2.3.1) इत्यधिकारात्।

147 *शि.वि.* 8.260

148 अपादाने पञ्चमी (*पा.सू.* 2.3.28)।

सहसहचराय स्वस्ति[149], तृणाय मन्यमाना[150], भवन्तीभ्यामेव रोचन्ते भवत्योः क्ष्वेलनानि[151], इदं रोचते युष्मभ्यम्[152]–इत्येतादृशाश्चामत्कारिकाः प्रयोगाः चतुर्थीविभक्तेरपि कविना समुस्थापिताः सन्ति।

पञ्चम्यां प्रकृष्टा प्रयोगाः पुनः – ऋते दुराचारात्[153], अपरः शिववीरात्[154], धर्मादपि निर्भीकान्[155], मन्दिरादारात्[156], वेशन्तादारात्[157], न निजकार्यान्निवर्तते[158] इत्यादिषु स्थलेषु शाब्दिकैः समास्वाद्याः।

षष्ठ्यां पुनः – असीनामेकमाकृष्य[159], प्रान्ते बद्धानामश्वानां कौचिच्चण्डवेगौ[160], भारतवर्षस्य स्मारयन्[161], दयतामखिलानां दामोदरः[162] इत्यादयो विशिष्टाः प्रयोगाः प्रेक्षावतां लोचनानि समुल्लासयन्ति।

प्रत्यार्थिनामाक्रमणं विधास्यति[163], दुराचारस्य न कोऽपि स्निह्यति[164] इत्यनयोः स्थलयोस्तु क्रमशः प्रत्यर्थिषु, दुराचारम्/दुराचाराय इतीमे रूपे एव प्रयोक्तुमुचिते। मन्दिरात् पश्चिमतः[165], मन्दिरात् पूर्वतः[166] इत्यत्र स्थलेऽपि मन्दिरस्येति षष्ठ्येव समुचिता, तत्र दिग्योगपञ्चमीं[167] प्रबाध्य षष्ठ्यतसर्थप्रत्ययेनेति[168] षष्ठीशास्त्रस्य जागरूकत्वात्।

149 *शि.वि.* 7.70

150 तत्रैव 9.150

151 तत्रैव 7.135

152 तत्रैव 9.81

153 तत्रैव 2.64

154 तत्रैव 3.115

155 तत्रैव 3.153

156 तत्रैव 3.153

157 तत्रैव 3.153

158 तत्रैव 4.166

159 तत्रैव 1.37

160 तत्रैव 3.130

161 तत्रैव 1.49

162 तत्रैव 12.338

163 तत्रैव 7.174

164 तत्रैव 12.366

165 तत्रैव 4.178

166 तत्रैव 10.113

167 अन्यारादितरर्ते॰ (*पा.सू.* 2.3.29)।

168 *पा.सू.* 2.3.30

एवमेव कुमारीं ममार्पयितुम्[169] इत्यत्रापि मह्यमिति प्रयोज्यम्, दानार्थकधातूनां योगे चतुर्थ्याः[170] एव सङ्गतत्वात्।

सप्तम्यां विभक्तौ निम्लोचति मार्तण्डमण्डले[171], समापितसायन्तनकृत्ये गुरौ[172], अस्तमिते मरीचिमालिनि[173], कथयत्सु रुदत्सु वर्गेषु[174], समुद्रशायिनि निर्विवेदयिषुः[175] इत्याद्याः हृद्याः प्रयोगाः काव्यकृत्प्रवरेण प्रस्तुताः।

समासाः

समासाः समुपवर्णनाप्रधानानां साहित्यिकवाक्यानां प्राणभूताः मन्यन्ते। समासेषु विशिष्य तत्पुरुषबहुव्रीहिभ्यां दीर्घदीर्घतराणि ललितललितानि पदकदम्बकानि संगुम्फ्य कविकुरङ्गाः काव्यसौन्दर्यं परां काष्ठां नयन्ति। कविर्व्यासाम्बिकादत्तोऽपि लघुलघूनां प्रसादगुणोपेतानां समस्तपदानां प्रयोगे परमं पाटवं धत्ते। कविरयं तत्र तत्र प्रसङ्गे प्रायशः समेषां समासानां विशिष्टानि निदर्शनानि प्रस्तौति। तथा हि –

अव्ययीभावे-निर्मक्षिकं[176], निश्शंकं[177], संमुखे[178], सोत्प्रासेन[179], प्रतिगोपुरं प्रतिपल्लि[180], आलङ्कम् आविन्ध्यं च[181], अनुतीरम्[182], उपकण्ठम्[183] इत्यादिषु स्थलेषु विशिष्टानि सामासिककार्याणि आकलयितुं शक्यानि।

---

[169] *शि.वि.* 11.209

[170] चतुर्थी सम्प्रदाने (*पा.सू.* 2.3.13)।

[171] *शि.वि.* 7.166

[172] तत्रैव 1.113

[173] तत्रैव 5.114

[174] तत्रैव 1.28

[175] तत्रैव 2.48

[176] तत्रैव 1.33

[177] तत्रैव 10.118

[178] तत्रैव 2.78, 9.95

[179] तत्रैव 11.240

[180] तत्रैव 5.16

[181] तत्रैव 12.373

[182] तत्रैव 11.238

[183] तत्रैव 12.349

तत्पुरुषे–परस्सहस्राः[184], कवोष्णम्[185], शोकाधिकः[186], महाव्रताश्रमाः[187], दिनकतिपयैः[188], स्वेदाक्तौ कपोलौ[189], दास्याः पुत्राः[190], प्रेमवार्ताः[191], टिड्ढाणञ्पण्डितः[192] इत्यादयो विशिष्टाः प्रयोगाः दृष्टिगोचरीभवन्ति।

बहुव्रीहिसमासेन कविरयं लघुलघूनां विशेषणानां प्रस्तुतिभिः काव्यवस्तूनि पटुतया पुष्णन्नवलोक्यते। यथा – निर्झरझर्झरध्वनिध्वनितदिगन्तरः फलपटलास्वादचपलितचञ्चुपतङ्गकुलाक्रमणाधिकविनतशाखशाखिसमूहव्याप्तः सुन्दरकन्दरः पर्वतखण्डः[193], चन्दनचर्चितभालः कपूरागुरुक्षोदच्छुरितवक्षोबाहुदण्डः ब्रह्मचारी[194], समाच्छादितललाटकपोलनासाग्रोत्तरोष्ठः[195], कमनीयकपोलपालिः प्रसन्नवदनाम्भोजप्रदर्शितदृढसिद्धान्तोत्साहः[196], समिद्धक्रोधाः[197], धारितहारितपरिधानाम्, श्लथद्वसनाम्[198] इत्यादीनि। किञ्च सतीर्थ्यः[199], द्वित्राः[200], पञ्चषाः[201], कुन्दकोरकाग्रदतीम्[202], लशुनगन्धिभिर्निश्वासैः[203], इष्वासपाणिं[204], कुसुमधन्वनः[205] इत्यादौ बहुव्रीहिसमासनिबन्धनानि विशिष्टकार्याणि कविना अनायासं स्मार्यन्ते।

---

[184] *शि.वि.* 1.6
[185] तत्रैव 1.41
[186] तत्रैव 3.115
[187] तत्रैव 3.155
[188] तत्रैव 3.57
[189] तत्रैव 12.369
[190] तत्रैव 7.163
[191] तत्रैव 8.220
[192] तत्रैव 6.74
[193] तत्रैव 1.7
[194] तत्रैव 1.8
[195] तत्रैव 4.163
[196] तत्रैव 4.163
[197] तत्रैव 7.189
[198] तत्रैव 9.4
[199] तत्रैव 1.8
[200] तत्रैव 1.6
[201] तत्रैव 3.49
[202] तत्रैव 1.16
[203] तत्रैव 1.38
[204] तत्रैव 11.262
[205] तत्रैव 12.344

द्वन्द्वे-कविः केषुचित् स्थलेषु दीर्घदीर्घाणि दुर्लभतराणि इतरेतरद्वन्द्वोदाहरणानि दर्शयन्नुपलभ्यते, यथा-कुतूकुतुपकर्करीकण्डोलकटकटाहकम्बिकडम्बान्[206], गण्डशैलपरिक्रमण-अधित्यकाधि-रोहण-उपत्यकालङ्घन-तटिनीतरणाद्यायासदीक्षादक्षेण पथा[207], दौन्दुभिक-वैणविक-वैणिक-मार्दङ्गिक-मौरजिक-पाणिघैः[208] इत्यादीनि। एवमेव आगतप्रत्यागतं विदधानः[209], हस्तपादं प्रक्षाल्य[210], यातायातं कुर्वन्[211]-इत्यादिषु स्थलेषु समाहारद्वन्द्वस्यापि विशिष्टाः प्रयोगाः साक्षात्कर्तुं सुशकाः।

मातृपितृविहीनायाः[112], मातृपितृसुखम्[213] इत्यत्र स्थलयोः आनङभावस्तु कवेश्चिन्त्य एव, आनङ् ऋतो द्वन्द्वे[214] इतितद्विधायकशास्त्रस्य जागरूकत्वात्। तथा च स्वयमपि कविः मातापितृभ्यामदत्तम्[215] इत्यादिषु नैकत्र स्थलेषु आनङागमविशिष्टानि द्वन्द्ववाक्यानि प्रयुञ्जानो दृश्यते।

क्वचित् क्वचित् कविना उपन्यासेऽस्मिन् एकशेषस्यापि उपयोग उपदर्शितः, यथा-तदेतस्याः परिमार्गणीयानि पितरौ गृहं च[216], पितरौ[217], सहपितरौ[218] इत्यादिषु स्थलेषु।

तद्धिताः

कविना व्यासेन तद्धितान्तपदानां प्रयोगेऽपि प्रकामपाटवं प्रदर्शितम्। तत्रापि केषाञ्चित् प्रत्ययानां कविरयं परमप्रियो दृश्यते। तद् यथा - च्विप्रत्ययान्तपदानां मालिकायाः सुषमा काव्येऽस्मिन् निभाल्यताम् -

---

206 *शि.वि.* 2.76

207 तत्रैव 3.157

208 तत्रैव 11.296

209 तत्रैव 1.50

210 तत्रैव 4.178

211 तत्रैव 5.42

212 तत्रैव 7.144, 155

213 तत्रैव 7.146

214 *पा.सू.* 6.3.25

215 *शि.वि.* 9.22

216 तत्रैव 1.10

217 तत्रैव 3.113

218 तत्रैव 3.21

मरूकरोति, जनपदीकरोति, काननीकरोति[219], मन्दुरीक्रियन्ते[220], अरुणीक्रियमाणः[221], तनूभूतं तमः[222], निरभीषूकृत्य[223], भूमिसात्कृतानि[224], अग्निसात्कुर्वन्[225], भस्मसात्[226], शूलाकुर्वतः[227], दुःखाकुरुतम्[228] इत्यादि।

एवमेव भावप्रत्ययान्तेषु–नेदिष्ठता[229], उदारता[230], सारवत्ता[231], मधुरिमा[232], महिमा[233], मञ्जिमा[234], क्रशिमान[235], धवलिमान[236], कालिमानम्[237], चाकचक्य[238], वैधुर्य[239], साहचर्यम्[240], इत्यादीनि, इतच्प्रत्ययान्तेषु–तारकित[241], पुलकितः[242], कण्टकितम्[243], आर्द्रितम्[244], दुःखिताम्[245], इत्यादीनि चोदाहरणानि प्रेक्षितुं शक्यानि।

[219] *शि.वि.* 1.24
[220] तत्रैव 1.25
[221] तत्रैव 12.347
[222] तत्रैव 12.268
[223] तत्रैव 12.288
[224] तत्रैव 1.30
[225] तत्रैव 2.75, 111
[226] तत्रैव 10.57
[227] तत्रैव 2.76, 3.114, 7.162
[228] तत्रैव 3.145, 7.140
[229] तत्रैव 12.336
[230] तत्रैव 4.103
[231] तत्रैव 6.100
[232] तत्रैव 7.227
[233] तत्रैव 6.75
[234] तत्रैव 9.10, 2.48
[235] तत्रैव 6.119
[236] तत्रैव 7.139
[237] तत्रैव 2.74
[238] तत्रैव 1.27
[239] तत्रैव 6.93
[240] तत्रैव 6.43
[241] तत्रैव 3.136
[242] तत्रैव 6.63
[243] तत्रैव 6.110
[244] तत्रैव 7.129
[245] तत्रैव 7.150

किञ्च प्रयोगानेताननतिरिच्यापि कविना प्रायशः सर्वेभ्यः तद्धित-प्रकरणेभ्यश्चामत्कारिकाणि उदाहरणानि यथावसरं काव्येऽस्मिन्नुपस्थापितानि। तानि यथा – त्वादृशाः[246], अस्मादृक्षाणाम्[247], आश्वीनो ग्रामः[248], आस्माकीनैः[249], स्वदेशीयानाम्[250], भावत्कौ[251], श्रैमत्कः[252], स्वाभाविकम्[253], मार्मिकः[254], नैशीथो ध्वनिः[255], सौरतान् विद्रोहिणः[256], वयस्यैः[257], अध्वन्यः[258], आजानेयेन धावितुम्[259], क्षोदिष्ठम् गरीयांसः[260], षोडशवर्षदेशीयः[261], सप्तवर्षकल्पाम्[262], पञ्चाशत्तमः[263], महाराष्ट्राः[264], यतरः ततरः[265], सहस्रधा[266], गव्यूतिः[267], परेद्युः[268], कथानकानि[269], मुमुदेतमाम्[270], अस्मितमाम्[271] इत्यादीनि।

---

246 *शि.वि.* 6.73
247 तत्रैव 6.105
248 तत्रैव 8.337
249 तत्रैव 9.60, 2.78
250 तत्रैव 9.45
251 तत्रैव 9.38
252 तत्रैव 11.149
253 तत्रैव भूमिका।
254 तत्रैव भूमिका।
255 तत्रैव 7.180
256 तत्रैव 8.268
257 तत्रैव 12.216
258 तत्रैव 12.364
259 तत्रैव 11.241
260 तत्रैव भूमिका।
261 तत्रैव 4.62
262 तत्रैव 1.9
263 तत्रैव 2.22
264 तत्रैव 5.23
265 तत्रैव 6.108
266 तत्रैव 7.140
267 तत्रैव 8.210
268 तत्रैव 9.37, 10.155
269 तत्रैव 9.43
270 तत्रैव 11.240
271 तत्रैव 8.202

मरीचिमालिनः[272], चतुरङ्गिणी सेना[273], उदञ्चितरोममाली[274], यवनवधव्यसनिनि[275], मूलच्छेदकौतुकिनः[276], स्विन्नसर्वाङ्गिण्यौ[277], अन्तरङ्गित्वगर्विण्यौ[278], निष्कपटप्रणयिनी[279], महाराष्ट्रधराधनी[280], रघुवीराभिमानिनी[281]इत्यादिषु स्थलेषु कविना कृतः इनिप्रत्ययप्रयोगस्तु अतिरिक्त एव, तत्र तत्रोक्तस्थलेषु बहुव्रीहिसमासेनैव मतुबर्थलाभसम्भवात्। तथा चोक्त-मभियुक्तैरपि – न कर्मधारयान्मत्वर्थीयो बहुव्रीहिश्चेदर्थप्रतिपत्तिकरः[282]। संबोभवीतितमाम्[283], मोमुद्यतेतमाम्[284], अधिकं भाग्यवत्तरः[285]इत्येषां स्थाने संबोभवीति, मोमुद्यते, भाग्यवत्तर इत्येतावतामेव प्रयोग उचितः, आद्ययोः यङ्प्रत्ययेन, अन्ते च तरप्प्रययेनैव अतिशयार्थलाभसम्भवे[286]तमपः अधिकशब्दस्य च व्यर्थत्वात्, पौनरुक्त्याच्च। किञ्च पारम्परीणः[287], सांमुखीनः[288], शौरसेनेषु[289], पाञ्चालेषु मैथिलेषु[290]इत्येतेषु स्थलेषु आदिवृद्धिरपि असमीचीनैव प्रतिभाति, आद्ययोः विहिते खप्रत्यये वृद्धिनिमित्तत्वाभावात्, अन्ते च प्रत्ययस्य जनपदे लुबि[291]ति लुप्तत्वाद् आदिवृद्धेः अशक्यत्वात्। कथावशेषकृतः[292]

---

272 *शि.वि.* 1.2, 5.14

273 तत्रैव 1.29, 6.93

274 तत्रैव 3.117

275 तत्रैव 1.41

276 तत्रैव 9.46

277 तत्रैव 7.133

278 तत्रैव 7.137

279 तत्रैव 10.121

280 तत्रैव 9.36

281 तत्रैव 10.122

282 व्याप्तिपञ्चकम्, माथुरीव्याख्या, आरम्भे – 'साध्याभाववदवृत्तित्वम्' इत्यत्र।

283 *शि.वि.* 2.78

284 तत्रैव 12.348

285 तत्रैव भूमिका।

286 धातोरेकाचो हलादेः क्रियासमभिहारे यङ् (*पा.सू.* 3.1.22), द्विवचनविभज्योपपदे तरबीयसुनौ (*पा.सू.* 5.3.57)।

287 *शि.वि.* 12.339, 6.83

288 तत्रैव 11.179, 11.236

289 तत्रैव 6.81

290 तत्रैव 6.181

291 *पा.सू.* 4.2.81

292 *शि.वि.* 10.105

इत्यत्र च्विप्रत्ययप्रयुक्तयोः इत्वदोर्घयोर[293] भावोऽपि चिन्त्य एव भाति, तत्स्थाने कथावशेषीकृत इति रूपमेव सम्यक्। पिच्छलीभवदि[294]ति स्थाने पिच्छिलीभवद् इति रूपमेव साधु, तत्र इलच्प्रत्ययस्य विहितत्वात्[295]। किञ्च श्वो रात्रौ[296], ह्यो रात्रौ[297], अद्यतनी रजनी[298]इत्यादीनां स्थानेष्वपि आगामिन्यां रात्रौ, व्यतीतायां रात्रौ, इयं रजनी इत्येते प्रयोगाः साधुतराः प्रतिभान्ति, अस्मिन् द्यवि इति अद्य इति व्युत्पत्त्या[299] दिवसस्य रात्रिभिन्नत्वात्। पूर्वं पर्यटितचरम्[300] इत्यत्र पुनः चरट्प्रत्ययेनैव[301] पूर्वार्थे लब्धे पूर्वपदप्रयोगः पुनरुक्तिदूषित एव।

तिङन्ताः

क्रियापदे शब्दविदां परीक्षा इति प्रसिद्धेरनुरूपं कविना व्यासेन प्रायशः सर्वविधानि पूर्वोत्तरतिङन्तरूपाणि यथाप्रसङ्गं शिवराजविजये सहजतया समुपयुक्तानि दृश्यन्ते। तत्र पूर्वतिङन्तानां प्रयोगक्रमे प्रायशः समेषां लकाराणां धातुरूपाणि कविना प्रयुज्यन्ते। तथाहि –

यथा लट्लकारे – निर्वक्ति[302], विभनक्ति[303], उपतिष्ठन्ते[304], अवचिनोमि[305], स्वपिति[306], वेत्ति[307] इत्यादीनि।

---

293 अस्य च्वौ (*पा.सू.* 7.2.32), च्वौ च (*पा.सू.* 7.4.26) इत्याभ्याम् ।

294 *शि.वि.* 12.253

295 लोमादिपामादिपिच्छादिभ्यः शनेलचः (*पा.सू.* 5.2.100)।

296 *शि.वि.* 9.36

297 *शि.वि.* 8.210

298 तत्रैव 4.196

299 सद्यःपरुत्परारि० (*पा.सू.* 5.3.22) इति निपातनात्।

300 *शि.वि.* 6.67

301 भूतपूर्वे चरट् (*पा.सू.* 5.3.93)।

302 *शि.वि.* भूमिका।

303 तत्रैव 1.4

304 तत्रैव 1.5

305 तत्रैव 1.5

306 तत्रैव 1.10

307 तत्रैव 1.10

लिट्लकारे – निश्चक्राम[308], आरेभे[309], इयेष, निपपात[310], अपससार[311], आरुरोह[312] इत्यादीनि।

लुट्लकारे – अवलोकयितासि कथयितासि[313], श्वो द्रष्टा[314] इत्यादीनि।

लृट्लकारे – वर्त्तिष्यन्ते भोत्स्यति[315], संवत्स्र्यथ[316], विनङ्क्ष्यति[317], योत्स्ये[318], समाप्स्यति[319] इत्यादीनि।

लोट्लकारे – भुङ्क्ष्व[320], भिन्धि छिन्धि[321], त्यज[322], त्रायस्व[323], विविनक्तु[324], क्रीणीध्वम्[325] इत्यादीनि।

लङ्लकारे – प्राविशत्[326], समतिष्ठत[327], आर्पयत्[328], अयुध्यत[329], आविध्यन्[330], समरक्षन्[331] इत्यादीनि।

---

308 *शि.वि.* 1.5

309 तत्रैव 1.6

310 तत्रैव 1.10

311 तत्रैव 1.17

312 तत्रैव 1.18

313 *शि.वि.* भूमिका। 6.75

314 तत्रैव 6.77

315 *शि.वि.* 6.112

316 तत्रैव 7.134

317 तत्रैव 7.143

318 तत्रैव 7.161

319 तत्रैव 11.264

320 तत्रैव 12.277

321 तत्रैव 12.345

322 तत्रैव 12.359

323 तत्रैव 4.194

324 तत्रैव 5.12

325 तत्रैव 6.66

326 तत्रैव 6.73

327 तत्रैव 6.76

328 तत्रैव 11.187

329 तत्रैव 11.221

330 तत्रैव 11.246

331 तत्रैव 1.16

लिङ्लकारे - संवर्तेय[332], परीक्षेय[333], विदध्यु:[334], रोचेत[335], जानीयात्[336], निश्चिनुयाम्[337] इत्यादीनि।

लुङ्लकारे - व्यधिषत[338], समरौत्सीत्[339], अजागरी:[340], अनैषी:[341], अश्रौषम्[342], अरोदी:[343] इत्यादीनि।

लृङ्लकारे - प्राप्स्यत् अकरिष्यत् अकलयिष्यत्[344], व्यरचयिष्यत्[345], व्यवाहरिष्यम् समधेक्ष्यम्[346] इत्यादीनि च।

किञ्च व्यासाम्बिकादत्तो मा-मास्मोपपदयोः लोट्लङ्लुङ्लकारान् काव्ये नैकत्र प्रायुङ्क्त, यथा - मा स्म भूत् मा स्म पुषत्[347], मा स्म आरोपयः मा स्म कार्षी:[348], मा स्म अवधीरय[349], मा स्प्राक्षी:[350] इत्यादिषु स्थलेषु।

अथ उत्तरतिङन्तपदानां प्रयोगेऽपि कवेर्भूयानाग्रहो दरीदृश्यते। एषामनायासप्रयोगे कविना साफल्यमपि अधिगतम्। तथाहि -

---

332 *शि.वि.* 1.28

333 तत्रैव 1.28

334 तत्रैव 1.28

335 तत्रैव 6.109

336 *शि.वि.* 6.161

337 तत्रैव 6.165

338 तत्रैव भूमिका।

339 *शि.वि.* भूमिका।

340 तत्रैव 1.9

341 तत्रैव 1.10

342 तत्रैव 1.15

343 तत्रैव 1.16

344 तत्रैव 12.294

345 तत्रैव 12.296

346 तत्रैव 9.38

347 तत्रैव भूमिका।

348 तत्रैव 1.16

349 तत्रैव 1.22

350 तत्रैव 1.28

यथा – णिजन्तेषु – जनयति[351], पातय मज्जय खण्डय कर्तय ज्वलय[352], अदीदलन्[353], साधयेयम् पातयेयम्[354], न्यवीविदत्[355], प्रावीविशत्[356] इत्यादीनि।

सन्नन्तेषु – चिखेदयिषामि[357], शुश्रूषते[358], पिपृच्छिषामि[359], जिगमिषामः[360], दिदृक्षते[361], विवक्षति[362] इत्यादीनि।

यङन्त-यङ्लुगन्तेषु – चर्कर्ति बर्भर्ति जर्हर्ति[363], दोधूयन्ते[364], वर्वर्ति[365], संबोभवीति[366], जाज्वल्यते[367] इत्यादीनि।

नामधातुषु – विधुरयसि[368], अश्वयाम्बभूव[369], कलङ्कयति[370], पाशयति[371], विरहयाम्बभूव[372], चटुलयन्ति[373], इत्यादीनि।

---

351 *शि.वि.* 1.4
352 तत्रैव 1.28
353 तत्रैव 1.32
354 तत्रैव 1.33
355 तत्रैव 2.60
356 *शि.वि.* भूमिका। 2.63
357 तत्रैव 1.24
358 तत्रैव 1.26
359 तत्रैव 1.34
360 तत्रैव 2.48
361 तत्रैव 2.62
362 *शि.वि.* 2.71
363 तत्रैव 1.4
364 तत्रैव 1.33
365 तत्रैव 3.121
366 तत्रैव 4.193
367 तत्रैव 5.22
368 तत्रैव 1.26
369 तत्रैव 1.30
370 तत्रैव 1.3
371 तत्रैव 3.114
372 तत्रैव 3.27
373 तत्रैव 3.181

कर्मकर्तृषु - तप्यते[374], तप्येत[375], विदीर्यते[376] इत्यादीनि।

भावकर्मसु - प्रशस्यते समभावि[377], अदर्शि[378], ध्यायन्ते भर्ज्यन्ते अपह्नियन्ते लुण्ठ्यन्ते समुद्धूयन्ते[379], व्ययाजिषत अतापिषत हन्यन्ते विदीर्यन्ते समृद्यन्ते[380] इत्यादीनि।

लकारार्थेषु - श्वः नीयते[381] इत्यादीनि च।

पूर्वोत्तरतिङन्तपदप्रयोगक्रमे कवेर्व्यासस्य कानिचन पदानि चिन्त्यान्यपि दृश्यन्ते। तथाहि - जारयन्ति[382] इति स्थाने जरयन्ति इत्येव साधु स्यात्, तत्र मित्त्वप्रयुक्तह्रस्वप्रसङ्गनात्[383]। विक्रीणामि[384], प्रतिजानामि[385], प्रत्यज्ञासीत्[386], समज्ञासीत्[387], उपातिष्ठत्[388], समद्राक्षीत्[389], नियुनक्ति[390], नियुनज्मि[391], समश्रौषीत्[392], समपृच्छत्[393], समपृच्छम्[394] इत्येतेषां स्थाने

---

[374] *शि.वि.* 9.9

[375] तत्रैव 9.95

[376] तत्रैव 9.41, 46

[377] तत्रैव भूमिका।

[378] तत्रैव 1.10

[379] *श.वि.*भूमिका। 1.10

[380] तत्रैव 1.23

[381] तत्रैव 2.98

[382] तत्रैव भूमिका।

[383] घटादयो मितः (गणसूत्रम्), मितां ह्रस्वः (*पा.सू.* 6.4.92)।

[384] *शि.वि.* 1.28

[385] तत्रैव 2.70, 10.115, 11.218

[386] तत्रैव 7.156, 7.172

[387] तत्रैव 7.185

[388] तत्रैव 2.103

[389] तत्रैव 4.174

[390] तत्रैव 4.174

[391] तत्रैव 7.171

[392] तत्रैव 6.101

[393] तत्रैव 6.113, 10.118

[394] तत्रैव 8.248

विक्रीणे[395], प्रतिजाने[396] – इत्यादीनि आत्मनेपदविशिष्टानि, अशंसत[397], प्रशशंसिरे[398], पिपासामहे[399], संवत्स्र्यते[400], चिक्रीडिरे[401], क्षयते[402], ह्रसते[403], विवक्षते[404] इत्येतेषां स्थाने अशंसत्[405], प्रशशंसुः[406] इत्यादीनि[407] परस्मैपदविशिष्टानि च तत्तत्सूत्रनिर्दिष्टानि रूपाण्येव प्रयोक्तुमुचितानि। एवमेव प्रतिरुन्धेः[408], विश्वसेव[409], सहयुञ्जेरन्[410], विश्वसेयम्[411], समुच्छ्‌वसेयम्[412] इत्येतेषां प्रयोगाणां स्थानेऽपि प्रतिरुन्ध्याः, विश्वस्याव इत्यादीनि रूपाण्येव प्रयोज्यानि, तत्र-तत्र रुधाद्यदादित्वप्रयुक्तश्नम्लुग्विकरणविधानै[413]स्तत्तद्रूपाणामेव साधुत्वात्। अथवा, स्थलेष्वेतेषु गणकार्यमनित्यमि[414]ति परिभाषया कथञ्चित् समाधानं विधातुं शक्यते, न विश्वसेदविश्वस्तम्[415], इत्यादिप्रयोगवत्। किञ्च अबाधित[416], जरीजृम्भन्ते[417], कलयति[418],

---

[395] परिव्यवेभ्यः क्रियः (*पा.स.* 1.3.18)।

[396] सम्प्रतिभ्यामनाध्याने (*पा.सू.* 1.3.46)।

[397] *शि.वि.* 10.101

[398] तत्रैव 11.244

[399] तत्रैव 6.88

[400] तत्रैव 9.48

[401] तत्रैव 11.212

[402] तत्रैव 11.225

[403] तत्रैव 11.231

[404] *शि.वि.* 12.332

[405] शंसु स्तुतौ (धातुसं. 728, भ्वादिः, *सि.कौ.*)।

[406] शंसु स्तुतौ (धातुसं. 728, भ्वादिः, *सि.कौ.*)।

[407] पिपासामः, संवत्स्र्यति, चिक्रीडुः इत्यादीनि।

[408] *शि.वि.* 2.55

[409] तत्रैव 3.145

[410] तत्रैव 6.57

[411] तत्रैव 12.282

[412] तत्रैव 12.327

[413] रुधादिभ्यः शनम् (*पा.सू.* 3.1.78), अदिप्रभृतिभ्यः शपः (*पा.सू.* 2.4.72)।

[414] परिभाषेन्दुशेखरः परिभाषा संख्या 96

[415] मूलं मृग्यम्।

[416] *शि.वि.* 3.127

[417] तत्रैव 5.3

[418] तत्रैव 6.61

जाग्रत[419], चिक्रीडन्ति[420], विनुनोदयिष्यामि[421], म्रियेय[422], कर्णौ स्फुट्येते[423], आश्लिषत्[424], क्रमत:[425], भोजयिष्यते[426], आमूमुचत्[427], जहर्षु:[428], व्यत्यापयामि[429] इत्येतेषां प्रयोगाणामपि असाधुत्वमेव प्रतिभाति, तत्तत्सूत्रनियमै: तत्र तत्र स्थाने क्रमश: अबाधि[430], जरीजृभ्यन्ते[431], कलयसि[432], जागृत[433], चेक्रीड्यते/चेक्रीडन्ति[434], विनुनोदयिषिष्यामि[435], मार्येय[436], स्फुटत:[437], आश्लिक्षत्[438], क्राम्यत:/क्रामत:[439], भोक्ष्यते[440], अमुञ्चत्[441], जहृषु:[442], व्यतिगमयामि[443] इत्येतेषामेव रूपाणामौचित्यात्। मा स्म गमत्[444] इत्यत्र प्रकरणानुरूपम् आडागमविशिष्टं मा

---

419 *शि.वि.* 6.70

420 तत्रैव 6.94

421 तत्रैव 7.113

422 तत्रैव 2.102

423 तत्रैव 9.46

424 तत्रैव 10.122

425 तत्रैव 11.236

426 तत्रैव 11.244

427 तत्रैव 11.184

428 तत्रैव 12.294

429 *शि.वि.* 7.144

430 चिणो लुक् (*पा.सू.* 6.4.104) इति तलोपात्।

431 यङि तथैव रूपौचित्यात्।

432 प्रस्तुतप्रसङ्गे युष्मदा साहचर्यात्।

433 लोण्मध्यमबहुवचने तथैव रूपौचित्यात्।

434 यङ्लुकि गुणस्यावश्यम्भावात्।

435 सनि इडागमात्।

436 प्रकृतप्रसङ्गे णिजर्थप्रेरणाया: सत्त्वात्।

437 दिवादौ स्फुट-धातोरपाठात् कर्तृवाच्ये तादृग्रूपानौचित्यात्।

438 आलिङ्गनेऽर्थे श्लिष् आलिङ्गने (*पा.सू.* 3.1.46) इति नियमात् तथैव रूपात्।

439 तादृशरूपयोरेव लटि औचित्यात्।

440 णिजर्थस्यासत्त्वात्।

441 णिजर्थस्यासत्त्वात्।

442 असंयोगाल्लिट् कित् (*पा.सू.* 1.2.5) इति नियमात् झौ गुणप्रतिषेधात्।

443 णौ गमिरबोधने (*पा.सू.* 2.4.46) इति नियमात्।

444 *शि.वि.* 1.40

स्मागमत् इत्येवोचितम्। समशयिष्ट[445], समबध्नन्[446], समकार्षुः[447] इत्येतेषु स्थलेषु तत्तदुपसर्गविरहिताः अशयिष्ट, अबध्नन्, अकार्षुरिति प्रयोगाः एव समीचीनाः, तत्र तत्र समुपसर्गसंयोजनेन अर्थान्तराणां प्रसिद्धत्वात्, अत्र च प्रकरणेषु तथार्थाभावात्। अत्यन्तं चेखिद्यते[448] इत्यत्र अत्यन्तमिति पुनरुक्तमेव, तदर्थस्य तिङन्तगतयङ्प्रत्ययेनैव[449] लाभसम्भवात्। एवमेव मोमुद्यन्तेतमाम्[450], संबोभवीतितमाम्[451] इत्यनयोः स्थलयोरपि अतिशयार्थवाचिनस्तमप्प्रत्ययस्य[452] पौनरुक्त्यप्रयुक्तं वैयर्थ्यं स्पष्टमेव।

कृदन्ताः

कविर्व्यासः कृदन्तपदानां वैविध्यपूर्णप्रयोगेष्वपि काव्येऽस्मिन् परमं साफल्यमासीसदत्। निदर्शनार्थं - यङन्तयङ्लुगन्तादिभ्यः, स्वतन्त्रेभ्यश्च धातुभ्यः शानच्प्रत्ययान्तपदानां कविनोपस्थापिता मालिका नितरां निभालनीया। तथाहि -

भज्यमान[453]–भुज्यमान[454]–अनुगम्यमान[455]–समुद्धूयमान[456]–दरीदृश्यमान[457]–बेभिद्यमान[458]–मामद्यमान[459]–तोद्यमान[460]–बंभज्यमान[461]–संचरीक्रियमाण[462]–सोस्रूयमाण–सरीस्रियमाण[463]–

---

445 *शि.वि.* 7.163

446 तत्रैव 9.77

447 तत्रैव 7.184

448 तत्रैव 9.61

449 धातोरेकाचः० (*पा.सू.* 3.1.22)।

450 *शि.वि.* 2.348

451 तत्रैव 2.79

452 तिङश्च (*पा.सू.* 5.3.56)।

453 *शि.वि.* 1.24

454 तत्रैव 2.45

455 तत्रैव 1.37

456 तत्रैव 2.46

457 तत्रैव 7.126

458 तत्रैव 8.229

459 तत्रैव 8.259

460 तत्रैव 9.109

461 *शि.वि.* 9.47

462 तत्रैव 12.277

463 तत्रैव 12.350

प्रतिष्ठासमाना[464]दीनि।

नानाविधानां ल्यबन्तपदानां प्रयोगेऽपि कवेर्महती समभिरुचिः प्रकाशमायाति काव्येऽस्मिन्, यथा – विरचय्य[465]–विरहय्य[466]–अविगणय्य[467]–आकलय्य[468] विस्तीर्य[469]–आज्ञाप्य[470]–उत्तार्य[471]–उत्कीर्य[472]–संशृङ्गार्य[473]–सन्धाय[474]– विधाय[475]–आदाय[476]–आधाय[477]–प्रभृतीनि।

सन्नन्तधातुभ्यः उप्रत्ययस्य प्रयोगाः अपि नैकत्र निदर्शनीयाः, यथा – रिरचयिषुः[478], शुश्रूषुः[479], आरिराधयिषुः[480], युयुत्सुः[481], आजिहीर्षुः[482], चिक्रीडिषुः[483] इत्यादयः।

स्वतन्त्रेभ्यः क्यजाद्यन्तेभ्यश्च धातुभ्यः क्तप्रत्ययानां प्रयोगोऽपि कवेर्विशिष्टमुल्लेखमर्हति। यथा – सुप्तः[484], कूजितं पूजितं पूरितं[485], विसृष्टेषु[486], अवलीढः[487], खुरखुरायितः[488],

---

464 *शि.वि.* 9.59
465 तत्रैव भूमिका।
466 तत्रैव 1.20
467 तत्रैव 1.20
468 तत्रैव 2.72
469 तत्रैव 3.154
470 तत्रैव 3.155
471 तत्रैव 3.160
472 तत्रैव 5.40
473 तत्रैव 9.221
474 तत्रैव 1.6
475 *शि.वि.* 1.6
476 तत्रैव 2.58
477 तत्रैव 2.58
478 तत्रैव भूमिका।
479 तत्रैव 1.14
480 तत्रैव 1.37
481 तत्रैव 1.40
482 तत्रैव 1.41
483 तत्रैव 2.47
484 तत्रैव 1.5
485 तत्रैव 1.7
486 तत्रैव 1.14
487 तत्रैव 1.16
488 *शि.वि.* 10.160

खणखणायित:[489], धमद्धमकित:[490] इत्यादय:।

एवमेव अन्येषामपि तुमुन्नादिकृत्प्रत्ययान्तपदानां कविना यथावसरं प्रस्तुता: चामत्कारिका: प्रयोगा: प्रस्तुते गद्यकाव्ये आस्वादयितुं शक्या:। केचन उदाहरणार्थं – योद्धुम्[491], उपन्यस्तुं[492], समन्वेष्टुं[493], कूर्दनं[494], मरणं[495], चुलुकनं[496], समापनीयानि[497], पूजनीयं[498], निर्वहणीया[499], संशृण्वन्[500], कवोष्णयन्[501], ध्यायन्[502], भित्त्वा[503], बद्ध्वा[504], भुक्त्वा[505], नमस्या[506], संस्था[507], श्रावं-श्रावम्[508], आलोकम्-आलोकं[509], सहवासिनाम्[510], जयजयेतिवादिन:[511], व्यर्थहत्या[512],

---

489 *शि.वि.* 12.371

490 तत्रैव 5.17

491 तत्रैव 1.35

492 तत्रैव 1.37

493 तत्रैव 3.118

494 तत्रैव 2.45

495 तत्रैव 2.80

496 तत्रैव 8.226

497 तत्रैव भूमिका।

498 तत्रैव 3.119

499 तत्रैव 3.151

500 *शि.वि.* 4.194

501 तत्रैव 5.5

502 तत्रैव 8.245

503 तत्रैव 1.20

504 तत्रैव 2.81

505 तत्रैव 2.101

506 तत्रैव भूमिका।

507 तत्रैव 1.20

508 तत्रैव 5.41

509 तत्रैव 2.87

510 तत्रैव 6.47

511 तत्रैव 8.223

512 तत्रैव 7.190

भटम्मन्या:[513], यायजूकैः[514], दुष्करम्[515], प्रणतवन्तौ[516], कर्णेजपस्य[517], पतद्ग्राहः[518], उपेयुषः[519] इत्यादयः।

कृदन्तपदानां प्रयोगप्रसङ्गेऽपि कवेः केचन प्रयोगाश्चिन्त्यतां यान्ति। यथा – आकर्षयन्निव[520], सिसेवयिषूणां[521], चिचर्वयिषन्निव[522], लुलुण्ठयिषन्[523] इत्येतेषु प्रयोगेषु णिच्प्रत्ययस्य अनौचित्यमेव, मूलधातुभ्य एव विवक्षितार्थलाभात् अत्र च णिजर्थप्रेरणायाः अप्रासङ्गिकत्वात्। आह्वयमानाम्[524] इतिस्थाने आह्वयन्तीम् इति प्रयोग एवोचितः, स्पर्धायामाङः[525] इतिसूत्रनिर्देशेन आङ्विशिष्टस्य ह्वेञः स्पर्धाह्वानार्थकत्वात्, अत्र च दूराह्वानमात्रस्य प्रसङ्गात्। प्रशंसमानौ[526], क्रन्दमानम्[527], खादमानाः[528] इत्येतेषु स्थलेषु आत्मनेपदत्वप्रयुक्तः शानच्प्रत्ययो[529]ऽप्यसङ्गत एव, तत्तन्मूलधातूनां परस्मैपदित्वेन शतृप्रत्ययस्यैवोचितत्वात्। क्रियासमभिहारेण चङ्क्रम्यमाणम् [530]इत्यत्रापि क्रियासमभिहारेणेति पुनरुक्तमेव, तदर्थस्य क्रियापदगतयङ्प्रत्ययेनैव लब्धत्वात्। दन्दल्यमानेन[531] इति प्रयोगस्तु दन्दह्यमानम् इत्यादिप्रयोगसादृश्यबुद्ध्यैव कविना कृतः प्रतिभाति, तत्र दलधातोर्यङि अभ्यासे नुमागमस्याविधानात्। आपिप्रच्छिषमाणम्[532] इतिस्थाने आपिपृच्छिषमाणम्

---

513 *शि.वि.* 12.372

514 तत्रैव 1.25

515 तत्रैव भूमिका।

516 *शि.वि.* 3.155

517 तत्रैव 4.174

518 तत्रैव 8.197

519 तत्रैव 10.142

520 तत्रैव 2.81

521 तत्रैव 10.143

522 तत्रैव 11.236

523 तत्रैव 11.237

524 तत्रैव 7.163

525 *पा.सू.* 1.3.31

526 *शि.वि.* 3.146

527 तत्रैव 8.244

528 तत्रैव 10.144

529 लटः शतृशानचौ० (*पा.सू.* 2.2.124)।

530 *शि.वि.* 3.140

531 तत्रैव 9.47

532 तत्रैव 7.173

इत्येवोचितम्, तत्र ग्रहिज्ये[533]ति सम्प्रसारणस्य अवश्यम्भावात्। किञ्च आपिप्रच्छिषमाणम्[534], आपृच्छमानः[535], आपृच्छमाना[536] इत्यत्र आङुपसर्गस्य, विलम्बमानः[537] इत्यत्र व्युपसर्गस्य, सहवासिनाम्[538] इत्यत्र सहोपपदस्य चाप्यनौचित्यमेव प्रतिभाति, तत्तदुपसर्गादिसंगोगे अर्थान्तराणां प्रसिद्धत्वात्। क्रमतः[539] इति स्थाने क्राम्यतः/क्रामतः इत्येवोचितम्, क्रमः परस्मैपदेष्विति[540]नियमात् दीर्घरूपयोरेवौचित्यात्। हत्यामनिच्छद्भिः[541]इत्येष प्रयोगोऽप्यनुपपन्न एव, हनस्त चे[542]ति सूत्रनियमात् हनः सुप्युपपदे एव क्यब्विधानात्। उद्बद्धुम्[543] इति स्थानेऽपि उद्बन्धुम् इत्येव प्रयोज्यम्, तुमुनि नलोपासम्भवात्। लिखितुम्[544] इति प्रयोगापेक्षयाऽपि लेखितुमित्येव साधु, तत्र लघूपधगुणस्या[545]वश्यकर्तव्यत्वात्।

इतरे भाषाप्रयोगाः

व्याकरणशास्त्रस्य तत्तत्प्रकरणसम्बद्धान् चामत्कारिकप्रयोगानतिरिच्य कविनाऽम्बिकादत्तेन केचिदितरेऽपि सुरभारतीशब्दभाण्डागारसमृद्धिजनकाः अभिनवाः भाषाप्रयोगाः शिवराजविजये समाचरिताः। तथाहि –

कविनाऽनेन गद्यप्रबन्धेऽस्मिन् नैकधा कोषगतानि अबहुप्रयुक्तानि पदानि तत्र तत्र प्रसङ्गे सफलतया समवतारितानि, यथा – दम्भोलिः(वज्रम्)[546], वसुमती(पृथ्वी)[547],

---

533 *पा.सू.* 6.1.16
534 *शि.वि.* 7.173
535 तत्रैव 8.265
536 तत्रैव 9.18
537 तत्रैव 11.230
538 तत्रैव 6.47
539 *शि.वि.* 11.236
540 *पा.सू.* 7.3.76
541 *शि.वि.* 9.60
542 *पा.सू.* 3.1.160
543 *शि.वि.* 9.20
544 तत्रैव 12.288
545 पुगन्तलघूपधस्य च (*पा.सू.* 7.3.86)।
546 *शि.वि.* 1.23
547 तत्रैव 2.48

जम्भारातिः(इन्द्रः)[548], कलविङ्कः(चटका)[549], अपीच्यदर्शनम्(सुन्दरम्)[550] इत्यादीनि।

ध्वनिसंकेतकानां तत्तदनुकरणशब्दानां प्रयोगे तत्र तत्र कविर्नितरां पटुत्वमावहति, यथा – हाहाकारम्[551], फूत्कारैः[552], हुडुक्कारः[553], खडखडायित–[554], खुरखुरायित–[555], खणखणायित–[556], सगुडगुडाशब्दं[557], सखडखडाशब्दं[558], सखिलखिलाशब्दं[559], धमद्ध मद्दोधूयमानः[560], फरफरायमाणः[561], खटखटाप्रधानम् [562]इत्यादयः।

कविरेष भाषान्तराणां सस्कृते सुसम्भावितानिच्छायापदानि नैकत्रात्र प्रबन्धे सफलतया प्रस्तौति, यथा – महामदः (महमूद)[563], दग्धमुखः (मुँहजला)[564], पुण्यनगरं (पुणे)[565], महामदगणिः (महमूद गनी)[566], अवरङ्गजीवः (औरंगजेब)[567], मज्जितस्थानम् (मस्ज़िद)[568], मोहावर्तखानः (मोहब्बत खाँ)[569], मोहरमः (मोहर्रम)[570], रामयानम्

---

548 *शि.वि.* 3.114
549 तत्रैव 4.161
550 तत्रैव 5.32
551 तत्रैव 1.28
552 तत्रैव 2.75
553 तत्रैव 2.95
554 तत्रैव 10.126
555 तत्रैव 10.160
556 तत्रैव 12.371
557 *शि.वि.* 5.15
558 तत्रैव 5.19
559 तत्रैव 11.235
560 तत्रैव 2.96
561 तत्रैव 3.150
562 तत्रैव 2.111
563 तत्रैव 1.26
564 तत्रैव 1.29
565 *शि.वि.* 2.45
566 तत्रैव 5.23
567 तत्रैव 10.132
568 तत्रैव 11.242
569 तत्रैव 12.371
570 तत्रैव 6.50

(रमजान)[571], मौलिविः (मौलवी)[572], शास्तिखानः (शाइस्ता खाँ)[573], चान्द्रखानः (चाँद खाँ)[574], रसनारी (रोशनआरा)[575], मायाजिह्वः (मुअज्जम)[576] इत्यादीनि।

बहुत्र भाषायां प्रचलितानि अपभ्रष्टानि नामानि कविः शाब्दिकदृशा सुपरिष्कृत्यैव प्रयुङ्क्ते । यथा – यशस्विसिंहः (जसवन्त सिंह)[577], मुरेश्वरः (मोरेश्वर)[578], स्तन्यजीवः (तानाजी)[579], अन्नजीवदत्तः (अन्नाजी दत्तोवा)[580], शिवराजः (शिवाजी)[581] इत्यादीनि।

आङ्ग्लहिन्द्यादिभाषासु प्रथिताः सुललिताः लोकोक्तीः कविर्व्यासो बहुत्र संस्कृतेन सफलतया अनूद्य व्यवहरति, यथा – कार्यं वा साधयेयं, देहं वा पातयेयम् (do or die)[582], घृतेन स्नातु भवद्रसना (आपके मुँह में घी-शक्कर)[583], एकमेकं चैकादश भवन्ति (एक-एक ग्यारह होते हैं)[584], सत्यं, दुग्धदग्धो जनस्तक्रमपि व्यजनैर्वीजयित्वा पिबति (सच है, दूध का जला छाँछ भी पंखा झल-झलकर पीता है)[585], अत्रुटितकेशाग्रो यातः (बिना बाल बांका हुए चला गया)[586] इत्यादीः।

काव्येऽस्मिन् नैकेषां भावानां सहजतयाऽभिव्यक्तये कविना तत्र तत्र प्रसङ्गेषु प्रदर्शिताः पदवीप्साः अपि नितरां निभालनीयाः, यथा – मन्दिरे मन्दिरे जयजयध्वनिः, तीर्थे तीर्थे घण्टानादः, मठे मठे वेदघोषः(व्याप्तौ)[587], श्यामश्यामैः गुच्छगुच्छैः

---

571 *शि.वि.* 6.50

572 तत्रैव 6.51

573 तत्रैव 6.76

574 तत्रैव 6.76

575 तत्रैव 8.193

576 तत्रैव 8.262

577 तत्रैव 6.80

578 तत्रैव 7.168

579 तत्रैव 12.303

580 तत्रैव 7.168

581 *शि.वि.* – गद्यबन्धाभिधानम्।

582 तत्रैव 1.33

583 तत्रैव 2.74

584 तत्रैव 12.328

585 *शि.वि.* – गद्यबन्धाभिधानम्। 12.353

586 तत्रैव 12.353

587 तत्रैव 1.18

कुञ्चितकुञ्चितैः कचकलापैः[588], मन्दमन्दं मुग्धमुग्धं मधुरमधुरं किञ्चिद् गायति[589], गहनगहनैः कोमलकोमलैः मधुरमधुरैः वाचां विलासैर्मनो हरसि (प्रशंसायाम्)[590], अलमलं विरमतं-विरमतं पतामि (भये)[591], हरिद्रा-हरिद्रा, लशुनं-लशुनं, मरिचं-मरिचं, चुक्रं-चुक्रं, वितुन्नकं-वितुन्नकं, शृङ्गवेरं-शृङ्गवेरं, रामठं-रामठं, मत्स्यण्डी-मत्स्यण्डी, मत्स्याः-मत्स्याः, कुक्कुटाण्डं-कुक्कुटाण्डं, पललं-पललम् इति कलकलैः (त्वरायाम्)[592], आम् आम् आम् . . . साधु साधु, महानेष पण्डितः (चाटूक्तौ)[593] इत्यादयः।

उपर्युक्तेषु भाषाप्रयोगेषु कविरयं क्वचित् क्वचिच्चिन्त्यानपि प्रयोगानाचरन्नुपलभ्यते। तथाहि - वार्ताः कर्तुं[594], प्रसादमोदकं[595], सतर्को भव[596] इत्येतेषु स्थलेषु वृत्तान्त[597]-प्रसन्नता[598]-सयुक्त्य[599]र्थेषु कोषेण निर्धारितान् वार्ताप्रसादसतर्कशब्दान् कविरयं लोकप्रचलितेष्वर्थान्तरेषु[600] प्रयुञ्जानो दृश्यते। समागमस्थानम्[601], सुरतनगरे[602] इत्यनयोः अश्लीलार्थपरतया कोषेण घोषितयोः शब्दयोः प्रयोगं कविः अर्थान्तरयोरनुतिष्ठति। भयभीताः[603], द्वौ स्तम्भौ[604], द्वौ भावत्कौ[605], परितः परिसर्पिणो जनान्[606], घनघटा[607]

---

588 *शि.वि.* – गद्यबन्धाभिधानम्। 4.162

589 तत्रैव 1.62

590 तत्रैव 6.96

591 तत्रैव 7.131

592 तत्रैव 1.75

593 तत्रैव 5.37

594 तत्रैव 5.37

595 तत्रैव 4.194

596 तत्रैव 11.246

597 वार्ता प्रवृत्तिर्वृत्तान्तः (*अमरकोषः* 1.9)।

598 प्रसादस्तु प्रसन्नता (*अमरकोष*: 1.6)।

599 अध्याहारस्तर्क ऊहः (*अमरकोष*: 1.8)।

600 सम्भाषणनैवेद्यसावधानार्थेष्वित्यर्थः।

601 *शि.वि.* 2.107

602 *शि.वि.* 8.248

603 तत्रैव 1.15

604 तत्रैव 7.120

605 तत्रैव 9.38

606 तत्रैव 8.231

607 तत्रैव 11.261

इत्येतेषु स्थलेषु पुनरुक्तिः स्पष्टैव। स्वपितुः, स्वमातुः[608] इत्यादिनि स्थले स्वशब्दोऽपि अतिरिक्त एव। लेखप्रकाण्डः[609], मण्डनाः[610], अधरम्[611], दाराः अपहरन्ति[612], ज्वालाजालः[613]इत्यादिषु स्थलेषु लिङ्गव्युत्क्रमो[614]ऽप्यवलोक्यते। तारकमण्डलम्[615] इत्यत्रापि तारकाशब्द एव कोषनिर्दिष्टः[616], न तु तारकशब्दः[617]।

उपसंहृतिः

कविर्व्यासाम्बिकादत्तः आधुनिकसंस्कृतसाहित्यजगतः सुप्रतिष्ठितो गद्यकारः। अनेन कविना पण्डितपछारेत्यपरनामधेयं गुप्ताशुद्धिप्रदर्शनम्, अन्यानि च कतिचन शब्दशास्त्रोपकारकाणि कृतिरत्नानि विरचय्य स्वीयं शाब्दिकप्रवरत्वमपि सुतरां प्रतिष्ठापितम्। एतत्प्रतिष्ठानुरूपमेव च स्वीये सर्वोत्कृष्टे शिवराजविजयकाव्ये अनेन सन्धिसमासादिभ्यः तत्तद्व्याकरण-प्रकरणेभ्यश्चामत्कारिकाः प्रयोगाः सहजतया समाचरिताः। व्याकरणस्य विशिष्टानां प्रयोगाणां व्यवहारावसरे कवेरस्य केचन प्रयोगाः प्रस्तुतायां समीक्षायां प्राथमिकदृष्ट्या चिन्त्यत्वेन प्रदर्शिताः सन्ति। प्रयोगानेतांश्च पुरस्कृत्य प्रेक्षावतां वस्तुस्थितिविमर्शको नीरक्षीरविवेकविभूषितो दयादृक्पातः, समाधानप्रधानश्च परामर्शः सादरमामन्त्र्यते।

गच्छतः स्खलनं क्वापि भवत्येव प्रमादतः।
हसन्ति दुर्जनास्तत्र समादधति सज्जनाः।।[618]

इत्यभियुक्तोक्तपद्धत्या प्रथममेषां प्रामाणिकत्वेन प्रतीयमानानां दुर्घटप्रयोगाणां सुघटीकरणार्थं प्रयासोऽपेक्ष्यते। तथा च सत्यपि प्रयासे चिन्त्यप्रयोगाणां साधुत्ववैधुर्ये उक्तप्रयोगान् परिष्कृत्य काव्यस्यास्य संशोधितं संस्करणमेकं प्रकाशयितुमावश्यकम्। यतो हि गद्यप्रबन्धोऽयम् आधुनिकसंस्कृतगद्यकाव्यानामादर्शभूतः नैकत्र पाठ्यपुस्तकेषु अनुशीलनार्थं निर्धारितः। अत्र च प्रामादिकेषु पदेषु सत्सु जनास्तथैवानुकुर्युः –

---

608 *शि.वि.* 8.22

609 तत्रैव भूमिका।

610 तत्रैव भूमिका।

611 तत्रैव 2.68

612 तत्रैव 6.102

613 तत्रैव 9.25

614 प्रकाण्डम्, मण्डनम्, अधरः, दारान्, जालम् इत्येतानि रूपाण्युचितानि।

615 *शि.वि.* 4.189

616 नक्षत्रमृक्षं भं तारा तारकाप्युडु वास्त्रियाम्। (*अमरकोषः* 1.6)।

617 न च ङ्यापोः संज्ञाच्छन्दसोर्बहुलम् (*पा.सू.* 6.3.63) इति ह्रस्वः, संज्ञाच्छन्दसोरभावात्।

618 परम्परीणं पद्यम्, मूलं मृग्यम्।

यद् यदाचरति श्रेष्ठस्तत्तदेवेतरो जनः।
स यत् प्रमाणं कुरुते लोकस्तदनुवर्तते।।[619]

इत्यादिगीतावचनात् । न चैवम् एतादृशप्रयोगेषु सत्सु काव्यस्यास्य दूषितत्वेन परिहेयत्वं प्रतिपादयितुं शक्यम्, इतरथाऽस्य नानागुणगणविभूषितत्वात्। तथा चोक्तमभियुक्तैः –

कीटानुविद्धरत्नादिसाधारण्येन काव्यता।
दुष्टेष्वपि मता, यत्र रसाद्यनुगमः स्फुटः।।[620]

इत्यलम्।

---

[619] श्रीमद्भगवद्गीता 3.21

[620] साहित्यदर्पणस्य प्रथमे परिच्छेदे उद्धृतं पद्यम्, मूलमन्वेष्यम्।

Contributors

Ajotikar, Anuja	Indian Institute of Technology, Bombay anujaajotikar@gmail.com
Arya, Vedmitra	University of Delhi aaryavedmitra@gmail.com
Ben-Dor, Sharon	sharonbendor@yahoo.com
Cardona, George	University of Pennsylvania cardonagj@verizon.net, cardona@sas.upenn.edu
Dharurkar, Chinmay	Indian Institute of Technology Bombay chinmayvijay@gmail.com
Jha, Paramanand	University of Delhi paramjha2010@gmail.com
Katira, Dipesh	Indian Institute of Technology Bombay dipesh.katira@gmail.com
Kulkarni, Malhar	Indian Institute of Technology, Bombay malharku@gmail.com, malhar@iitb.ac.in
Milewska, Iwona	Jagiellonian University milewska.iwona@gmail.com
Ogawa, Hideyo	HiroshimaUniversity hogawa@hiroshima-u.ac.jp, hogawa8822@gmail.com
Pontillo, Tiziana	University of Cagliari Pontillo@unica.it

Scharf, Peter M.	Université Paris Diderot. peter.scharf@univ-paris-diderot.fr peter.scharf@inria.fr
Sharma, Subodh	Rashtriya Sanskrit Sansthan, Dehradun subodhsharma62@gmail.com, subodhsharma62@rediffmail.com
Tomonari, Yuki	University of Tokyo mitriibhaavii@gmail.com
Yagi, Toru	Kyoto University tyagi@ogu-m.jp